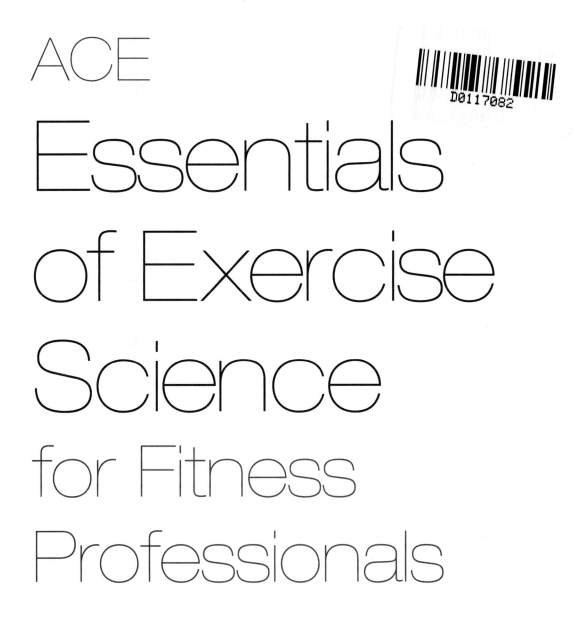

ACE
Essentials of Exercise Science
for Fitness Professionals

American Council on Exercise®

Editors
Cedric X. Bryant, Ph.D., FACSM
Daniel J. Green

Library of Congress Catalog Card Number: 2009911191

ISBN 978-1-890720-58-2

P Q R S

Distributed by:
American Council on Exercise
4851 Paramount Drive
San Diego, CA 92123
(858) 576-6500
(858) 576-6564 FAX
ACEfitness.org

Project Editor: Daniel J. Green

Technical Editor: Cedric X. Bryant, Ph.D., FACSM

Cover Design & Art Direction: Karen McGuire

Associate Editor: Marion Webb

Special Contributor & Proofreader: Sabrena Jo

Production: Nancy Garcia

Photography: Dennis Dal Covey

Anatomical Illustrations: James Staunton

Index: Kathi Unger

Chapter Models: Fabio Comana, Todd Galati, Jessica Matthews, Alexandra Morrison, Beckie Page, Leslie R. Thomas, Matthew Zuniga

Acknowledgments:
Thanks to the entire American Council on Exercise staff for their support and guidance through the process of creating this manual.

NOTICE

The fitness industry is ever-changing. As new research and clinical experience broaden our knowledge, changes in programming and standards are required. The authors and the publisher of this work have checked with sources believed to be reliable in their efforts to provide information that is complete and generally in accord with the standards accepted at the time of publication. However, in view of the possibility of human error or changes in industry standards, neither the authors nor the publisher nor any other party who has been involved in the preparation or publication of this work warrants that the information contained herein is in every respect accurate or complete, and they are not responsible for any errors or omissions or the results obtained from the use of such information. Readers are encouraged to confirm the information contained herein with other sources.

TABLE OF CONTENTS

FOREWORD

ACE Essentials of Exercise Science for Fitness Professionals presents the foundational knowledge that all fitness professionals need to be successful. For example, Group Fitness Instructors cannot design balanced workouts without a solid understanding of human anatomy—particularly the role of agonist and antagonist muscles during various movements. Personal Trainers must have detailed knowledge of the physiology of training if they are to design appropriate, effective, and safe long-term exercise programs for their clients. And Health Coaches blend the art and science of behavior change with an in-depth understanding of the powerful role lifestyle medicine plays in the prevention and management of chronic disease.

The publication of this book marks the first time that the American Council on Exercise has created a text of core content that is universal to all fitness professionals. While this is not meant to be a comprehensive exercise science textbook—the broad science of human anatomy, for example, cannot be covered in its entirety in a single chapter—it synthesizes the topics in a way that is specifically tailored to the practice of being a fitness professional.

In addition to serving as a trusted resource throughout your fitness career, this book represents the first step toward becoming an ACE certified Fitness Professional, which is itself a stepping-stone to a rewarding and fruitful career. I wish you good luck as you set out on this path to success. Make good use of this textbook and the study guides contained within each chapter, and be sure to visit ACEfitness.org or contact ACE's in-house professionals should you need any additional help. ACE is committed to your success and to the success of each of your clients or class participants. Together, we can help get the world moving toward new levels of health and fitness.

Scott Goudeseune
Chief Executive Officer

INTRODUCTION

The five chapters that comprise *ACE Essentials of Exercise Science for Fitness Professionals* constitute the core science background that all fitness professionals need to be successful, regardless of which ACE certification they choose to pursue.

Chapter 1: Human Anatomy covers the seven physiological systems of the human body that all fitness professionals must understand: the cardiovascular, respiratory, digestive, skeletal, neuromuscular, muscular, and endocrine systems. Many newcomers to the fitness industry are surprised by the detailed anatomical content that is presented in ACE's textbooks, but fitness professionals must gain an understanding of how these systems impact—and are impacted by—the ability to perform physical activity if they are to be successful.

Chapter 2: Exercise Physiology introduces the concept of physical fitness and presents the acute and chronic adaptations to exercise. In addition, this chapter covers the environmental considerations that fitness professionals must take into account regarding exercising in the heat, cold, altitude, or air pollution. Finally, specific topics related to exercise physiology in youth, older adults, and pregnant women are presented.

Chapter 3: Fundamentals of Applied Kinesiology presents biomechanical principles applied to human movement, and divides the body into three regions: the lower extremity, the spine and pelvis, and the upper extremity. Additional topics include balance and alignment and age- and obesity-related biomechanical considerations.

Chapter 4: Nutrition offers nutrition and hydration guidelines that fitness professionals can use with clients without overstepping their scope of practice, including the government-issued *Dietary Guidelines* and MyPlate Food Guidance System. Basic tools are also presented that fitness professionals can share with their clients, such as how to read a food guide label and how to make smarter choices when eating outside the home. Nutritional guidelines for several special populations are discussed as well.

Chapter 5: Physiology of Training covers both the acute responses to physical activity—how the body reacts to a single bout of exercise—and the chronic adaptations to exercise—how the body changes in response to a regular or consistent exercise routine. In addition, this chapter explains various techniques used in flexibility training and the body's response to each.

To help you target your studies, each chapter includes a study guide that will test your recall of the key topics and ideas. In addition, these study guides will give you an idea of what to expect from ACE's certification exams, as each chapter includes multiple-choice questions that mimic the style and scope of questions on the actual ACE exams. We wish you good luck as you take this first step on what will undoubtedly be a rewarding journey.

Cedric X. Bryant, Ph.D., FACSM
President and Chief Science Officer

Daniel J. Green
Project Editor

SABRENA JO, M.S., *has been actively involved in the fitness industry since 1987, focusing on teaching group exercise, owning and operating her own personal-training business, and managing fitness departments in commercial fitness facilities. Jo is a former full-time faculty member in the Kinesiology and Physical Education Department at California State University, Long Beach. She has a bachelor's degree in exercise science as well as a master's degree in physical education/biomechanics from the University of Kansas, and has numerous fitness certifications. Jo, an ACE-certified Personal Trainer and Group Fitness Instructor and ACE Faculty Member, educates other fitness professionals about current industry topics through speaking engagements at local establishments and national conferences, as well as through educational videos. She is a spokesperson for ACE and is involved in curriculum development for ACE continuing education programs.*

Human Anatomy

Sabrena Jo

The study of the human body has its origins in prehistoric times, making it one of the oldest known sciences. The term anatomy comes from the Greek word *anatomē,* which means "dissection" or "to cut apart." Originally, anatomical understanding came largely from observations of dissected plants and animals. The proper understanding of a structure, however, must include knowledge of function in the living organism (i.e., physiology). Therefore, anatomy is almost inseparable from physiology, which is sometimes called functional anatomy. In this chapter, human anatomy is presented as the science of studying the body's structures and how these structures operate through various systems.

The study of anatomy spans many disciplines, and finding consistency between the disciplines is sometimes challenging. Therefore, readers might discover discrepancies between anatomy textbooks, such as the origin and insertion of the same muscle listed slightly differently in two separate texts. This chapter presents essential anatomy concepts that are important for fitness professionals to know in order to perform their jobs effectively. The material offered here provides an excellent foundation for fitness professionals, but is not meant to be a detailed text for the vast study of anatomical science. To further their understanding of anatomy, fitness professionals may also want to study a textbook devoted entirely to anatomy.

Anatomical structures were originally named in Greek, Latin, and Arabic. With knowledge of the important anatomical, directional, and regional terms associated with the structures of the body, people often find that most tissues are named quite descriptively (Table 1-1). A good example is the comparison between the biceps brachii and biceps femoris muscles. Biceps refers to a "two-headed muscle." Therefore, both muscles are composed of two heads. The location of each muscle, however, is quite different. The word brachii comes from the root term "brachium," which means muscle of the arm, whereas the word femoris comes from "femur," which is the large bone of the thigh. The biceps brachii is a muscle of the front, upper arm and the biceps femoris is a muscle found in the back of the thigh. Table 1-2 provides a list of common anatomical terminology, which will help individuals decipher the root words, and thus, the meaning of bodily structures.

Table 1-1

Anatomical, Directional, and Regional Terms

Anterior (ventral)	Toward the front
Posterior (dorsal)	Toward the back
Superior	Toward the head
Inferior	Away from the head
Medial	Toward the midline of the body
Lateral	Away from the midline of the body
Proximal	Toward the attached end of the limb, origin of the structure, or midline of the body
Distal	Away from the attached end of the limb, origin of the structure, or midline of the body
Superficial	External; located close to or on the body surface
Deep	Internal; located further beneath the body surface than the superficial structures
Cervical	Regional term referring to the neck
Thoracic	Regional term referring to the portion of the body between the neck and the abdomen; also known as the chest (thorax)
Lumbar	Regional term referring to the portion of the back between the abdomen and the pelvis
Plantar	The sole or bottom of the feet
Dorsal	The top surface of the feet and hands
Palmar	The anterior or ventral surface of the hands
Sagittal plane	A longitudinal (imaginary) line that divides the body or any of its parts into right and left sections
Frontal plane	A longitudinal (imaginary) section that divides the body into anterior and posterior parts; lies at a right angle to the sagittal plane
Transverse plane	Also known as the horizontal plane; an imaginary line that divides the body or any of its parts into superior and inferior sections

Table 1-2

Common Anatomical (Medical) Terminology

Root	Meaning	Term	Definition
arthro	joint	arthritis	inflammation in a joint
bi	two	biceps	two-headed muscle
brachium	arm	brachialis	muscle of the arm
cardio	heart	cardiology	the study of the heart
cephalo	head	cephalic	pertaining to the head
chondro	cartilage	chondroectomy	excision of a cartilage
costo	rib	costochondral	pertaining to a rib and its cartilage
dermo	skin	dermatitis	inflammation of the skin
hemo, hemat	blood	hemorrhage	internal or external bleeding
ilio	ilium	ilium	the wide, upper part of the pelvic bone
myo	muscle	myositis	inflammation of a muscle
os, osteo	bone	osteomalacia	softening of the bone
pulmo	lung	pulmonary artery	vessel that brings blood to the lungs
thoraco	chest	thorax	chest
tri	three	triceps	three-headed muscle

Naming the various parts of the human body required anatomists to develop a reference position, so that structures and areas of the body could be described in relation to each other. This **anatomical position** refers to a person standing erect with the head, eyes, and palms facing forward. The feet are together with the toes pointing forward and the arms are hanging by the sides. A representation of anatomical position is given in Figure 1-1, along with the anatomical planes of motion.

There are four structural levels in the body: cells, tissues, organs, and systems. The most basic structures are the cells. They make up the tissues, which are the next most complex level. Fitness professionals should gain a basic understanding of the structure

Figure 1-1
Anatomical position and planes of motion

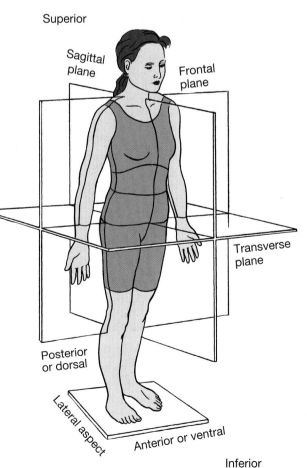

and function of muscular, nervous, and **connective tissues.** In terms of complexity, the next structural level in the body consists of the organs. An organ is formed by two or more tissues combining to serve as a specialized physiologic center for the body. The stomach, for example, is an organ lined with **epithelial tissue** (a tissue that lines various body cavities), and its walls are formed by muscle tissue. Its specific physiological function is to prepare ingested food for **digestion.**

At the highest structural level, the body is composed of systems. Organs that function cooperatively and have a common purpose (such as the digestion and **absorption** of food) are said to be part of a body system. For instance, the mouth, **esophagus,** stomach, and intestines are all part of the digestive system. Fitness professionals should be familiar with the following systems: cardiovascular, respiratory, digestive, skeletal, nervous, muscular, and endocrine.

Cardiovascular System

The cardiovascular, or circulatory, system is a closed-circuit system composed of the heart, blood vessels, and blood. Blood continuously travels a circular route through the heart into the **arteries,** then to the **capillaries,** into the **veins,** and back to the heart. Together with the respiratory system, the heart and blood vessels deliver oxygen and nutrients to the body's tissues while also removing waste, such as carbon dioxide and metabolic by-products.

Blood, the fluid component of the cardiovascular system, links the internal environment of the body to the external environment by transporting materials between the two environments as well as among the various cells and tissues. The liquid component of blood, called **plasma,** is responsible for carrying **hormones,** plasma proteins, food materials (e.g., **carbohydrates, amino acids, lipids**), **ions** (e.g., sodium, chloride, bicarbonate), and gases (e.g.,

ACE Essentials of Exercise Science for Fitness Professionals

oxygen, nitrogen, carbon dioxide) throughout the body. The portion of the blood that is not plasma contains the formed elements, which include red blood cells, various types of white blood cells, and **platelets.**

Given that blood "feeds" virtually all tissues, its primary function is transportation. In addition, the cardiovascular system plays an important role in temperature regulation and acid–base balance.

Blood is transported throughout the body via blood vessels. The categories of blood vessels include the following:

- Arteries and **arterioles,** which carry oxygen-rich blood away from the heart
- Veins and **venules,** which return oxygen-poor blood to the heart
- Capillaries, which provide sites for gas, nutrient, and waste exchange between the blood and tissues

As blood leaves the heart to nourish the body, it is carried by the arteries (Figure 1-2a). Large arteries, such as the **aorta** and its major branches, are thick and elastic and are passively stretched as the blood is ejected from the heart. **Arteriosclerosis** (i.e., hardening of the arteries

Figure 1-2a
Major arteries of the body (anterior view)

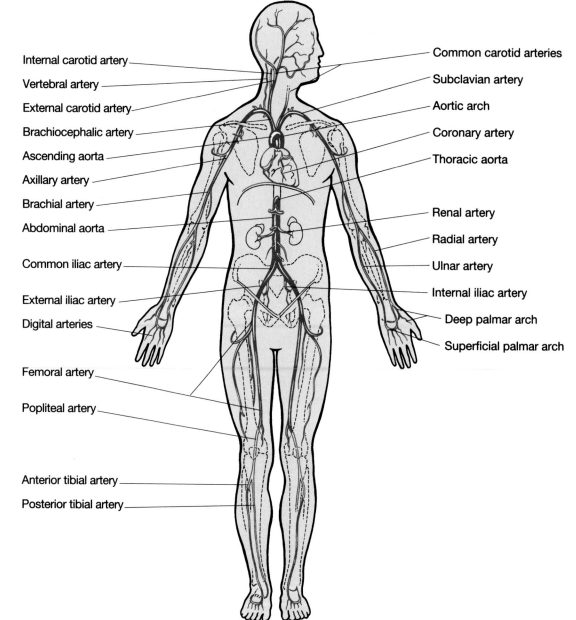

Internal carotid artery

Vertebral artery

External carotid artery

Brachiocephalic artery

Ascending aorta

Axillary artery

Brachial artery

Abdominal aorta

Common iliac artery

External iliac artery

Digital arteries

Femoral artery

Popliteal artery

Anterior tibial artery

Posterior tibial artery

Common carotid arteries

Subclavian artery

Aortic arch

Coronary artery

Thoracic aorta

Renal artery

Radial artery

Ulnar artery

Internal iliac artery

Deep palmar arch

Superficial palmar arch

and narrowing of the arteries due to plaque accumulation), which is commonly seen in older adults, contributes to arterial rigidity and decreases the arteries' ability to expand. This condition gives way to an increase in blood pressure, which is commonly associated with aging. As arteries lead away from the heart, they branch extensively to form a "tree" of smaller, microscopic vessels called arterioles. Eventually, the arterioles develop into "beds" of much smaller structures, the capillaries. Capillaries have extremely thin walls, and, consequently,

allow the exchange of materials between the blood and the **interstitial fluid** between the cells. Blood passes from the capillary beds to small venous vessels called venules. As venules lead back to the heart, they increase in size and become veins (Figure 1-2b). The walls of veins are thinner and less elastic than arterial walls. Commonly found inside the veins of the lower limbs are valves that allow blood to flow in only one direction—toward the heart. Blood leaving the major veins—the superior and inferior vena cava—empties directly into the

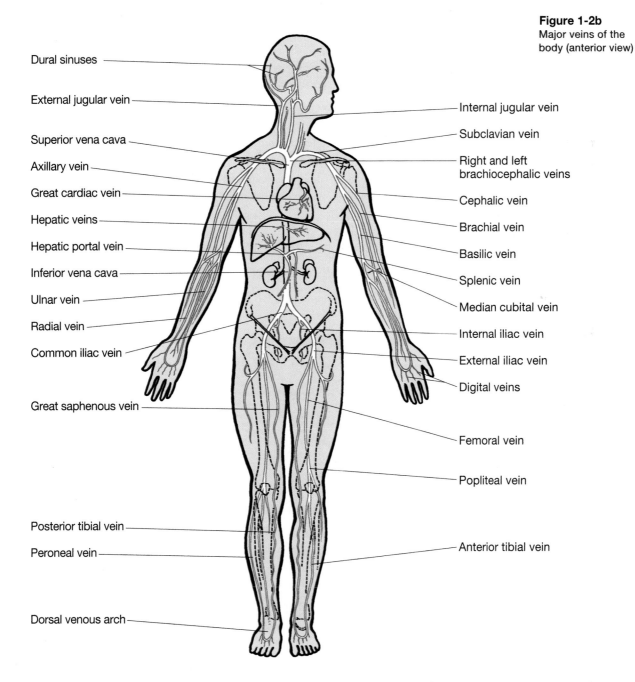

Figure 1-2b
Major veins of the body (anterior view)

Dural sinuses

External jugular vein

Superior vena cava

Axillary vein

Great cardiac vein

Hepatic veins

Hepatic portal vein

Inferior vena cava

Ulnar vein

Radial vein

Common iliac vein

Great saphenous vein

Posterior tibial vein

Peroneal vein

Dorsal venous arch

Internal jugular vein

Subclavian vein

Right and left brachiocephalic veins

Cephalic vein

Brachial vein

Basilic vein

Splenic vein

Median cubital vein

Internal iliac vein

External iliac vein

Digital veins

Femoral vein

Popliteal vein

Anterior tibial vein

heart, where it is transported to the lungs to pick up a fresh supply of oxygen.

The heart serves as a pump, pushing the blood throughout the body. It is located between the lungs and lies just left of center, behind the sternum. The adult heart is approximately the size of a closed fist. It is divided into four chambers and is often considered two pumps in one, as the right two chambers are responsible for pulmonary circulation and the left two chambers are responsible for systemic circulation. The chambers of the heart consist of two atria and two **ventricles.** The atria are small and located superior to the ventricles, which make up the bulk of the heart. The right **atrium** and the right ventricle form the right pump, while the left atrium and left ventricle combine to form the left pump (Figure 1-3). The right and left sides of the heart are separated by a muscular wall, called the interventricular septum, which prevents the mixing of blood from the two sides of the heart.

To function as a pump, the heart must have both receiving and propulsion chambers and valves, which direct blood flow through the heart. Blood movement within the heart is from the atria (the receiving chambers) to the ventricles (the propulsion chambers) and from the ventricles to the arteries. Backward movement of blood within the heart is prevented by four one-way valves.

The right and left atrioventricular valves connect the atria with the right and left ventricles, respectively. Backflow from the arteries into the ventricles is prevented by the pulmonary semilunar valve (right ventricle) and the aortic semilunar valve (left ventricle).

The right side of the heart receives blood that is partially depleted of its oxygen content and contains an elevated level of carbon dioxide after having passed through the cells. This blood is then pushed into the lungs, where it releases its carbon dioxide in exchange for oxygen. This is called the **pulmonary circuit.** The left side of the heart receives newly oxygenated blood from the lungs and pumps it to the various tissues of the body through the **systemic circuit.** The specific pathway of blood through the heart starts as venous blood (blood coming back to the heart through the veins). All the blood from the venous system enters the

Figure 1-3
Structure of the heart and flow of blood within it

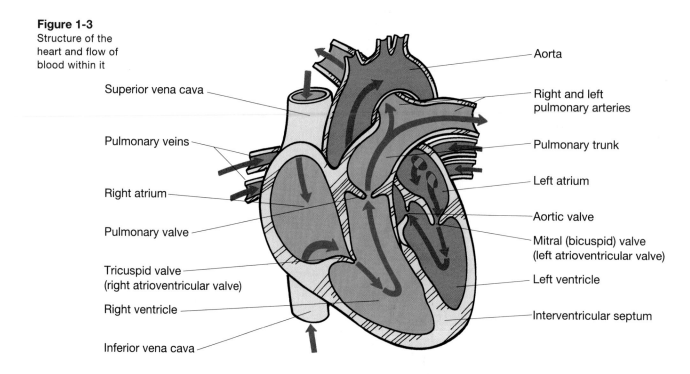

Aorta

Superior vena cava

Right and left pulmonary arteries

Pulmonary veins

Pulmonary trunk

Right atrium

Left atrium

Pulmonary valve

Aortic valve

Mitral (bicuspid) valve (left atrioventricular valve)

Tricuspid valve (right atrioventricular valve)

Left ventricle

Right ventricle

Interventricular septum

Inferior vena cava

right atrium first. From there, blood enters the right ventricle, which pumps it to the lungs through the pulmonary arteries (the exception to arteries carrying oxygen-rich blood). In the lungs, the blood picks up a fresh supply of oxygen and gives off carbon dioxide. The oxygenated blood returns from the lungs to the left atrium through the pulmonary veins (the exception to veins carrying oxygen-poor blood). From the left atrium, blood enters the left ventricle, and is then pumped through the aorta to the rest of the body (except for the lungs).

The **cardiac cycle** is the period from the beginning of one heartbeat to the beginning of the next. The right and left sides of the heart perform their pumping actions simultaneously. In other words, when the heart beats, both atria contract together to empty the blood into the ventricles.

Approximately 0.1 seconds after the atria contract, both ventricles contract to deliver blood to the pulmonary and systemic circuits. The repeating phases of contraction and relaxation are called **systole** and **diastole.** Systole refers to the contraction phase of the cardiac cycle, during which blood leaves the ventricles, while diastole refers to the relaxation phase of the cardiac cycle, during which blood fills the ventricles.

Respiratory System

The structures of the respiratory system make it possible for the body to exchange gases between the external environment and the tissues. Specifically, the respiratory system provides a means to replace oxygen and remove carbon dioxide from the blood. In addition, it makes vocalization possible and plays an important role in the regulation of the acid–base balance during exercise. The respiratory system is made up of the nose, nasal cavity, **pharynx, larynx, trachea, bronchi,** and lungs. Together, these structures form a group of passages that filter air and transport it into the lungs, where gas exchange occurs within microscopic air sacs called **alveoli** (Figure 1-4).

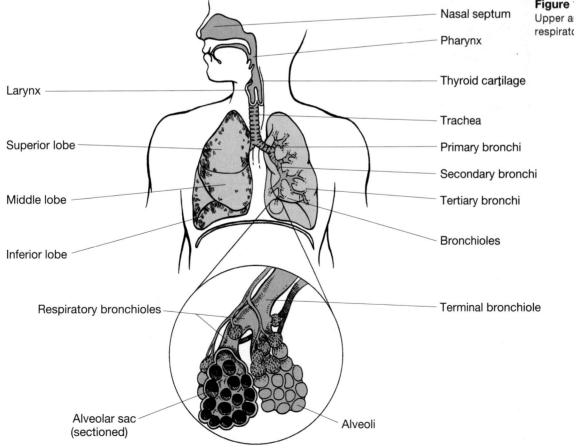

Larynx

Superior lobe

Middle lobe

Inferior lobe

Respiratory bronchioles

Alveolar sac (sectioned)

Nasal septum

Pharynx

Thyroid cartilage

Trachea

Primary bronchi

Secondary bronchi

Tertiary bronchi

Bronchioles

Terminal bronchiole

Alveoli

Figure 1-4
Upper and lower respiratory pathways

Air enters the respiratory system through both the nostrils and the mouth. The air is warmed and passed through the pharynx (throat), and then the larynx (the area of the "Adam's apple"). Humans normally breathe approximately 5 to 6 liters of air per minute through the nose when at rest, but use the mouth as the primary passageway for air when ventilation is increased to approximately 20 to 30 liters per minute during exercise. From the larynx, air travels through the trachea (windpipe), which extends to the fifth or sixth thoracic vertebrae, where it divides into two smaller branches: the right and left primary bronchi. The primary bronchi divide into smaller secondary bronchi, one for each lobe of the lung. The secondary bronchi then branch into many tertiary bronchi that repeatedly branch further, resulting in tiny **bronchioles.** The bronchioles continue to branch to form terminal bronchioles, which ultimately divide into even smaller respiratory bronchioles that end in clusters of alveoli (i.e., thin-walled air sacs).

The lungs contain approximately 300 million alveoli, which provide an enormous surface area for gas exchange. It is estimated that the total surface area available for diffusion in the human lung is about the size of a tennis court.

The lungs are encased within the rib cage. These paired, cone-shaped structures house the primary, secondary, and tertiary bronchi, as well as the various bronchioles and alveoli. The two lungs are separated by a space called the **mediastinum,** which contains several important organs, including the heart, aorta, esophagus, and part of the trachea. The lungs rest on top of the most important muscle of **inspiration,** the diaphragm, which is the only skeletal muscle considered essential for life. When the diaphragm contracts, it forces the abdominal contents downward and forward, while the external intercostals (groups of muscles that run between the ribs) lift the ribs outward. This action reduces the pressure in the membranes surrounding the lungs

and, in turn, causes the lungs to expand. This expansion allows airflow into the lungs. At rest, the diaphragm and external intercostals perform most of the work of inspiration. However, during physical activity, accessory muscles of inspiration are recruited, including the pectoralis minor, scalenes, and sternocleidomastoid. By assisting the diaphragm and external intercostals in the effort to further increase the volume of the **thorax,** these muscles aid in inspiration. **Expiration** occurs passively during normal, quiet breathing, requiring no assistance from muscle action. However, during exercise, expiration becomes active. Important muscles of expiration, such as the rectus abdominis, internal obliques, serratus posterior, and internal intercostals, are activated to help pull the rib cage downward and force air from the lungs by squeezing the abdominal organs upward against the diaphragm.

The muscles of respiration adapt to regular exercise training, as do the locomotor skeletal muscles. Regular endurance exercise increases the oxidative capacity of respiratory muscles, which improves respiratory muscle endurance. This is important because respiratory muscles have been shown to fatigue with exercise, adversely affecting the ability to breathe during both moderate- and high-intensity activities. Improving respiratory muscle endurance enhances exercise performance at various intensities.

Digestive System

Each cell in the body requires a constant source of energy to perform its specific function. People obtain energy from ingested food that has been mechanically or chemically processed by the body so that it can ultimately pass through the wall of the **gastrointestinal (GI) tract** and enter the bloodstream. The vascular system carries food molecules through the hepatic portal vein to the liver before distributing them throughout the body. After entering the cells, the digested food molecules may be reassembled into proteins, carbohydrates, and fats, or may be used in the production of energy to support body activity. The digestive system carries out six basic processes:

- Ingestion of food into the mouth
- Movement of food along the digestive tract
- Mechanical preparation of food for digestion
- **Chemical digestion** of food
- Absorption of digested food into the circulatory and **lymphatic systems**
- Elimination of indigestible substances and waste products from the body by defecation

The Lymphatic System

The lymphatic system is composed of an extensive network of capillaries, collecting vessels, lymph nodes, and lymphoid organs, and serves to return excess fluid from between the cells (interstitial fluid) back to the bloodstream, thereby preventing swelling of the intercellular spaces (edema). Lymph fluid is very similar to blood, except that it contains no red blood cells or platelets, as these components cannot escape through the blood-vessel walls. Once lymph enters the blood through specialized vessels called lymphatic capillaries, it circulates through the arteries, blood capillaries, and veins. There are four important functions of the lymphatic system:

- Destruction of bacteria and other foreign substances that are present in lymph nodes
- Specific immune responses that aid in manufacturing antibodies to destroy bacteria and foreign substances
- The return of interstitial fluid to the bloodstream
- Prevention of excessive accumulation of tissue fluid and filtered proteins by drainage into highly permeable lymphatic capillaries in the connective tissues

At its most basic structural level, the digestive system consists of a tube—called the GI tract—that extends from the mouth to the **anus.** When food is in the GI tract, it is considered to be outside of the body. To enter the body, the ingested food must cross the cells that line the wall of the digestive tract; many substances pass through the GI tract without being absorbed. Although the GI tract is one continuous tube, it is divided into several separate regions, each of which performs specialized functions in the digestive process. These regions include the mouth, pharynx, esophagus, stomach, small intestine, and large intestine (Figure 1-5).

Food enters the body through the mouth, where the mechanical process of chewing breaks large pieces of food into smaller ones. Saliva blends with these pieces to ease swallowing and dissolve some of the food particles, thereby allowing the food to be tasted by the taste buds on the tongue. Furthermore, secretions from the salivary glands contain an enzyme that initiates carbohydrate digestion. Food that is swallowed passes through the mouth to the pharynx, which serves as a common passageway for both the respiratory

Figure 1-5
The gastrointestinal (GI) tract

This image was provided by KidsHealth, one of the largest resources online for medically reviewed health information written for parents, kids, and teens. www.KidsHealth.org; www.TeensHealth.org. ©1995–2009. The Nemours Foundation/ KidsHealth. Reprinted with permission.

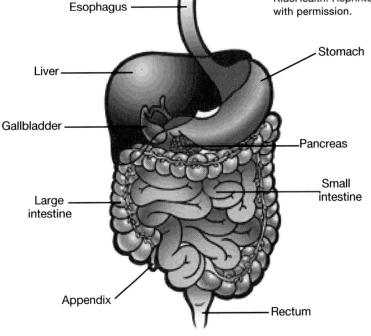

Esophagus

Liver

Gallbladder

Large intestine

Appendix

Stomach

Pancreas

Small intestine

Rectum

and digestive systems. The act of swallowing causes food to slide across the **epiglottis,** bypassing the entrance to the lungs. This is important because the epiglottis closes off the trachea to prevent choking when swallowing. After a mouthful of food has been swallowed, it is called a **bolus.**

Next, the bolus slides down the esophagus—a muscular tube that connects the pharynx with the stomach. Located behind the trachea, the esophagus passes through the mediastinum of the thorax and continues on to the diaphragm, where it ultimately empties into the stomach. Waves of contractions, called peristalses (singular = **peristalsis**), move the food through the esophagus, where it enters the stomach through the **cardiac sphincter,** which sits at the upper portion of the stomach. The stomach prepares ingested food by chemical and mechanical means for passage into the small intestine. The chemical action consists of specialized stomach cells that produce secretions to break down food particles; these secretions also protect the stomach cells from being broken down. The mechanical action occurs when the stomach grinds the food into a suspension of particles to create a thick liquid mixture known as **chyme.** The stomach stores chyme until it can be emptied into the small intestine at a rate appropriate for optimal digestion and absorption. Chyme leaves the stomach and enters the small intestine through the **pyloric sphincter.**

The small intestine is the primary site for digestion and absorption of food, including the energy-providing nutrients (protein, carbohydrate, and fat), **vitamins, minerals,** and water. Therefore, it is important for the stomach to store food and pass it into the small intestine at a rate that does not exceed the small intestine's capacity. In general, it takes hours to digest and absorb a meal that took only minutes to consume. Measuring a length of approximately 21 feet (6.4 meters), the small intestine is divided into three segments—the **duodenum** [the first 8 inches (20.3 cm)], the **jejunum** [8 feet (2.4 meters)], and the **ileum** [12 feet (3.7 meters)].

As it passes through the duodenum, chyme is exposed to **bile** from the liver and gallbladder (which aids in the digestion of fat), and pancreatic enzymes (which aid in the digestion of protein, carbohydrate, and fat). In the small intestine, a process similar to peristalsis, called segmentation, not only pushes the chyme, but also periodically squeezes it momentarily, thereby forcing the intestinal contents backward a few inches and allowing the digestive juices and absorbing cells to make better contact with the nutrients. Most absorption of food molecules occurs in the duodenum and the jejunum through the surfaces of microscopic, hair-like projections called **villi** and **microvilli.** Each projection has its own capillary network and lymph vessel, so as food molecules move across them, the nutrients can immediately pass through into the bloodstream and body fluids.

By the time chyme reaches the large intestine (sometimes called the **colon**), digestion and absorption are mostly complete. The large intestine, which is approximately 5 feet (1.5 meters) long, is called "large" because its diameter is greater than that of the small intestine. The final absorption of water and salt occurs in the large intestine, leaving semisolid waste that is passed out of the body through the anus. Fiber and other indigestible substances in the diet provide bulk against which the muscles of the colon can work to expel the waste. Transit time of a meal through the digestive system (from mouth to colon) can take several hours and depends on the nutrient composition of the meal.

The kidney is another organ related to digestion, but it is actually part of its own distinct system (the urinary system). The kidneys are located on each side of the vertebral column in the posterior abdominal cavity. They are the body's main excretory organs and are critically important for maintaining the body's internal environment within a range that is optimal for survival of the cells. The kidneys carry out their functions by eliminating from the body a variety of metabolic products, such as urea, uric acid, and creatinine, and by excreting or conserving water and **electrolytes.** As blood flows through the kidneys, some of the plasma is filtered out. As the filtrate flows along, water, electrolytes, **glucose,** amino acids, and other important substances are reabsorbed and returned to the blood. Hormones regulate the reabsorption and secretion processes within the kidneys and allow them to exert a high degree of control over which materials get excreted or reabsorbed. When the reabsorption and secretion processes are completed, the remaining fluid in the kidneys is transported to the bladder and excreted as urine.

Skeletal System

The human skeleton is an active, living tissue that performs several important functions: support, movement, protection, storage, and formation of blood cells (**hemopoiesis**). The body has a total of 206 bones, most of which are paired (e.g., right and left femurs, right and left tibias) (Figure 1-6). The structural functions of bone include giving support to the soft tissues of the body and

Figure 1-6
Skeletal system

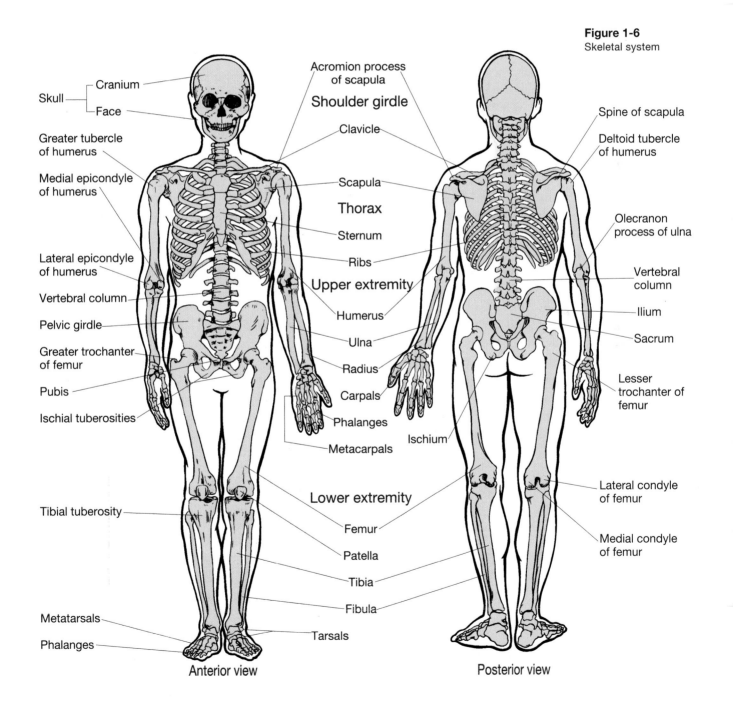

Skull ── Cranium
         └ Face

Greater tubercle of humerus

Medial epicondyle of humerus

Lateral epicondyle of humerus

Vertebral column

Pelvic girdle

Greater trochanter of femur

Pubis

Ischial tuberosities

Tibial tuberosity

Metatarsals

Phalanges

Anterior view

Acromion process of scapula

Shoulder girdle

Clavicle

Scapula

Thorax

Sternum

Ribs

Upper extremity

Humerus

Ulna

Radius

Carpals

Phalanges

Metacarpals

Ischium

Lower extremity

Femur

Patella

Tibia

Fibula

Tarsals

Spine of scapula

Deltoid tubercle of humerus

Olecranon process of ulna

Vertebral column

Ilium

Sacrum

Lesser trochanter of femur

Lateral condyle of femur

Medial condyle of femur

Posterior view

providing attachment sites for most muscles, which play an important role in movement. Many of the body's muscles attach to bone, and when the muscles contract, the bones move at their **articulations** (joints). The skeleton also provides protection for many of the body's organs. For example, the skull encases the brain, the vertebrae form a canal around the spinal cord, the rib cage protects the heart and lungs, and the bony pelvis guards the urinary bladder and internal reproductive organs. The skeleton is also a storehouse for two essential minerals—calcium and phosphorous—that are necessary for the proper functioning of other body systems. In addition, fat, sodium, potassium, and other minerals are stored in the bones. Recall that bones are not static structures. They are constantly breaking down to release minerals and other substances into the blood, while simultaneously rebuilding to provide the body with flexible, yet sturdy, structural support. After birth, the skeleton is a production site for blood cells found within the circulatory system (e.g., red blood cells, certain white blood cells, platelets).

The various shapes of bones determine how they are classified (i.e., long, short, flat, irregular). Long bones are so named because they are longer than they are wide, which means that they have a long axis. Most of the bones of the limbs are classified as long bones (e.g., humerus, radius, ulna, femur, tibia, fibula, phalanges). Bones that are approximately the same length and width are called short bones (e.g., carpals, tarsals). Flat bones are thin and typically curved. They include some of the bones of the skull, the ribs, and the sternum. Bones that do not fit into the previous categories are classified as irregular bones because of their diverse shapes (e.g., hip bones, vertebrae, certain skull bones).

Bones are composed of a dense outer layer, called compact or **cortical bone,** and a honeycomb-like inner structure, called spongy or **trabecular bone.** The cortical shell makes up roughly 75% of the skeleton, whereas the trabecular network makes up the remaining 25%. Cortical bone is essential, because it provides strength, **tendon** attachment sites for muscles, and organ protection without excessive weight. Trabecular bone serves two vital purposes. It provides a large surface area for mineral exchange and helps to maintain skeletal strength and integrity. It is particularly abundant in the vertebrae and at the ends of long bones, sites that are under continuous stress from motion and weightbearing. Areas containing a large percentage of trabecular tissue are most likely to fracture when the bone is weakened due to a disease such as **osteoporosis.**

A closer look at a typical long bone reveals its many structures (Figure 1-7). The shaft, called the **diaphysis,** is located between the two ends, which are named the **proximal** and **distal** epiphyses (singular = **epiphysis**). The hollow space inside the diaphysis is called the medullary cavity, which is used as a storage site for fat and is sometimes called the yellow bone marrow cavity. It is lined by a thin connective tissue layer called the **endosteum.** The diaphysis and outer layers of the epiphyses are made of cortical bone, whereas trabecular bone is concentrated in the central regions of the epiphyses. Certain long bones contain red marrow—which is essential in the manufacture and maturation of red blood cells, most white blood cells, and platelets—in the trabecular tissue of their epiphyses. An **epiphyseal cartilage,** also called a "growth plate," separates the diaphysis and epiphysis in children and young adults, providing a means for the bone to increase in length. In adults, when skeletal growth has been completed, the epiphyseal cartilage is replaced by bone and the area is called the epiphyseal line. A dense connective-tissue layer called the **periosteum** covers the outer surface of bone and is well supplied with blood vessels and nerves, some of which enter the bone.

Throughout life, the human skeleton is being continuously broken down while simultaneously being restored. In fact, most of the adult skeleton is replaced

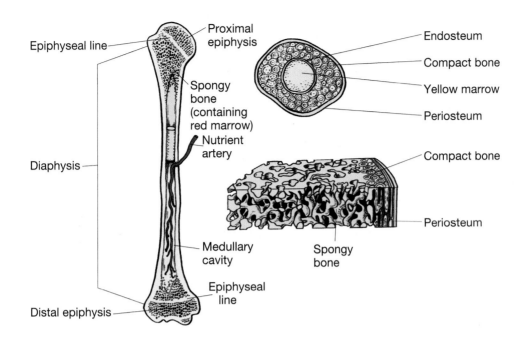

Figure 1-7
Long bone gross
anatomy

approximately every 10 years. In adults, a process called remodeling is responsible for the continual reshaping and rebuilding of the skeleton in response to internal and external signals from specialized bone cells that either build bone (**osteoblasts**) or break it down (**osteoclasts**). Remodeling is vital for bone health for several reasons. First, the remodeling process repairs damage to the skeleton that can result from repeated stresses. It also prevents the accumulation of too much old bone, which can lose its resilience and become brittle. Furthermore, remodeling plays an important role in removing calcium and phosphorous from the bones when these minerals are deficient in the diet or when an increased need exists due to pregnancy or lactation.

Although the size and shape of the skeleton is genetically determined, it can be greatly affected by loading or impact from physical activity. Ultimately, a bone's size and shape fits best with its function. In other words, "form follows function." **Wolff's law** indicates that changes in bone structure coincide with changes in bone function. That is, when the skeleton is subjected to stressful forces, such as those that occur with exercise, it responds by laying down more bone tissue, thereby increasing its

density. Conversely, when individuals experience prolonged periods of bed rest due to illness or injury, their bones lose mineral and become less dense. Maintaining adequate bone density is an important issue for all adults. Fitness professionals can play a crucial role in helping people preserve bone tissue by educating them about the importance of exercise and proper nutrition.

Axial Skeleton

Of the 206 bones that make up the skeleton, 74 are categorized as the axial skeleton (Table 1-3). Consisting of the skull, vertebral column, sternum, and ribs, the axial skeleton's most important functions are to provide the main axial support for the body and protect the **central nervous system (CNS)** and the organs of the thorax. Fitness professionals should have a fundamental knowledge of the structure of the vertebral column, since the mechanics of the spine affect all exercise performance. The vertebral column consists of 33 vertebrae, which are categorized by regions (Figure 1-8). The upper region (neck area) of the spine contains seven cervical vertebrae, which are the smallest and most delicate. The mid-region, below the cervical vertebrae, contains 12 thoracic vertebrae that are each

Table 1-3

Bones in the Axial and Appendicular Skeletons

Axial Skeleton	Number of Bones
Skull	
Cranium	8
Face	14
Hyoid	1
Vertebral Column	26
Thorax	
Sternum	1
Ribs	24
(Auditory ossicles)*	6
Total	80

Appendicular Skeleton	Number of Bones
Lower Extremity	
Phalanges	28
Metatarsals	10
Tarsals	14
Patella	2
Tibia	2
Fibula	2
Femur	2
Pelvic Girdle	
Hip or pelvis (os coxae = ilium, ischium, pubis)	2
Shoulder Girdle	
Clavicle	2
Scapula	2
Upper Extremity	
Phalanges	28
Metacarpals	10
Carpals	16
Radius	2
Ulna	2
Humerus	2
Total	126

* The auditory ossicles, three per ear, are not considered part of the axial or appendicular skeletons, but rather a separate group of bones. They were placed in the axial skeleton group for convenience.

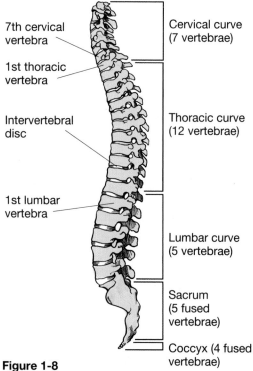

7th cervical vertebra

1st thoracic vertebra

Intervertebral disc

1st lumbar vertebra

Cervical curve (7 vertebrae)

Thoracic curve (12 vertebrae)

Lumbar curve (5 vertebrae)

Sacrum (5 fused vertebrae)

Coccyx (4 fused vertebrae)

Figure 1-8
Vertebral column (lateral view)

attached to a rib. The lower region consists of five lumbar vertebrae, the sacrum (five fused vertebrae), and the coccyx (four fused vertebrae). The lumbar vertebrae are the largest and heaviest vertebrae due to their role in continuously receiving ground reaction forces and axial compression forces.

Appendicular Skeleton

The remaining 126 bones are categorized as the appendicular skeleton, which includes the bones of the upper and lower limbs and the pectoral (shoulder) and pelvic (hip) girdles (see Table 1-3). The pectoral and pelvic girdles represent the means by which the appendicular skeleton articulates (joins together) with the axial skeleton. The pectoral girdle (clavicle and scapula) attaches to the axial skeleton only at the sternum, providing little support for the upper-body structures. Still, the support is sufficient, because the upper limbs do not bear the body's weight. This minimal connection with the axial skeleton allows the pectoral girdle to express a wide range of movements at the shoulder. In contrast, the pelvic girdle (ilium, ischium, and pubis—known collectively as the os coxae) does support the body's weight. Therefore, it has more extensive attachments to the axial skeleton through its articulation with the sacrum (see Figure 1-6). Furthermore, each side of the pelvic girdle is united by a strong joint made of cartilage called the pubic symphysis.

Articulations

The bones of the skeleton come together at articulations (joints.) When two bones meet at a junction, they are said to "articulate" with each other (e.g., the femur articulates inferiorly with the tibia). While most joints allow movement between two bones, some permit little, if any, movement. The three main types of joints are fibrous, cartilaginous, and synovial. Fibrous joints are held tightly together by fibrous connective tissue and allow little or no movement. They are classified as synarthroidal (syn = together; arthro = joint). In other words, synarthroidal joints are considered immovable joints and include the sutures of the skull and the joint between the distal ends of the tibia and fibula (Figure 1-9). In cartilaginous joints, the bones are connected by cartilage and little or no movement is allowed. A characteristic of one type of cartilaginous joint, a symphysis, is the fibrocartilaginous pad, or disk, that separates the two bones. The junction of the two pubic bones (pubic symphysis) and the junctions between the bodies of adjacent vertebrae (see Figure 1-8) are examples of symphyses.

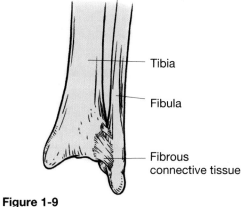

Figure 1-9
Example of a fibrous joint

Tibia

Fibula

Fibrous connective tissue

The most common type of joint in the body is the synovial joint, which is freely moveable. Because of this freedom, synovial joints are classified as diarthroses (diarthrosis means "through joint"). Synovial joints have four characteristic traits: an articular cartilage, an articular capsule, a synovial membrane, and synovial fluid. Articular cartilage refers to the hyaline cartilage (from the Greek word *hyalos,* meaning glass) that covers the end surfaces of long bones. The articular capsule encloses the joint with a double-layered membrane. The outer layer is composed of a dense fibrous tissue that forms **ligaments** to strengthen the joint. The inner layer is the synovial membrane, which is well supplied with capillaries and produces a thick fluid called synovial fluid. The fluid nourishes the articular cartilages and lubricates the joint surfaces. Some synovial joints also have articular disks made of fibrocartilage, such as the menisci in the knee. The medial and lateral meniscus help absorb shock in the knee, increase joint stability, direct synovial fluid to aid in nourishment of the knee, and increase joint contact surface area, thereby decreasing overall pressure on the joint.

Movements of Synovial Joints

Synovial joints move depending on the shapes of their bony structures and their articular surfaces. A joint's **axis of rotation** allows it to move in various planes, where the plane of movement is generally perpendicular to the axis. The axis of rotation is an imaginary line that forms a right angle to the plane of movement about which a joint rotates. For example, the bones of the elbow allow the forearm to move anteriorly and posteriorly (**sagittal plane**) around an imaginary horizontal line that passes through it from side to side (mediolateral axis of rotation) (Figure 1-10). To review which planes of movement are perpendicular to each other, see Figure 1-1. Some joints have more than one axis of rotation, allowing them to move in various planes. Joints that move in one plane only and have one axis of rotation are called

Figure 1-10
Movement of synovial (diarthrodial) joints

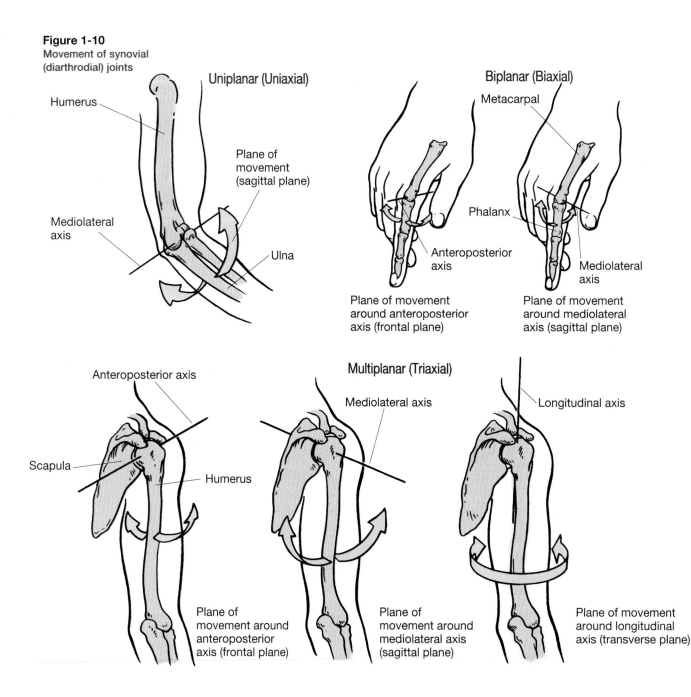

uniplanar or uniaxial joints. These joints are also called "hinge" joints, because hinges (like those on a door) allow movement in only one plane. The ankles and elbows are examples of uniaxial joints.

Joints that allow movement in two planes that are perpendicular to each other are called biplanar or biaxial joints. Examples of biaxial joints are the foot (calcaneocuboid joint), knee, hand, and wrist. Biaxial joint movement can be observed when the index finger (first phalanx) moves anteriorly and posteriorly

(sagittal plane movement around a mediolateral axis) and laterally and medially (**frontal plane** movement around an anteroposterior axis) (see Figure 1-10). Still other joints permit movement in three axes of rotation. These are called mulitplanar or triaxial joints and include the hip, thumb, and shoulder. The shoulder, for example, allows the humerus to move anteriorly and posteriorly; laterally and medially; and rotate internally and externally (**transverse plane** movement around a longitudinal axis) (see Figure 1-10). A summary of the major joints in the body, classified by type and movements, is presented in Table 1-4.

There are four general groups of movements that occur in synovial joints throughout the body: gliding, angular, **circumduction,** and rotation. In gliding, the surfaces of two adjoining bones move back and forth upon each other. An example of a gliding joint is the articulation between the head of a rib and the body of its associated vertebra. Angular movement describes an increase or decrease in the angle between two adjoining bones. There are four angular movements defined for synovial joints: **flexion, extension, abduction,** and **adduction.** Flexion describes movement in which the bones comprising a joint move toward each other in the sagittal plane, decreasing the joint angle between them. An example is bringing the forearm upward toward the upper arm, as in elbow flexion. Extension is the opposite of flexion and causes the angle between two adjoining bones to increase in the sagittal plane. An example is starting with the calf upward toward the back of the thigh and moving it downward away from the thigh, as in knee extension (Figure 1-11).

Abduction occurs when a part of the body is moved away from the midline of the body, such as lifting an arm or leg away from the side of the body. Adduction is the opposite of abduction and refers to movement of a body part toward

Table 1-4

Major Joints in the Body

Region/Joint	Type	Number of Axes of Rotation	Movements Possible
Lower Extremity			
Foot (metatarsophalangeal)	Synovial (condyloid)	2	Flexion & extension; abduction & adduction; circumduction
Ankle (talocrural)	Synovial (hinge)	1	Plantarflexion & dorsiflexion
Between distal tibia & fibula	Fibrous	0	Slight movement possible
Knee (tibia & femur)	Synovial (modified hinge)	2	Flexion & extension; internal & external rotation
Hip	Synovial (ball & socket)	3	Flexion & extension; abduction & adduction; internal & external rotation
Upper Extremity			
Hand (metacarpophalangeal)	Synovial (condyloid)	2	Flexion & extension; abduction & adduction; circumduction
Thumb	Synovial (saddle)	3	Flexion & extension; abduction & adduction; circumduction; opposition
Wrist (radiocarpal)	Synovial	2	Flexion & extension; abduction & adduction; circumduction
Proximal radioulnar	Synovial (pivot)	1	Pronation & supination
Elbow (ulna & humerus)	Synovial (hinge)	1	Flexion & extension
Shoulder	Synovial (ball & socket)	3	Flexion & extension; abduction & adduction; circumduction; internal & external rotation
Ribs & sternum	Cartilaginous	0	Slight movement possible

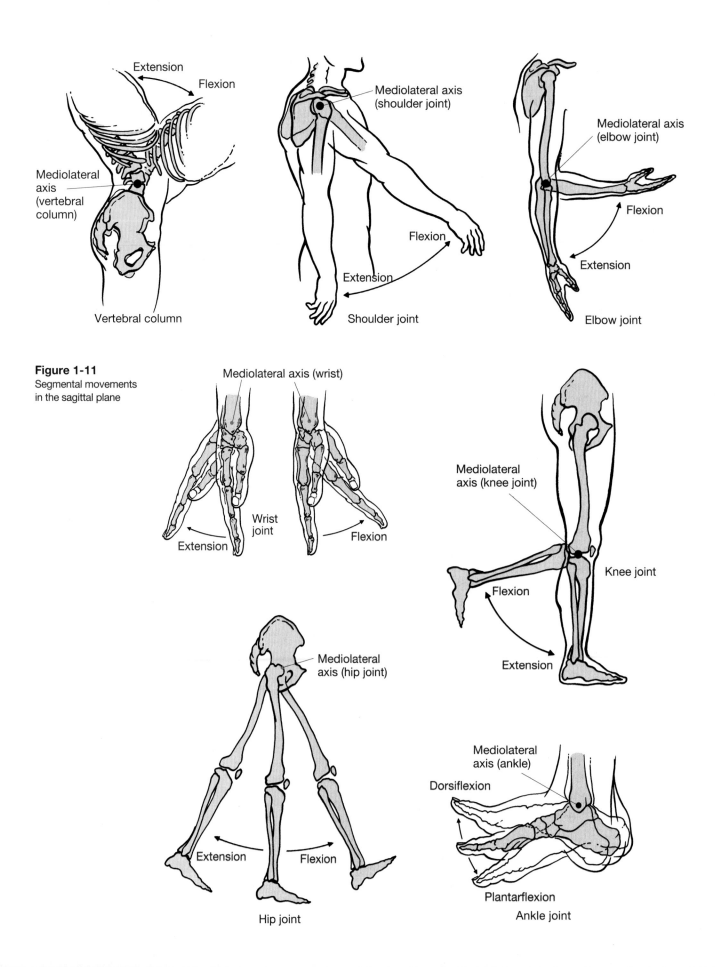

Figure 1-11
Segmental movements
in the sagittal plane

the midline of the body, such as lowering an arm or leg from an abducted position toward the side of the body (Figure 1-12). In the case of the fingers and toes, the reference point for abduction and adduction is the midline of the hand and foot, respectively. For example, abduction of the fingers occurs when they move away from the third digit of the hand (i.e., spreading the fingers apart). Conversely, adduction of the fingers refers to the digits moving out of abduction toward the third digit. Abduction of the toes is accomplished by moving them away from the second toe (i.e., spreading the toes apart) and adduction occurs when the toes move

out of abduction toward the second toe. All abduction and adduction movements occur in the frontal plane.

Certain joints, such as the shoulder and hip, are capable of incorporating all four angular movements to create one motion called circumduction. That is, the movement is actually a sequential combination of flexion, extension, abduction, and adduction. An easy way to remember circumduction is to picture a swimmer performing arm circles as a warm-up prior to diving in the pool. The circular motion represents circumduction of the shoulder joints.

Rotation describes motion of a bone around a central (longitudinal) axis. From

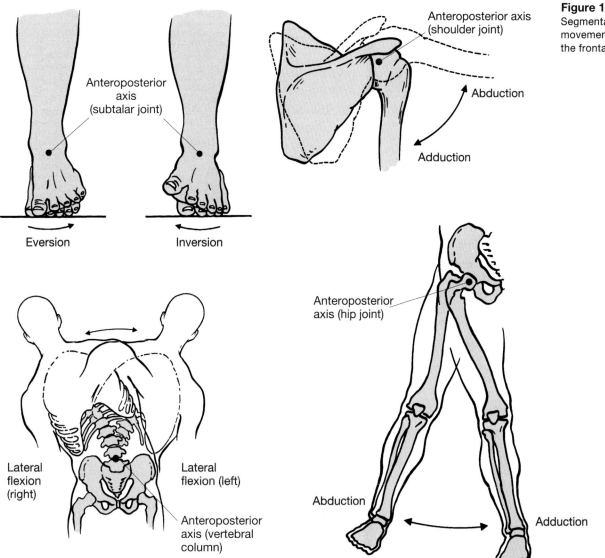

Figure 1-12
Segmental movements in the frontal plane

ACE Essentials of Exercise Science for Fitness Professionals

the anatomical position, movement of the anterior surface of the humerus or femur inward is called internal (medial) rotation. Conversely, movement of the anterior surface of humerus or femur outward is called external (lateral) rotation. A specific type of rotation, called **pronation** and **supination,** occurs at the radioulnar joint. Rotating the forearm outward so the palm faces anteriorly is supination, whereas rotation of the forearm inward so the palm faces posteriorly is pronation. Anatomical position, therefore, requires supination of the forearm (see Figure 1-1). Rotation around a longitudinal axis occurs in the transverse plane. This also includes rotation of the spine (Figure 1-13). A summary of the synovial joint fundamental movements is presented in Table 1-5.

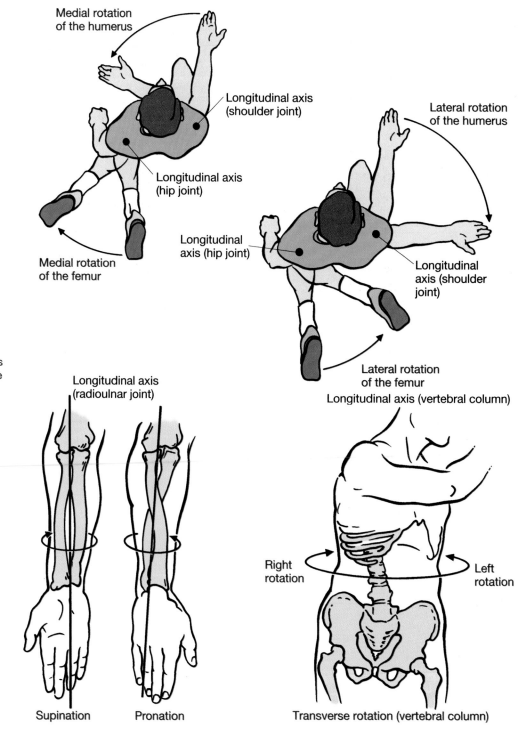

Figure 1-13
Segmental movements in the transverse plane

Table 1-5

Fundamental Movements (From Anatomical Position)

Plane	Action	Definition
Sagittal	Flexion	Decreasing the angle between two bones
	Extension	Increasing the angle between two bones
	Dorsiflexion	Moving the top of the foot toward the shin (only at the ankle joint)
	Plantarflexion	Moving the sole of the foot downward; "pointing the toes" (only at the ankle)
Frontal	Abduction	Motion away from the midline of the body (or part)
	Adduction	Motion toward the midline of the body (or part)
	Elevation	Moving to a superior position (only at the scapula)
	Depression	Moving to an inferior position (only at the scapula)
	Inversion	Lifting the medial border of the foot (only at the subtalar joint)
	Eversion	Lifting the lateral border of the foot (only at the subtalar joint)
Transverse	Rotation	Internal (inward) or external (outward) turning about the vertical axis of bone
	Pronation*	Rotating the hand and wrist medially from the elbow
	Supination†	Rotating the hand and wrist laterally from the elbow
	Horizontal flexion (adduction)	From a 90-degree abducted shoulder or hip position, the humerus or femur, respectively, is flexed (adducted) in toward the midline of the body in the transverse plane
	Horizontal extension (abduction)	The return of the humerus or femur from horizontal flexion (adduction)
Multiplanar	Circumduction	Motion that describes a "cone"; combines flexion, extension, abduction, and adduction in sequence
	Opposition	Thumb movement unique to humans and primates

*Pronation of the foot is a combination of eversion and abduction, raising the lateral edge of the foot.
†Supination of the foot is a combination of inversion and adduction, raising the medial edge of the foot.

Nervous System

The overall function of the nervous system is to collect information about conditions in relation to the body's external state, analyze this information, and initialize appropriate responses to fulfill specific needs. In other words, the nervous system gathers information, stores it, and controls various bodily systems in response to this input. The muscular system, which is composed of more than 600 individual muscles, is responsible for movement of various body parts. Connective tissue, which is intricately associated with the neuromuscular system, provides structure, cohesion, and support to the muscles and nerves it surrounds. The connection of the muscles to the brain and spinal cord through a network of nerve circuits that direct the ebb and flow of muscular energy is referred to as the neuromuscular system.

Neural Organization

The nervous system is separated into various divisions based on either structural or functional characteristics. Keep in mind that these divisions—which are called nervous systems themselves—are still part of a single, overall nervous system. In terms of structure, the nervous system is divided into two parts: the CNS and the **peripheral nervous system (PNS).** The CNS consists of the brain and spinal cord, which are both encased and protected by bony structures—the skull and the vertebral column, respectively. The CNS is responsible for receiving sensory input from the PNS and formulating responses to this input. This makes the CNS the integrative and control center of the nervous system. The PNS is composed of all the nervous structures located outside of the CNS, namely the nerves and **ganglia** (nerve cell bodies associated with the nerves). In part, the PNS is made up of pairings of nerves that branch out from the brain and spinal cord from different regions. Twelve pairs of cranial nerves, which arise from the brain and brain stem, exit the cranial cavity through **foramina** (small holes) in the skull. Thirty-one pairs of spinal nerves, which arise from the spinal cord, exit the vertebral column through intervertebral foramina. Named for the region of the spine where they originate and the vertebral level from

which they emerge, the paired spinal nerves are classified as eight cervical, 12 thoracic, five lumbar, five sacral, and one coccygeal (Figure 1-14). A list of the spinal nerve roots and the muscles they innervate is presented in Table 1-6.

In terms of function, the PNS is separated into two categories: the afferent (sensory) division and the efferent (motor) division. The afferent division carries nerve impulses to the CNS from receptors located in the skin, **fasciae,** joints, and visceral organs. In other words, afferent sensory data is incoming information. In contrast, the efferent division handles outgoing information and can be divided into the **somatic** and **autonomic nervous systems.** The somatic nervous system is mostly under conscious control and carries nerve impulses

Figure 1-14
Spinal cord and spinal nerves (posterior view)

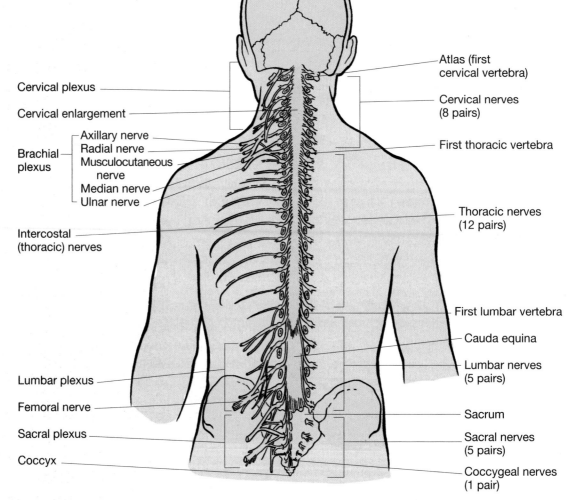

Table 1-6

Selected Spinal Nerve Roots and Major Muscles Innervated

Nerve Root	Muscles Innervated
C5	Biceps brachii, deltoid, supraspinatus, infraspinatus
C6	Brachioradialis, supinator, extensor carpi radialis longus and brevis, extensor carpi ulnaris
C7	Triceps brachii, flexor carpi radialis, flexor carpi ulnaris
C8	Extensor pollicis longus and brevis, adductor pollicis longus
T1	Intrinsic muscles of the hand (lumbricals, interossei)
L2	Psoas major and minor, adductor magnus, adductor longus, adductor brevis
L3	Rectus femoris, vastus lateralis, vastus medialis, vastus intermedius, psoas major and minor
L4	Anterior tibialis, posterior tibialis
L5	Extensor hallucis longus, extensor digitorum longus, peroneus longus and brevis, gluteus maximus, gluteus medius
S1	Gastrocnemius, soleus, biceps femoris, semitendinosus, semimembranosus, gluteus maximus
S2	Gluteus maximus, flexor hallucis longus, flexor digitorum longus
S4	Bladder, rectum

flight" response, this activation affects nearly every organ to enable the body to stop storing energy and mobilize all resources to respond to the stressful event or activity. The **parasympathetic nervous system** aids in controlling normal functions when the body is relaxed; it aids in digesting food, storing energy, and promoting growth.

Structures of the Nervous System

The most basic structural and functional component of the nervous system is the neuron (nerve cell). The neuron is composed of a cell body (soma) and one or more processes—fibrous extensions called **dendrites** and **axons** (Figure 1-15). Dendrites conduct electrical impulses toward the cell body, while axons transmit electrical signals away from the cell body. Neurons may have hundreds of the branching dendrites, depending on the neuron type, but each neuron has only one axon. For an electrical impulse to travel through the nervous system, it must be passed from one neuron to the next. Most neurons do not have direct contact with each other.

Instead, neurons remain separated from each other by a small space called a **synapse.** To carry the impulse across the synapse from one neuron to the other, the first neuron releases a chemical transmitter substance

from the CNS to the skeletal muscles. In some instances, muscle contractions brought on by the somatic nervous system are not consciously controlled, such as in the case of a reflex response. The autonomic nervous system is made up of nerves that transmit impulses to the smooth muscles, cardiac muscle, and glands. These visceral motor impulses generally cannot be consciously controlled. The autonomic nervous system is further divided into the sympathetic and parasympathetic divisions. The **sympathetic nervous system** is activated when there is a stressor or an emergency, such as severe pain, anger, or fear. Called the "fight or

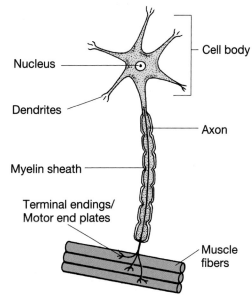

Figure 1-15
Basic anatomical structure of a motor neuron (or nerve cell) and motor end plate

Cell body

Nucleus

Dendrites

Axon

Myelin sheath

Terminal endings/ Motor end plates

Muscle fibers

that attaches to receptors located on the membrane of the second neuron.

Most axons are covered with a fatty substance called **myelin,** which insulates the axon and keeps the electrical current from migrating outside of the neuron. A nerve is made up of the processes of many neurons held together by connective tissue sheaths. Sensory nerves carry impulses to the CNS, whereas motor nerves carry nerve impulses from the CNS to the PNS. Motor neurons form a **neuromuscular junction** with the skeletal muscles they supply.

Proprioception

The sense of knowing where the body is in relation to its various segments and the external environment is called **proprioception.** The sensory information gathered to achieve this kinesthetic awareness comes from structures called **proprioceptors,** which are receptors located in the skin, in and around the joints and muscles, and in the inner ear. Cutaneous receptors are located in the skin and send sensory information regarding pressure, touch, and movement of the hairs on the skin. Joint receptors are located in the joint capsules and the surrounding ligaments. They transmit sensory information relating to positions, velocities, and accelerations occurring at the joints. In addition, pressure receptors within the joints provide added information about pressure changes that is used for important postural adjustments and normal gait.

Pacinian corpuscles are receptors located **deep** within the skin and the joint capsule that are sensitive to pressure. **Meissner's corpuscles** are receptors located in the **superficial** layers of the skin that are responsive to light touch. While most researchers agree that these skin receptors do not play a large part in proprioception, it is believed that injured individuals who have experienced joint and ligament receptor damage benefit from increased reliance on cutaneous receptors for proprioception. **Golgi-Mazzoni corpuscles** are located

within the joint capsule and are responsive to joint compression. Thus, any weightbearing activity stimulates these receptors. Another type of proprioceptor, the musculotendinous receptor, is involved in muscular control and coordination. There are two such types of receptors—the **Golgi tendon organ (GTO)** and the **muscle spindle**. Connected to approximately 15 to 20 muscle fibers and located between the muscle belly and its tendon, the GTO senses increased tension within its associated muscle when the muscle contracts or is stretched. One of the GTO's functions when it senses muscle contraction is to cause an inhibition of the contraction (**autogenic inhibition**). It has been theorized that this function adjusts muscle output in response to fatigue. That is, when muscle tension is reduced due to fatigue, GTO output is also reduced, which lowers its inhibitory effect in its own muscle and allows the muscle to increase its contractile ability. Furthermore, GTO activation results in an enhanced contraction of the opposing (**antagonist**) muscle group. Both of these properties have important implications in flexibility because a muscle can be stretched more fully and easily when the GTOs have inhibited the muscle's contraction and allowed the antagonistic muscle group to contract more readily.

A second type of musculotendinous receptor, the muscle spindle, is located mostly in the muscle belly and lies parallel to the muscle fibers. This arrangement causes the muscle spindle to stretch when the muscle itself experiences a stretch force, thereby exciting the muscle spindle and causing a reflexive contraction in the muscle known as the stretch reflex. The muscle spindle's reflex contraction of its associated muscle simultaneously causes the antagonist muscle group to relax (**reciprocal inhibition**). For example, if the gastrocnemius is stretched rapidly, the muscle spindles within the muscle belly cause it to contract. At the same time, if the opposing muscle group (anterior tibialis) is contracting, the muscle spindle reflex causes it to relax. The muscle spindles and the GTOs work together through their reflexive actions to regulate muscle stiffness, and therefore, contribute largely to the body's sense of postural control (Figure 1-16).

Autogenic inhibition and reciprocal inhibition are directly associated with stretching. A practical application of autogenic inhibition is observed during **static stretching.** Low-force, long-duration static stretches evoke a temporary increase in muscle tension due to muscle lengthening. After seven to 10 seconds of a low-force stretch, the increase in muscle tension activates a GTO response. Under GTO activation, muscle spindle activity within the stretched muscle is temporarily inhibited, allowing further muscle stretching. After the removal of the stretch stimulus, however, the muscle spindle quickly reestablishes its stretch threshold. A practical application of reciprocal inhibition is observed during **proprioceptive neuromuscular facilitation (PNF)** (see Chapter 5). Low-grade muscle contractions (50% of maximum force) of an antagonist muscle for six to 15 seconds inhibit or reduce muscle spindle activity within the **agonist** muscle. This reduces muscle tonicity, allowing that muscle to be stretched. For example, activation of the gluteus maximus can temporarily inhibit muscle spindle activity within the iliopsoas. For range-of-motion improvement, it is important to initiate a stretch immediately following inhibition of the muscle spindle (as is the case with PNF stretching) due to its rate of recovery.

The body relies on the **vestibular system** for sensory information related to the position of the head in space and sudden changes in the directional movement of the head. Located in the inner ear, the vestibular system is composed of three fluid-containing semicircular canals that lie at right angles to each other. Each canal contains sensory hair cells that detect the movement of the fluid in the canals. When the angular position of the head changes, fluid rushes over the hair cells and causes them to bend. This response

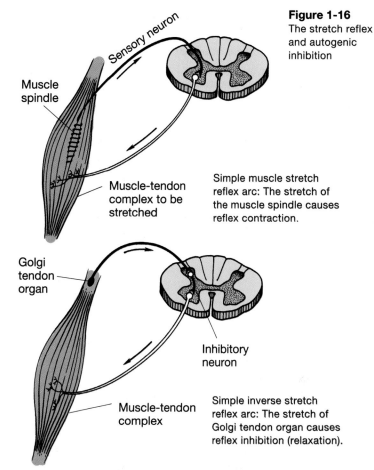

Figure 1-16
The stretch reflex and autogenic inhibition

Simple muscle stretch reflex arc: The stretch of the muscle spindle causes reflex contraction.

Simple inverse stretch reflex arc: The stretch of Golgi tendon organ causes reflex inhibition (relaxation).

signals to the CNS the direction of the head's rotation and the position of the head during movement. The vestibular system functions to coordinate many motor responses and helps stabilize the eyes to maintain postural stability during stance and locomotion.

Muscular System

Muscle tissue is categorized into different types based on its function, is controlled both voluntarily and involuntarily, and is able to produce various levels of force based on its size and shape. One property that all muscle tissue has in common is its ability to contract and develop tension. There are three types of muscle tissue—skeletal muscle, smooth muscle, and cardiac muscle. Skeletal muscle attaches to the skeleton and, through contraction, exerts force on the bones and moves them. Skeletal muscle is considered voluntary muscle because it is normally under the conscious control of the individual. When viewed under a microscope, skeletal muscle tissue exhibits alternating light and dark bands, giving it a striped appearance. This characteristic is the reason skeletal muscle is also called striated muscle.

Smooth muscle is found in the walls of hollow organs and tubes, such as the stomach, intestines, and blood vessels, and functions to regulate the movement of materials through the body. It is named smooth muscle because it lacks the striated appearance of skeletal muscle. Because it is not under conscious control, it is considered involuntary. Cardiac muscle forms the wall of the heart and is a very specialized tissue that functions to maintain the constant pumping action of the heart. Cardiac tissue is involuntary, like smooth muscle, and is striated in appearance, just like skeletal muscle.

Muscle Function

The skeletal muscle's role in movement and physical activity is the main focus of this section. Before going into detail about skeletal muscle structure and function, a brief discussion about certain connective tissues is necessary. At each end of the belly of most skeletal muscles, a specialized form of connective tissue, called a tendon, attaches the muscle to the bones. Tendons are typically defined as either tendons of **origin** or tendons of **insertion.** The tendon of origin is usually attached to the proximal bone of a joint, which is typically the less mobile of the two bones that make up the joint. In contrast, the tendon of insertion is typically attached to the more distal bone of a joint, which is usually the more moveable of the two bones that make up the joint. When describing the attachment sites of muscles, it is common to state the origin and insertion of the muscle. For example, the brachialis muscle originates on the anterior humerus and inserts on the ulnar tuberosity and coronoid process of the ulna.

Understanding the origins and insertions of the major muscle groups is important for all fitness professionals. Fundamentally, skeletal muscles perform their required tasks by pulling on bones to create joint movement. That is, when a muscle contracts, its origin and insertion attachments move closer together. In contrast, when a muscle is stretched, its origin and insertion points move farther apart. Correct anatomical knowledge of muscle attachments is crucial when designing safe and effective exercise programs, but there is more to consider. Each joint movement incorporates all of the supporting structures surrounding it. Pairings of muscles called agonists and antagonists help to illustrate this point. A muscle that creates a major movement is called a **prime mover,** or agonist. The muscle on the opposite side of the joint is called an opposing muscle, or antagonist. For example, the quadriceps muscle group in the front of the thigh produces knee extension. When the quadriceps contracts to extend the knee, it is considered the agonist muscle group, whereas on the opposite side of the joint, the hamstrings (antagonist) is being stretched. This type of functional pairing of muscle groups is found throughout the body.

When visually comparing the various skeletal muscles, it is evident that they come in different shapes and muscle-fiber arrangements (Figure 1-17). These characteristics vary from muscle to muscle because of functionality. In some muscles, the muscle fibers run parallel to the long axis of the muscle, forming a long, strap-like arrangement. This type of muscle is classified as a longitudinal muscle, and although it is capable of producing considerable movement, it is relatively weak compared to other muscle-fiber arrangements. The sartorius muscle of the thigh is an example of a longitudinal muscle. Other muscles have a tendon that runs the entire length of the muscle, with the muscle fibers inserting diagonally into the tendon. In some muscles of this type, all of the muscle fibers insert onto one side of the tendon (unipennate), and in others, the muscle fibers insert obliquely onto each side of the tendon (bipennate). Unipennate (e.g., anterior tibialis) and bipennate (e.g., rectus femoris) muscles typically produce less movement than longitudinal muscles, but are capable of creating greater force during contraction. In multipennate muscles, the muscle fibers have a complex arrangement that involves the convergence of several tendons. The deltoid muscle of the shoulder is a multipennate muscle.

Muscle-fiber Types

Skeletal muscle can be divided into two general categories based on how quickly it contracts: **fast-twitch muscle fibers** and **slow-twitch muscle fibers.** Slow-twitch fibers (also called slow-oxidative or **type I muscle fibers**) contain relatively large amounts of **mitochondria** and are surrounded by more capillaries than fast-twitch fibers. Additionally, slow-twitch fibers contain higher concentrations of myoglobin than do fast-twitch fibers (also called **type II muscle fibers**). The high concentration of **myoglobin,** the large number of capillaries, and the high mitochondrial content make slow-twitch fibers resistant to fatigue and capable of sustaining aerobic metabolism. As the name implies, slow-twitch fibers contract more slowly than fast-twitch fibers. Furthermore, slow-twitch fibers create lower force outputs and are more efficient than fast-twitch fibers.

It is generally agreed that there are two subtypes of fast-twitch fibers—identified as type IIx and IIa. Traditionally, the fastest type of skeletal muscle fiber in humans has been called the type IIb fiber. However, research in the late 1980s led to the discovery of new properties in the skeletal fast-twitch muscle fibers of both rodents and humans, which has prompted scientists to re-label these fibers as type IIx (Pette, 2001). Type IIx muscle fibers (sometimes called fast-glycolytic fibers) contain a relatively small amount of mitochondria, have a limited capacity for aerobic metabolism, and fatigue more easily than slow-twitch fibers. In fact, these fibers cannot sustain their effort for more than a few seconds. However, they possess a high number of glycolytic enzymes, which provide them with a considerable anaerobic capacity. Type IIx fibers are the largest and fastest, and are capable of producing the most force of all the skeletal muscle fibers, but are notably less efficient than slow-twitch fibers (Shoepe et al., 2003). A second subtype of fast-twitch muscle fibers is the type IIa fiber (also called intermediate or fast-oxidative glycolytic fibers). These fibers possess speed, fatigue resistance, and force-production capabilities somewhere between slow-twitch and type IIx fibers. They are also used for strength and power activities, but can sustain an effort for longer than the type IIx fibers—up to three minutes in highly trained athletes. Type IIa fibers are unique in that they are highly adaptable. That is, with endurance training, they can increase their oxidative capacity to levels similar to those observed in slow-twitch fibers.

A muscle's fiber-type composition is typically an equal mixture of both fast- and

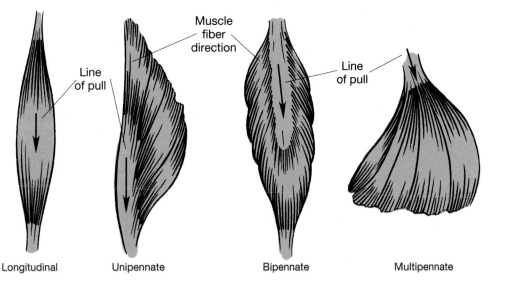

Figure 1-17
Muscle fiber arrangements

Longitudinal   Unipennate   Bipennate   Multipennate

slow-twitch fibers, though some muscle groups are known to be made up of primarily fast- or slow-twitch fibers. The percentage of specific fiber types contained in skeletal muscle may be influenced by genetics, hormones, and the activity and exercise habits of the individual. Fiber composition of skeletal muscles is thought to play an important role in sport and exercise performance. It is commonly believed that successful power athletes possess a relatively large percentage of fast-twitch fibers, whereas endurance athletes generally possess a large percentage of slow-twitch fibers. However, it should be noted that muscle-fiber composition is only one variable that determines success in overall physical performance.

Muscle Contraction

Skeletal muscle is composed of tiny, individual muscle cells, called muscle fibers. Muscle fibers are held in place by thin sheets of connective tissue membranes called fasciae (singular = fascia). The fascia that encases the entire muscle is known as the **epimysium.** Within the epimysium are bundles of muscle fibers grouped together in a fibrous sheath of fascia known as the **perimysium.** Within the perimysium are individual muscle fibers wrapped in a fascia called **endomysium** (Figure 1-18).

Muscle-fiber Microanatomy

As noted earlier, when highly magnified with a microscope, skeletal muscle fibers have a cross-striated appearance with alternating light and dark bands. Each muscle fiber contains several hundred to several thousand threadlike **myofibrils** (protein filaments) that run parallel to each other and extend lengthwise throughout the cell. The dark bands, called A bands, contain the protein filament **myosin.** The light bands, or I bands, are where the protein filament **actin** is located. Actin filaments also extend into the A bands, where they overlap with the myosin filaments. Crossing the center of each I band is a dense Z line that divides the myofibrils into a series of repeating segments called **sarcomeres.** The sarcomere is considered the functional contracting unit of skeletal muscle, and is the portion of a myofibril that is found between two Z lines. In the center of a sarcomere is a lighter, somewhat less dense area called the H zone. This region is lighter in color, because actin does not extend into this area and the myosin filament becomes thinner in this middle region. A thin, darker M line crosses the center of the H zone. The H zone contains only myosin filaments. Actin filaments are found in the I band and in the part of the A band, up to the H zone. Actin filaments attach directly to the Z lines. The myosin filaments

Figure 1-18
Organization
of muscle

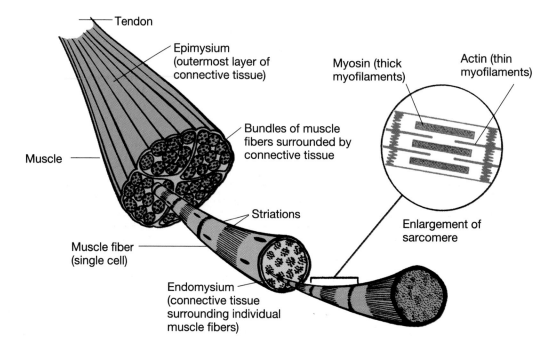

have tiny projections called cross-bridges that reach out at an angle toward the actin filaments.

Sliding Filament Model

When a muscle fiber contracts, the energy used to drive the contraction comes primarily from a substance within the cell called **adenosine triphosphate (ATP).** Muscle contraction occurs when the brain and spinal cord direct motor neurons to release a **neurotransmitter** called **acetylcholine** at the neuromuscular junction. Once the acetylcholine is detected, calcium is released into the area surrounding the fiber. The calcium exposes binding sites along the actin filament for the myosin filament. As long as there is sufficient ATP, the myosin filaments bind with receptor sites on the actin filaments and cross-bridges are formed. The myosin pulls the actin toward the center and the sarcomere shortens (i.e., the Z lines are pulled closer together) (Figure 1-19). Because all of the sarcomeres shorten simultaneously, the overall length of the muscle fiber is shortened. If multiple muscle fibers are stimulated to contract at the same time, the entire muscle will contract.

Naming Skeletal Muscles

Certain criteria are used in the naming of a muscle, such as its shape, size, and location in the body. These criteria facilitate finding muscles and learning about their specific locations:

- *Shape:* The names of certain muscles include references to their shape (e.g., the rhomboid muscles resemble the geometric shape of a rhomboid).
- *Action:* Some muscle names include references to their actions in the body (e.g., the extensor digitorum longus muscle extends the toes).
- *Location:* Certain muscles have a reference to location in their names (e.g., the posterior tibialis muscle is located on the back side of the tibia).

Figure 1-19
The sliding filament theory

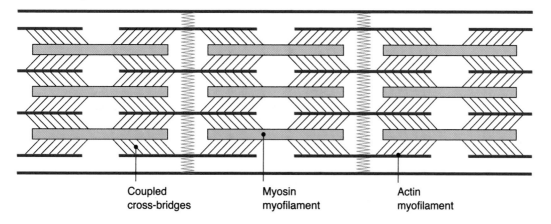

Myofibril at rest

Uncoupled cross-bridges   Myosin myofilament   Actin myofilament

Contracted myofibril

Coupled cross-bridges   Myosin myofilament   Actin myofilament

- *Attachments:* The points of origin and insertion of some muscles can be deciphered in their names (e.g., the coracobrachialis muscle originates on the coracoid process of the scapula and inserts on the brachium, which means arm).
- *Number of divisions:* Muscle names sometimes refer to the number of divisions that make up their structure [e.g., the triceps brachii muscle is an arm muscle consisting of three (tri) heads].
- *Size relationships:* Sometimes muscle names describe a muscle's size in relation to others (e.g., the gluteus maximus is a larger muscle than the gluteus minimus).

Connective Tissue

Connective tissue is the material between the cells of the body that gives tissues form and strength. This "cellular glue" is also involved in delivering nutrients to the tissue. Connective tissue is made up of dozens of proteins, including **collagen,** the most abundant protein in the body. The two major physical properties of collagen fibers are their **tensile strength** and relative **inextensibility.** In other words, structures containing large amounts of collagen tend to limit motion and resist stretch. Thus, collagen fibers are the main constituents of tissues such as ligaments and tendons that are subjected to a pulling force.

One of the mechanisms behind collagen's great tensile strength and relative inextensibility is its banded, or striated, structure (much like the pattern observed in muscle tissue). When viewed under a microscope, the collagen of a tendon is arranged in wavy bundles called **fascicles.** The fascicle is composed of fibrils, which in turn consist of bundles of subfibrils. Each subfibril is composed of bundles of collagen filaments. In addition to a striated pattern, connective tissues contain wavelike folds of collagen fibers known as **crimp.** The mechanical properties of collagen fibers are such that each fibril behaves as a mechanical spring, thus each fiber is a collection of springs. When a fiber is pulled, its crimp straightens and its length increases. As in a mechanical spring, energy is stored within the fiber, and

it is the release of this energy that returns the fiber to its resting state when the stretch force is removed.

Compared to a sarcomere, a collagenous fiber is relatively inextensible. Collagen fibers may undergo an extension of about 3%, until the slack in their wavy bundles (crimp) is taken up. If the stretch continues, a critical point will be reached where the tissue ruptures.

Like collagen, structures called elastic fibers are made up of amino acids. The term **elastin** has been used to describe the structural make-up of these extensible fibers. Unlike collagen, elastic fibers are responsible for determining the possible range of extensibility of muscle cells. Researchers have found a large amount of elastic tissue in the connective tissue that surrounds the sarcomere. Elastic fibers also are found in numerous other organs and structures where their roles include disseminating mechanical stress, enhancing coordination, maintaining tone during muscular relaxation, defending against excessive forces, and assisting organs in returning to their undeformed state once all forces have been removed. As their name implies, elastic fibers succumb readily to stretching, and when released they return to their former length. Only when elastic fibers are stretched to more than 150% of their original length do they reach their rupture point.

Similar to other soft tissue structures, elastic fibers deteriorate with age. Elastic fibers can submit to fragmentation, fraying, and calcification due to the aging process. These alterations may be in part responsible for the loss of resiliency and increased joint rigidity experienced by older individuals.

Elastic fibers are almost always found together with collagen fibers. These two connective tissues work together to support and facilitate joint movement. Elastic fibers are responsible for reverse elasticity (i.e., the ability of a stretched material to return to its original resting state). Collagen, on the other hand, provides the rigidity that limits the deformations of the elastic elements and gives tissues their tensile strength and relative inextensibility. In tissues containing large amounts of collagen, rigidity, stability, tensile strength, and restricted range of motion are observed.

While various forms of connective tissue are found throughout the body, the structures related most to the practical applications of personal training are tendons, ligaments, and fasciae. Tendons are tough, cord-like tissues that connect muscles to bones. Their primary function is to transmit force from muscle to bone, thereby producing motion. Tendons consist of fibrils that are usually oriented toward the direction of normal physiological stress. The amount of deformation that occurs in a tendon when a stretch load is applied is called a load-deformation curve. The wavy bundles of collagen in tendons straighten when a low level of stretch force is applied. Further stretch results in deformation of the tendon that is linearly related to the amount of tension applied. When stretched within a certain range, tendons will return to their original lengths when unloaded. Stretching the tendon beyond its "yield point" results in permanent length changes and microtrauma to the tendon's structural integrity.

Ligaments function primarily to support a joint by attaching bone to bone. Unlike tendons, ligaments take on various shapes, such as cords, bands, or sheets, depending on their location. Ligaments possess a greater mixture of elastic and fine collagenous fibers woven together than their tendinous counterparts. This results in a tissue that is pliant and flexible that allows freedom of movement, but is also strong, tough, and inextensible so as not to yield easily to applied forces. Whereas tendons provide approximately 10% of the resistance experienced during joint movement, the ligaments and joint capsule (a sac-like structure that encloses the ends of bones at a joint) contribute about 47% of the total resistance to movement.

In gross anatomy, fascia is a term typically used to designate all fibrous connective tissue not otherwise specifically named. There are three general categories of fascia. Superficial fascia lies directly below the skin and usually contains a collection of fat. Deep fascia lies directly beneath the superficial fascia and is tougher, tighter, and more compact than the superficial fascia. It encases muscles, bones, nerves, blood vessels, and organs. Finally, subserous fascia forms the fibrous layer of serous membranes that cover and support the innermost body cavities. Examples include the pleura around the lungs, the pericardium around the heart, and the peritoneum around the abdominal cavity and organs.

Intramuscular fascia (deep fascia) is directly related to flexibility and **range of motion.** Its three main functions are:

- To provide a framework that ensures proper alignment of muscle fibers, blood vessels, and nerves
- To enable the safe and effective transmission of forces throughout the whole muscle
- To provide the necessary lubricated surfaces between muscle fibers that allow muscles to change shape during contraction and elongation

During a passive stretching movement, fascia contributes 41% of the total resistance to joint range of motion. Thus, fascia is second only to the joint capsule (ligaments) in terms of resistance to movement.

Factors That Contribute to Flexibility

Muscle and connective tissue are two important determinants of flexibility. The tightness of these soft-tissue structures is a major contributor to both static and dynamic flexibility. Muscle is a complex structure—composed of progressively smaller units—that is very adaptable to the stresses placed upon it. Connective tissue structures contain a wide variety of specialized cells that perform functions including protection, storage, binding, connection, and general support and repair. The following represents the relative contribution of soft tissues to the total resistance encountered by the joint during movement through its range of motion:

- Joint capsule (ligaments)—47%
- Muscle (fascia)—41%
- Tendons—10%
- Skin—2%

Age

For a muscle fiber to be lengthened, an external force must act upon it. Forces include gravity, momentum, antagonistic muscle contractions (active stretch), and the force provided by another person or one's own body (passive stretch). To stretch effectively without risking injury, the sarcomere should be elongated to a length at which there is a slight overlap of the filaments, with at least one cross-bridge maintained between the actin and myosin. This length has been found to be approximately 50 to 67% more than resting length, which allows movement through wide ranges of motion.

A significant contributor to range-of-motion limitation is the effect of aging on muscle tissue. The aging process inevitably brings about a decrease in normal muscle function, including strength, endurance, flexibility, and agility. These functions are even more adversely affected when inactivity, disease, and injury (which are commonly associated with aging) are present. Part of the decline in age-related muscle function is due to the progressive atrophy, or wasting away, of muscle tissue. This loss is due to the reduction in both size and number of the muscle fibers. As muscle fibers atrophy, they are replaced by fatty and fibrous (collagen) tissue. Collagen is a primary component of connective tissue that exhibits a low compliance, which contributes to the stiffening and decreased mobility of aging muscle. Furthermore, the water content of the soft tissues of older adults diminishes due to the aging process. Collectively, these changes appear to be partly responsible for the flexibility loss due to aging.

Importantly, this loss appears to be minimized in those who remain physically active. A program of regular physical activity can contribute significantly to joint stability and flexibility for individuals of any age. Resistance training enhances the tensile strength of tendons and ligaments, and stretching exercises maintain the suppleness of tendons, ligaments, and muscles, thus allowing a full range of motion at each joint.

Gender

In general, females are more flexible than males. Several factors, including anatomical and physiological differences, may account for the disparity in flexibility between the sexes. Specifically, the pelvic regions of men and women are shaped differently. When compared to women's pelvic bones, men's pelvic bones are generally heavier and rougher; the cavity is not as spacious; the sacrosciatic notch, pubic arch, and sacrum are narrower; and the acetabula are closer together than women's. Women have broader and shallower hips than men, which allows for a greater potential for range of motion in the pelvic region. Furthermore, women usually have a greater range of extension in the elbow due to having a shorter upper curve of the olecranon process of the elbow than men. It has also been suggested that girls have greater potential for flexibility after puberty because of their lower center of gravity and shorter leg length compared with boys.

Joint Structure and Past Injury

Bony structures can restrict the end point in a joint's range of motion. In many instances, joints rely on bony prominences to stop movements at normal end points in the range. However, an elbow that has been fractured through the joint might lay down excess calcium in the joint space, causing the joint to lose its ability to fully extend. Additionally, skin might be a contributor to limited movement. For example, an individual who has had some type of injury or surgery involving a tearing, incision, or laceration of the skin, particularly over a joint, will have inelastic scar tissue formed at that site. This scar tissue is incapable of stretching with joint movement. Over time, however, skin contractures caused by scarring of ligaments, joint capsules, and musculotendinous units can see improved elasticity through stretching.

Tissue Temperature

To most effectively stretch a muscle, intramuscular temperature should be increased prior to stretching. A warm-up immediately prior to activity provides the body with a period of adjustment from rest to exercise and should be designed to improve performance and decrease the chance of injury by preparing the individual mentally and physically for activity. Increasing the temperature enhances the ability of collagen and elastin components within the musculotendinous unit to deform and the ability of the GTOs to reflexively relax through autogenic inhibition. The optimal temperature of muscle to achieve these benefits appears to be 103° F (39° C).

The most common and recommended method of elevating body temperature and reducing tissue viscosity is self-initiated active movement. A warm-up may include activities such as light calisthenics, walking, jogging, or stationary bicycling. The warm-up activities should be intense enough to increase the body's core temperature and cause some sweating, but not so intense as to cause fatigue.

Cooling down provides the body a period of adjustment from exercise to rest, and may be defined as a group of low-intensity exercises performed immediately after an activity. The main objectives of a cool-down are to facilitate muscular relaxation, promote the removal of muscular waste products by the blood, reduce muscular soreness, and allow the cardiovascular system to adjust to lowered demand. It is recommended that stretching be incorporated immediately after the cool-down period of a workout because this is when tissue temperatures will be highest.

Circadian Variations

The term circadian is Latin (*circa* = about; *dies* = day) and refers to a time period of approximately 24 hours. It is well-established that most physiological functions exhibit circadian rhythms. That is, they demonstrate maximum and minimum function at specific times of day. Blood pressure, body temperature, heart rate, hormone levels, alertness, and responsiveness oscillate as a function of circadian rhythms. Furthermore, joint stiffness has been associated with specific times of day. For example, a significant increase in flexibility in the afternoon is typically observed compared with measurements taken in the early morning hours.

Human stature, or height, also has been proven to fluctuate throughout the day, with average daily changes of up to 0.6 inches (1.5 cm). This fluctuation is relevant to flexibility because it may influence **posture,** range of motion, mechanical efficiency, risk of injury, perception of stiffness, and low-back pain. The vertebral column becomes shorter during the day and regains its normal length throughout the night. One explanation for this height loss directly relates to the fluid content of the intervertebral disks. The cartilaginous disks located between each spinal vertebra are considered osmotic structures in which a free exchange of fluid occurs through the semi-permeable end plates of the disks. During the day, when the vertebral column is vertical and the disks are subjected to dynamic muscular forces, the gravitational force of the body's weight, and hydrostatic pressure, fluid is squeezed out of the disk (disk dehydration), resulting in narrowing of the space between the vertebrae. During sleep, when the spinal column is horizontal, the disks are rehydrated due to the osmotic pressure exceeding the hydrostatic pressure and disk compression. In this state, the disks absorb fluids from the surrounding area and normal body length is renewed.

The increased hydration of intervertebral disks during sleep, and the subsequent swelling of the disks upon waking, has three significant implications for the flexibility of the lumbar spine:

- This swelling accounts for the increased stiffness in the spine during lumbar flexion upon wakening.
- The lumbar disks and ligaments are at greater risk for injury in the early morning.
- Range of motion increases later in the day.

Consequently, a program to increase flexibility, specifically for the spine, should be performed later in the day to decrease the risk of injury to the disks and their surrounding structures.

Muscles of the Upper Extremity

Although not a complete review of every muscle in the upper extremity, this section covers the most commonly used major muscle groups contributing to movement at the scapula, shoulder, elbow, and wrist.

*Major Muscles That
Act at the Shoulder Girdle*

The shoulder girdle consists of the articulations between the medial end of each clavicle with the sternum, the lateral end of each clavicle with the scapula, the scapula with the soft tissues of the thorax, and the scapula with the head of the humerus. The muscles that act on the scapula are those of the shoulder girdle. Since the scapulae have no bony articulation with the rib cage, the scapulothoracic "joint" is supported with soft tissues. Thus, the main function of shoulder-girdle muscles is to fixate the scapula. When the scapula is immobilized, it serves as a stable point of origin for the muscles that move the humerus. There are four posterior muscles that anchor the scapula (trapezius, rhomboid major, rhomboid minor, and levator scapulae) and two anterior muscles (pectoralis minor and serratus anterior).

The shape of the trapezius allows it to perform several distinct actions. If the upper portion contracts, the scapula is elevated, as in shrugging the shoulders. In contrast, if the lower portion contracts, **depression** of the scapula occurs. When all parts of the

trapezius are working together, they tend to pull upward and adduct the scapula at the same time. If the scapula is fixed, the trapezius assists in neck extension. Additionally, the trapezius stabilizes the scapula for deltoid action, since it is used in preventing the glenoid fossa from being pulled downward during the lifting of objects or when carrying an object on the tip of the shoulder, such as the strap of a purse. The rhomboid muscles are responsible for adducting and downwardly rotating the scapula. Further, from a more functional perspective, both rhomboid major and minor muscles are used in pull-up movements. As an individual hangs from a horizontal bar, suspended by the hands, the scapulae tend to be pulled away from the top of the chest. When the pull-up movement begins, the rhomboids draw the medial border of the scapulae down and back toward the spinal column.

The levator scapulae muscles are so named because of their primary function of elevating the superior medial portion of the scapula. In addition to assisting the upper trapezius during elevation of the scapula, the levator scapulae muscles bilaterally extend the neck or unilaterally flex the neck to one side when the scapulae are anchored by the pectoralis minor (Figure 1-20). The two anterior muscles of

Figure 1-20
Superficial and deep muscles that act at the scapulothoracic articulation

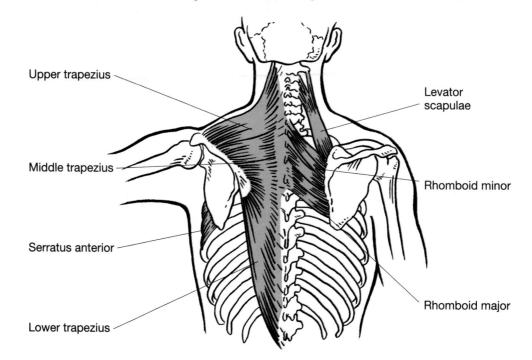

the shoulder girdle also work to stabilize the scapula. Additionally, the pectoralis minor and serratus anterior function to abduct the scapulae during pushing movements with the hands. The pectoralis minor acts as an antagonist to the trapezius, rhomboids, and levator scapulae, whereas the serratus anterior acts as an antagonist to the rhomboids (Figure 1-21). The origins, insertions, primary functions, and examples of exercises to develop the muscles of the shoulder girdle are presented in Table 1-7.

Major Muscles That Act at the Shoulder

The most mobile joint in the body, the shoulder joint consists of the articulation of the head of the humerus with the glenoid fossa and the associated cartilage of the scapula. Nine muscles cross the shoulder joint and insert on the humerus, with seven of the nine muscles arising from the scapulae (supraspinatus, infraspinatus, subscapularis, teres minor, deltoid, teres major, and coracobrachialis). Two arise from the axial skeleton and have no attachments on the scapulae (pectoralis major and latissimus dorsi). The supraspinatus, infraspinatus, subscapularis, and teres minor derive their names from the portion of the scapula from which they originate. This group of four muscles is called the rotator cuff, and can be remembered using the acronym **SITS** (Figure 1-22).

The rotator-cuff muscles surround the head of the humerus, with the primary stabilizing function of holding the humeral head in the glenoid fossa. The lack of bone supporting the

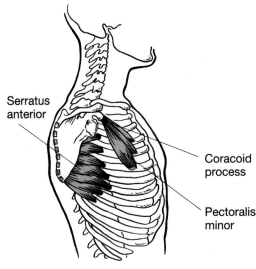

Figure 1-21
Anterior shoulder-girdle muscles

Serratus anterior

Coracoid process

Pectoralis minor

Table 1-7				
Major Muscles That Act at the Shoulder Girdle				
Muscle	**Origin**	**Insertion**	**Primary Function(s)**	**Selected Exercises**
Trapezius	Occipital bone, spines of 7th cervical and thoracic vertebrae	Lateral third of clavicle, acromion process, and spine of scapula	Upper: upward rotation and elevation of scapula Middle: upward rotation and adduction of scapula Lower: depression of scapula	Upright rows, shoulder shrugs
Levator scapulae	Transverse processes of first four cervical vertebrae	Upper vertebral border of scapula	Elevation of scapula	Shoulder shrugs
Rhomboid major and minor	Spines of 7th cervical through 5th thoracic vertebrae	Middle to lower vertebral border of scapula	Adduction, downward rotation, and elevation of scapula	Chin-ups, supported dumbbell bent-over rows
Pectoralis minor	Anterior surface of ribs 3 through 5	Coracoid process of scapula	Stabilization, depression, downward rotation, and abduction of the scapula	Push-ups, incline bench press, regular bench press, cable crossover chest flys
Serratus anterior	Lateral, anterior surface of ribs 1 through 9	Ventral surface of vertebral border of scapula	Stabilization, abduction, and upward rotation of the scapula	Push-ups, incline bench press, pull-overs

Figure 1-22
Rotator cuff
muscles

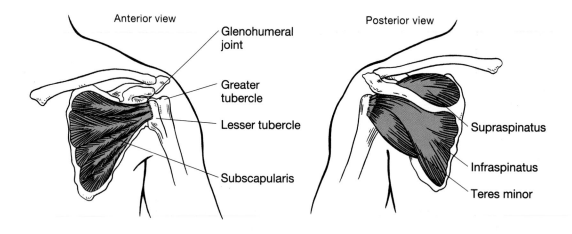

shoulder joint requires that these muscles and their associated tendons work as stabilizers to prevent **subluxation** or dislocation of the humeral head from the glenoid fossa. The supraspinatus holds the head of the humerus in the glenoid fossa from a superior position and can be easily injured, especially with throwing movements. It crosses the upper part of the shoulder joint and assists the deltoid during abduction of the arm. The infraspinatus works with another rotator-cuff muscle, the teres minor, when the rhomboids stabilize the scapula by flattening it to the back so that the humerus may be externally rotated. Both muscles help hold the head of the humerus in the glenoid cavity in addition

to externally rotating it. The subscapularis is the only rotator cuff muscle to originate on the anterior portion of the scapula. In addition to its function of helping to stabilize the shoulder joint, it acts as a medial rotator of the arm. The subscapularis also requires help from the rhomboids in stabilizing the scapulae to make it effective in its actions.

The deltoid is a large muscle that forms a cap over and around the shoulder (Figure 1-23). Because its fibers pass in front of, directly over, and in the back of the shoulder, the deltoid's actions are varied, with some of the actions being antagonistic to each other. The anterior fibers flex and internally rotate the humerus, whereas the posterior fibers extend and laterally

Figure 1-23
Superficial shoulder
muscles

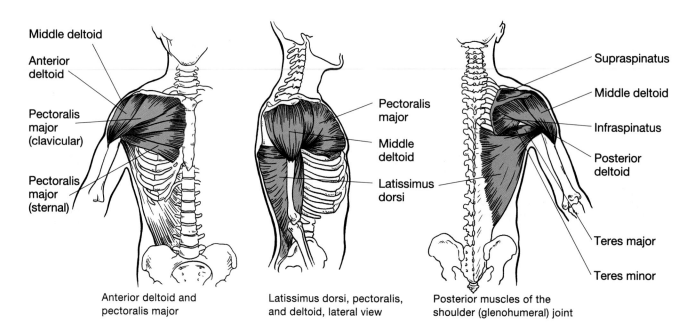

rotate the humerus. For proper functioning, the trapezius fixes the scapula as the deltoid pulls on the humerus. Thus, any movement of the humerus on the scapula will involve all or part of the deltoid.

The teres major arises from the lower medial portion of the scapula and primarily acts to internally rotate the humerus (Figure 1-24). This muscle is effective only when the rhomboids stabilize the scapula. Otherwise, the scapula would move forward to meet the arm when the teres major contracts. The teres major works with the latissimus dorsi and is sometimes called the "little lat." The coracobrachialis is the remaining muscle that originates on the scapula. Its location in front of the shoulder allows it to assist in flexion and adduction of the humerus (Figure 1-25).

The remaining two muscles that act at the shoulder joint, the latissimus dorsi and pectoralis major, originate from the axial skeleton. Located in the mid- to lower-back, the latissimus dorsi is the widest muscle of the posterior trunk (see Figure 1-24). It is one of the most important and powerful extensor muscles of the humerus. Additionally, it acts to adduct and internally rotate the humerus. When the insertion is fixed, such as when hanging by the arms, the latissimus dorsi can anteriorly tilt the pelvis as well as assist in lateral flexion of the spine. The pectoralis major is a large, fan-shaped muscle that lies on top of the smaller pectoralis minor (Figure 1-26). Its position on the anterior chest wall allows it to effectively work together with the latissimus dorsi to adduct the humerus from a raised, abducted

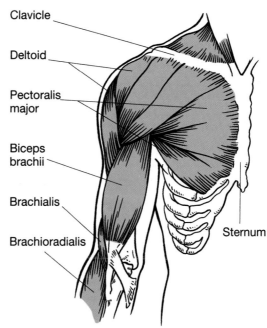

Coracobrachialis

Figure 1-25
Deep muscle that originates on the shoulder blade (scapula) and assists in flexion and adduction of the arm

Reprinted with permission from Golding, L. & Golding, S. (2003). *Fitness Professional's Guide to Musculoskeletal Anatomy and Human Movement*. Monterey, Calif.: Healthy Learning.

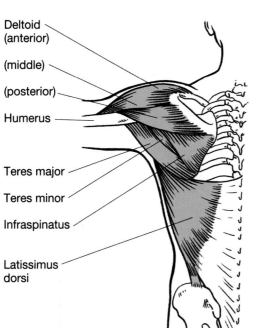

Deltoid (anterior)

(middle)

(posterior)

Humerus

Teres major

Teres minor

Infraspinatus

Latissimus dorsi

Figure 1-24
Superficial musculature of the superior and inferior shoulder joint, prime movers for shoulder abduction (deltoid) and adduction (latissimus dorsi and teres major)

Redrawn from Luttgens, K., Deutsch, H., & Hamilton, N. (1992). *Kinesiology* (8th ed.). Madison, Wis.: Brown & Benchmark. Reprinted with permission from The McGraw-Hill Companies.

Clavicle

Deltoid

Pectoralis major

Biceps brachii

Brachialis

Brachioradialis

Sternum

Figure 1-26
Superficial musculature of the anterior chest, shoulder, and arm

position. It also works to internally rotate the humerus. Because its tendon of insertion twists such that the fibers of the clavicular portion insert below those of its sternocostal portion, the pectoralis major can also extend and flex the shoulder. The clavicular portion flexes an extended shoulder, whereas the sternocostal portion extends a flexed shoulder. The origins, insertions, primary functions, and examples of exercises to develop the muscles that act at the shoulder are presented in Table 1-8.

Major Muscles That Act at the Elbow

The articulations of the distal end of the humerus with the proximal ends of the radius and ulna comprise the elbow joint. Additionally, the articulation of the radius and ulna with each other must be considered, since these two bones are responsible for pronation and supination of the forearm. Actions that occur at the elbow joint primarily come from contractions of muscles located in the upper arm. Two upper-arm anterior muscles (biceps

brachii and brachialis) and one posterior upper-arm muscle (triceps brachii) are responsible for the most powerful forearm movements. As the name implies, the biceps brachii has two heads, both of which originate on the scapula. Because of its scapular attachments, it can assist as a weak flexor of the shoulder. When the forearm is supinated, the biceps brachii acts as a strong flexor of the elbow. However, because of its insertion on the radius, the biceps brachii also acts to supinate the forearm when the forearm is pronated. Lying deep to the biceps brachii, the brachialis is another strong flexor of the forearm. The brachialis pulls on the ulna, which does not rotate, making it the only pure flexor of the elbow (see Figure 1-26). The brachioradialis, the bulk of which is located in the forearm, also acts to flex the elbow. This action of flexion by the brachioradialis is favored when the mid-position between pronation and supination of the forearm is assumed. The triceps brachii muscle is a three-headed structure and the only muscle located

Table 1-8

Major Muscles That Act at the Shoulder

Muscle	Origin	Insertion	Primary Function(s)	Selected Exercises
Pectoralis major	Clavicle, sternum, and first six costal cartilages	Greater tubercle of humerus	Flexion, extension, adduction, internal rotation, and horizontal adduction	Push-ups, pull-ups, incline bench press, regular bench press, climbing a rope, all types of throwing, tennis serve
Deltoid	Anterior, lateral clavicle, border of the acromion, and lower edge of spine of the scapula	Deltoid tubercle of humerus on mid-lateral surface	Entire muscle: abduction Anterior fibers: flexion, internal rotation, and horizontal adduction Posterior fibers: external rotation and horizontal abduction	Lateral "butterfly" (abduction) exercises; anterior deltoid has similar functions to the pectoralis major
Latissimus dorsi	Spines of lower six thoracic vertebrae and all lumbar vertebrae, crests of ilium and sacrum, lower four ribs, and inferior angle of scapulae	Medial side of intertubercular groove of humerus	Extension, adduction, horizontal abduction, and internal rotation	Chin-ups, rope climbing, dips on parallel bars, rowing, any exercise that involves pulling the arms downward against resistance (e.g., "lat" pull-downs on exercise machine)
Rotator cuff	Various aspects of scapula	All insert on greater tubercle of humerus except for the subscapularis, which inserts on the lesser tubercle of the humerus	Infraspinatus and teres minor: external rotation Subscapularis: internal rotation Supraspinatus: abduction All contribute to the stability of the humeral head	Exercises that involve internal and external rotation (e.g., tennis serve, throwing a baseball)
Teres major	Posterior inferior lateral border of scapula, just superior to inferior angle	Intertubercular groove of the humerus	Extension, adduction, and internal rotation	Chin-ups, seated rows, "lat" pull-downs, rope climbing

in the posterior compartment of the upper arm (Figure 1-27). One of its portions—the long head—originates from the scapula, allowing it to act as a weak extensor of the shoulder. All three heads converge into one tendon that inserts on the olecranon process of the ulna. The triceps brachii acts as the primary extensor of the elbow. The origins, insertions, primary functions, and examples of exercises to develop the muscles that act at the elbow are presented in Table 1-9.

Major Muscles That Act at the Wrist

The articulations of the distal ends of the radius and ulna with the carpal bones of the hand comprise the wrist joint. Most of the muscles that function at the wrist have their origins on the humerus, thereby making the bulk of their structures toward the proximal end of the forearm. Although these muscles cross the elbow joint, they have only very slight actions at the elbow.

The muscles that act at the wrist can be

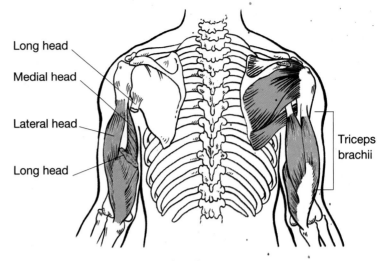

Figure 1-27
Triceps: long, medial, and lateral heads

divided into two main groups based on location and function (Figure 1-28). The muscles of the anterior group serve as flexors of the wrist and pronators of the forearm and originate mostly on the medial epicondyle of the humerus. They include the flexor carpi radialis, flexor carpi ulnaris, palmaris longus, pronator teres, and pronator quadratus. The

Table 1-9

Major Muscles That Act at the Elbow and Forearm

Muscle	Origin	Insertion	Primary Function(s)	Selected Exercises
Biceps brachii	Long head: tubercle above glenoid cavity; Short head: coracoid process of scapula	Radial tuberosity	Flexion at elbow; supination at forearm	Arm curls, chin-ups, rock climbing, upright rowing
Brachialis	Anterior humerus	Ulnar tuberosity and coronoid process of ulna	Flexion at elbow	Same as for biceps brachii
Brachioradialis	Distal ⅔ of lateral condyloid ridge of humerus	Styloid process of radius	Flexion at elbow; supination at forearm	Same as for biceps brachii
Triceps brachii	Long head: lower edge of glenoid cavity of scapula; Lateral head: posterior humerus; Short head: distal ⅔ of posterior humerus	Olecranon process of ulna	Extension at elbow; arm extension (long head)	Push-ups, dips, bench press, shoulder press
Pronator teres	Epicondyle of medial humerus	Middle ⅓ of lateral radius	Flexion at elbow and pronation at forearm	Pronation of forearm with dumbbell
Pronator quadratus	Distal anterior surface of ulna	Distal anterior surface of radius	Pronation at forearm	Resisted pronation
Supinator	Lateral, posterior epicondyle of humerus and supinator crest of ulna	Proximal, lateral surface of radius	Supination at forearm	Resisted supination

muscles of the posterior group of the forearm serve as extensors of the wrist and supinators of the forearm and originate mostly on the lateral epicondyle of the humerus. They include the extensor carpi radialis longus, extensor carpi ulnaris, extensor carpi radialis brevis, and supinator. The origins, insertions, primary functions, and examples of exercises to develop the muscles that act at the wrist are presented in Table 1-10.

Muscles of the Torso

Muscles That Act at the Trunk

The major muscles of the trunk that support, stabilize, and move the spine are presented in this section. These include the muscles of the

Figure 1-28
Muscles of the wrist

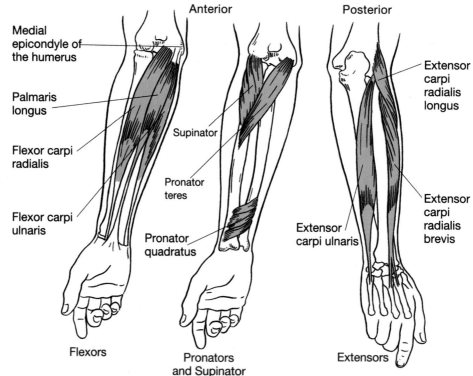

Medial epicondyle of the humerus

Palmaris longus

Flexor carpi radialis

Flexor carpi ulnaris

Anterior

Supinator

Pronator teres

Pronator quadratus

Posterior

Extensor carpi radialis longus

Extensor carpi radialis brevis

Extensor carpi ulnaris

Flexors

Pronators and Supinator

Extensors

Table 1-10

Major Muscles That Act at the Wrist

Muscle	Origin	Insertion	Primary Function(s)	Selected Exercises
Flexor carpi radialis	Medial epicondyle of humerus	Anterior base of 2nd and 3rd metacarpals	Flexion	Wrist curls; grip-strengthening exercises for racquet sports
Flexor carpi ulnaris	Medial epicondyle of humerus, medial olecranon process, and upper, posterior ulna	5th metacarpal	Flexion	Same as flexor carpi radialis
Extensor carpi radialis longus	Lateral epicondyle of humerus	Posterior base of 2nd metacarpal	Extension	"Reverse" wrist curls; racquet sports, particularly tennis
Extensor carpi ulnaris	Lateral epicondyle of humerus and middle ½ of posterior ulna	Posterior base of 5th metacarpal	Extension	Same as extensor carpi radialis longus
Palmaris longus	Medial epicondyle of humerus	Palmar aponeurosis	Flexion	Wrist curls

abdominal wall (rectus abdominis, external obliques, internal obliques, and transverse abdominis) and the muscles that are located on the posterior surface of the spine (erector spinae and multifidi). The abdominal wall has no skeletal structures to support it, and therefore must rely on strength from the multidirectional layers of muscles comprising it. The rectus abdominis is a superficial, flat muscle that is located on the anterior aspect of the abdominal wall (Figure 1-29). It runs vertically from the pubis to the ribcage and functions mainly as a flexor of the spine. Additionally, the rectus abdominis controls the tilt of the pelvis by

pulling the pubis upward, preventing anterior pelvic tilt. The external oblique makes up the outermost layer of the abdominal wall and primarily serves to rotate and assist in bilaterally flexing the spine. Its fibers run medially and downward in the same direction as a person's hands when they are put into his or her front coat pockets. The internal oblique lies beneath the external oblique and acts to rotate and assist in bilaterally flexing the spine. Its fibers run upward and medially, opposing those of the external oblique (Figure 1-30). The oblique muscles work together to rotate the trunk. Rotation of the trunk to the right

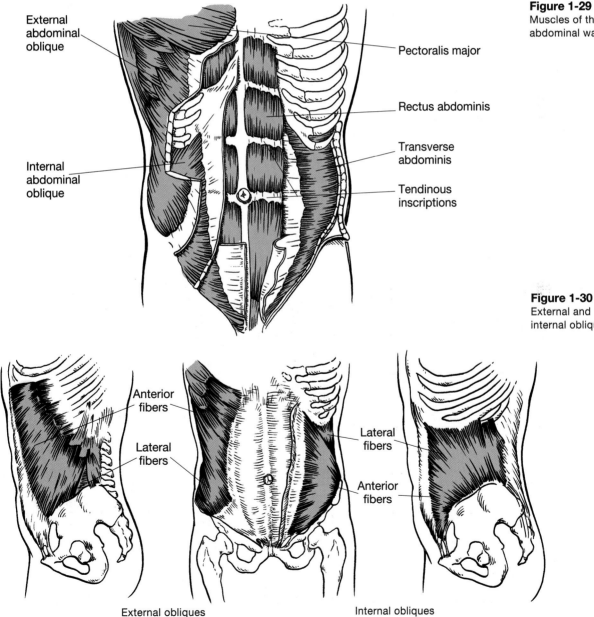

External abdominal oblique

Internal abdominal oblique

Pectoralis major

Rectus abdominis

Transverse abdominis

Tendinous inscriptions

Figure 1-29
Muscles of the abdominal wall

Figure 1-30
External and internal obliques

Anterior fibers

Lateral fibers

Lateral fibers

Anterior fibers

External obliques

Internal obliques

involves simultaneous contraction of the right internal oblique and the left external oblique. The deepest muscle of the abdominal wall is the transverse abdominis, which has fibers that run horizontally, encircling the abdominal cavity (see Figure 1-29). The transverse abdominis acts to compress the abdominal cavity, stabilize the lumbar and pelvic regions, and assist in forced expiration. This muscle tightens the thoracolumbar fascia and helps stabilize the sacroiliac joints. Because its fibers are oriented horizontally, their contraction reduces the diameter of the abdomen (i.e., "sucking in the gut"). Collectively, the muscles of the abdominal wall aid in forced expiration during heavy breathing by exerting pressure on the abdominal contents, thereby forcing the diaphragm upward.

The posterior longitudinal muscle that runs vertically from the sacrum to the skull is known as the erector spinae and has three subdivisions that form separate columns along the back—the iliocostalis, the spinalis, and the longissimus (Figure 1-31). The most lateral column, the iliocostalis, inserts on the ribs. The most medial column, the spinalis,

inserts on the vertebrae. The column of the longissimus is located between the iliocostalis and the spinalis. The erector spinae muscle groups are further divided into lumborum, thoracis, cervicis, and capitis portions, which derive their names from their points of insertion on or near certain vertebrae. The erector spinae act to extend the spine when they act bilaterally. If they contract unilaterally, they act as lateral flexors of the spine. The multifidi (plural for multifidus) are deep to the erector spinae and can span between one to three vertebrae from origin to insertion (see Figure 3-25 on page 131). Since they span only a few joints, the multifidi are able to affect only local segments of the spine and provide support (i.e., stability) rather than prime movement. The origins, insertions, primary functions, and examples of exercises to develop the muscles that act at the trunk are presented in Table 1-11.

Muscles of the Lower Extremity

Compared to the musculature of the upper limbs, the muscles of the lower extremity tend to be bulkier and more powerful to serve their function in locomotion. The muscles of the lower limbs create somewhat less movement than those of the upper limbs, but they provide relatively more strength and stability. Additionally, the pelvis is fully supported by the skeleton, whereas the shoulder girdle relies more on soft-tissue structures for stability and strength. Although this section does not offer a complete review of every muscle in the lower extremity, it covers the most commonly used major muscle groups that contribute to movement at the hip, knee, and ankle.

Muscles That Act at the Hip

The hip joint is made up of the articulation of the head of the femur with the acetabulum (the cup-shaped space created by the adjoining of the three pelvic bones—the ilium, ischium, and pubis). An anterior view of the hips and pelvis reveals nine muscles—iliopsoas, sartorius, rectus femoris, tensor fascia latae, pectineus, adductor brevis, adductor longus, adductor magnus,

Figure 1-31
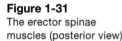
The erector spinae muscles (posterior view)

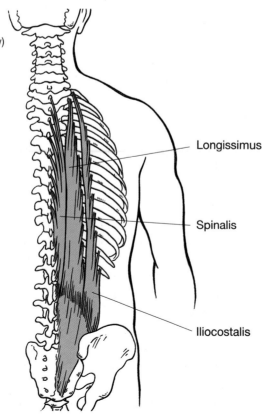

Longissimus

Spinalis

Iliocostalis

Table 1-11

Major Muscles That Act at the Trunk

Muscle	Origin	Insertion	Primary Function(s)	Selected Exercises
Rectus abdominis	Pubic crest	Cartilage of 5th through 7th ribs	Flexion and lateral flexion of the trunk	Bent-knee sit-ups, partial curl-ups, pelvic tilts
External oblique	Anterior, lateral borders of lower 8 ribs	Anterior half of ilium, pubic crest, and anterior fascia	Contralateral rotation, lateral flexion, and forward flexion (both sides)	Twisting bent-knee curl-ups (rotation opposite) and curl-ups
Internal oblique	Lumbodorsal fascia, iliac crest, and anterior fascia	Cartilage of last 3 to 4 ribs, linea alba, and superior ramis of pubis	Ipsilateral rotation, lateral flexion, and forward flexion (both sides)	Twisting bent-knee curl-ups (rotation same side) and curl-ups
Transverse abdominis	Iliac crest, lumbar fascia, cartilages of last 6 ribs, and anterior fascia	Xiphoid process of sternum, anterior fascia, and pubis	Compresses abdomen	Prone plank and "drawing in" maneuver
Erector spinae	Posterior iliac crest, sacrum, ribs, and vertebrae	Angles of ribs, transverse processes of all ribs	Extension (both sides) and lateral flexion	Squat, dead lift, prone back extension exercises
Multifidi	Posterior surface of the sacrum, articular processes of the lumbar vertebrae, transverse processes of the thoracic vertebrae, articular processes of C3-7	The spinous processes spanning 1 to 4 vertebrae above the origin	Contributes to spinal stability during trunk extension, rotation, and side-bending	Birddog

and gracilis. A posterior viewpoint shows 12 muscles—gluteus maximus, gluteus medius, gluteus minimus, six deep lateral rotators, and three hamstrings muscles.

Most of the muscles that act at the hip arise from the pelvis. One muscle, the psoas major, originates from the lumbar vertebrae and shares a tendon with the iliacus muscle, which arises from the ilium. Because these two muscles converge and insert on the femur with the same tendon, they are often referred to as the iliopsoas muscle (Figure 1-32). The main actions of the iliopsoas are flexion and external rotation of the femur. When the thigh is fixed, such as when rising from a supine position to a sitting position, the iliopsoas pulls on the lumbar vertebrae and flexes the spine and pelvis on the femur. When the trunk is fixed, such as when an individual is lying supine and lifting the legs up from the floor, the iliopsoas flexes the femur on the pelvis. In this position, the lumbar attachments of the psoas pull on the vertebrae and can create excessive lordosis and low-back pain in individuals who do not have enough abdominal strength to counterbalance this force. The abdominals can be used to prevent this low-back discomfort by pulling upward on the pelvis and thus "flattening" the back.

Arising from the anterior ilium and inserting on the medial tibia, the sartorius is the longest muscle in the body (see Figure 1-32). It crosses both the hip and the knee and produces flexion at both joints when activated. This muscle is sometimes referred to as the "tailor" muscle because it is very much involved in sitting cross-legged, which at one time was called the tailor's position. In fact, sartorius is Latin for "tailor." The rectus femoris originates just below the sartorius on

ACE Essentials of Exercise Science for Fitness Professionals

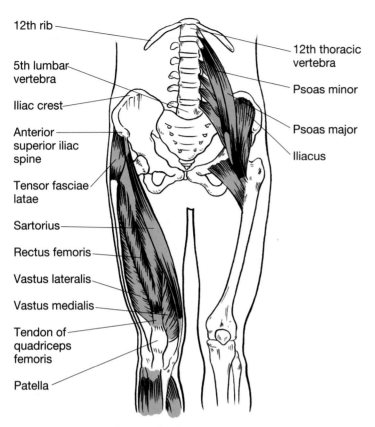

12th rib

5th lumbar vertebra

Iliac crest

Anterior superior iliac spine

Tensor fasciae latae

Sartorius

Rectus femoris

Vastus lateralis

Vastus medialis

Tendon of quadriceps femoris

Patella

12th thoracic vertebra

Psoas minor

Psoas major

Iliacus

Figure 1-32
Anterior musculature of the hip and knee, prime movers for hip flexion (iliacus, psoas major and minor) and knee extension

the anterior ilium and inserts into the patellar tendon (Figure 1-33). This muscle is part of the quadriceps femoris muscle group and is the only one that acts at both the hip and the knee; the other quadriceps muscles act only at the knee. The rectus femoris produces flexion at the hip and extension at the knee. Although the tensor fasciae latae is a lateral hip muscle, it can be viewed while looking at the pelvis anteriorly (see Figure 1-32). It inserts on the iliotibial tract, which is a strong band of connective tissue that extends from the lateral hip downward to the lateral knee. The tensor fasciae latae primarily serves to stabilize the knee by tightening the iliotibial tract. From the supine position, raising the leg with the thigh internally rotated calls it into action. The pectineus is a short muscle that crosses the anterior hip (Figure 1-34). Due to its angle of pull, it is a flexor, strong adductor, and external rotator of the hip. Another group of muscles that can be viewed anteriorly that act on the hip is the adductor group. As their names indicate, the adductor brevis, longus, and magnus act to adduct the hip. Another hip adductor, the gracilis, also assists in flexing the knee (see Figure 1-34).

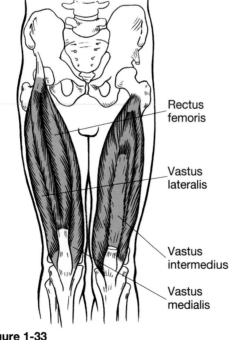

Rectus femoris

Vastus lateralis

Vastus intermedius

Vastus medialis

Figure 1-33
Quadriceps muscles

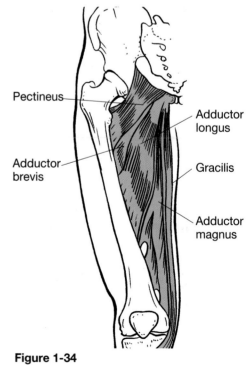

Pectineus

Adductor brevis

Adductor longus

Gracilis

Adductor magnus

Figure 1-34
Medial muscles of the hip that are responsible for adduction

The muscles that are observed when looking at the pelvis posteriorly mainly act to extend the hip and externally rotate the femur. Three gluteal muscles serve to give shape to the buttocks and provide a powerful means for movement. The gluteus maximus is the largest and most superficial posterior hip muscle (Figure 1-35). Because its tendon of insertion passes behind the hip, the gluteus maximus acts as an extensor and external rotator of the hip. When movement between the pelvis and femur approaches and goes beyond 15 degrees of extension, the gluteus maximus acts as an extensor and rotator of the hip. It is not used extensively in ordinary walking. However, a strong action of the gluteus maximus occurs in running, hopping, and jumping.

Deep to the gluteus maximus is the smaller gluteus medius. Its tendon of insertion crosses over the top of the hip joint, making it a hip abductor. Deep to the gluteus medius is the still smaller gluteus minimus. Its tendon of insertion passes in front of the hip joint, thereby allowing it to internally rotate the femur (Figure 1-36). In terms of function, both the gluteus medius and minimus have important roles in walking. As the weight of the body is suspended on one leg, these muscles prevent the opposite hip from sagging. As the body ages, these muscles tend to lose their effectiveness, but they may be strengthened by activities that require an individual to transfer weight from one foot to the other.

A group of six posterior hip muscles called the deep lateral rotators is responsible for externally rotating the femur in the acetabulum. They are the piriformis, gemellus inferior, gemellus superior, obturator internus, obturator externus, and quadratus femoris (Figure 1-37). Of interest is the most superior of the lateral rotators, the piriformis. The sciatic nerve may pass through or just inferior to the piriformis and in some individuals is associated with **sciatica,** an irritation of the sciatic nerve that causes pain, tingling, or weakness in the lower extremity.

Three muscles in the posterior thigh are responsible for extending the hip. They

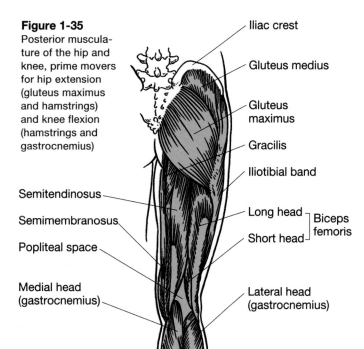

Figure 1-35
Posterior musculature of the hip and knee, prime movers for hip extension (gluteus maximus and hamstrings) and knee flexion (hamstrings and gastrocnemius)

Iliac crest

Gluteus medius

Gluteus maximus

Gracilis

Iliotibial band

Long head ⎤ Biceps
Short head ⎦ femoris

Lateral head (gastrocnemius)

Semitendinosus

Semimembranosus

Popliteal space

Medial head (gastrocnemius)

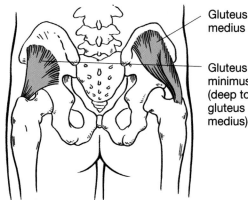

Gluteus medius

Gluteus minimus (deep to gluteus medius)

Figure 1-36
Abductors of the posterior hip

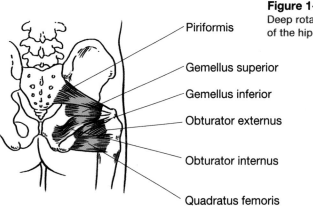

Piriformis

Figure 1-37
Deep rotators of the hip

Gemellus superior

Gemellus inferior

Obturator externus

Obturator internus

Quadratus femoris

Table 1-12

Major Muscles That Act at the Hip Joint

Muscle	Origin	Insertion	Primary Function(s)	Selected Exercises
Iliopsoas: Iliacus and psoas major and minor	Transverse processes of T12 and L1 through L5; iliac crest and fossa	Lesser trochanter of femur	Flexion and external rotation	Straight-leg sit-ups, running with knees lifted up high, leg raises, hanging knee raises
Rectus femoris	Anterior-inferior spine of ilium and upper lift of acetabulum	Superior aspect of patella and patellar tendon	Flexion	Running, leg press, squat, jumping rope
Gluteus maximus	Posterior $\frac{1}{4}$ of iliac crest and sacrum	Gluteal line of femur and iliotibial band	Extension and external rotation; Superior fibers: abduction	Cycling, plyometrics, jumping rope, squats, stair-climbing machine
Biceps femoris	Long head: ischial tuberosity; Short head: lower, lateral linea aspera	Lateral condyle of tibia and head of fibula	Extension, abduction, and slight external rotation	Cycling, hamstring curls with knee in external rotation
Semitendinosus	Ischial tuberosity	Proximal anterior-medial aspect of tibia	Extension, adduction, and slight internal rotation	Same as biceps femoris
Semimembranosus	Ischial tuberosity	Posterior aspect of medial tibial condyle	Extension, adduction, and slight internal rotation	Same as biceps femoris
Gluteus medius and minimus	Lateral surface of ilium	Greater trochanter of femur	Abduction (all fibers); Anterior fibers: internal rotation; Posterior fibers: external rotation	Side-lying leg raises, walking, running
Adductor magnus	Pubic ramus and ischial tuberosity	Medial aspects of femur	Adduction	Side-lying bottom-leg raises, resisted adduction
Adductor brevis and longus	Pubic ramus and ischial tuberosity	Linea aspera of femur	Adduction	Side-lying bottom-leg raises, resisted adduction
Tensor fasciae latae	Anterior iliac crest and ilium just below crest	Iliotibial band	Flexion, abduction, and internal rotation	Hanging knee raises, side-lying leg raises, running
Sartorius	Anterior superior iliac spine	Proximal anterior medial tibia just below the tuberosity	Flexion and external rotation of the hip; flexion of the knee	Knee lift with hip external rotation, wide stance onto bench
Pectineus	Superior pubic ramus	Lesser trochanter and linea aspera of femur	Flexion, adduction, and external rotation	Hanging knee raises, side-lying bottom-leg raises, resisted external rotation of the thigh
Six deep external (lateral) rotators: Piriformis, obturator internus, obturator externus, superior gemellus, inferior gemellus, and quadratus femoris	Multiple origin points for six muscles on pubis, ischium, sacrum, and obturator foramen	On and just below greater trochanter, and trochanteric fossa of femur	External rotation	Resisted external rotation of the thigh
Gracilis	Pubic symphysis and arch	Medial tibia just below the condyle	Adduction	Side-lying bottom-leg raises, resisted adduction

are referred to as the hamstring muscle group and consist of the biceps femoris, semimembranosus, and semitendinosus (see Figure 1-35). The origins, insertions, primary functions, and examples of exercises to develop the muscles that act at the hip are presented in Table 1-12.

Muscles That Act at the Knee

The articulations of the distal femur with the proximal tibia and fibula comprise the knee joint. The muscles located in the thigh are responsible for movement at the knee. The thigh muscles are grouped by fasciae into anterior, posterior, and medial compartments.

The anterior compartment is also called the extensor compartment, because the muscles in this location primarily extend the knee. There are five muscles in the anterior compartment of the thigh. Four of them (rectus femoris, vastus intermedius, vastus lateralis, and vastus medialis) are collectively called the quadriceps femoris (see Figure 1-33). They are individually named and originate from different areas, but they all converge and share one tendon of insertion, the patellar tendon. The quadriceps femoris is responsible for extending the knee. As mentioned earlier, one of the muscles, the rectus femoris, also crosses the hip joint and contributes to hip flexion. The fifth muscle of the anterior compartment is the sartorius, which was mentioned earlier for its action at the hip. Recall that because of its position as it crosses the knee, it assists in knee flexion.

The posterior, or flexor, compartment consists of the hamstring muscles. These muscles were mentioned earlier for their action of extension at the hip. They are also the primary flexors of the knee. The tendons of insertion of the semimembranosus and semitendinosus pass medially behind the knee, whereas the biceps femoris tendon passes laterally behind the knee. The triangular space created between these tendons on the posterior aspect of the knee is called the popliteal space (see Figure 1-35).

The medial compartment of the thigh is also referred to as the adductor compartment. Five muscles comprise the adductor compartment (adductors magnus, longus, and brevis;

pectineus; and gracilis). These muscles were mentioned earlier for their role in adducting the hip joint. In addition to adduction of the hip, the gracilis contributes to flexion at the knee. The origins, insertions, primary functions, and examples of exercises to develop the muscles that act at the knee are presented in Table 1-13.

Muscles That Act at the Ankle and Foot

The ankle joint, which is composed of the articulations between the distal tibia, distal fibula, and proximal talus, acts as a hinge, allowing only **dorsiflexion** and **plantarflexion.** The articulation of the talus and the calcaneus is referred to as the subtalar joint, which allows inversion and eversion of the foot. The muscles contained in the lower leg control movements at the ankle and foot. The lower leg has four separate compartments that are divided by connective tissue. The anterior compartment contains muscles that extend the toes and dorsiflex and/or invert the foot. The posterior compartments consist of muscles that plantarflex the foot and/or flex the toes. The lateral compartment is made up of muscles that act to plantarflex and/or evert the foot.

The anterior compartment, which is made up of muscles including the anterior tibialis, extensor hallucis longus, extensor digitorum longus, and peroneus tertius, is located just lateral to the thick shaft of the tibia (Figure 1-38). The structures of the posterior compartment include the superficial gastrocnemius, soleus, and plantaris muscles, and the deep popliteus, flexor hallucis longus, flexor digitorum longus, and posterior tibialis muscles (Figure 1-39). The gastrocnemius and soleus are powerful plantarflexors that make up the bulk of the calf and share a common insertion, the Achilles tendon. The heads of the gastrocnemius have their origins on the femur and cross the posterior knee. This makes the gastrocnemius, a two-joint muscle, responsible for flexing the knee in addition to plantarflexing the ankle.

The gastrocnemius is more effective at knee flexion when plantarflexion is minimal, such as when performing a prone-lying hamstring curl, and less effective at plantarflexion when

Table 1-13

Major Muscles That Act at the Knee Joint

Muscle	Origin	Insertion	Primary Function(s)	Selected Exercises
Rectus femoris	Anterior-inferior spine of ilium and upper lip of acetabulum	Superior aspect of patella and patellar tendon	Extension (most effective when the hip is extended)	Cycling, leg press machine, squats, vertical jumping, stair climbing, jumping rope, plyometrics
Vastus lateralis, intermedius, and medialis	Along the surfaces of the lateral, anterior, and medial femur	Patella and tibial tuberosity via the patellar tendon	Extension	Same as for rectus femoris, resisted knee extension
Biceps femoris	Long head: ischial tuberosity; Short head: lower, lateral linea aspera	Lateral condyle of tibia and head of fibula	Flexion and external rotation	Cycling, lunging, hamstring curls
Semitendinosus	Ischial tuberosity	Proximal anterior medial aspect of tibia	Flexion and internal rotation	Same as biceps femoris
Semimem-branosus	Ischial tuberosity	Posterior aspect of medial tibial condyle	Flexion and internal rotation	Same as biceps femoris
Gracilis	Pubic symphysis and pubic arch	Medial tibia just below the condyle	Flexion	Side-lying bottom-leg raises, resisted adduction
Sartorius	Anterior superior iliac spine	Proximal anterior medial tibia just below the tuberosity	Flexion and external rotation of the hip; flexion of the knee	Knee lift with hip external rotation, wide stance onto bench
Popliteus	Lateral condyle of the femur	Proximal tibia	Knee flexion; internal rotation of the lower leg to "unlock the knee"	Same as biceps femoris

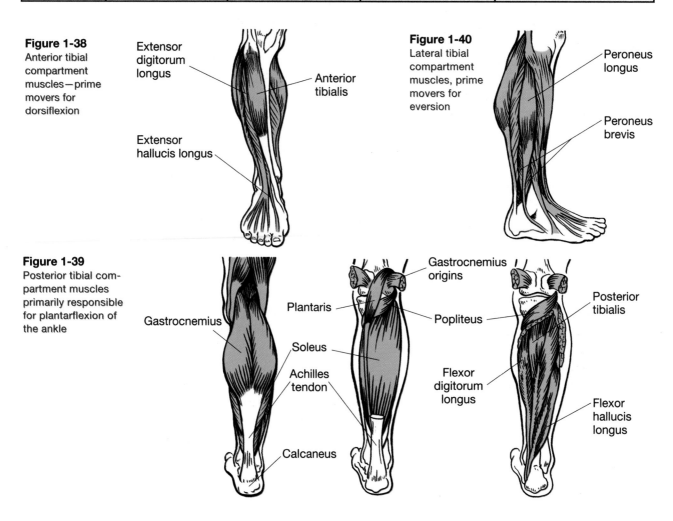

Figure 1-38
Anterior tibial compartment muscles—prime movers for dorsiflexion

Extensor digitorum longus

Anterior tibialis

Extensor hallucis longus

Figure 1-40
Lateral tibial compartment muscles, prime movers for eversion

Peroneus longus

Peroneus brevis

Figure 1-39
Posterior tibial compartment muscles primarily responsible for plantarflexion of the ankle

Gastrocnemius

Plantaris

Soleus

Achilles tendon

Calcaneus

Gastrocnemius origins

Popliteus

Flexor digitorum longus

Posterior tibialis

Flexor hallucis longus

the knee is bent. The gastrocnemius is the primary focus during standing calf work, whereas the soleus is the primary focus of seated calf exercises. The lateral compartment of the leg contains the peroneus longus and brevis (Figure 1-40). The origins, insertions, primary functions, and examples of exercises to develop the muscles that act at the ankle and foot are presented in Table 1-14.

Endocrine System

The endocrine system, which is made up of various glands throughout the body, is responsible for regulating bodily activities through the production of hormones. Hormones are chemical substances that generally fit into one of two categories: steroid-derived hormones and hormones synthesized from amino acids. The cells of the endocrine glands release their hormones directly into the bloodstream, where they are delivered to target organs. The principal endocrine glands are the pituitary, thyroid, parathyroids, adrenals, pancreas, and gonads.

The pituitary gland is often referred to as the "master gland," because of its regulatory effect on several other endocrine glands and its importance in controlling a number of diverse bodily functions. It is located beneath the brain and divided into anterior and posterior lobes. The posterior lobe releases a hormone called **vasopressin,** which acts on the kidneys and is considered an antidiuretic (i.e., a substance that inhibits urine production, thereby aiding in the retention of bodily fluid). The posterior portion also releases oxytocin, a hormone that stimulates the smooth muscles of the reproductive organs and intestines.

The anterior portion of the pituitary gland releases six hormones that affect various important bodily functions: follicle-stimulating hormone (FSH), luteinizing hormone (LH), thyroid-stimulating hormone (TSH), **adrenocorticotropin hormone (ACTH),** growth hormone (GH), and prolactin. FSH and LH are called gonadotropins because of their effects on the gonads (ovaries and testes). These substances control the secretion of **estrogen** and **progesterone** in the ovaries and the production

of **testosterone** in the testicles. TSH stimulates the synthesis and release of thyroxine from the thyroid gland, which helps control the rate at which all cells utilize oxygen. ACTH controls the secretion in the adrenal gland of hormones that influence the metabolism of carbohydrates, sodium, and potassium. ACTH also controls the rate at which substances are exchanged between the blood and tissues. GH specifically stimulates growth of the skeletal system, but also general growth.

Additionally, GH promotes the entrance of amino acids into the body's cells for their incorporation into protein and releases fatty acids into the blood for use as energy. GH has also been shown to promote the formation of glucose and its release into the blood. Another anterior pituitary hormone, prolactin, is involved in the initiation and maintenance of breast-milk production and secretion in females.

The thyroid gland is located anterior to the upper part of the trachea, and is among the largest endocrine organs in the body. Mentioned earlier for its functions controlled by the pituitary gland, the thyroid gland releases three hormones: thyroxine, triiodothyronine, and calcitonin.

Thyroxine and triiodothyronine are iodine-containing hormones that are released by the thyroid to regulate the metabolism of carbohydrates, proteins, and lipids, thereby increasing the body's oxygen consumption and heat production. The third hormone, calcitonin, lowers blood calcium and phosphate levels by accelerating the absorption of calcium by the bones. The parathyroid glands are four structures located on the posterior surface of the thyroid gland. These glands release parathyroid hormone (PTH), which is primarily responsible for controlling the levels of calcium and phosphorus in the blood through its actions on the kidneys and the skeleton. PTH increases bone resorption, which functions to break down bone calcium for its release into the blood. Further, PTH works synergistically with vitamin D to maintain the body's calcium levels.

The adrenal glands appear as two pyramid-shaped organs located close to the superior border of each kidney. Each gland consists of

Table 1-14

Major Muscles That Act at the Ankle and Foot

Muscle	Origin	Insertion	Primary Function(s)	Selected Exercises
Anterior tibialis	Proximal ⅔ of lateral tibia	Medial aspect of 1st cuneiform and base of 1st metatarsal	Dorsiflexion at ankle; inversion at foot	Cycling with toe clips, resisted inversion (with dorsiflexion)
Peroneus longus	Lateral surface of head of tibia, head of fibula, and proximal ⅔ 2/of lateral fibula	Inferior aspects of medial tarsal (1st cuneiform) and base of 1st metatarsal	Plantarflexion at ankle; eversion at foot	Resisted eversion of foot
Peroneus brevis	Distal ⅔ of lateral fibula	Base of the 5th metatarsal	Plantarflexion at ankle; eversion at foot	Resisted eversion of foot
Gastrocnemius	Posterior surfaces of femoral condyles	Posterior surface of calcaneus via Achilles tendon	Plantarflexion at ankle; flexion at knee	Hill running, jumping rope, calf raises, cycling, stair climbing
Soleus	Proximal ⅔ of posterior surfaces of tibia and fibula and popliteal line	Posterior surface of calcaneus via Achilles tendon	Plantarflexion at ankle	Virtually the same as for gastrocnemius; bent-knee toe raises with resistance
Posterior tibialis	Posterior surface of the lateral tibia and medial fibula	Lower medial surfaces of medial tarsals and metatarsals	Plantarflexion at ankle; inversion at foot	Resisted inversion of foot with plantarflexion
Extensor hallucis longus	Anterior middle fibula	Dorsal surface of the distal phalanx of the great toe	Dorsiflexion and inversion of the foot; extension of the great toe	Resisted inversion with dorsiflexion
Extensor digitorum longus	Lateral condyle of tibia, proximal ¾ of the fibula	Dorsal surface of the phalanges of toes 2 through 5	Dorsiflexion and eversion of foot; extension of toes 2 through 5	Resisted eversion with dorsiflexion longus
Peroneus tertius	Distal ⅓ of the anterior/lateral fibula	Dorsal surface of the base of the 5th metatarsal	Dorsiflexion and eversion of the foot	Resisted eversion with dorsiflexion
Plantaris	Posterior surface of the femur above the lateral condyle	Posterior surface of calcaneus via Achilles tendon	Flexion of the knee; plantarflexion of the foot	Same as gastrocnemius
Flexor hallucis longus	Distal ⅔ of the fibula	Plantar surface of distal phalanx of great toe	Flexion of the great toe; plantarflexion and inversion of the foot	Resisted inversion with plantarflexion
Flexor digitorum longus	Posterior middle ⅓ of tibia	Plantar surfaces of distal phalanges of toes 2 through 5	Flexion of toes 2 through 5; plantarflexion and inversion of the foot	Resisted inversion with plantarflexion

two distinct parts: the medulla (inner portion) and the cortex (outer portion). The adrenal medulla and the adrenal cortex are so distinct that each portion is, in effect, its own distinct endocrine organ. The adrenal medulla produces two hormones: **epinephrine** (adrenaline) and **norepinephrine** (noradrenaline). These substances function cooperatively to prepare the body for emergencies or stressful events. Epinephrine acts to elevate blood glucose levels; increase the rate, force, and amplitude of the heartbeat; and dilate blood vessels that feed the heart, lungs, and skeletal muscles. The release of norepinephrine causes an increase in heart rate and in the force of contraction of the cardiac muscle. It also contributes to constriction of blood vessels in most areas of the body. The adrenal cortex secretes mineralocorticoids associated with sodium and potassium metabolism, glucocorticoids that aid in the utilization of glucose and mobilization of fatty acids, and gonadocorticoids, including testosterone, estrogen, and progesterone.

The pancreas lies just below the stomach and, in addition to its role in producing digestive enzymes, functions as an endocrine gland that produces hormones involved in regulating carbohydrate metabolism. The pancreas secretes **insulin,** which acts to facilitate the uptake and utilization of glucose (blood sugar) by cells and prevent the breakdown of **glycogen** (the storage form of glucose) in the liver and muscle. This function makes insulin a powerful hypoglycemic agent—that is, it decreases the blood sugar level. Insulin also plays a role in lipid and protein metabolism, as it favors lipid formation and storage and facilitates the movement of amino acids into cells. The pancreas secretes another hormone, **glucagon,** which generally opposes the actions of insulin. Glucagon decreases glucose oxidation and increases the blood

sugar level (hyperglycemia). Its main action appears to be stimulation of the breakdown of glycogen in the liver for its release into the bloodstream.

The gonads are the endocrine glands that produce hormones that promote sex-specific physical characteristics and regulate reproductive function. The sex hormones testosterone and estrogen are found in both males and females, but in varying concentrations. In males, testosterone is produced in the testes and acts to initiate sperm production, stimulate the development of male secondary sex characteristics, and promote tissue building. In females, the ovaries are the primary source for the production of estrogen, which regulates ovulation, menstruation, the physiological adjustments during pregnancy, and the appearance of female secondary sex characteristics. Furthermore, estrogen affects the blood vessels, bones, lungs, liver, intestines, prostate, and testes. Table 1-15 lists the major endocrine glands and summarizes some selected effects of their associated hormones.

Summary

Fitness professionals are required to design programs and group fitness classes that are safe and effective and that accomplish the desired fitness and/or personal goals of clients or participants. Without a fundamental understanding of human anatomy, this task is nearly impossible. Anatomical terminology and the five major anatomical systems—cardiovascular, respiratory, nervous, skeletal, and muscular—were presented. This information should enable fitness professionals to identify specific exercises and physical activities that will efficiently accomplish the fitness goals of their clients or class participants.

Table 1-15

Major Endocrine Glands and Their Hormones

Gland	Hormones	Selected Effects
Pituitary	Antidiuretic hormone	Reduces urinary excretion of water
	Oxytocin	Stimulates the contraction of the smooth muscle of the uterus and intestines
	Follicle stimulating hormone (FSH) and luteinizing hormone (LH)	Stimulate gonads to secrete sex hormones
	Thyroid stimulating hormone (TSH)	Stimulates thyroid gland to secrete thyroid hormones
	Adrenocorticotropin hormone (ACTH)	Stimulates adrenal glands to secrete glucocorticoids
	Growth hormone (GH)	Stimulates general growth and skeletal growth, and promotes metabolic functions
	Prolactin	Initiates and maintains breast-milk secretion in females
Thyroid	Thyroxine and triiodothyronine	Increases oxygen consumption and heat production, and affects many metabolic functions
	Calcitonin	Decreases blood calcium and phosphate levels
Parathyroids	Parathyroid hormone (PTH)	Raises plasma calcium levels and lowers plasma phosphate levels
Adrenals	Epinephrine	Affects carbohydrate metabolism, generally promoting hyperglycemia. Constricts vessels in the skin, mucous membranes, and kidneys, but dilates vessels in skeletal muscle
	Norepinephrine	Increases heart rate and force of contraction of the myocardium, and constricts blood vessels in most areas of the body
	Mineralocorticoids (e.g., aldosterone)	Promote reabsorption of sodium and excretion of potassium in the kidneys
	Glucocorticoids (e.g., cortisol)	Promote protein and triglyceride breakdown
Pancreas	Insulin	Causes liver and muscle cells to take up glucose and store it in the form of glycogen; encourages fat cells to take on blood lipids and turn them into triglycerides; also has several other anabolic effects throughout the body
	Glucagon	Causes the liver to convert stored glycogen into glucose and release it into the bloodstream

References

Pette, D. (2001). Historical perspectives: Plasticity of mammalian skeletal muscle. *Journal of Applied Physiology,* 90, 3, 1119–1124.

Shoepe, T. et al. (2003). Functional adaptability of muscle fibers to long-term resistance exercise. *Medicine & Science in Sports & Exercise,* 35, 6, 944–951.

Suggested Reading

Behnke, R.S. (2006). *Kinetic Anatomy.* Champaign, Ill.: Human Kinetics.

Calais-Germain, B. (1993). *Anatomy of Movement.* Seattle, Wa: Eastland Press, Inc.

Delavier, F. (2005). *Strength Training Anatomy.* Champaign, Ill.: Human Kinetics.

Golding, L.A. & Golding, M.G. (2003). *Musculoskeletal Anatomy and Human Movement.* Monterey, Calif.: Healthy Learning.

Houglum, P.A. (2006). *Therapeutic Exercise for Musculoskeletal Injuries* (2nd ed.). Champaign, Ill.: Human Kinetics.

Travell, J.G. & Simons, D.G. (1999). *Myofascial Pain and Dysfunction: The Trigger Point Manual* (2nd ed.). Baltimore, Md.: Williams & Wilkins.

STUDY GUIDE

Chapter 1
Human Anatomy

Getting Started

This chapter describes the structure and function of five major systems within the human body: the cardiovascular system, the respiratory system, the nervous system, the skeletal system, and the muscular system. After reading this chapter, you should have a better understanding of:

- Basic anatomical terminology
- The functional anatomy of the heart
- The major arteries and veins
- The central and peripheral nervous systems
- The axial and appendicular skeletal systems
- The structure and function of the neuromuscular and muscular systems
- The structure and type of movements allowed by joints
- Fundamental movements of the human body
- Muscle names and locations
- The principal endocrine glands

Expand Your Knowledge

I. Match the anatomical, directional, and regional terms to their descriptions.

a. _____ anterior

b. _____ superficial

c. _____ superior

d. _____ proximal

e. _____ medial

f. _____ frontal plane

g. _____ sagittal plane

h. _____ transverse plane

1. Divides the body into anterior and posterior parts
2. External; located close to or on the surface
3. Toward the midline of the body
4. Toward the front
5. Toward the attached end of the limb, origin of the structure, or midline of the body
6. Divides the body or any of its parts into superior and inferior sections
7. Divides the body or any of its parts into right and left sections
8. Toward the head

II. Aside from distributing oxygen and nutrients to the cells, list the other major functions of the cardiovascular system.

a. _____

_____

b. _____

_____

c. _____

_____

III. Provide the labels for the following diagram of the heart. Then, indicate the chronological order of blood flow, beginning with blood entering through the superior and inferior vena cava.

a. _____   1. _____

b. _____   2. _____

c. _____   3. _____

d. _____   4. _____

e. _____   5. _____

f. _____   6. _____

g. _____   7. _____

h. _____   8. _____

i. _____   9. _____

j. _____   10. _____

k. _____   11. _____

l. _____   12. _____

m. _____   13. _____

n. _____

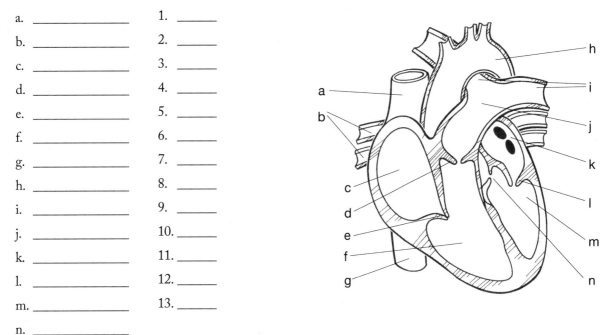

IV. Number the following steps in the process of oxygen delivery to the capillaries of the lungs in order, beginning as oxygen is taken into the mouth and nose.

a. ___ through the pharynx

b. ___ gas exchange in the lungs

c. ___ through the primary bronchi

d. ___ through the trachea

e. ___ through the bronchioles

f. ___ through the larynx

g. ___ through the secondary bronchi

h. ___ through the alveoli

V.   Describe the major differences between the following pairs of words or phrases.

   a. Central nervous system and peripheral nervous system _____

   _____

   _____

   b. Axial skeleton and appendicular skeleton _____

   _____

   _____

   c. Formed elements and plasma _____

   _____

   _____

   d. Skeletal muscle and both cardiac and visceral muscle _____

   _____

   _____

   e. Arteries and veins _____

   _____

   _____

VI. Describe the major characteristics of the following joint categories.

   a. Synovial _____

   _____

   b. Cartilaginous _____

   _____

   c. Fibrous _____

   _____

VII. Name the type and describe the possible movements at the following joints.

   a. Thumb _____

   _____

   b. Hip _____

   _____

   c. Knee _____

   _____

   d. Elbow _____

   _____

   e. Hand _____

   _____

VIII. List the three forms of connective tissue related most to the practical application of personal training, briefly explain their roles during physical activity, and identify their relative contribution to the resistance experienced during joint movement.

a. _____

_____

_____

b. _____

_____

_____

c. _____

_____

_____

IX. Briefly explain how each of the following factors contributes to or affects flexibility.

a. Age _____

_____

_____

_____

b. Gender _____

_____

_____

_____

c. Joint structure and past injury _____

_____

_____

_____

d. Tissue temperature _____

_____

_____

_____

e. Circadian variations _____

_____

_____

_____

X.   Identify the muscles on the following illustrations as indicated.

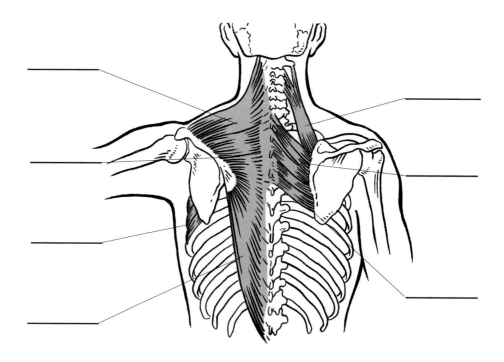

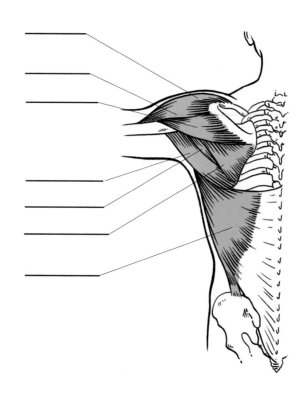

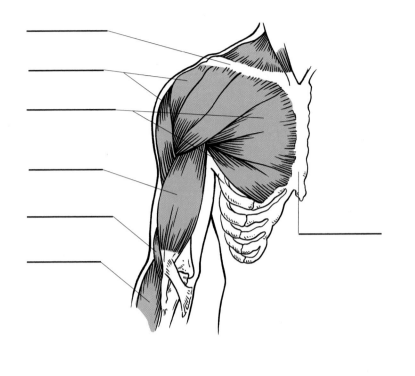

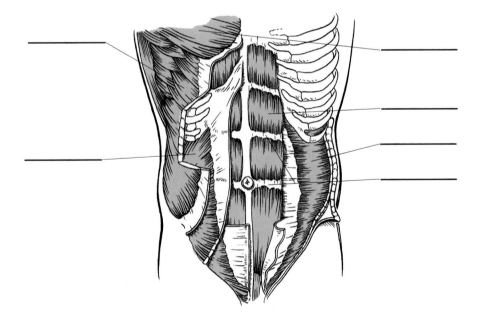

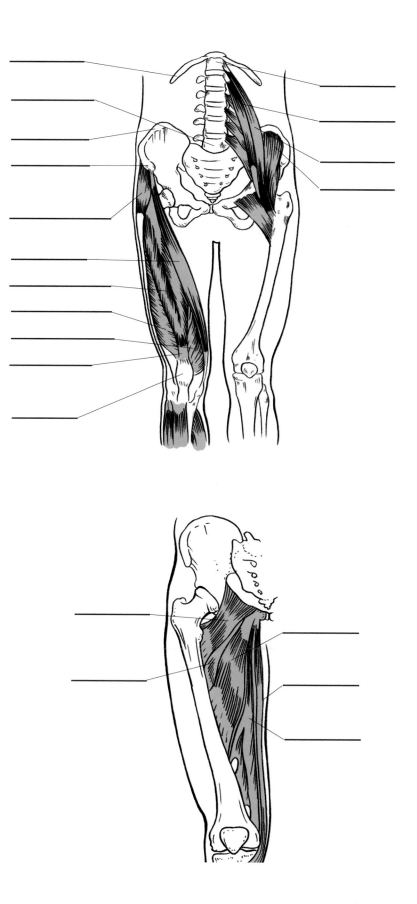

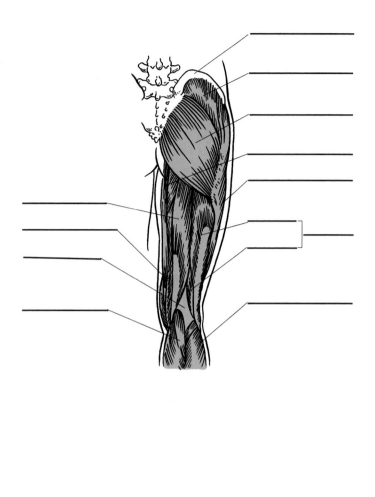

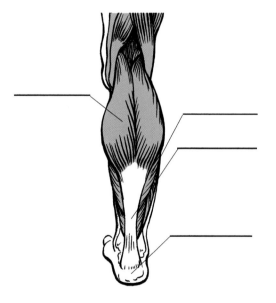

Show What You Know

I.   Explain the dangers of working past the "burning" feeling that results when muscles are heavily exercised or in a state of fatigue. _____

_____

_____

_____

_____

_____

II. Name the primary muscles or muscle groups that are utilized during the following movements.

a. Leg extension at the knee _____

_____

b. Adduction at the shoulder _____

_____

c. Lateral flexion at the trunk _____

_____

d. Plantarflexion at the ankle _____

_____

e. Flexion at the elbow _____

_____

f. Adduction of the scapula _____

_____

Multiple Choice

1. Which blood vessels carry blood that is rich in oxygen from the lungs back to the heart?

    A. Coronary arteries

    B. Pulmonary arteries

    C. Coronary veins

    D. Pulmonary veins

2. Which muscle or muscle group is **MOST** important for respiration in humans?

    A. Internal intercostals

    B. Diaphragm

    C. External intercostals

    D. Transverse abdominis

3. It is important for fitness professionals to have a general understanding of Wolff's law because it explains how _____.

    A. Regular endurance exercise increases the oxidative capacity of the respiratory muscles

    B. Intervertebral disks are better prepared for external loads following rehydration during sleep

    C. Bones increase density in response to the stress applied through weightbearing exercise

    D. Functional training improves kinesthetic awareness by stimulating the proprioceptors in the joints

4. Golgi tendon organs (GTOs) can affect a static stretch by causing _____.

    A. Relaxation of the muscle(s) being stretched through autogenic inhibition

    B. Contraction of the muscle(s) being stretched through autogenic inhibition

    C. Relaxation of the antagonist(s) through reciprocal inhibition

    D. Contraction of the antagonist(s) through reciprocal inhibition

5. What organ is **PRIMARILY** responsible for the digestion and absorption of nutrients?

    A. Stomach

    B. Pancreas

    C. Small intestine

    D. Large intestine

6. The forward-backward movements of the arms and legs during walking occur in which plane of movement?
   A. Frontal
   B. Sagittal
   C. Longitudinal
   D. Transverse

7. Which type of muscle fiber is the **MOST** highly adaptable to different training stimuli, making it able to increase oxidative capacities or increase force production and speed?
   A. Type I
   B. Type IIa
   C. Type IIb
   D. Type IIx

8. During dynamic and static stretching, which of the following soft tissues contributes **LEAST** to the total resistance encountered by the joint during movement through its range of motion?
   A. Muscle fascia
   B. Tendons
   C. Skin
   D. Joint capsule

9. Which muscles are prime movers for the shoulder joint adduction performed during a wide-grip pull-up?
   A. Trapezius and rhomboids
   B. Deltoid and latissimus dorsi
   C. Teres major and serratus anterior
   D. Pectoralis major and latissimus dorsi

10. How does the pancreas help regulate blood glucose levels?
    A. It secretes glucagon to increase blood glucose levels and insulin to increase glucose uptake by the cells
    B. It releases glucocorticoids that aid in the utilization of glucose and metabolism of fatty acids
    C. It secretes insulin to increase blood glucose levels and stimulate uptake of the glucose by the cells
    D. It releases pancreatic enzymes into the small intestine to aid in the digestion of protein, carbohydrate, and fat

JOHN P. PORCARI, Ph.D., is a professor in the Department of Exercise and Sports Science and executive director of the La Crosse Exercise and Health Program at the University of Wisconsin–La Crosse. He is a fellow of the American College of Sports Medicine and of the American Association of Cardiovascular and Pulmonary Rehabilitation (AACVPR) and was the President of AACVPR in 2002–2003. Dr. Porcari's research interests have focused on the acute and training responses to exercising on a variety of exercise modalities, particularly new fitness products. He has authored more than 75 peer-reviewed publications and made more than 150 national presentations dealing with health and fitness.

CARL FOSTER, Ph.D., is a professor in the Department of Exercise and Sports Science and director of the Human Performance Laboratory at the University of Wisconsin–La Crosse (UWL). He is a fellow of the American College of Sports Medicine (ACSM) and of the American Association of Cardiovascular and Pulmonary Rehabilitation. He was the 2005–2006 President of ACSM. Dr. Foster's research interests range from high-performance physiology (he is the head of sports science for U.S. Speedskating) to clinical exercise physiology (he is the research director for the Clinical Exercise Physiology graduate program at UWL). He has published more than 250 scientific papers and book chapters and 22 longer works (e.g., books, monographs, position stands, videos).

CHAPTER 2

Exercise Physiology

John P. Porcari & Carl Foster

Whenever the human body increases its activity level, energy is required to fuel this movement, and the body has to make adaptations to provide this energy to the tissues. The study of **exercise physiology** provides an understanding of how the body responds to the acute and chronic demands placed on it by the increased energy demands of exercise. It is essential that fitness professionals understand the basics of exercise physiology so that they can design safe and effective exercise programs and classes.

Benefits of Physical Activity

There are many established benefits of being physically active, many of them related to the prevention or treatment of most major diseases. It has often been said that if exercise could be packaged in a pill, it would be the most widely prescribed medication in the world. Some of the benefits of regular exercise include improved cardiovascular function, lowered **systolic** and **diastolic blood pressure**, decreased body weight and fat mass, improved **lipid** profile, improved **glucose** control, decreased **anxiety** and **depression**, enhanced feelings of well-being, decreased incidence of several cancers (e.g., colon, breast, prostate), and decreased incidence of **osteoporosis.** Epidemiological studies have shown that regular exercisers live two to four years longer than **sedentary** individuals. The benefits of exercise are particularly pronounced when sedentary individuals adopt even a minimal exercise program, but benefits continue to accrue whenever more exercise is performed. Although there is some debate over the precise dose of exercise necessary to achieve health benefits, there is wide agreement that if everyone performed 30 minutes of moderate-intensity exercise daily (e.g., a two-mile walk), the incidence of most of the chronic "diseases of civilization" (or lifestyle diseases) would decrease dramatically. From this foundation, it may be argued that the focus of the exercise profession into the foreseeable future will likely be on strategies to get people to start exercising and to keep exercising regularly, rather than on the development of high levels of fitness.

The Concept of Physical Fitness

Given that the basic understanding of the exercise community is grounded in the concept of **physical fitness,** it is important to define what is meant by this commonly used term that has historically meant different things to different people. Much of the recent research on the benefits of exercise has focused on the role of physical activity in enhancing health status, as opposed to physical fitness. Physical activity can be defined as any bodily movement that comes about from the contraction of skeletal muscle and that increases energy expenditure. Many everyday activities are included under the umbrella of physical activity, including gardening, raking leaves, and performing household chores, as well as what might be thought of as formal exercise. Exercise is considered to be a more structured form of physical activity that has a specific purpose in

mind. In many cases, exercise is designed to improve specific aspects of physical fitness, which can be defined as a set of attributes that allow individuals to perform physical activity with greater ease. A high level of physical fitness enables people to perform their required daily tasks without fatigue, thus enabling them to participate in additional pleasurable activities for personal enjoyment. Increased physical fitness is often reflected by physiological adaptations, such as a lowered **heart rate (HR)** during a standardized exercise task or an improved ability to mobilize and use body fuels. A high level of physical fitness also implies optimal physical performance and good health, because the amount and intensity of exercise necessary to improve physical fitness is much higher than the amount and intensity of exercise necessary to have a meaningful impact on health. However, the overwhelming story coming out of the research literature in the past 25 years has been that it is not necessary to perform the volume (and particularly the intensity) of exercise necessary to cause large physiological adaptations in order to become much healthier.

Physical fitness is generally considered to have four major components, though many experts include **mind/body vitality** as a fifth component:

- Muscular fitness involves **muscular strength** and **muscular endurance.** Muscular strength, which is the maximal force that a muscle or muscle group can exert during a contraction, is essential for normal everyday functioning, as individuals are required to lift and carry objects (e.g., groceries, suitcases) in their daily lives. Adequate muscular strength may become even more important as people age. Some elderly individuals, for instance, are not able to walk up stairs or even get up out of a chair due to inadequate lower-body strength. Longitudinal studies of masters runners (i.e., athletes who are at least 40 years of age) by the late Dr. Michael Pollock have indicated that in the absence of systematically performed resistance exercise, a loss of muscle mass (and thus, of muscular strength) is a routine finding with aging (Pollock et al., 1997, 1987). Fortunately, these same studies indicate that this trend could be prevented by performing regular resistance exercise. Muscular endurance, the second component of muscular fitness, is the ability of a muscle or muscle group to exert force against a resistance over a sustained period of time. Muscular endurance is assessed by measuring the length of time (duration) a muscle can exert force without fatigue, or by measuring the number of times (repetitions) that a given task can be performed without fatigue. Many everyday activities require a significant amount of muscular endurance (e.g., walking up stairs, shoveling snow).

- **Cardiovascular** or **cardiorespiratory endurance** (sometimes referred to as **aerobic** power or aerobic fitness) is the maximal capacity of the heart, blood vessels, and lungs to deliver oxygen and nutrients to the working muscles so that energy can be produced. The higher a person's cardiorespiratory endurance, the more physical work he or she can perform before becoming fatigued. Efficient functioning of the cardiorespiratory system is essential for physical activities such as walking, running, swimming, and cycling. In addition, the effect of physical activity on the reductions in the incidence of many of the diseases of civilization is arguably related more to improvements in cardiorespiratory endurance than to any of the other components of physical fitness. This is likely attributable to the requirement to recruit a large muscle mass during the kinds of whole-body training that leads to improved cardiorespiratory endurance.
- **Flexibility** is the ability to move joints through their normal full **range of motion (ROM)**. An adequate degree of flexibility is important to prevent musculoskeletal injuries, to maintain correct body posture, and to allow people to complete everyday bending and reaching tasks.
- **Body composition** refers to the makeup of the body in relation to proportions of **lean body mass** and body fat. Lean body mass consists of the muscles, bones, nervous tissue, skin, blood, and organs. These tissues have a relatively high metabolic rate and make a positive contribution to physical performance. Lean body mass often decreases with aging, inactivity, and many disease states. As a general principle, any time the lean body mass increases, it can be thought of as positive for health and fitness. The primary role of body fat, or **adipose tissue,** the other component of body composition, is to store energy for later use. Body fat is further classified into **essential fat** and **storage fat.** Essential body fat is that amount of **fat** thought to be necessary for maintenance of life and reproductive function; 2 to 5% body fat is generally thought to be essential for men, while 10 to 13% is thought to be essential for women. The differences in these sex-specific essential-fat levels are due to the energy reserve necessary for childbearing, with the extra fat being located primarily in the breasts and pelvic regions. Excess body-fat storage is referred to as **overweight** or **obesity** and has been associated with a wide variety of health disorders, including **hypertension, type 2 diabetes,** and an increased incidence of **coronary artery disease.**

Physiology of the Cardiorespiratory System

Cardiorespiratory endurance is defined as the capacity of the heart and lungs to deliver blood and oxygen to the working muscles during exercise. A person's capacity to perform aerobic exercise depends largely on the interaction of the cardiovascular and respiratory systems as they provide oxygen to be transported in the blood to the active cells so that **carbohydrates** and **fatty acids** can be converted to **adenosine triphosphate (ATP)** for muscular contraction. These two systems are also important for the removal of metabolic waste products, such as carbon dioxide and **lactate,** and for the dissipation of the heat produced by metabolic processes. There are three basic processes that must interact to provide adequate blood and nutrients to the tissues:

- Getting oxygen into the blood—a function of **pulmonary ventilation** coupled with the oxygen-carrying capacity of the blood
- Delivering oxygen to the active tissues—a function of **cardiac output**
- Extracting oxygen from the blood to complete the metabolic production of ATP—a function of localizing the delivery of the cardiac output to the active muscles and the oxidative **enzymes** located within the active cells

Oxygen-carrying Capacity

The oxygen-carrying capacity of blood is determined primarily by two variables: (1) the ability to adequately ventilate the **alveoli** in the lungs and (2) the **hemoglobin (Hb)** concentration of the blood. Pulmonary ventilation is a function of both the rate and depth (**tidal volume**) of breathing. At the onset of exercise, both tidal volume and breathing rate increase. This increase in ventilation volume brings more oxygen into the lungs, where it can be absorbed into the blood. Because the alveoli are essentially blind pouches (i.e., air flows in and out of them via the same bronchial tubes), it is particularly important to maintain an adequate tidal volume during even heavy exercise so that the gas concentrations in the alveoli can be effectively exchanged. If this does not happen, and the oxygen (O_2) concentration in the alveoli is too low and the carbon dioxide (CO_2) concentration is too high, the tendency for the gases to move in the desired direction (from alveoli to pulmonary **capillaries,** or from pulmonary capillaries to alveoli, respectively) is reduced.

In normal individuals, **respiration** does not limit exercise performance. However, individuals with **emphysema** (degradation of the alveoli) or **asthma** (constriction of the breathing passages) cannot move enough air through their lungs to adequately aerate the alveoli and thereby oxygenate the blood. As a result, the blood leaving the lungs is not sufficiently loaded with oxygen and exercise capacity is diminished. Additionally, because the brain is very sensitive to the CO_2 concentration in the blood, a failure to adequately ventilate the lungs will result in elevated blood CO_2 concentration, with the result being that the exerciser will feel an urgent need to stop exercising.

Hemoglobin is a **protein** in red blood cells that is specifically adapted to bond with (i.e., carry) oxygen molecules. When oxygen enters the lungs, it diffuses through the pulmonary membranes into the bloodstream, where it binds to hemoglobin. The oxygen is then carried within the bloodstream throughout the body. Individuals with low hemoglobin concentrations (i.e., **anemia**) cannot carry as much oxygen in their blood as individuals with high hemoglobin concentrations. For example, in people with anemia (i.e., less than 12 g of Hb per 100 mL of blood), the blood's oxygen-carrying capacity is severely limited, and they fatigue very easily. In the warmer, more acidic, and lower O_2 environment of the exercising muscles, hemoglobin reverses its tendency to bind with O_2 and releases it to the tissues. In most healthy individuals, the oxygen-carrying capacity of the blood is not a limiting factor in the performance of aerobic exercise.

Oxygen Delivery

Probably the most important factor in cardiorespiratory endurance is the delivery of blood to the active cells, which is a function of cardiac output. Cardiac output ($\dot{Q}$) is the product of HR (in beats per minute) and **stroke volume (SV),** or the quantity of blood pumped per heartbeat:

$$\dot{Q} = HR \times SV$$

At rest, cardiac output averages approximately 5 liters (1.3 gallons) per minute. During maximal exercise, this number normally increases to 20 to 25 liters per minute (~5 to 6.5 gallons) and can increase to up to 30 to 40 liters (~8 to 10.5 gallons) per minute in highly trained individuals. The increase in cardiac output is brought about by increases in both HR and SV. HR generally increases in a linear fashion up to maximal levels, while SV increases up to approximately 40 to 50% of an individual's maximal capacity and then plateaus. The increase in SV is brought about by increases in both venous return and in the contractile force of the heart (represented by the **ejection fraction,** or the percentage of the end diastolic volume that is ejected with each contraction of the heart). The ejection fraction is normally 50 to 60% at rest and increases to 60 to 80% during exercise. In individuals with **cardiovascular disease,** the ejection fraction may be reduced after the loss of heart muscle tissue following a **myocardial infarction.** In individuals with **ischemia** during exercise (inadequate blood flow to the heart because of narrowed coronary arteries), the ejection fraction may be normal at rest and then decrease with exercise. This is because ischemic tissue (i.e., tissue receiving too little blood flow to restore ATP aerobically) loses much of its contractility. An everyday situation that most people would recognize is sleeping on one's arm. The tingling feeling and inability to move the arm properly (as a result of lack of blood flow to the arm due to body position) is comparable to what happens to the heart tissue when myocardial ischemia occurs.

Oxygen Extraction

The third important factor in determining cardiorespiratory endurance is the extraction of oxygen from the blood at the cellular level for the aerobic production of ATP. The amount of oxygen extracted is largely a function of muscle-fiber type and the availability of specialized oxidative enzymes. For example, **slow-twitch muscle fibers** are specifically adapted for **oxygen extraction** and utilization due to their high levels of oxidative enzymes. Aerobic production

of ATP takes place in the **mitochondria** of the cells. One of the most important adaptations to training is an increase in the number and size of the mitochondria, with a corresponding increase in the levels of oxidative enzymes used to aerobically produce ATP. Even more important is the ability of the circulation to selectively increase the percentage of the increased cardiac output that is delivered to the exercising muscles and to actually decrease blood flow to the **viscera.** This means that the increased cardiac output is used very efficiently. This redistribution of blood flow is accomplished by active **vasoconstriction** in the viscera and inactive muscles and active **vasodilation** in the active muscles (regulated by metabolites produced in the active muscles).

Bioenergetics of Exercise

The human body's cells require a continuous supply of energy to function. Ultimately, the food that people eat supplies this energy. However, the cells do not directly use the energy contained in food. Rather, they need ATP, which is the immediately usable form of chemical energy needed for all cellular function, including muscular contraction. While a small amount of ATP is actually stored within the muscles, the majority of the ATP used for muscular contraction is synthesized from foods consumed.

Foods are made up of carbohydrates, fats, and proteins. The process of **digestion** breaks these nutrients down to their simplest components (glucose, fatty acids, and **amino acids**), which are absorbed into the blood and transported to metabolically active cells, such as nerve or muscle cells. These substances either immediately enter a metabolic pathway to produce ATP or are stored for later use. For example, excess glucose will be stored as **glycogen** in muscle or liver cells, or it will be converted to fat and stored in adipose tissue (body fat). Fatty acids that are not immediately used for ATP production will also be stored as adipose tissue. In contrast, relatively little

ACE Essentials of Exercise Science for Fitness Professionals

of the protein (amino acids) a person eats is used for energy production. Instead, it is used for the growth or repair of cellular structures or is excreted as waste products. However, amino acids can be converted to glucose in the liver (**gluconeogenesis**) and used in either nerve or muscle. In starvation states, protein from the body tissues can be broken down (catabolized) and converted to glucose in the liver. Figure 2-1 summarizes the fate of the carbohydrates, fats, and protein that people eat.

Foods consumed ultimately produce the chemical energy required for cellular function, but can only do so by being digested. Human ancestors had to exercise (hunt or gather) to obtain food. Accordingly, they developed the useful ability to store fat. In contemporary life, where food can be procured without exercise, this metabolic capacity has led to the obesity epidemic.

Stored ATP—The Immediate Energy Source

ATP is a complicated chemical structure made up of a substance called adenosine and three simpler groups of atoms called phosphate groups (P). Special high-energy bonds exist between the phosphate groups (Figure 2-2a). Breaking the phosphate bond releases energy (E) that the cell uses directly to perform its cellular function (Figure 2-2b). The specific cellular function performed depends on the type of cell. In a muscle cell, the breakdown of ATP allows the mechanical work known as muscular contraction. If ATP is not available, muscle contraction stops. Because being able to exercise was so critical to human ancestors' ability to procure food, pursue mates, or escape predators, much of human physiology is organized to provide an uninterrupted source of ATP.

While ATP can be stored within the cells, the amount stored and immediately available for muscle contraction is extremely limited, and is sufficient for only a few seconds of muscular work. Therefore, ATP must be continuously resynthesized, which occurs in several ways using one of three energy systems, all of which are always active. The response occurs more or less immediately via the phosphagen system, somewhat more slowly with the **anaerobic** production of ATP from carbohydrate, or still more slowly

Figure 2-1
Foods consumed ultimately produce the chemical energy required for cellular function

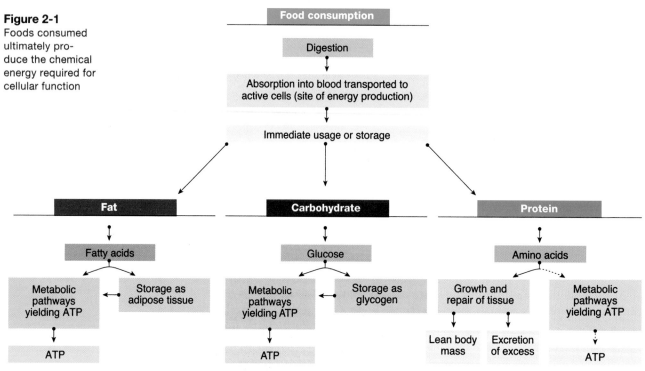

Note: ATP = Adenosine triphosphate

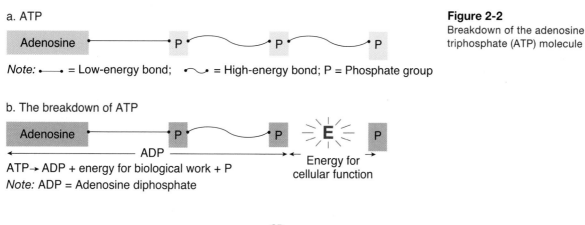

Figure 2-2
Breakdown of the adenosine triphosphate (ATP) molecule

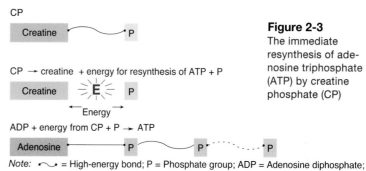

Figure 2-3
The immediate resynthesis of adenosine triphosphate (ATP) by creatine phosphate (CP)

with the aerobic production of ATP from either carbohydrate or fat. All three energy pathways are always active, but their relative activity varies from movement to movement, depending on the momentary level of muscular activity.

The Phosphagen System

Creatine phosphate (CP) is another high-energy phosphate compound found within muscle cells. Together, ATP and CP are referred to as the **phosphagens.** When ATP is broken down for muscular contraction, it is resynthesized very quickly from the breakdown of CP. The energy released from breaking the high-energy phosphate bond in CP is used to reconstitute ATP from **adenosine diphosphate (ADP)** and P (the phosphate group broken off from ATP) (Figure 2-3). The process is so efficient that the concentration of ATP barely decreases even during the most vigorous exercise (e.g., running 100 meters). The concentration of CP, on the other hand, can quickly drop to very low levels as CP is used in reconstituting ATP. During very heavy exercise, two ADP can be combined to make ATP and **adenosine monophosphate (AMP)** (the myokinase reaction). This is important because it provides an additional pathway for the rapid resynthesis of ATP and because AMP may be an important signaling molecule in terms of telling the body that it needs to adapt to training in a way that increases ATP production.

The total amount of ATP and CP stored in muscle is very small, and thus the amount of energy available for muscular contraction is extremely limited. There is probably enough energy available from the phosphagens for only about 10 seconds of all-out exertion, if there were not continual resynthesis of ATP.

However, this energy is instantaneously available for muscular contraction, and therefore is essential at the onset of physical activity and during short-term, high-intensity activities such as sprinting, performing a weight-lifting movement, or throwing a ball.

Anaerobic Production of ATP From Carbohydrate

The anaerobic production of ATP from carbohydrate is known as **anaerobic glycolysis.** Anaerobic literally means "without the presence of oxygen," and **glycolysis** refers to the breakdown of glucose (or its storage form, glycogen). Thus, anaerobic glycolysis is a metabolic pathway that does not require oxygen, the purpose of which is to use the energy contained in glucose (or glycogen) for

ACE Essentials of Exercise Science for Fitness Professionals

the formation of ATP. Anaerobic glycolysis provides a convenient intermediate energy system between the phosphagen system and the aerobic production of ATP.

Anaerobic glycolysis is capable of producing ATP quite rapidly, and thus is required when energy (ATP) is needed to perform activities requiring large bursts of energy over somewhat longer periods of time than the phosphagen system will allow (typically one to three minutes). This metabolic pathway occurs within the cytoplasm of the cell and involves the incomplete breakdown of glucose (or glycogen) to a simpler substance called **pyruvate.** Pyruvate may then be used in the mitochondria by the aerobic energy system. However, if exercise intensity is very high and adequate amounts of oxygen are not available, pyruvate can be converted into lactate, as indicated in Figure 2-4a. Lactate may be transported out of the active cell and used for energy by other cells in the body. This allows for the continued production of pyruvate via anaerobic glycoloysis, resulting in a steady supply of ATP.

The formation of lactate poses a significant problem, because its accumulation is associated with changes in muscle pH (acidity), which contributes to muscle fatigue. If the removal of lactate by the circulatory system and other inactive structures (i.e., inactive skeletal muscle, liver, myocardium) cannot keep pace with its production in the active muscles, temporary muscle fatigue may occur, with painful symptoms usually referred to as "the burn." Thus, anaerobic glycolysis can only be used to a limited extent during sustained activity, but provides the main source of ATP for high-intensity exercise lasting up to a maximum of approximately three minutes.

Aerobic Production of ATP From Carbohydrate or Fat

The aerobic production of ATP is used for activities requiring sustained energy production. As aerobic literally means "in the presence of oxygen," aerobic metabolic pathways require a continuous supply of oxygen delivered by the circulatory system. Without oxygen, these pathways cannot produce ATP, as the metabolic fuels (carbohydrate and fat) are burned in the presence of oxygen. However, instead of light and heat that come with the burning of wood or oil, the energy produced by this burning is in the form of ATP, the chemical that the rest of the body can use for energy, along with some residual heat. The efficiency of cellular respiration is only about 25%, with most of the energy produced actually wasted as heat.

This metabolic pathway, called **aerobic glycolysis** or **oxidative glycolysis**, occurs within highly specialized cell structures called the mitochondria, which are often called the powerhouses of the cell. They contain specific enzymes (oxidative enzymes) needed by the cell to utilize oxygen. This highly efficient metabolic process is limited mainly by the capacity of the cardiorespiratory system to deliver oxygen to the active cells. When sufficient oxygen is available, pyruvate is converted into **acetyl-CoA,** which enters the **Kreb's cycle** and the electron-transport system, produces substantial amounts of ATP (Figure 2-4b), and produces CO_2 and H_2O, which are easily removed waste products.

Figure 2-4
Production of adenosine triphosphate (ATP) via anaerobic and aerobic glycolysis and beta oxidation

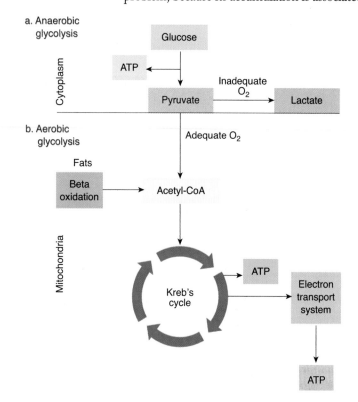

Aerobic pathways are also available to break down fatty acids (the digested component of dietary fat) for the production of ATP. This metabolic pathway, called fatty acid oxidation, or **beta oxidation** (see Figure 2-4b), also occurs within the mitochondria and requires a continuous supply of oxygen. The aerobic metabolism of fat yields a very large amount of ATP. Therefore, fat is said to have a high caloric density. A calorie is a unit of energy. Fat yields 9 kilocalories of energy per gram compared to 4 kilocalories of energy yielded per gram of glucose. This difference is the reason why body fat is such an excellent source of stored energy (and is so hard to lose).

At rest, the body uses both glucose and fatty acids for energy production via aerobic pathways. The cardiorespiratory system can easily supply the oxygen necessary for this low rate of energy metabolism. During exercise, however, supplying the required amount of oxygen rapidly enough becomes more difficult. Because glucose metabolism requires less oxygen than fatty-acid metabolism, the body will use more glucose and less fat for energy production as exercise intensity increases. The **respiratory exchange ratio (RER)** is a marker of the proportion of fat or carbohydrate that is being used for fuel at different exercise intensities. The RER is a ratio of carbon dioxide produced relative to the amount of oxygen consumed, and is measured using analyzers that evaluate the O_2 and CO_2 concentrations in expired air during steady-state exercise.

> Respiratory exchange ratio = Carbon dioxide produced/Oxygen consumed

Table 2-1 provides RER values indicative of fuel use. When pure fat is being used as fuel, the RER value is 0.70. When pure carbohydrate (glucose) is being used for fuel, the RER is 1.00. At rest, RER values average approximately 0.75, indicating that the body is burning approximately 85% fat and 15% carbohydrate for fuel. As exercise intensity increases, the RER value also increases, reflecting a shift from primarily fat metabolism

Table 2-1		
Percentage of Carbohydrate or Fat Burned as Fuel Based on the Respiratory Exchange Ratio (RER)		
RER	**Carbohydrate**	**Fat**
0.70	0	100
0.71	1	99
0.72	4	96
0.73	8	92
0.74	11	89
0.75	15	85
0.76	18	82
0.77	21	79
0.78	25	75
0.79	28	72
0.80	32	68
0.81	35	65
0.82	39	61
0.83	42	58
0.84	45	55
0.85	49	51
0.86	52	48
0.87	56	44
0.88	59	41
0.89	62	38
0.90	66	34
0.91	69	31
0.92	73	27
0.93	76	24
0.94	80	20
0.95	83	17
0.96	86	14
0.97	90	10
0.98	93	7
0.99	97	3
1.00	100	0

to primarily carbohydrate metabolism. For example, at a common submaximal intensity of approximately 60% of **maximum heart rate (MHR),** RER values might be approximately 0.83, indicating that 58% of the energy is coming from fat and 42% is coming from carbohydrates. If the exercise intensity increases to 85% of MHR, the RER value would probably be in the range of 0.92, with 73% of the fuel coming from carbohydrates and only 27% coming from fat metabolism. The RER is only indicative of fuel use during steady-state conditions. During incremental exercise, the RER is influenced by the buffering of acid metabolites and does *not* represent fuel use at all.

Fact or Fiction:
Does Low-intensity Exercise Burn the Most Fat?

A very common misconception in the exercise literature is that low-intensity exercise is the best way to lose body weight and, more specifically, body fat. This misconception is based on the RER chart found in Table 2-1. Below an RER value of 0.86, a higher percentage of fat is being burned for fuel. Thus, it has been thought that by exercising at a low intensity (the lower the intensity of exercise, the lower the RER value), more fat would be burned for fuel and the fat stores would selectively decrease. This notion does not make sense mathematically and, more importantly, has never been proven in the laboratory.

To test this hypothesis, researchers at the University of Wisconsin, La Crosse, had subjects perform two 30-minute bouts of exercise: a relatively low-intensity bout (RER = 0.88) and a relatively high-intensity bout (RER = 0.93) (Porcari, 1994). The results, which are presented in Figure 2-5, show that for the low-intensity exercise, subjects burned a total of 240 calories, with 96 of those calories (41%) coming from fat. During the high-intensity bout, a total of 450 calories were burned, with 108 of those calories (24%) coming from fat. Therefore, during the low-intensity bout, there was a higher percentage of calories coming from fat, but the total *number* of fat calories was less than during the high-intensity trial. It is important to remember that the total number of calories burned is what determines weight loss, regardless of the source of those calories.

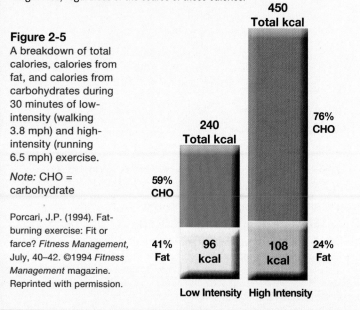

Figure 2-5
A breakdown of total calories, calories from fat, and calories from carbohydrates during 30 minutes of low-intensity (walking 3.8 mph) and high-intensity (running 6.5 mph) exercise.

Note: CHO = carbohydrate

Porcari, J.P. (1994). Fat-burning exercise: Fit or farce? *Fitness Management,* July, 40–42. ©1994 *Fitness Management* magazine. Reprinted with permission.

It should be noted that no mention has been made of the use of protein as a fuel source, and that an RER value for protein is not included in Table 2-1. In a well-fed individual, only a negligible amount of protein is used to fuel muscular contraction. Exceptions to this rule are seen during the later stages of an exhausting exercise event (e.g., an ultramarathon) or in some clinical conditions, such as **diabetes,** where the body actually breaks down, or catabolizes, protein for fuel. Figure 2-6 provides an overview of the metabolic pathways of macronutrient utilization.

Aerobic Capacity and Oxygen Metabolism

Since the primary mechanism for creating energy is from the oxidation of glucose and fatty acids, quantifying an individual's **oxygen consumption** is an excellent measure of his or her ability to perform sustained endurance exercise. The more oxygen an individual can take in, transport, and utilize, the more physical work he or she can perform. Oxygen consumption can be determined using specialized metabolic carts by measuring the volume of air that an individual is breathing, as well as the concentrations of oxygen and carbon dioxide exhaled (Figure 2-7).

When oxygen consumption is measured at maximal levels of exertion, it is referred to as **maximal aerobic capacity,** or $\dot{V}O_2max$, which is typically represented as milliliters of oxygen consumed per kilogram of body weight per minute (mL/kg/min). The dividing of oxygen consumption by body weight makes this a "relative" measurement. A larger person will invariably consume more oxygen to perform a given amount of work than a smaller person, just because he or she has a larger body to move. Dividing by body weight allows comparisons to be made between individuals of different body sizes, and is indicative of how well they can move their bodies (e.g., walking and running).

Oxygen consumption can also be represented in absolute terms: liters of oxygen consumed per minute (L/min). This method is most commonly used to calculate how many calories are being expended during a particular activity. Approximately 5 kilocalories (kcal) of energy are burned for every liter of oxygen consumed. For example, if someone were exercising at a level that requires 2 liters of oxygen per minute, he or she would be burning 10 kcal/min (2 L/min x 5 kcal/L = 10 kcal/min). Many

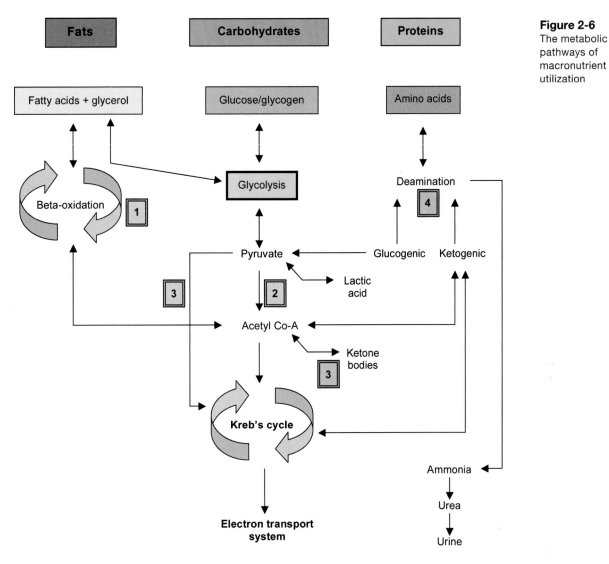

Figure 2-6
The metabolic pathways of macronutrient utilization

The following key points provide a general summary to better understand macronutrient roles in metabolism:

Number 1: Triglycerides (e.g., stored fat) are hydrolyzed to glycerol and free fatty acids. Because acetyl-CoA is a small carbon structure, the long-chain fatty acids must first be reduced to two-carbon structures via a fragmenting process called beta-oxidation. These two-carbon fragments are then converted to acetyl-CoA, where they have their point of entry into the Kreb's cycle.

Number 2: Note the multi- and unidirectional signs throughout all metabolic pathways, in particular the reaction where pyruvate forms acetyl-CoA. Once formed, it cannot be reconstituted back to pyruvate. The reaction of converting pyruvate to acetyl-CoA is irreversible, which explains why free fatty acids from fats cannot be utilized to form glucose. On the other hand, excess dietary carbohydrates that are not utilized for energy purposes can be converted to glycerol and enter the beta-oxidation process in reverse, manufacturing the two components needed to manufacture triglycerides. Consequently, excess carbohydrates can be converted to fat.

Number 3: Pyruvate additionally serves an important role as a precursor to the manufacture of an intermediate product of the Kreb's cycle that facilitates fat metabolism. Reductions in available pyruvate, as witnessed with carbohydrate-restricted diets or carbohydrate depletion, may impede the body's ability to properly metabolize fats. The accumulation of partially metabolized fats will result in the manufacture of ketone bodies as a means to rid the body of accumulated acetyl-CoA, a potential toxin. Likewise, the accumulation of ketone bodies can pose significant health risks to individuals (e.g., gout, kidney stones, kidney failure). Carbohydrates (pyruvate), therefore, are essential to properly metabolize fats.

Number 4: Proteins must first undergo deamination to remove the amino group before they can be metabolized. They are defined as either glucogenic or ketogenic, based on their point of entry into the pathways. Glucogenic amino acids can be converted to pyruvate, and therefore have the capacity to generate glucose via gluconeogenesis. Ketogenic amino acids, however, are converted to acetyl-CoA and enter the Kreb's cycle, and therefore can only be used to generate energy.

Figure 2-7
Example of a specialized metabolic cart system used to determine oxygen consumption

books contain tables of the number of calories burned during various activities. To measure these values, researchers had subjects perform each activity and measured how much oxygen they were consuming, which was then converted to caloric-expenditure values. This was most likely done using a portable metabolic analyzer. It should also be noted that on most of those charts, the number of calories burned varies quite substantially based on body weight, because larger people consume more oxygen than smaller people when performing any amount of work. Many of these tables are related and presented in terms of a reference 70-kg (154-pound) man. For smaller or larger people, the caloric expenditure estimate must be adjusted for body weight.

Acute Responses to Aerobic Exercise

Aerobic exercise is best characterized as large-muscle, rhythmic activities (e.g., walking, jogging, aerobics, swimming, cross-country skiing) that can be sustained without undue fatigue for at least 20 minutes. Such movement patterns depend on the oxidative metabolic pathways to create ATP, and the goal of the body is to be in a **steady state,** where the energy needs are being met aerobically. The other metabolic pathways (i.e., the phosphagen system and anaerobic glycolysis) are used primarily to produce energy at the onset of these types of activities.

Figure 2-8 highlights the changes that take place with regard to oxygen consumption during aerobic exercise. When aerobic exercise begins, the body rapidly responds to increase the oxygen consumed to produce the ATP necessary to meet the molecular demands. At rest, the body is primarily under the control of the **parasympathetic nervous system,** which keeps heart rate, blood pressure, and metabolism low. With the onset of exercise, the parasympathetic system is inhibited (e.g., **vagal withdrawal**) and sympathetic stimulation (i.e., the "fight or flight" mechanism) increases

Figure 2-8
Oxygen consumption during aerobic exercise

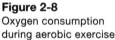

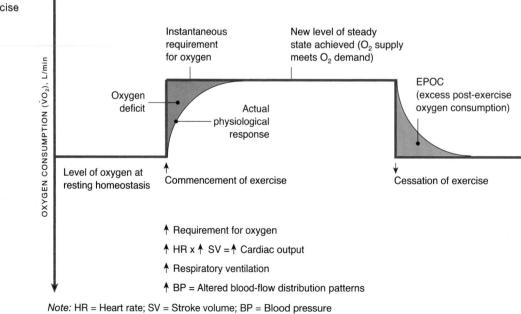

Note: HR = Heart rate; SV = Stroke volume; BP = Blood pressure

and has many effects on the body. In addition to sending nervous signals to stimulate the cardiovascular system, signals are sent to the adrenal glands to release **epinephrine** and **norepinephrine** into the bloodstream. The purpose of these sympathetic **hormones,** which are also called **catecholamines,** is to stimulate the body to adjust to the increased metabolic demands of exercise. Cardiac output increases to deliver more blood to the active muscle cells. This increase is accomplished by an increase in both HR and stroke volume.

The heavy bold line in Figure 2-8 indicates the level of $\dot{V}O_2$ required at rest and the near instantaneous increase that occurs with the beginning of exercise (at the upward arrow). The line returns to the resting level when exercise is stopped (at the downward arrow). The actual $\dot{V}O_2$ that results from the physiological responses to aerobic exercise is indicated by the sloping line in Figure 2-8. Notice that actual $\dot{V}O_2$ does not immediately meet the physiological requirement for oxygen. Instead, an oxygen deficit occurs.

The physiological responses that occur with the beginning of exercise take approximately two to four minutes to meet the increased metabolic demands for oxygen. During this time, the anaerobic metabolic systems—which are capable of producing energy more rapidly—produce the energy needed to carry out the exercise. During this period, the phosphagens are depleted and lactate accumulates. When the cardiorespiratory system has fully responded, a new level of oxygen consumption is achieved. If the exercise intensity is not too high relative to the body's ability to provide oxygen to the muscles, a steady state is achieved. The transition from rest to steady-state exercise is often uncomfortable for many people, particularly if the O_2 deficit is large. Once a steady state is reached, individuals usually feel more comfortable. Many people refer to this as having "caught their second wind."

With cessation of exercise, the requirement for oxygen returns to the initial resting level. Again, however, the body responds more slowly. As cardiac output, blood pressure, and respiratory ventilation return to resting

levels, oxygen consumption slowly declines as well, but is still elevated above resting levels. This is called **excess post-exercise oxygen consumption (EPOC).** The energy produced during this time is used to replenish the depleted phosphagens, to eliminate accumulated lactate if it has not already been cleared from the blood, and to restore other homeostatic conditions (e.g., thermoregulation, tissue resynthesis). If nothing else, the increase in temperature that occurs with exercise will increase the metabolic rate (e.g., the **Q10 effect,** or the doubling of the metabolic rate with every 10° C increase in body temperature). As the body returns to normal temperature, the metabolic rate will return to normal.

If exercise intensity is so high that the body cannot meet all of the metabolic demands of the muscles via steady-state aerobic metabolism, the muscles have to supplement ATP production via anaerobic metabolism. When this occurs, the person is said to have exceeded the **anaerobic threshold (AT).** When someone exceeds the AT, lactate accumulates progressively in the blood, the oxygen deficit and corresponding EPOC are extremely high, and exercise cannot be performed for more than a few minutes. It is also at this point that **hyperventilation** begins to occur. As the body tries to buffer acid metabolites (i.e., remove them from the system), one of the by-products, CO_2, provides a powerful stimulus to the respiratory system, and the body increases respiration in an attempt to

Many texts use varied terminology related to the metabolic markers used to describe the physiological response to cardiorespiratory exercise. In this manual, VT1 and VT2 will be used, but it is important that the fitness professional be able to recognize the other terms when reviewing the literature:

- The first ventilatory threshold (VT1) is also referred to as the lactate threshold and the anaerobic threshold
- The second ventilatory threshold (VT2) is also referred to as the **respiratory compensation threshold (RCT)** and the **onset of blood lactate accumulation (OBLA)**

Another potential source of confusion involves the term "anaerobic threshold," which has come to mean different things in various parts of the world based on the way it was used in early research on the topic. This is another reason ACE has chosen to utilize VT1 and VT2 throughout this manual.

ACE Essentials of Exercise Science for Fitness Professionals

"blow off" the excess CO_2. This increase in respiration is often generically referred to as the **ventilatory threshold (VT)** and can be used as an indirect indicator of the AT. Actually, there are two fairly distinct changes in the breathing pattern during incremental exercise. The first change in breathing pattern, which is sometimes called the **first ventilatory threshold (VT1)**, occurs at approximately the first time that lactate begins to accumulate in the blood, represents hyperventilation relative to $\dot{V}O_2$, and is caused by the need to blow off the extra CO_2 produced by the buffering of acid metabolites. There is a second disproportionate increase in ventilation, the **second ventilatory threshold (VT2)**, which occurs at the point where lactate is rapidly increasing with intensity, and represents hyperventilation even relative to the extra CO_2 that is being produced. It probably represents the point at which blowing off CO_2 is no longer adequate to buffer the increase in acidity that is occurring with progressively intense exercise (Figure 2-9) (see Chapter 5 for more information on ventilatory regulation and minute ventilation). In well-trained individuals, VT1 is approximately the highest intensity that can be sustained for one to two hours of exercise. In elite marathon runners, VT1 is very close to their competitive pace. The VT2 is the highest intensity that can be sustained for 30 to 60

Figure 2-9
Ventilatory effects during aerobic exercise

minutes in well-trained individuals. A variety of studies have examined the training of athletes in terms of the intensities associated with VT1 and VT2. As a general principle, serious athletes perform 70 to 80% of their training at intensities at less than VT1, approximately 10 to 15% at intensities between VT1 and VT2, and approximately 5 to 10% at intensities greater than VT2. Research has indicated that very fit non-athletes (basically performing less than seven hours of training per week), may perform up to 25% of their training at intensities between VT1 and VT2 (Kristjansson et al., 2008). In beginning or less-committed exercisers, both safety concerns and the better compliance associated with lower-intensity exercise make it fair to suggest that VT1 may represent the upper-limit exercise intensity for the health/fitness exerciser. An interesting observation emerging from this research is that the exercise intensity associated with the ability to talk comfortably (i.e., the **talk test**) is highly related to VT1. As long as the exerciser can speak comfortably, he or she is almost always below VT1. The first point at which it becomes noticeably more difficult to speak approximates the intensity of VT1, and the point at which speaking is definitely not comfortable approximates the intensity of VT2.

During aerobic exercise, HR increases in a linear fashion and is proportional to the increase in oxygen consumption that occurs with increased amounts of physical work. Stroke volume also increases up to about 40 to 50% of an individual's maximal aerobic capacity and then plateaus. Systolic blood pressure also increases as a result of the increase in contractile strength of the heart and is very important in blood-flow distribution because it provides the driving force that pushes blood through the circulatory system. Similar to HR, systolic blood pressure increases in a linear fashion throughout the range of exercise intensities. Diastolic blood pressure, which is a measure of the pressure in the **arteries** during the relaxation phase (**diastole**) of the cardiac cycle, stays the same or decreases slightly because of the

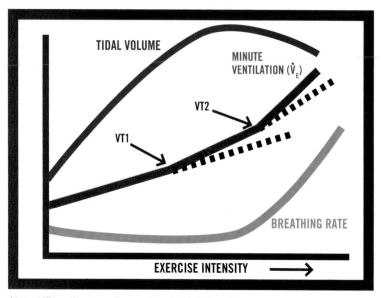

Note: VT1 = First ventilatory threshold; VT2 = Second ventilatory threshold; $\dot{V}_E$ = Minute ventilation

vasodilation of the blood vessels within the working muscles (Figure 2-10). More blood is allowed to enter the muscles with each heartbeat, so less blood is "trapped" in the arteries between heartbeats. Pulmonary ventilation also increases to provide more oxygen to the red blood cells in the lungs.

Much of the cardiovascular advantage in well-trained individuals and athletes is seen in the stroke volume due to a greater pumping capacity of the heart. This is analogous to a trained skeletal muscle being larger and stronger. The very high values for stroke volume in athletes are probably attributable to inherited differences (e.g. similar to basketball players being selected because they are inherently tall). However, most of the improvement in cardiac output that occurs with training is attributable to increases in stroke volume.

Blood-flow patterns also change during exercise according to metabolic need. Blood is shunted to the active muscles (to produce ATP for contraction) and to the skin during light-intensity exercise to dissipate the metabolic heat produced (reduced blood flow to the skin is seen during high-intensity exercise), while the amount of blood flowing to less-active organs such as the kidney and intestinal tract decreases (Table 2-2). Additionally, epinephrine causes the release of glucose from the liver, a process called **glycogenolysis,** which allows blood glucose levels to remain high to provide fuel for the exercising muscles.

Chronic Training Adaptations to Aerobic Exercise

The benefits of any type of exercise-training program are said to follow the **SAID principle** (specific adaptation to imposed demands). The concept of the SAID principle is that the body will adapt to the specific challenges imposed upon it, as long as the program progressively overloads the system being trained. When performed appropriately, a regular program of aerobic exercise can have significant physiological benefits in as

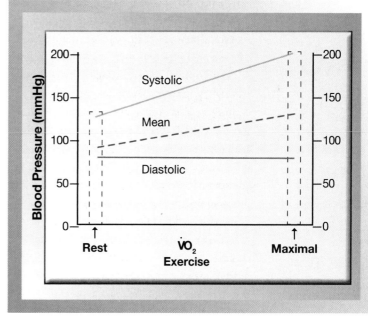

Figure 2-10
Normal responses to blood pressure during exercise

Table 2-2

Blood Flow Distribution at Rest and During Exercise

Organ	Rest	Maximal Exercise
Muscles	15–20%	84%
Liver	27%	2%
Heart	4%	4%
Skin	6%*	2%*
Brain	14%	4%
Kidneys	22%	1%
Other	7%	3%

*During light-intensity exercise in warm climates, skin blood flow might reach 12–14%. Reduced flow is seen during high-intensity exercise.

little as eight to 12 weeks. Changes to the cardiorespiratory system include improvements in cardiac efficiency (increased SV and a lower HR), increased respiratory capacity, and, ultimately, an increase in **maximal oxygen consumption.** These improvements provide individuals with a greater physiological reserve and allow them to perform everyday activities with less stress and strain. Regular exercise has also been shown to result in lowered blood pressure in moderately hypertensive individuals. This results in less work for the heart muscle and puts less stress on the blood vessels.

The benefits of aerobic exercise are not limited to the cardiovascular and respiratory systems. Studies have shown that weightbearing exercise promotes improved bone density, which is a key factor in the prevention of osteoporosis, particularly in women. Improvements in the control of blood glucose and blood lipids (e.g., **cholesterol, triglycerides**) are also associated with consistent physical activity. One of the primary reasons why many people exercise is to control body weight. Exercise burns calories, but just as importantly, exercise serves to maintain or increase lean body mass, which is vital for maintaining resting metabolic rate. It is the decrease in muscle mass that contributes to the fall in metabolic rate as people age or go on very restrictive diets. And, finally, the psychological benefits of exercise cannot be overlooked. Exercise has long been associated with lower levels of anxiety and depression and a higher quality of life.

Neuromuscular Physiology

The basic anatomical unit of the nervous system is the **neuron,** or nerve cell. There are two kinds of neurons: sensory and motor. **Sensory neurons** convey electrochemical impulses from sensory organs in the periphery (such as the skin) to the spinal cord and the brain [i.e., the **central nervous system (CNS)**]. **Motor neurons** conduct impulses from the CNS to the periphery. Because the motor neurons carry electrical impulses from the CNS to the muscle cells, they signal the muscles to contract or relax and, therefore, regulate muscular movement. The endings of the motor neuron connect, or **synapse,** with muscle cells in the periphery of the body. This motor neuron–muscle cell synapse is called the **neuromuscular junction,** or **motor end plate** (Figure 2-11). The basic functional unit of the neuromuscular system is the **motor unit,** which consists of one motor neuron and the muscle cells that it innervates. The number of muscle cells that a motor neuron innervates can vary tremendously, depending upon the precision and accuracy required of that muscle. For example, the eye

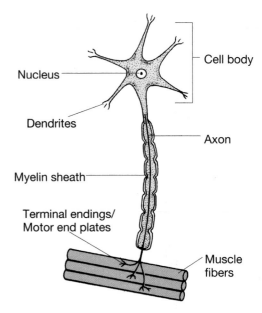

Figure 2-11
Basic anatomical structure of a motor neuron (or nerve cell) and motor end plate

muscles, which require very fine adjustments, may have as few as one muscle fiber in a motor unit. In contrast, the quadriceps muscles, which generate high forces, may have more than a thousand muscle fibers per motor unit.

Muscles are composed of several kinds of fibers that differ in their ability to utilize the metabolic pathways previously described. **Fast-twitch (FT) muscle fibers** are rather poorly equipped in terms of the oxygen-delivery system, but have an outstanding capacity for the phosphagen system and a very high capacity for anaerobic glycolysis. Therefore, FT fibers are specialized for anaerobic metabolism. They are recruited by the nervous system predominantly for rapid, powerful movements such as jumping, throwing, and sprinting. Typically, FT motor units innervate more muscle fibers, allowing for greater muscle force production. Refer to Chapter 5 for more detailed information regarding fast-twitch muscle fiber types.

Slow-twitch (ST) muscle fibers, on the other hand, are exceptionally well equipped for oxygen delivery and have a large quantity of aerobic, or oxidative, enzymes. Although they do not have a highly developed mechanism for use of the phosphagens or anaerobic glycolysis,

ST fibers have a large number of mitochondria and, consequently, are particularly well designed for aerobic glycolysis and fatty-acid oxidation. Thus, ST fibers are recruited primarily for low-intensity, longer-duration activities such as walking, jogging, and swimming. Additionally, muscles that need to be especially fatigue resistant (e.g., postural muscles) are usually ST fibers.

Most people have roughly equal percentages of the two fiber types. Persons who excel in activities characterized by sudden bursts of energy, but who tire relatively rapidly, are probably born with a large percentage of FT fibers. Persons who are best at lower-intensity endurance activities are probably born with a large percentage of ST fibers. There are also a number of "intermediate" muscle fibers that have a fairly high capacity for both fast anaerobic and slow aerobic movements (see "Muscle-fiber Types," page 27). There is some evidence that very high-level athletes may have a high proportion of these "super fibers," more from selection than from training.

Muscle-fiber distribution (fast twitch, intermediate, or slow twitch) is determined to a large extent by genetic makeup. This is not to say, however, that muscle-fiber type is unresponsive to activity. All three types of muscle fiber are highly trainable. That is, they are capable of adapting to the specific metabolic demands placed on them. A person who regularly engages in low-intensity endurance activities improves his or her aerobic capacity. Although all three types of muscle fiber will show some improvement in aerobic ability, the ST fibers will be most responsive to this kind of training and will show the largest improvement in aerobic capacity. If, on the other hand, short-duration, high-intensity exercise such as interval training is performed regularly, other metabolic pathways will be emphasized, and the capabilities of the FT fibers to perform anaerobically will be enhanced. ST fibers are less responsive to this kind of training. It is worth noting that muscle fibers are recruited sequentially, in response to the need for muscle force generation. Thus,

ST fibers are recruited first, then FT fibers. FT fibers can only adapt to training if they are recruited during higher-intensity exercise. Thus, to improve the endurance of FT fibers, it is necessary to train at higher intensities. This can be accomplished fairly easily by performing very short high-intensity interval training (e.g., 15 seconds of hard exercise followed by 30 seconds of easy exercise).

Muscular **hypertrophy** is often associated with a strength-development program. This hypertrophy is the result of an increase in the size of individual muscle cells. The increase in size is due to a proliferation of **actin** and **myosin** myofilaments within the **myofibrils,** especially within the FT muscle fibers. One common misconception is that women will develop "large" muscles if they strength train. Generally speaking, women do not experience muscular hypertrophy to the same extent as men, because the male hormone **testosterone** is important in synthesizing the contractile proteins. Nevertheless, women will increase substantially in strength in response to a progressive strength-training program.

Training for muscular endurance is specific to both ST and FT muscle fibers and motor units. Training increases the concentration of oxidative enzymes that extract oxygen from the blood in both types of fibers, thus making energy production more efficient. An increase in tissue **vascularity,** or an increase in the number and size of blood vessels, often accompanies this type of program. Increased vascularity enhances blood supply and, consequently, oxygen delivery to the myofibrils. It also aids in transporting metabolites, such as lactate, away from the contracting muscle.

Hormonal Responses to Exercise

The endocrine system plays a major role in regulating the body's response to exercise and training by releasing various hormones via glandular secretion. Hormones are released into the circulation generally, rather than being released via ducts

ACE Essentials of Exercise Science for Fitness Professionals

into specific spaces (e.g., tears are released via tear ducts). For example, testosterone magnifies the normal increase in protein synthesis that occurs with training. Hormones circulate generally and only have actions on specific receptors on specific tissues. After binding to specific receptors on a target cell, these hormones perform a number of functions in the body, such as regulating cellular metabolism, facilitating the cardiovascular responses to exercise, facilitating transport across cell membranes (e.g., **insulin**), inducing secretory activity [e.g., **adrenocorticotropin hormone (ACTH),** causing the release of **cortisol**], and modulating protein synthesis. Even though the hormonal response to exercise is very complex, the integrated response of the various systems provides the changes necessary to help the body make the acute and chronic adaptations to exercise training.

- **Growth hormone (GH)** is secreted by the anterior pituitary gland and facilitates protein synthesis in the body, mostly by helping the cell transport nutrients from outside the cell to the interior where they may be incorporated into cell proteins. Many of growth hormone's effects are mediated by **insulin-like growth factors** (IGF-1 and IGF-2), which are synthesized in the liver as a result of GH release during exercise.
- **Antidiuretic hormone (ADH),** which is also called **vasopressin,** is released by the posterior pituitary gland during exercise. As its name implies, the primary function of ADH is to reduce urinary excretion of water in response to the dehydrating effects of sweating during exercise. This helps preserve the plasma volume and the **osmolality** (i.e., saltiness) of the blood. Conversely, if a person is too hydrated, ADH can be reduced, allowing for increased urine production, again preserving a very narrow range of osmolality in the blood and tissues.
- Epinephrine and norepinephrine are called catecholamines and are released by the adrenal medulla as part of the sympathetic response to exercise (the "fight or flight" mechanism). Epinephrine and norepinephrine play two major roles: to increase cardiac output by increasing HR and contractility during exercise and to cause glycogenolysis in the liver (i.e., glycogen breakdown), so that more glucose can be released into the bloodstream for use by the actively working muscles.
- **Aldosterone** and cortisol are two of the main hormones released by the adrenal cortex. Aldosterone acts to limit sodium excretion in the urine to maintain electrolyte balance during exercise. Cortisol is a **glucocorticoid** and plays a major role in maintaining blood glucose during prolonged exercise by promoting protein and triglyceride breakdown. Cortisol is also a major stress hormone and is elevated when the body is under too much stress, either from too much exercise or inadequate regeneration.
- Insulin and **glucagon** are both secreted by the cells of the **islets of Langerhans** in the pancreas, yet they have opposite effects. When blood glucose is high (e.g., after a meal), insulin is released from the **beta cells** in the islets of Langerhans to facilitate glucose removal from the blood to facilitate glucose entry into the tissues and bring blood glucose back to within a normal range. When blood glucose levels are low (e.g., during prolonged endurance exercise), glucagon is released from the **alpha cells** in the islets of Langerhans to stimulate glucose release from the liver to increase blood glucose. Glucagon also causes the release of free fatty acids from adipose tissue so that they can be used as fuel.
- Testosterone (released by the testes) and **estrogen** (released by the ovaries) are the primary male and female sex hormones, respectively. Testosterone is responsible for the masculine characteristics (**androgenic** effects) and also has **anabolic** (muscle-building) effects. Because of potent anabolic effects, testosterone and its

derivatives are often abused in attempts to enhance athletic performance. Estrogen is responsible for the feminine characteristics and also plays a major role in bone formation and maintenance. Excessively high levels of chronic exercise training and low body weight may decrease estrogen levels to the point where some female athletes no longer have their menstrual cycle, a condition called **amenorrhea.** This condition has been associated with osteoporosis and an increased risk of bone fractures. The **female athlete triad** consists of osteoporosis, disordered eating, and amenorrhea. Although some researchers do not feel that the female athlete triad is a discrete disorder, the best current evidence, as incorporated in a position stand from the American College of Sports Medicine (ACSM), supports its existence (ACSM, 2007).

Environmental Considerations When Exercising

Exercising under extreme environmental conditions can add significant stress to the cardiovascular system. Special precautions need to be taken when exercising in the heat or cold or at high altitude.

Exercising in the Heat

Exercising in the heat poses a significant threat to individuals if they do not take adequate precautions. The danger of heat overload is compounded if people are not adequately hydrated prior to starting exercise, wear excessive clothing, or are overweight or obese. For example, heat-induced problems are very common in football, where a number of issues combine to illustrate this point. The weight of the football padding adds to the external work that the person has to do. This added work increases the amount of heat build-up and increases the amount of sweating and **dehydration.** The football padding also makes it difficult to dissipate the heat, as the heat effectively gets trapped beneath the

padding. A similar phenomenon occurs when people are overweight or obese. The added body fat lies over the muscles and effectively traps the heat from escaping.

Considerable metabolic heat is produced during exercise. To reduce this internal heat load, blood is brought to the skin surface (i.e., **peripheral vasodilation**) to be cooled. When the sweat glands secrete water onto the skin, it is evaporated, which serves to cool the underlying blood. If environmental conditions are favorable, these mechanisms will adequately prevent the body temperature from rising by more than about 2 to 3° F, even during heavy exercise. There is some evidence that during prolonged exercise there is a "stop now" temperature for most people. The value will be slightly different from person to person, but is approximately 104° F (40° C). Heat injuries usually occur when heat loss is compromised, as when wearing heavy clothing, or when the heat sensing mechanism fails (as with amphetamine use). There is evidence from South Africa that in the presence of heat injuries, the ability to turn off heat production is compromised even after exercise is stopped (Rae et al., 2008).

During exercise in the heat, however, dissipating internal body heat is more difficult, and external heat from the environment may significantly add to the total heat load. This results in a higher HR than normal at any level of exercise. For example, if a man walks at three miles per hour and his HR is 125 beats per minute, walking at the same speed in the heat may result in a HR of 135 to 140 beats per minute. Thus, exercisers (regardless of the type of exercise performed) will have to decrease their absolute workload in the heat to stay within their target HR zones.

This elevated HR comes about primarily for two reasons. First, as the body tries to cool down, the high degree of vasodilation in the vessels supplying the skin reduces venous return of blood to the heart, and SV declines. The heart attempts to maintain cardiac output by elevating HR. Second, sweating results in a considerable loss of body water. If lost fluids are not replenished, dehydration eventually results, and blood volume declines. This reduced blood volume also decreases venous return to the heart, leading to a higher HR to maintain cardiac output.

A hot humid, environment is the most stressful environment for exercising. When the air contains a large quantity of water vapor, sweat will not evaporate readily. Since the evaporative process is the most efficient mechanism for cooling the body, adequate cooling may not occur in humid conditions. Under these conditions, heat exhaustion and heat stroke become dangerous possibilities. Heat exhaustion usually develops in non-acclimatized individuals and is typically a result of inadequate circulatory adjustments to exercise coupled with fluid loss. Heat stroke is a complete failure of the heat-regulating mechanisms, with the core temperature exceeding 104° F (40° C). Both conditions require immediate medical attention. Symptoms of heat exhaustion and heat stroke, as well as treatment options, are presented in Table 2-3.

Table 2-4 combines measures of heat and humidity into a simple-to-use **heat index** that provides guidelines regarding when exercise can be safely undertaken, and when it should be avoided.

Fitness professionals should share the following tips with clients or class participants before they consider exercising in the heat:

- Begin exercising in the heat gradually. Becoming acclimated to exercising in the heat takes approximately seven to 10 days. Start by exercising for short periods of time each day.
- Always wear lightweight, well-ventilated clothing. Wear light-colored clothing if exercising in the sun, as white reflects heat better than other colors.
- Never wear impermeable or non-breathable garments. The notion that wearing rubber suits or non-breathable garments adds to weight loss is a myth, as the change in weight is due to fluid loss, not fat loss. Wearing impermeable clothing is a dangerous practice that could lead to significant heat stress and heat injury.
- Replace body fluids as they are lost. Drink fluids at regular intervals while exercising, but avoid overhydration, which can be as dangerous as dehydration. Frequent consumption of small amounts of fluid to minimize sweat-related weight loss is the best practice (see Table 4-6, page 181). While there are many commercially available sports drinks, rehydration with water is adequate except under extreme conditions where greater than 3% of a person's body weight is lost.
- Recording daily body weight is an excellent way to prevent accumulative dehydration. For example, if 5 pounds (2.27 kg) of body water is lost after aerobic exercise, this water should be replaced before exercising again the next day. If lost water has not been regained, exercise should be curtailed until the body is adequately rehydrated.
- Air movement is critical for adequate cooling. Even in cool conditions, if there is limited air movement (e.g., exercising on an indoor cycle, treadmill, or other equipment), the microclimate next to the body can become the same temperature as the body (~100° F, or 38° C), and saturated with water vapor from sweat (just like exercising in the tropics). This microclimate will prevent adequate heat loss, and thus put the exerciser at risk of a heat injury. Maintaining very good air movement around the exerciser allows the microclimate to be better regulated and facilitates heat loss.

Exercising in the Cold

The major problems encountered when exercising in the cold are associated with an excessive loss of body heat, which can result in **hypothermia** or frostbite. Additionally, the cold can also cause a generalized **vasoconstriction** that can increase peripheral resistance and blood pressure. This may cause

Table 2-3

Heat Exhaustion and Heat Stroke

	Signs and Symptoms	Treatment
Heat Exhaustion	Weak, rapid pulse Low blood pressure Headache Nausea Dizziness General weakness Paleness Cold clammy skin Profuse sweating Elevated body core temp ($\leq$104° F or 40° C)	Stop exercising Move to a cool, ventilated area Lay down and elevate feet 12–18 inches Give fluids Monitor temperature
Heat Stroke	Hot, dry skin Bright red skin color Rapid, strong pulse Labored breathing Elevated body core temp ($\geq$105° F or 41° C)	Stop exercising Remove as much clothing as feasible Try to cool the body immediately in any way possible (wet towels, ice packs/baths, fan, alcohol rubs) Give fluids Transport to emergency room immediately

Table 2-4

Heat Index

	Actual Thermometer Reading (°F) (°C given in parentheses)										
	70 (21)	75 (24)	80 (27)	85 (29)	90 (32)	95 (35)	100 (38)	105 (41)	110 (43)	115 (46)	120 (49)
Relative Humidity	Equivalent or Effective Temperature* (°F) (°C given in parentheses)										
0	64 (18)	69 (21)	73 (23)	78 (26)	83 (28)	87 (31)	91 (33)	95 (35)	99 (37)	103 (39)	107 (42)
10	65 (18)	70 (21)	75 (24)	80 (27)	85 (29)	90 (32)	95 (35)	100 (38)	105 (41)	111 (44)	116 (47)
20	66 (19)	72 (22)	77 (25)	82 (28)	87 (31)	93 (34)	99 (37)	105 (41)	112 (44)	120 (49)	130 (54)
30	67 (19)	73 (23)	78 (26)	84 (29)	90 (32)	96 (36)	104 (40)	113 (45)	123 (51)	135 (57)	148 (64)
40	68 (20)	74 (23)	79 (26)	86 (30)	93 (34)	101 (38)	110 (43)	123 (51)	137 (58)	151 (66)	
50	69 (21)	75 (24)	81 (27)	88 (31)	96 (36)	107 (42)	120 (49)	135 (57)	150 (66)		
60	70 (21)	76 (24)	82 (28)	90 (32)	100 (38)	114 (46)	132 (56)	149 (65)			
70	70 (21)	77 (25)	85 (29)	93 (34)	106 (41)	124 (51)	144 (62)				
80	71 (22)	78 (26)	86 (30)	97 (36)	113 (45)	136 (58)					
90	71 (22)	79 (26)	88 (31)	102 (39)	122 (50)						
100	72 (22)	80 (27)	91 (33)	108 (42)							

*Combined index of heat and humidity and what it feels like to the body

How to Use Heat Index
1. Locate temperature across top
2. Locate relative humidity down left side
3. Follow across and down to find Equivalent or Effective Temperature
4. Determine Heat Stress Risk on chart at right

Note: This Heat Index chart is designed to provide general guidelines for assessing the potential severity of heat stress. Individual reactions to heat will vary. In addition, studies indicate that susceptibility to heat disorders tends to increase among children and older adults. Exposure to full sunshine can increase Heat Index values by up to 15° F.

Apparent Temperature	Heat Stress Risk with Physical Activity and/or Prolonged Exposure
90–105 (32–41)	Heat cramps or heat exhaustion *possible*
106–130 (41–54)	Heat cramps or heat exhaustion *likely* Heat stroke *possible*
131–151 (54–66)	Heat stroke *highly likely*

problems in people who are hypertensive or who have heart disease. Following exercise, chilling can occur quickly if the body surface is wet with sweat and heat loss continues. There are documented cases of runners who ran in a cold environment, got sweaty, slowed from fatigue, and developed clinical hypothermia (increased heat losses from sweat and air movement coupled with decreased heat production from a reduced exercise intensity).

Heat loss from the body becomes greatly accelerated when there is a strong wind. The **windchill** factor can be quite significant. The windchill index presented in Table 2-5 provides the various combinations of temperature and wind velocity that can be used as guidelines when deciding if it is safe to exercise in a cold environment.

Fitness professionals should share the following tips with clients or class participants before they consider exercising in a cold environment.

- Wear several layers of clothing, so that garments can be removed or replaced as needed. As exercise intensity increases, remove outer garments. Then, during periods of rest, warm-up, cool-down, or low-intensity exercise, put them back on. A head covering is also important, because considerable body heat radiates from the head.
- Allow for adequate ventilation of sweat. Sweating during heavy exercise can soak inner garments. If **evaporation** does not readily occur, the wet garments can continue to drain the body of heat during rest periods, when retention of body heat is extremely important. In particularly cold outdoor environments, if there is any meaningful wind, it is better to begin an exercise bout going into the wind and finish with the wind at one's back. If the opposite happens, the exerciser can become quite sweaty when moving with the wind, and then have to return against the wind while facing increased heat losses from the effect of wet clothing.
- Select garment materials that allow the

Table 2-5

Windchill Factor Chart

	Actual Thermometer Reading (°F) (°C given in parentheses)											
Estimated wind speed (in mph) (km/h given in parentheses)	50 (10)	40 (4)	30 (-1)	20 (-7)	10 (-12)	0 (-18)	-10 (-23)	-20 (-29)	-30 (-34)	-40 (-40)	-50 (-46)	-60 (-51)
Equivalent or Effective Temperature (°F) (°C given in parentheses)												
calm	50 (10)	40 (4)	30 (-1)	20 (-7)	10 (-12)	0 (-18)	-10 (-23)	-20 (-29)	-30 (-34)	-40 (-40)	-50 (-46)	-60 (-51)
5 (8)	48 (9)	37 (3)	27 (-3)	16 (-9)	6 (-14)	-5 (-21)	-15 (-26)	-26 (-32)	-36 (-38)	-47 (-44)	-57 (-49)	-68 (-56)
10 (16)	40 (4)	28 (-2)	16 (-9)	4 (-16)	-9 (-23)	-24 (-31)	-33 (-36)	-46 (-43)	-58 (-50)	-70 (-57)	-83 (-64)	-95 (-71)
15 (24)	36 (2)	22 (-6)	9 (-13)	-5 (-21)	-18 (-28)	-32 (-36)	-45 (-43)	-58 (-50)	-72 (-58)	-85 (-65)	-99 (-78)	-112 (-80)
20 (32)	32 (0)	18 (-8)	4 (-16)	-10 (-23)	-25 (-32)	-39 (-39)	-53 (-47)	-67 (-55)	-82 (-63)	-96 (-71)	-110 (-79)	-124 (-87)
25 (40)	30 (-1)	16 (-9)	0 (-18)	-15 (-26)	-29 (-34)	-44 (-42)	-59 (-51)	-74 (-59)	-88 (-67)	-104 (-76)	-118 (-83)	-133 (-92)
30 (48)	28 (-2)	13 (-11)	-2 (-19)	-18 (-28)	-33 (-36)	-48 (-44)	-63 (-53)	-79 (-62)	-94 (-70)	-109 (-78)	-125 (-87)	-140 (-96)
35 (56)	27 (-3)	11 (-12)	-4 (-20)	-20 (-29)	-35 (-37)	-51 (-46)	-67 (-55)	-82 (-63)	-98 (-72)	-113 (-81)	-129 (-89)	-145 (-98)
40 (64)	26 (-3)	10 (-12)	-6 (-21)	-21 (-29)	-37 (-38)	-53 (-47)	-69 (-56)	-85 (-65)	-100 (-73)	-116 (-82)	-132 (-91)	-146 (-99)
[Wind speeds greater than 40 mph (64 km/h) have little additional effect.]	**GREEN**				**YELLOW**				**RED**			
	LITTLE DANGER (for properly clothed person). Maximum danger of false sense of security.				INCREASING DANGER Danger for freezing of exposed flesh				GREAT DANGER			

body to give off body heat during exercise and retain body heat during inactive periods. Cotton is a good choice for exercising in the heat because it readily soaks up sweat and allows evaporation. For those same reasons, however, cotton is a poor choice for exercising in the cold. Wool is an excellent choice when exercising in the cold because it maintains body heat even when wet. Newer synthetic materials (e.g., polypropylene) are also excellent choices, as they wick sweat away from the body, thereby preventing heat loss. When windchill is a problem, nylon materials are good for outerwear. Synthetic materials like Gore-Tex®, although much more expensive than nylon, are probably the best choice for outerwear because they can block the wind, are waterproof, and allow moisture to move away from the body.

• Replace body fluids in the cold, just as in the heat. Fluid replacement is also vitally important when exercising in cold air. Large amounts of water are lost from the body during even normal respiration, and this effect becomes magnified when exercising.

• Because sweat losses may not be as obvious as when exercising in the heat, monitoring of body weight over several days is recommended.

Exercising at Higher Altitudes

At moderate-to-high altitudes, the relative availability (i.e., **partial pressure**) of oxygen in the air is reduced. Because there is less pressure to drive the oxygen molecules into the blood as it passes through the lungs, the oxygen carried in the blood is reduced. Therefore, a person exercising at high altitude will not be able to deliver as much oxygen to the exercising muscles and exercise intensity will have to be reduced (e.g., the person will have to walk or run more slowly) to keep the HR in a target zone. Typically, the effect of altitude on performance is greatest on about the third day at altitude. The first phase of acclimatization takes place in approximately two weeks,

although it may take several months to fully acclimatize. Even after acclimatization, it is important to recognize that performance will not be as good at altitude as at sea level. In wind-resisted activities (e.g., running, cycling), the loss of air resistance may actually overcome the effect of the reduced ability to consume oxygen.

Signs and symptoms of altitude sickness include shortness of breath, headache, lightheadedness, and nausea. Generally, altitude sickness can be avoided by properly acclimatizing oneself by gradually increasing exercise and activity levels over the span of several days. The most common everyday experience of altitude sickness is when a person flies into a ski area and tries to ski immediately. Often by the end of the day, they have fairly severe altitude sickness that may take a couple of days to resolve. The higher the destination, the greater the risk, but a good strategy is to not exercise the first night at altitude. This helps many people avoid altitude sickness. A prolonged warm-up and cool-down and frequent exercise breaks at a lower intensity should help most people become accustomed to exercising at higher altitudes.

Exercising in Air Pollution

Some areas of the country have a high degree of airborne pollutants (i.e., smog) that can adversely affect exercise performance. These pollutants are the result of the combustion of fossil fuels and primarily include ozone, sulfur dioxide, and carbon monoxide. When these airborne particles are inhaled, they can have a number of deleterious effects on the body, such as irritating the airways and decreasing the oxygen-carrying capacity of the blood, both of which hamper performance. Inhaled air pollutants have been shown to be associated with the development of both cardiac and pulmonary disease. One area of risk that is often not well recognized is indoor ice arenas. An ice-preparation machine (or Zamboni) that is powered by propane may leave very high concentrations of pollutants in the air over the ice surface. Thus, while an exerciser is thinking that he or she is safe from the smog outside, he or she may actually be in a very polluted environment. In individuals with cardiovascular disease, prolonged exposure to air pollution can even induce ischemia and **angina.** The overall physiological effects are determined by the degree of exposure (or dose) to pollutants to which an individual is exposed. This dose is related to the amount of pollutants in the air, the length of exposure, and the amount of air breathed. Practical suggestions to minimize the effects of air pollution include exercising early in the morning to avoid the build-up of pollutants associated with increased vehicular traffic, and avoiding high-traffic urban areas. Similar to exercising in the heat or at altitude, exercise pace may need to be reduced to keep HR in the desired training range. Under extreme conditions, exercising indoors is probably the best choice.

Age

As a general principle, exercise performance improves from puberty until young adulthood. If activity levels are maintained (they often are not because of the professional and family demands of young adulthood), the ability to exercise and perform at a high level is usually well preserved into the early 30s. Following this period, there tends to be a slow decline in performance ability, independent of the reduction in activity levels (which are relatively much more important than aging per se). Even if an optimal situation in which structured athletic training is maintained, there appears to be a somewhat inevitable decline in performance ability beyond age 60. The performance losses with aging are mostly related to the reduction in activity levels, but also are attributable to the accumulation of injuries (both major and minor), losses of **connective tissue** elasticity, minor but cumulative changes in circulatory function (the MHR declines by approximately one beat per minute per year regardless of training, with a proportional decrease in maximal cardiac

output), and (at least in males) reductions in testosterone concentration, which reduce the effectiveness of the response to training. As a general principle, the combination of connective-tissue fragility and the loss of testosterone concentrations means that the response to training is slower in older individuals and that it takes longer to recover from intense training sessions. Thus, where a young, athletic person might be able to train at a high intensity three times each week, by middle age a person may only be able to train hard twice each week, or three times every two weeks.

In individuals who are comparatively sedentary, the risk of underlying cardiovascular disease is not trivial. Accordingly, there is a clearly documented risk of triggering a myocardial infarction when performing unaccustomed heavy exercise. Accordingly, in individuals over the age of about 45 (males) or 55 (females), particular care should be taken to avoid high-intensity workouts for the first several weeks of exercise, and to progress exercise entirely by duration [i.e., keep exercise at an intensity below VT1 (so the exerciser can always converse normally)]. After several weeks, exercise intensity can be progressed carefully.

Gender

The primary variances between males and females are related to the differences attributable to the hormones specific to each gender. Women will tend to have somewhat more body fat secondary to the presence of estrogen, and men will have more muscle mass attributable to the presence of testosterone. Additionally, testosterone magnifies the training response, so that the response to a given training stimulus is both larger and more rapid in men. Other than the differences related to the presence of testosterone and estrogen, the responses of men and women to exercise are remarkably similar, as even the size difference between men and women is hormonally attributable.

As part of a generally less robust ability to synthesize protein, in addition to menstrual blood losses, women typically have lower hemoglobin concentrations and are much more often **anemic** than men. This will reduce the oxygen-carrying capacity of the blood and will thereby reduce $\dot{V}O_2$max.

There is some evidence that women are generally weaker than men. Most of this difference can be attributed to the smaller muscle mass of women. However, in tests of upper- and lower-body strength, women are weaker than men in terms of upper-body strength even after adjustment for differences in muscle mass, whereas the differences in lower-body strength are almost entirely attributable to variances in muscle mass.

Pregnancy

Beyond the weight gain, the mechanical limitations to the change in body shape, and the diversion of part of the cardiac output to the developing baby, the unique effects of pregnancy on exercise performance are remarkably small. As a matter of course, exercised performance ability is going to be decreased as the pregnancy develops. Historically, there have been concerns that the increase in core temperature with exercise might endanger the developing baby or that the diversion of the cardiac output to the exercising muscles might in some way compromise the circulation to the baby. However, there is no contemporary evidence to support either concern. Further, reasonable extrapolation of the concept that humans emerged as hunter-gatherers, and that women were very physically active until late in pregnancy, suggests that the logic of concerns about hyperthermia or circulatory diversion are unreasonable. Nevertheless, common sense suggests that hard training or competition during pregnancy is likely to be counterproductive, and that during pregnancy exercise intensity and duration should be reduced to maintenance levels and guided by the comfort of the pregnant woman. Further, given that fetal nutrition is a paramount issue, attempts to reduce body fatness by creating a negative energy balance either through heavy exercise or dietary restriction are not recommended.

Summary

This chapter is designed to provide fitness professionals with a basic overview of exercise physiology. Considerable space has been devoted to the presentation of aerobic and anaerobic metabolism, because the principle of **specificity** clearly dictates that physiological adaptations are specific to encountered stresses. Fitness professionals must understand the various methods of applying progressive overload and the physiological adaptations that result. Too often, the exercising public falls victim to the poor advice of exercise leaders, coaches, and other "experts" who fail to apply the concept of exercise specificity because they simply do not understand basic exercise physiology principles.

References

American College of Sports Medicine (2007). The female athlete triad. *Medicine & Science in Sports & Exercise,* 39, 1867–1882.

Kristjansson, H. et al. (2008). Spontaneous training patterns in physically active non-athletes. *Journal of Cardiopulmonary Rehabilitation,* 28, 273.

Pollock, M.L. et al. (1997). Twenty year follow up of aerobic power and body composition of older track athletes. *Journal of Applied Physiology,* 82, 1508–1516.

Pollock, M.L. et al. (1987). Age and training: Effects on aerobic capacity and body composition. *Journal of Applied Physiology,* 62, 725–731.

Porcari, J.P. (1994). Fat-burning exercise: Fit or farce? *Fitness Management,* July, 40–42.

Rae, D.E. et al. (2008). Heatstroke during endurance exercise: Is there evidence for excessive endothermy? *Medicine & Science in Sports & Exercise,* 40, 1193–1204.

Suggested Reading

American College of Sports Medicine (2018). *ACSM's Guidelines for Exercise Testing and Prescription* (10th ed.). Philadelphia: Wolters Kluwer/ Lippincott Williams & Wilkins.

American College of Sports Medicine (2005). *ACSM's Resource Manual for Guidelines for Exercise Testing and Prescription* (5th ed.). Philadelphia: Lippincott Williams & Wilkins.

Howley, E.T. & Franks, B.D. (2007). *Health Fitness Instructor's Handbook* (5th ed.). Champaign, Ill.: Human Kinetics.

McArdle, W., Katch, F., & Katch, V. (2006). *Exercise Physiology* (6th ed.). Philadelphia: Lippincott Williams & Wilkins.

Plowman, S.A. & Smith, D.L. (2007). *Exercise Physiology for Health, Fitness, and Performance.* Boston: Allyn and Bacon.

Wilmore, J.H., Costill, D.L., & Kenney, W.L. (2008). *Physiology of Sport and Exercise* (4th ed.). Champaign, Ill.: Human Kinetics.

STUDY GUIDE

Chapter 2
Exercise Physiology

Getting Started

This chapter describes the relevant changes in the cells and tissues of the body that occur during exercise, and the long-term physical adaptations your clients can expect from an exercise program. After reading this chapter, you should have a better understanding of:

- The components necessary to achieve optimum fitness
- The physiology of the cardiopulmonary system
- The energy pathway systems
- The cardiopulmonary responses to exercise and aerobic training
- The physiological adaptations to strength training
- Hormonal responses to exercise
- Environmental considerations when exercising

Expand Your Knowledge

I. List the four major components of physical fitness.

a. _____

b. _____

c. _____

d. _____

II. Describe the major differences between the following pairs of words or phrases.

a. Muscular strength and muscular endurance _____

_____

_____

b. Essential fat and storage fat _____

_____

_____

c. Tidal volume and stroke volume _____

_____

_____

d. Aerobic glycolysis and anaerobic glycolysis _____

_____

_____

e. Heat exhaustion and heat stroke _____

_____

_____

f. First ventilatory threshold and second ventilatory threshold _____

_____

_____

III. Match each term with the associated descriptive statement.

a. _____ Beta oxidation

b. _____ Partial pressure

c. _____ Mitochondria

d. _____ Catecholamines

e. _____ Sympathetic stimulation

f. _____ Maximal aerobic capacity

g. _____ Creatine phosphate

h. _____ Adenosine triphosphate

i. _____ Lactate

j. _____ Respiratory exchange ratio

k. _____ First ventilatory threshold

l. _____ Second ventilatory threshold

1. Complicated chemical structure that when broken down releases energy for cellular work

2. The process that results in preparing the body for exercise; "fight or flight" mechanism

3. The relative amount and availability of an atmospheric gas at a given altitude

4. A metabolic by-product that causes changes in muscle pH and eventual muscle fatigue

5. The process of breaking down fatty acids for the production of ATP

6. The amount of carbon dioxide produced relative to the amount of oxygen consumed

7. The site for aerobic production of ATP

8. The greatest amount of oxygen an individual can take in, transport, and use for physical work

9. A category of hormones that stimulate the body to adjust to the increased metabolic demands of exercise

10. A high-energy compound found within muscle cells used to supply energy for intense, short-duration activities

11. The highest intensity that can be sustained for 30 to 60 minutes in well-trained individuals

12. The highest intensity that can be sustained for one to two hours in well-trained individuals

ACE Essentials of Exercise Science for Fitness Professionals

IV. List the three basic processes of the cardiorespiratory system that must be functioning properly to provide adequate blood and nutrients to the tissues.

a. _____

b. _____

c. _____

V. Fill in the space to the right of each letter by placing an (AR) if it describes an acute response to aerobic exercise or a (CA) if it describes a chronic adaptation to regular aerobic exercise training.

a. _____ Increased respiratory capacity

b. _____ Decreased blood pressure in moderately hypertensive individuals

c. _____ Increased cardiac output

d. _____ Lowered resting heart rate

e. _____ Increased aerobic capacity

f. _____ Increased systolic blood pressure

g. _____ Increased pulmonary ventilation

h. _____ Improved body composition

i. _____ Depletion of phosphagens and accumulation of lactate

j. _____ Decreased flow of blood to visceral organs

VI. Match the following hormones to their functions.

a. _____ Cortisol

b. _____ Estrogen

c. _____ Epinephrine

d. _____ Insulin

e. _____ Aldosterone

f. _____ Vasopressin

g. _____ Glucagon

h. _____ Growth hormone

1. Reduces the urinary excretion of water

2. Promotes protein and triglyceride breakdown during prolonged exercise

3. Facilitates protein synthesis in the body

4. Increases cardiac output and causes gylcogenolysis during exercise

5. Plays a major role in bone formation and maintenance

6. Causes the release of free fatty acids into the bloodstream

7. Limits sodium excretion in the urine to maintain electrolyte balance during exercise

8. Facilitates glucose removal from the blood

VII. Fill in the blanks.

a. At rest, respiratory exchange ratio values average approximately 0.75, which indicates the body is burning ____% fat and ____% carbohydrate.

b. In the study of body composition, _____ consists of muscles, bones, nervous tissue, skin, blood, and organs.

c. Cardiac output is the product of _____ and _____.

d. On average, _____ of energy are burned for every liter of oxygen consumed.

e. During exercise, _____ stays the same or decreases due to vasodilation of blood vessels.

f. The increased use of oxygen after an intense workout to restore the body's homeostatic conditions is called _____.

g. _____ are the nervous-system structures that conduct impulses from the central nervous system to the periphery.

h. Individuals who excel in activities characterized by sudden bursts of activity, but who tire relatively quickly, most likely have a larger percentage of _____.

i. A condition associated with low body weight and excessively high levels of chronic exercise training that can increase one's risk for osteoporosis is called _____.

j. _____ is the best time of day to exercise to minimize the effects of air pollutants associated with vehicular traffic.

VIII. Match the following terms to their associated formulas or common descriptive units of measurement.

a. _____ Respiratory exchange ratio

b. _____ Cardiac output

c. _____ Relative $\dot{V}O_2$max

d. _____ Absolute $\dot{V}O_2$max

1. L/min

2. Carbon dioxide produced/oxygen consumed

3. mL/kg/min

4. $\dot{Q}$ = HR x SV

IX. List the signs and symptoms of heat exhaustion and heat stroke.

Heat Exhaustion	Heat Stroke

X. Answer the following questions related to exercising in the heat or cold.

a. Why is it important to record daily body weights when exercising in hot environments? _____

_____

_____

b. Explain why cotton is a good choice for garments worn while exercising in the heat.

_____

_____

_____

c. Why is wearing several layers of clothing recommended for exercising in the cold?

_____

_____

_____

d. Explain the importance of allowing adequate ventilation for sweat during exercise in a cold environment. _____

_____

_____

XI. Indicate whether the following activities primarily rely on the aerobic (A) or anaerobic (AN) energy pathway.

a. _____ Bench press exercise for eight to 12 repetitions at 70 to 80% of one-repetition maximum

b. _____ Plyometric jump squat

c. _____ Cycling at 70% of heart-rate reserve for 20 minutes

d. _____ Sprinting at 90% $\dot{V}O_2$max for 60 seconds

e. _____ Sitting, taking notes

f. _____ Shot putting

Show What You Know

I.   You have two new clients, a husband and wife couple named Dorothy and Bob, who are currently performing 30 minutes of cardiorespiratory exercise four days per week. Dorothy works at a relatively light intensity (walking at 3.8 mph) and Bob exercises at a higher intensity (running at 6.5 mph). Even though she is working in the "fat-burning" zone, Dorothy is concerned that she is not losing body fat as effectively on her program as her husband is on his program. Explain to Dorothy how she could make her program more effective and why Bob may be progressing more quickly toward his goal than she is toward her goal. _____

_____

_____

_____

_____

_____

_____

_____

_____

_____

_____

_____

_____

_____

_____

_____

_____

_____

_____

II. Maria is a long-distance runner who wants you to train her to become more skilled in track-and-field events such as sprinting and jumping. Explain how adding interval training to her exercise regimen will help her reach her goals. _____

_____

_____

_____

_____

_____

_____

_____

_____

_____

_____

_____

_____

_____

_____

_____

_____

ACE Essentials of Exercise Science for Fitness Professionals

Multiple Choice

1. Which of the following is the **LEAST** important factor in determining cardiorespiratory endurance?

   A. Oxygen-carrying capacity of the blood

   B. Cardiac output

   C. Stored fat available for fuel

   D. Oxygen extraction at the cellular level

2. What is the primary energy system utilized during events lasting approximately 2 to 3 minutes, such as the 800-meter dash or 200-meter freestyle swim?

   A. Stored ATP

   B. Phosphagen system

   C. Anaerobic glycolysis

   D. Aerobic glycolysis

3. Which of the following is **CORRECT** regarding 30 minutes of steady-state exercise performed at an intensity where RER = 0.94 vs. an intensity where RER = 0.77?

   A. Carbohydrates are the primary fuel source while exercising at both intensities

   B. Exercising at an RER of 0.94 will burn more calories from fat due to the greater total caloric expenditure at this intensity

   C. Fats are the primary fuel source while exercising at both intensities

   D. Exercising at an RER of 0.77 will burn more calories from fat due to the higher percentage of fat being used for fuel

4. What is occurring physiologically when an individual reaches the first ventilatory threshold (VT1) during cardiorespiratory exercise?

   A. The individual is exercising in the optimal fat-burning zone

   B. Breathing changes dramatically as blood lactate rapidly increases

   C. The individual is exercising anaerobically above lactate threshold

   D. Breathing changes as lactate begins to accumulate in the blood

5. What changes to systolic and diastolic blood pressure (BP) are expected as intensity increases during submaximal cardiorespiratory exercise?

   A. Systolic BP increases while diastolic BP remains unchanged or decreases slightly

   B. Both systolic and diastolic BP increase with the increase in intensity

   C. Systolic BP remains unchanged or decreases slightly while diastolic BP increases

   D. Both systolic and diastolic BP remain relatively unchanged until near maximal efforts

6. After three months of performing cardiorespiratory exercise on most days of the week, which of the following changes would be **LEAST** expected?

    A. Increased blood glucose control

    B. Decreased stroke volume

    C. Increased blood lipid control

    D. Decreased resting heart rate

7. Which training program would be **MOST** effective for improving the capabilities of slow-twitch muscle fibers?

    A. Circuit training with 90-second work and 30-second recovery intervals

    B. Short-duration low-to-moderate intensity cardiorespiratory exercise

    C. High-intensity interval training with 15-second work and 60-second recovery intervals

    D. Long-duration moderate-intensity cardiorespiratory exercise

8. Why does resistance training result in greater hypertrophy gains for men than for women?

    A. Men usually exercise more vigorously than women

    B. Women have less testosterone than men

    C. Men have greater endurance than women

    D. Women typically use machines for resistance training

9. Which combination of environmental factors would warrant the **MOST** consideration for moving an outdoor exercise session to an indoor space for participant safety?

    A. Temperature = 95° F (35° C); relative humidity = 50%

    B. Temperature = 40° F (4° C); wind speed = 25 mph (40 km/h)

    C. Temperature = 70° F (21° C); relative humidity = 90%

    D. Temperature = 20° F (−7° C); wind speed = 5 mph (8 km/h)

10. Fatty acids are broken down for the production of ATP _____.

    A. By bile released from the liver and gallbladder

    B. After most glycogen reserves have been used

    C. Most effectively in fast-twitch muscle fibers

    D. Through beta oxidation in the mitochondria

ROD A. HARTER, PH.D., A.T.C., FACSM, *is an associate professor in the Department of Nutrition and Exercise Sciences at Oregon State University in Corvallis. Dr. Harter is a certified athletic trainer and a fellow of the American College of Sports Medicine. His areas of specialization include kinesiology, biomechanics, and sports medicine.*

SABRENA JO, M.S., *has been actively involved in the fitness industry since 1987, focusing on teaching group exercise, owning and operating her own personal-training business, and managing fitness departments in commercial fitness facilities. Jo is a former full-time faculty member in the Kinesiology and Physical Education Department at California State University, Long Beach. She has a bachelor's degree in exercise science as well as a master's degree in physical education/biomechanics from the University of Kansas, and has numerous fitness certifications. Jo, an ACE-certified Personal Trainer and Group Fitness Instructor and ACE Faculty Member, educates other fitness professionals about current industry topics through speaking engagements at local establishments and national conferences, as well as through educational videos. She is a spokesperson for ACE and is involved in curriculum development for ACE continuing education programs.*

CHAPTER 3

Fundamentals of
Applied Kinesiology

Rod A. Harter & Sabrena Jo

Kinesiology involves the study of human movement from biological and physical science perspectives. A common way for professors to describe kinesiology to their students is to have them imagine the human body as a living machine designed for the performance of work. To accomplish this work, there must be meaningful and purposeful integration of the anatomical, neurological, and physiological systems in accordance with the physical laws of nature. Understanding the principles and concepts of kinesiology will provide a framework with which to analyze the vast multitude of human movements, and to make decisions and judgments regarding the safety and effectiveness of a particular movement sequence or sport skill and its role in the accomplishment of a specific fitness or personal goal of a client or class participant. In this context, expertise in kinesiology will provide the tools to analyze common **activities of daily living (ADL),** as well as the specialized movements associated with exercise performance.

To use these tools, consider the body's daily activities, postures, and the mechanical stresses that it undergoes in these positions. Next, identify possible areas of weakness or tightness caused by those habitual positions and activities. Then, design activities to improve the body's function under those specific conditions. The result will be balanced fitness programs that not only include cardiovascular endurance, but also proper body mechanics, neutral postural alignment, and **muscular balance.**

Biomechanical Principles Applied to Human Movement

As an area of study, **biomechanics** involves the application of mechanics to living organisms (chiefly human beings) and the study of the effects of the forces applied. Within the study of mechanics, there are two major areas of interest to a fitness professional: **kinematics** and **kinetics.** Kinematics involves the study of the form, pattern, or sequence of movement without regard for the forces that may produce that motion. Kinetics is the branch of mechanics that describes the effects of forces on the body. From a kinesiology viewpoint, a force can be either internal (e.g., produced by muscles) or external (e.g., produced by gravity's pull on a barbell), and cause, modify, or oppose motion.

The analytical process within kinesiology can either be quantitative (mathematically derived) or qualitative (subjective). Biomechanics research laboratories at major universities, medical schools, and hospitals use state-of-the art equipment costing hundreds of thousands of dollars to perform precise quantitative analyses of movement. In contrast, current digital camera technology is relatively inexpensive and will allow a fitness professional to create a record of an individual's movement pattern at the beginning and later stages of learning a new skill or task (e.g., exercising on a stability ball). Sharing this visual record

with the individual, along with a critique of the movement, allows for self-analysis and improvement. A more common example of a "low-tech" kinesiological qualitative analysis is the real-time use of a mastery of kinesiological principles when training in an exercise facility with mirrored walls to give clients or class participants verbal cues for immediate self-correction when necessary.

Even though a fitness professional will use the naked eye rather than expensive digital cameras and computers to analyze human movement, he or she will still need to understand the physical laws that apply to the motion of all objects. While Sir Isaac Newton, a 17th century English mathematician, is perhaps best known for his conceptualization of the **law of gravity** after observing an apple falling from a tree to the ground, his formulation of three important natural laws that govern motion represents his greatest contribution to science. When taken together, Newton's laws of motion provide a better understanding of the interrelationships among forces, mass, and human movement—at individual joints or of the body as a whole.

Law of Inertia

Newton's first law of motion, known as the **law of inertia,** states that a body at rest will stay at rest and that a body in motion will stay in motion (with the same direction and velocity) unless acted upon by an external force. A body's inertial characteristics are proportional to its mass. Therefore, it is more difficult to start moving a heavy object than a light one. Similarly, if two objects are moving at the same velocity, it requires more effort to stop or slow the heavier object than the lighter one. For fitness professionals, resistance-training programs probably have the greatest association with Newton's first law. For example, the "sticking point" at the beginning of a biceps curl occurs in part due to the difficulty of overcoming the dumbbell's inertial property of being at rest, and in part due to the mechanical disadvantage of the human body to generate internal forces when the elbow is fully extended.

Law of Acceleration

The **law of acceleration,** Newton's second law, states that the force (F) acting on a body in a given direction is equal to the body's mass (m) multiplied by the body's acceleration (a) in that direction (F = ma). Newton's second law also relates to a moving body's momentum (M), in that a body's linear momentum is equal to its mass multiplied by its velocity (v) (M = mv). For a given mass, the application of additional force will accelerate the body to a higher velocity, thus creating greater momentum. For a given velocity, linear momentum will be increased if the mass of the body is increased. Angular momentum is governed by similar principles, but the motion performed is about an axis. If an individual is using a 10-pound (4.5-kg) dumbbell to slowly perform biceps curls, there will be less momentum produced than when moving that same weight at a faster rate. If the velocity of movement is held constant, but the person switches to a 15-pound (6.8-kg) dumbbell (greater mass, m), then momentum (M = mv) will increase proportionally.

Law of Reaction

Newton's third law, commonly referred to as the **law of reaction,** states that every **applied force** is accompanied by an equal and opposite reaction force. Said differently, for every action there is an equal and opposite reaction. This law has bearing on the ground-reaction forces (impact forces) that the body must absorb during activities such as step training, **plyometrics,** and jogging. According to Newton's principles, the ground exerts a force against the body equal to the force that the body applies to the ground as a person walks, jogs, or sprints. Step training and martial arts–derived exercise programs remain popular activities even though the magnitude of the ground-reaction forces associated with each may place an individual at risk for a variety

of overuse injuries. Athletic shoes designed specifically for step training have additional cushioning in the metatarsal region of the foot for injury prevention, as much of the vertically directed ground-reaction force is concentrated in the forefoot.

Motion and Forces

Motion

Motion is a change in an object's position in relation to another object. It is necessary to choose a reference point to determine whether an object is moving or at rest. For example, a sleeping baby in a car traveling 30 mph is at rest if the car seat is the reference point. If the road is the reference point, however, the baby is in motion.

To avoid confusion, it is also necessary to choose a reference point to analyze the motion of the body and its parts. Two primary reference points can be used in the body: joints and segments, which are body parts between two joints. For example, the upper-arm segment is between the shoulder and elbow, while the lower-leg segment is between the knee and ankle joints.

Four Types of Motion

There are four basic types of motion: rotary (Figure 3-1), translatory (Figure 3-2), curvilinear, and general plane motion.

If an object is tied down at a fixed point, it turns around that fixed point in rotary

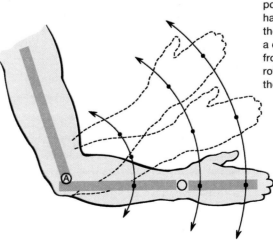

Figure 3-1
Rotary motion. Each point in the forearm/hand segment follows the same angle, at a constant distance from the axis of rotation (A), and at the same time.

Figure 3-2
Translatory motion. Each point on the forearm/hand segment moves in a parallel path through the same distance at the same time.

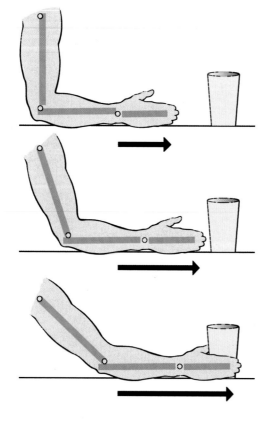

(angular) motion, much like a tetherball. Body segments generally move in rotary motion as they rotate around the joint at one end (the fixed point). When an object in motion is not tied down and moves in a straight line, it moves in translatory or linear motion; all parts move in the same direction and at the same speed.

However, many human movements combine translatory and rotary movements to accomplish certain tasks, such as reaching for an object. In this case, the forearm and hand move straight forward because of rotary motion at the shoulder and elbow. This creates a third type of motion: curvilinear motion, which is similar to the path of a ball thrown through the air. A small gliding motion within the joint (linear or translatory) combines with the more obvious rotary motion of the segment. The gliding within the joint slightly changes the **axis of rotation** throughout the movement, particularly at the knee and shoulder, and is an important part of normal movement patterns.

When motions at various joints are simultaneously linear and rotary, "general plane motion" occurs. The whole body is in linear motion when a person rides a bicycle, while some body segments also experience rotary motion around the joints (hips, knees, ankles). The body as a whole undergoes rotary motion during a somersault or a cartwheel. At the same time, the person is in linear motion across the floor. Table 3-1 provides a list of the fundamental movements with respect to **anatomical position.**

Forces

A force is something that tends to cause motion. Simply stated, it is a push or pull exerted by one object or substance on another. A force can be external to the body, such as gravity (the pull of the earth on a body), water, air (wind), other objects, or other people. Muscular forces are considered internal forces when the body as a whole is the reference point. However, when the joint or joint axis is the reference point, muscular forces are classified as "external" because they act outside the joint itself.

When describing human movement, people often refer to **motive** and **resistive forces.** A motive force causes an increase in speed or a change in direction. A resistive force resists the motion of another external force.

In weight training, the contracting muscle may be the motive force (tending to cause motion), while gravity (acting on the body segment and the dumbbell) is the resistive force in that it resists the motion of the motive force. This occurs in the up phase of a lifting motion such as a biceps curl. The contraction of the elbow flexors causes upward motion of the forearm, and the force of gravity acting on the dumbbell and the arm resists the upward movement. In the return phase of the same biceps curl, the opposite occurs: the motive force is gravity, which causes downward motion. The elbow flexor contraction in the return phase resists the downward motion and is the resistive force.

There are several terms used in kinesiology to describe the various muscular actions. When the muscle acts as the motive force, it shortens as it creates muscle tension. This is

Table 3-1

Fundamental Movements (From Anatomical Position)

Plane	Action	Definition
Sagittal	Flexion	Decreasing the angle between two bones
	Extension	Increasing the angle between two bones
	Hyperextension	Increasing the angle between two bones beyond anatomical position (continuing extension past neutral)
	Dorsiflexion	Moving the top of the foot toward the shin (ankle only)
	Plantarflexion	Moving the sole of the foot downward (ankle only)
Frontal	Abduction	Motion away from the midline of the body (or body part)
	Adduction	Motion toward the midline of the body (or body part)
	Elevation	Moving the scapula to a superior position
	Depression	Moving the scapula to an inferior position
	Inversion	Lifting the medial border of the foot (subtalar joint only)
	Eversion	Lifting the lateral border of the foot (subtalar joint only)
Transverse	Rotation	Medial (inward) or lateral (outward) turning about the vertical axis of bone in the transverse plane
	Pronation	Of the forearm, rotating the hand and wrist from the elbow to the palm-down position (elbow flexed) or back (elbow extended)
		Of the foot, rotation so that the sole of the foot faces somewhat laterally and the weight is borne on the inside edge of the foot
	Supination	Of the forearm, rotating the hand and wrist from the elbow to the palm-up position (elbow flexed) or forward (elbow extended)
		Of the foot, rotation so that the sole of the foot faces somewhat medially and the weight is borne on the outside edge of the foot
	Horizontal flexion (horizontal adduction)	From a 90-degree abducted arm position, the humerus moves toward the midline of the body in the transverse plane
	Horizontal extension (horizontal abduction)	The return of the humerus from horizontal flexion (adduction) to 90-degree abduction
Multiplanar	Circumduction	Motion that describes a "cone"; combines flexion, abduction, extension, and adduction in sequential order
	Opposition	Thumb movement unique to primates and humans that follows a semicircle toward the little finger

called a **concentric** action. When the muscle acts as the resistive force, it lengthens as it creates muscle tension. This is called an **eccentric** action. When muscle tension is created, but no apparent change in length occurs, the muscle action is called **isometric.**

People often refer to the tools used in strength training, such as free weights, variable-resistance machines, elastic bands or tubing, manual resistance, and body weight, as "resistance." It is important to remember, though, that they are the resistive force in one phase of the movement and the motive force in the other phase.

Levers and Torque

Body segments work as a system of **levers** as they rotate around the joints. A lever is a rigid bar with a fixed point around which it rotates when an external force is applied. The fixed point is called its **fulcrum**. In general, the center of a joint acts as a fulcrum for rotary motion of the body segments.

Rotary motion occurs in one of three planes of motion (Figure 3-3). When the body is in anatomical position, **flexion** and **extension** occur in the **sagittal plane, abduction** and **adduction** occur in the **frontal plane,** and internal and external rotation occur in the **transverse plane.**

The axis of rotation is the imaginary line or point about which the lever rotates. It intersects the center of the joint and is perpendicular to the plane of movement (Figure 3-4). The axis of rotation is in the frontal or **coronal plane** (side-to-side) for movements occurring in the sagittal plane. The axis of rotation is in the sagittal plane (anterior-posterior) for movements occurring in the frontal plane. The axis of rotation is called longitudinal (superior-inferior) for movements occurring in the transverse plane.

For rotation to occur, the motive force must contact the lever at some distance from the axis of rotation. If the motive force passes through the axis of rotation, no movement will occur.

The perpendicular distance from the axis of rotation to the line of applied force is called a lever arm. The lever arm length of the motive force (F) is the force arm (Fa). The lever arm length of the resistance (R) is

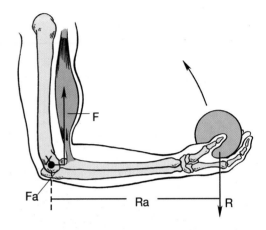

Figure 3-4
Example of a lever system in the human body

Note: X = axis of rotation; F (biceps contraction) = motive force; R (weight in hand) = resistance; Fa (biceps force x distance of biceps attachment from axis) = lever arm of the motive force; Ra (weight x distance from axis) = lever arm of the resistance.

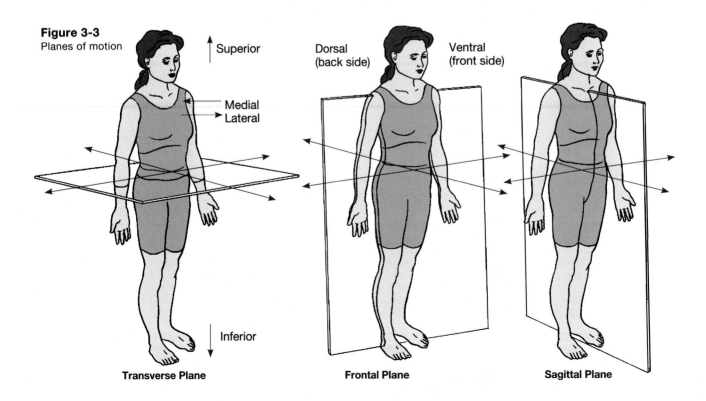

Figure 3-3
Planes of motion

Superior
Medial
Lateral
Inferior

Dorsal (back side)
Ventral (front side)

Transverse Plane

Frontal Plane

Sagittal Plane

the resistance arm (Ra). Equilibrium occurs (i.e., the lever is in balance) if the force times the force arm equals the resistance times the resistance arm (F x Fa = R x Ra).

When a force acts on a lever at some distance from the axis of rotation, a turning effect occurs. This turning effect is called **torque.** The magnitude of torque is found by multiplying the amount of force by the length of the lever arm (perpendicular distance from the axis of rotation). Therefore, F x Fa is the torque of the motive force, and R x Ra is the torque of the resistance. Rotation occurs in the direction of the greater torque.

Sample Torque Calculation

An individual holding a weight in his or her hand is asked to hold it steady at 90 degrees of elbow flexion. The force of the weight and the arm segment is considered to be 10 pounds. The elbow flexors are considered to act at a perpendicular distance from the elbow joint of 2 inches. The lever arm length of the weight + the arm segment is 15 inches. What is the torque of the elbow flexors in a balanced system? To calculate the torque of the elbow flexors, use the following equation:

R x Ra = F x Fa*

10 pounds x 15 inches = 150 pound-inches

In the balanced system, the torque of the resistance and the torque of the elbow flexors would be equal at 150 pound-inches. To answer the question of how much force must be created by the elbow flexors to hold the 10-pound weight steady, solve for F:

R x Ra = F x Fa
10 pounds x 15 inches = F x 2 inches
150 pound-inches = F x 2 inches
150 pound-inches / 2 inches = F
75 pounds = F

* R = Resistance; Ra = Resistance arm;
F = Motive force; Fa = Force arm

Lever Classes

The body operates as a system of levers (rigid bars rotating around fixed points). If a fitness professional possesses knowledge of the types and mechanics of levers, he or she will better understand the motion and workings of the human body.

There are three classes of levers, each determined by the relative location of its axis, force, and resistance. The first two classes are seen primarily outside the body (Figure 3-5). Levers such as a wheelbarrow and crow bar enable people to lift or push heavy objects with relatively small forces. In these levers, the motive force acts farther away from the axis of rotation than the resistive force, allowing smaller forces to easily move large amounts of resistance. A mechanical advantage is utilized with a long lever arm. A relatively small amount of force is needed at the end of a long lever arm as compared to the relatively large force needed at the end of a short lever arm to lift the same load.

Internally, the body operates primarily as a series of third-class levers in which the force (F) acts between the axis (X) and the resistance (R),

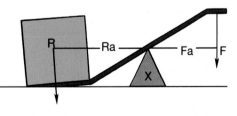

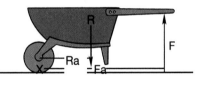

Figure 3-5
The first two classes of levers

Note: X = axis of rotation (fulcrum); R = resistance load; F = effort force; Fa = lever arm distance from the force to the axis (force arm); Ra = lever arm distance from the resistance to the axis (resistance arm). The product of force and force lever arm balances the product of the resistance and resistance lever arm in this example (F x Fa = R x Ra); therefore, the resulting torques (turning effects) are equal.

as in the example of the biceps action at the elbow in Figure 3-4. That is, the motive force has a short lever arm and the resistance has a long lever arm. In a third-class lever system, the motive force muscles are at a mechanical disadvantage and must create a strong force to lift small amounts of resistance. Since muscle attachments are typically close to the joint and use a short lever arm, while the bones are relatively long, with resistance applied at the end (long lever arm), the forces necessary to lift even small weights are larger than people usually think. For example, to abduct the arm to 80 degrees (lateral raise) with a 10-pound (4.5-kg) weight in the hand may require up to 300 pounds (136 kg) of tension in the deltoid. If the deltoid connected one inch farther down (creating a longer lever arm for the motive force) and the arm was two inches shorter (creating a shorter lever arm for the resistance), it would take much less muscular force to lift the same weight. This is why world-class weightlifters usually have relatively short arms and legs.

This is also why a lateral raise (abducting the shoulder to 80 degrees) is easier if the exerciser bends the elbow slightly or attaches the weight higher on the arm. When the lever arm of the resistance is shortened, the person can move it with much less tension in the deltoid. Fitness professionals can use the principles of levers when varying resistance for a client or class participant. To create more resistance with the same amount of weight, move the weight farther from the working joint. To lessen the resistance as fatigue occurs, move the weight closer to the working joint.

Muscles and Force Production

Although the body's lever system puts the muscles at a mechanical disadvantage in terms of force production for lifting heavy weights, it is very conducive to force production when high velocities of motion are involved. Since force equals mass times acceleration, muscular forces of the shoulders and arms can create significant striking or throwing forces but relatively small lifting forces. A strong contraction of upper-body muscles can provide considerable acceleration of the hand. With tools that extend the lever arm beyond the hand, such as an ax, significant forces can be achieved to accomplish a task such as splitting wood.

There also are anatomical and physiological factors that influence a muscle's ability to create force, such as the number and size of muscle fibers, fiber type and arrangement, as well as neurological training and recruitment. There are several kinds of muscle fiber arrangements, including penniform (unipennate, bipennate, multipennate) and longitudinal (Figure 3-6). Penniform muscles are designed for higher force production than longitudinal muscles. Most muscles in the body are penniform muscles, in which the fibers lie diagonal to the line of pull. (The line of pull is generally thought of as a

Figure 3-6
Muscle fiber arrangements

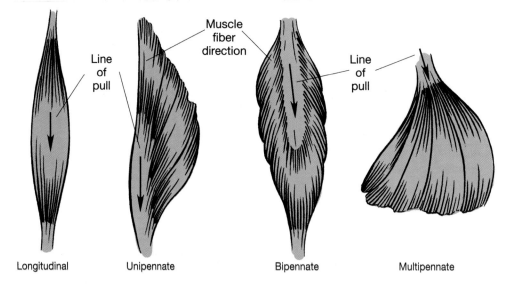

Longitudinal   Unipennate   Bipennate   Multipennate

straight line between the muscle's two points of attachment.) A penniform muscle allows a greater number of fibers to be packaged into a given cross-sectional area, making it possible for more fibers to contribute to force production. The quadriceps is an example of a penniform muscle that can produce significant amounts of force. (Its attachments also are relatively far from the moving joints.)

Longitudinal muscles are long and thin and have parallel fibers that run in the same direction as the length of the muscle. This type of fiber arrangement allows for speed of contraction. However, since the cross section of a longitudinal muscle is small, its force of contraction is small. The sartorius and the rectus abdominis are examples of longitudinal muscles.

Human Motion Terminology

Several terms are important to know when discussing human motion. They are usually one-word descriptions of movements, directions, relationships, and positions, so that discussions can be concise. There also are terms for muscle functions and the roles muscles play during movement.

An **agonist,** also called a **prime mover,** is a muscle that causes a desired motion. **Antagonists** are muscles that have the potential to oppose the action of the agonist. For example, if shoulder flexion is the desired action (without gravity as a factor), the shoulder flexors are the agonists and the shoulder extensors are the antagonists.

Synergist muscles assist the agonist in causing a desired action. They may act as joint stabilizers or may neutralize rotation or be activated when the external resistance increases or the agonist becomes fatigued. The term **co-contraction** describes when the agonist and antagonists contract together and a joint must be stabilized. It is an important component of functional or usable strength because the torso muscles must be able to stabilize the spine to safely move external resistance. The muscles that co-contract to protect a joint and maintain alignment are called stabilizers. Stimulating

strength and endurance of the stabilizers is a vital component of effective fitness training.

Terms for Types of Muscular Action

When a muscle contracts, it develops tension or force as cross-bridges within muscle fibers are formed and broken. There are several types of muscle actions, each of which is named after the muscle's apparent length during the action. A muscle may actually shorten (come together), lengthen (away from the middle), or remain the same length.

Static (Isometric) Action

In an isometric action, no visible movement occurs and the resistance matches the muscular tension. The resistance may come from the opposing muscle group (co-contraction) or from another force such as gravity, an immovable object, or weight-training equipment. Bodybuilders use isometric action when striking a pose to show their muscle development, and physical therapists use isometrics in rehabilitation following an injury when a joint must not move. Isometric action also is used in **proprioceptive neuromuscular facilitation (PNF)** stretching techniques (see page 241). Isometric muscle action can be used in **balance** and stabilization training and may be included in strength-training programs. Holding the torso upright in neutral position during a V-sit exercise (sitting on the floor with straight legs extended to form a V) and a brief hold at the top of a push-up are good examples. If isometric methods are used, the person must be able to take deep, fluid breaths throughout the individual muscle action.

Concentric (Shortening) Action

In a concentric action, the muscle shortens and overcomes the resistive force. For example, the biceps brachii act concentrically in the up phase of a biceps curl with a dumbbell.

Eccentric (Lengthening) Action

In an eccentric action, the muscle is producing force and is "lengthening," or returning to its resting length from a shortened position. The muscle "gives in" to, or is overwhelmed by, the external force and can be thought of as "putting on the brakes," or slowing the descent of a weight.

An eccentric action occurs when an external force exceeds the contractile force generated by a muscle. For example, the biceps brachii act eccentrically in the return phase of a biceps curl performed with a dumbbell.

An understanding of muscle actions is crucial to exercise analysis. Joint motion alone does not accurately reveal the muscle causing that motion.

Kinetic Chain Movement

Optimal performance of movement requires that the body's muscles work together to produce force while simultaneously stabilizing the joints. Typically, people who have weak stabilizer muscles (e.g., deep abdominals, hip stabilizers, scapula retractors) exhibit problems with performing proper, efficient movement, which may lead to pain and/or injury. Therefore, functional training (or purposeful exercise) that takes advantage of closed kinetic chain activity and focuses on the body's stabilizing musculature is often incorporated into rehabilitation and/or post-rehabilitation programs for these individuals.

A biomechanical concept that is commonly used in functional training involves the proposition that the body's joints make up a kinetic chain in which each joint represents a link. Drawing on this principle, exercises may be described as either open- or closed-chain movements. In a closed-chain movement, the end of the chain farthest from the body is fixed, such as a squat where the feet are fixed on the ground and the rest of the leg chain (i.e., ankles, knees, hips) moves. In an open-chain exercise, the end of the chain farthest from the body is free, such as a seated leg extension. Closed-chain exercises tend to emphasize compression of joints, which helps stabilize the joints, whereas open-chain exercises tend to involve more shearing forces at the joints. Furthermore, closed-chain exercises involve more muscles and joints than open-chain exercises, which leads

to better neuromuscular coordination and overall **stability** at the joints.

An example of a program that develops functional strength and **range of motion** is a conditioning routine that incorporates squats, lunges, multidirectional reaches, and overhead presses to enhance an older adult's everyday activities. Squatting and lunging are essential to human movement, as these tasks are required to stand up from a chair or stoop down to pick up a pair of shoes. Multidirectional reaches (i.e., reaching one or both arms in front of, to the side of, or behind the body) are important for training balance and postural control during dynamic activities. Balance training is crucial for older adults who find their balance capabilities declining with age. Overhead presses (i.e., shoulder presses) are tied closely to function in older adults because age-associated declines in upper-body strength often make the simplest tasks, such as putting away groceries on a top shelf, a substantial effort.

Mobility and Stability

Movement involves integrated action along the kinetic chain, where action at one segment affects successive segments within the chain. Joint **mobility** is the range of uninhibited movement around a joint or body segment. Joint stability is the ability to maintain or control joint movement or position. Both joint mobility and stability are attained by the interaction of all components surrounding the joints and the neuromuscular system. Joint mobility must never be attained by compromising joint stability.

Flawed movement patterns, poor **posture,** improper exercise technique, and poorly designed exercise equipment may force unnatural joint movements and muscle actions, thereby overtaxing muscles and increasing the potential for muscle imbalance. These types of misalignments and compensated movements due to faulty mechanics ultimately result in injury. Thus, fitness professionals must be especially attuned to individuals' posture and movement patterns and must ensure that proper technique is utilized in each exercise session.

Balance and Alignment

To understand human motion and design appropriate exercises, fitness professionals must understand several other mechanical principles that relate to the body's balance and alignment: **center of gravity (COG)**, the **line of gravity,** and **base of support (BOS).**

Center of Gravity

To track an object's motion, its COG must be identified. In a rigid object of uniform density, like a baseball, this point is at its geometric center. The location of the COG in the ever-changing human body is more difficult to find. The body's COG is the point at which its mass is considered to concentrate and where it is balanced on either side in all planes (frontal, sagittal, transverse). Gravity is also enacting its constant downward pull through this point. Thus, a body's center of mass is considered to be its COG.

In an average person, this point is generally located at the level of the second

sacral vertebra, but it changes from person to person, depending on build. It also changes with a person's position in space and depends on whether he or she is supporting external weight. See Figure 3-7 for various locations of a person's COG.

Line of Gravity and Base of Support

Gravity acts on a body in a straight line through its COG toward the center of the earth. This line of gravitational pull is called the line of gravity. To maintain balance without moving, a person's line of gravity must fall within the base of support, the area beneath the body that is encompassed when one continuous line connects all points of the body that are in contact with the ground (e.g., the space between the feet if a person is standing). A large, wide base of support is more stable than a small, narrow one (Figure 3-8). Thus, standing with one's feet apart and toes turned out is more stable than placing them parallel and close together. This is why a person with balance problems will automatically stand and walk with the feet apart. To work on balance with a client or class participant, the fitness professional can make the individual's base of support narrower to

Figure 3-7
Center of gravity

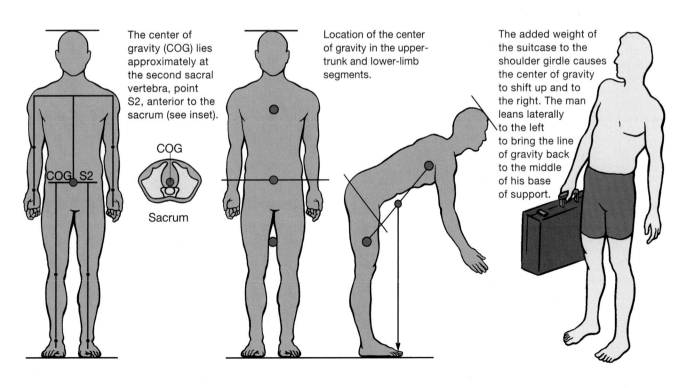

The center of gravity (COG) lies approximately at the second sacral vertebra, point S2, anterior to the sacrum (see inset).

COG / S2

COG

Sacrum

Location of the center of gravity in the upper-trunk and lower-limb segments.

The added weight of the suitcase to the shoulder girdle causes the center of gravity to shift up and to the right. The man leans laterally to the left to bring the line of gravity back to the middle of his base of support.

stimulate adaptation to the imposed demand.

For a person to stand without excessive muscular effort or strain, the body parts must be equally distributed about the line of gravity (within the base of support). Such balanced, neutral alignment prevents excessive stress on muscles and ligaments. An important goal of exercise and training is to stimulate and reinforce neutral, symmetrical alignment about the line of gravity (static balance).

Linear and rotary motion of the whole body (walking, running, doing a flip or a dive) involve shifting the line of gravity beyond the base of support, then moving to reestablish a new base of support beneath it. The muscles exert forces to rotate and move, then reestablish equilibrium (dynamic balance).

Kinesiology of the Lower Extremity

In this chapter, movements of the lower extremity are defined as those that occur at the hip, knee, and ankle joints. The normal ranges of motion for these joints are presented in Figure 3-9. The subsequent

Figure 3-8
A wide base of support allows a wide excursion of the line of gravity (LOG) without permitting it to fall outside the base of support.

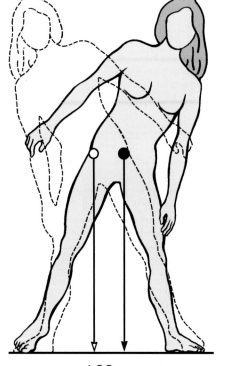

LOG

sections provide details regarding the functions of the primary muscles in the lower extremity and examples of exercises to develop strength and improve flexibility.

Anterior Hip Muscles: Hip Flexors

The most important muscles, or prime movers, for hip flexion are the iliopsoas, rectus femoris, sartorius, and tensor fasciae latae. These muscles act synergistically to cause hip flexion, as in a straight-leg raise or knee lift. They also act eccentrically to control hip extension, such as in the downward phase of a straight-leg raise or knee lift. The iliopsoas is actually three muscles—the iliacus, psoas major, and psoas minor (absent in about 40% of people)—that function together as one unit. The iliacus gets its name from the Latin root *ilium*, meaning groin or flank. The iliacus has its **origin** on the inner surface of the ilium bone of the hip (near the sacroiliac joint) and inserts into the lesser trochanter of the femur. The psoas major and psoas minor originate on the transverse processes of the five lumbar vertebrae and attach to the femur at the lesser trochanter. Given the origin of the psoas muscles in the low back and attachment to the proximal femur, they have poor mechanical efficiency (leverage) when recruited to raise or lower the mass of a straight leg. In most people, the abdominals are not strong enough to balance the large force created by the psoas to keep the spine in neutral position during a straight-leg lift. This is one reason why straight-leg sit-ups and leg-lowering exercises are not recommended. Because of its origin at the lumbar spine, psoas tightness (inflexibility) or **hypertrophy** can result in passive **hyperextension** of the lumbar spine, a condition known as **lordosis**. Tightness in the iliopsoas can also be attributed to a lack of stretching exercises and poor standing and sitting postures.

To stretch the iliopsoas, have the individual stand in a forward lunge position with the front knee flexed and the back leg straight with the foot flat on the floor

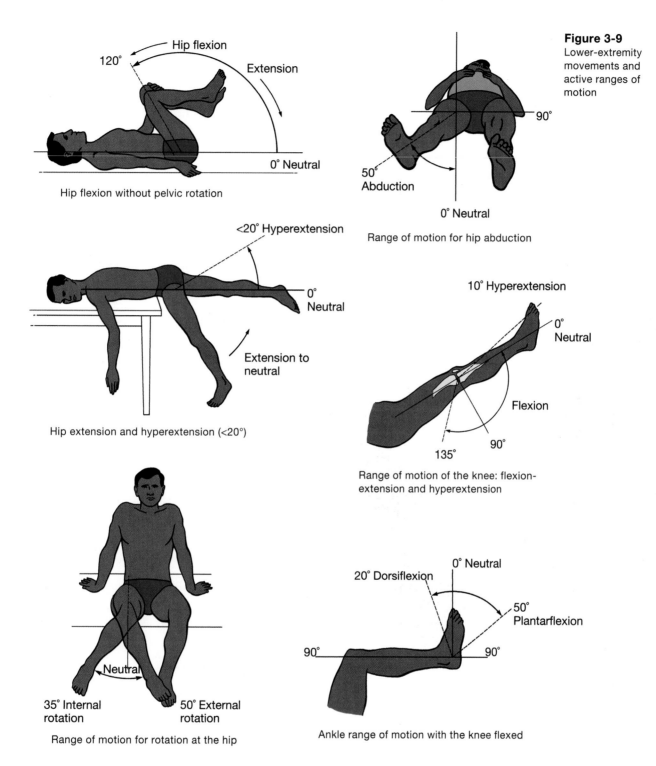

Figure 3-9
Lower-extremity movements and active ranges of motion

Hip flexion without pelvic rotation

Range of motion for hip abduction

Hip extension and hyperextension (<20°)

Range of motion of the knee: flexion-extension and hyperextension

Range of motion for rotation at the hip

Ankle range of motion with the knee flexed

(Figure 3-10). Instruct him or her in how to activate the abdominal muscles to slightly flex the lumbar spine and hold this position for at least 15 seconds. Careful supervision of this activity is important, as the tendency is to hyperextend the lumbar spine during this stretch, putting unwanted compressive loads on the joints of the lumbar spine. To strengthen the iliopsoas, the individual can perform a resisted knee lift (Figure 3-11). Most healthy active people have adequate strength in their hip flexors through ADL such as walking and stair climbing. As people age, there is a tendency to become less active, and the decreased stride length and hip flexion range of motion observed in many

a. Straight-leg hip flexor stretch for the right leg

b. The exerciser can flex the front leg at the knee for a deeper stretch of the right iliopsoas and rectus femoris muscles.

Figure 3-10
Hip flexor stretch

older adults during walking is the direct result of the loss of hip flexor muscular strength.

The rectus femoris is the only one of the four muscles of the quadriceps femoris that crosses the hip joint. This muscle works at both the knee and hip; concentric action of the rectus femoris results in hip flexion, knee extension, or both simultaneously. An effective exercise to strengthen this muscle is the standing straight-leg raise, producing an overload in both hip flexion and knee extension. To stretch the rectus femoris, the individual can perform the iliopsoas lunge stretch, then lower the body so that the back knee bends.

The sartorius is the longest muscle in the body, originating from the anterior superior iliac spine (ASIS) and inserting onto the medial tibia, just below the knee. This multijoint muscle flexes, abducts, and externally rotates the hip while flexing and internally rotating the knee. Just lateral to the sartorius is the tensor fasciae latae (TFL), a short muscle with a very long tendon that combines with tendon fibers from the lower fibers of the gluteus maximus to form the

Figure 3-11
Hip flexor (iliopsoas) strengthening exercise

iliotibial (IT) band. The TFL originates on the ASIS and inserts on the lateral tibia just below the knee. Sprinters typically have highly developed TFL muscles from the explosive hip flexion action required when coming out the starting blocks at the beginning of a race.

Posterior Hip Muscles: Hip Extensors

The primary hip extensors are the hamstrings (biceps femoris, semitendinosus, and semimembranosus) and the gluteus maximus. Working concentrically, these muscles extend the hip joint against gravity, such as during a prone leg lift. They are also activated eccentrically to control hip flexion (e.g., motion during the downward phase of a squat or lunge) (Figure 3-12).

Electromyographic studies show that during normal walking and other low-intensity movements, the hamstrings act as prime movers for hip extension. There also is some electrical activity in the gluteus maximus muscle. During higher-intensity activities such as stationary cycling, stair climbing, and sprinting, in which greater hip ranges of motion and more powerful hip extension are required, the gluteus maximus plays the primary role. Other activities, such as indoor cycling classes, jumping rope, and power walking on hilly terrain, also recruit the gluteus.

Figure 3-12
Eccentric action of the gluteus maximus and hamstrings controls the downward phase of the squat into hip flexion.

If an individual lists "buns of steel" as a fitness goal, be sure to include moderate- to higher-intensity activities that extend and hyperextend the hip. One guideline for choosing activities that involve the gluteus maximus is to select exercises that require at least 90 degrees of hip flexion. These activities tend to be more vigorous and require firing of the gluteus maximus to provide the extra force needed to help the hamstrings accomplish the task of extending the hip through such a large range of motion.

Lateral Hip Muscles: Hip Abductors and External Rotators

The abductors and external rotators of the hip are found posterior and lateral to the hip joint in an area commonly referred to as the buttocks. The three gluteal muscles—gluteus medius, gluteus minimus, and the superior fibers of the gluteus maximus—are the primary hip abductors and are assisted by the TFL (Figures 3-13 and 3-14). The gluteus medius is the largest of the hip abductor muscles, two times larger than the gluteus minimus; the TFL is the smallest (Clark & Haynor, 1987).

The origins of these muscles are superior to the joint; therefore, when these muscles act concentrically, the hip is pulled away from the midline of the body into abduction. Recall that the function of a muscle depends on the orientation (line of pull) of its fibers in relation to the joint at which it is acting. The primary function of the gluteus maximus is hip extension, while the main action of the gluteus medius is hip abduction. However, about one-third of the fibers of the gluteus maximus cross the hip superior to the functional axis of the joint, while the other two-thirds of the muscle fibers cross inferior to the joint axis, making these fibers ideal for abduction and adduction. This means that concentric activation of those fibers of the gluteus maximus superior to the joint axis will produce abduction, while the inferior fibers will cause adduction. In a similar anatomical paradigm, the anterior fibers of the gluteus medius attach medially to the hip joint axis for rotation, and produce internal rotation when acting concentrically. The posterior fibers of the gluteus medius insert lateral to the hip's axis for rotation, and thus will create external rotation when activated concentrically.

There are six external rotators of the hip located deep to the gluteus maximus. From superior to inferior, these muscles are the piriformis, superior gemellus, obturator

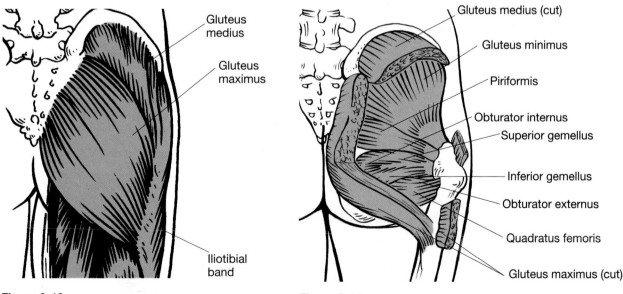

Figure 3-13
Superficial gluteal muscles of the hip

Gluteus medius
Gluteus maximus
Iliotibial band

Figure 3-14
Gluteal muscles and six external rotators of the hip

Gluteus medius (cut)
Gluteus minimus
Piriformis
Obturator internus
Superior gemellus
Inferior gemellus
Obturator externus
Quadratus femoris
Gluteus maximus (cut)

ACE Essentials of Exercise Science for Fitness Professionals

internus, inferior gemellus, obturator externus, and quadratus femoris (see Figure 3-14). The orientation of the muscle fibers in this group is horizontal and this, coupled with their position posterior to the joint, makes them highly efficient external rotators of the hip. When the hip is extended, the gluteus maximus also functions as an external rotator.

The optimal arc of motion for the gluteus medius to produce hip abduction is between 0 and 40 degrees of hip flexion, as its mechanical efficiency as an abductor diminishes beyond that range. When abduction exercises are performed with the hip flexed more than 40 degrees, the six small external rotators of the hip take on the role of prime movers (Lundy, 2006).

To stretch the external rotator muscles, have the individual lie flat on his or her back and pull the flexed knee and hip diagonally across the body (Figure 3-15). This position involves adduction and internal rotation, which effectively stretches these muscles.

An understanding of concentric and eccentric muscle actions is critical for the proper design of exercise programs or classes. If the movement direction is opposite the pull of gravity, the active muscle is working concentrically; if the direction of movement is the same as the pull of gravity, then the muscle is working eccentrically. However, when gravity is "eliminated" during movements that occur perpendicular to the pull of gravity, or parallel to the floor, each muscle group acts concentrically to produce the desired motion. When resistance is added through the use of elastic bands or stability balls, the same principles apply in all planes

of motion; concentric muscle actions occur if the movement increases the resistance in the elastic tubing, and eccentric muscle actions occur if the motion decreases the resistance offered by the elastic tubing.

Figure 3-16 employs a series of hip abduction and adduction exercises to provide examples of how body position can modify the influence of gravity. In Figure 3-16a, side-lying leg lifts are depicted. The initial action is hip abduction upward against gravity's downward pull. No motion will occur until sufficient internal muscle forces are created. Therefore, the hip abductors are acting concentrically as agonists. In the downward phase of the leg lift, the hip joint action is adduction. This joint motion occurs slowly in the same direction as gravity's pull; therefore, the hip abductors are working eccentrically as agonists to control hip adduction. The hip abductors are the prime movers for the hip abduction and adduction motions seen in this activity. The hip adductors serve as the prime movers for the hip adduction and abduction motions when the lower leg is extended and raised against the force of gravity (Figure 3-16b).

Figure 3-16c shows a **supine** hip abduction/adduction exercise with the hips extended, knees flexed, and feet flat on the floor. The hip abductors contract concentrically as the legs move further apart (abduction), with the hip adductors contracting eccentrically to control the movement and stabilize the hips. The hip adductors contract concentrically to bring the legs back together (adduction), as the hip abductors contract eccentrically to control the movement and stabilize the hips. The hip and knee extensors contract isometrically throughout this exercise to maintain the glute bridge position.

In the final example (Figure 3-16d), elastic tubing is utilized so that concentric muscle actions of the hip abductors occur when the exerciser moves the legs away from midline, increasing the resistance in the elastic tubing. Conversely, eccentric muscle actions occur in the hip abductors

Figure 3-15
Stretching of the deep external rotators of the right hip. The exerciser should keep the shoulders and back flat and pull the flexed hip and knee across the torso.

Fundamentals of Applied Kinesiology

Figure 3-16
Concentric and eccentric hip muscle actions

a. Side-lying leg lifts (upper leg): abductors work concentrically in the upward phase and eccentrically in the downward phase

b. Side-lying leg lifts (lower leg): adductors work concentrically in the upward phase and eccentrically in the downward phase

c. Supine hip abduction/adduction with the hips extended: abduction of the hip joints occurs as the legs move further apart, while the adductors control the movement of the legs together

d. Concentric (legs apart) action of the hip abductors with elastic resistance

during the return to the starting position (adduction), against the force supplied by the elastic band at the lower leg.

Medial Hip Muscles: Hip Adductors and Internal Rotators

The muscles that produce adduction and internal rotation are located anterior, inferior, and medial to the hip joint. In this case, the muscle names clearly indicate their function—the primary adductors are the adductor magnus, adductor longus, and adductor brevis. See Figures 3-16b&c for good examples of exercises that recruit the adductors of the hip.

Because of the anatomical configuration of the hip, there are no true primary internal rotators of the hip for movements starting from the anatomical position, because no single muscle has a superior mechanical advantage over another to produce internal rotation torque (Neumann, 2003). As the hip joint is increasingly flexed toward

90 degrees, the most important internal rotators of the hip are the adductor longus and brevis muscles, gluteus medius and minimus, pectineus, and tensor fasciae latae. Lindsay et al. (1992) point out that the changes in the mechanical advantage (leverage) of the internal rotators improves dramatically when strength is tested in a flexed-hip versus an extended-hip position, increasing maximum internal rotation torque by as much as 50%.

The inner thigh is an area of concern for many people. Many people want to lose the fat that has accumulated along the medial thigh and improve both the muscle tone and strength of their adductors. It is important to educate people that spot reduction of fat does not work, regardless of what they see on television infomercials. To decrease body-fat stores along the inner thigh or anywhere else in the body, daily caloric expenditure must consistently exceed daily caloric intake. Irrespective of gender, accumulating 60 minutes of physical activity on most days of the week will most effectively help with weight loss and help decrease body-fat percentage.

Anterior Knee Muscles: Knee Extensors

The large muscle on the front of the thigh, the quadriceps femoris, is the prime mover for knee extension when acting concentrically. As the Latin roots of its name implies, the quadriceps femoris is composed of four different muscles located on the femur that work together to extend the knee. Three of the four muscles—the vastus lateralis, vastus medialis, and vastus intermedius—originate on the proximal femur. The rectus femoris is the only one of the quadriceps that crosses the hip joint and produces hip flexion when acting concentrically, a function made possible by its

origin on the anterior inferior iliac spine. The quadriceps muscles combine distally to form the patellar tendon, the second largest tendon in the body. The patella, the largest sesamoid ("seed-like") bone in the body, is found within the patellar tendon and acts like a pulley to increase the mechanical advantage of the quadriceps by as much as 30% at some knee-joint angles.

During relaxed standing, there is little activity in the quadriceps to keep the knees extended, as most of the body weight is borne statically on the joint surfaces of the lower extremity. When moving from a standing position to a seated position, the quadriceps act eccentrically to allow knee flexion, thereby permitting a controlled (safe) descent of the body into the chair. When getting up from a chair, the quadriceps muscles act concentrically as prime movers to extend the knee. In the varied ADL, strong quadriceps

Squats and Lunges: Is "Never Let the Knees Go Past the Toes" an Appropriate Movement Cue?

While it is appropriate to avoid excessive forward movement of the knee during squatting and lunging movements, it is a myth that exercisers should "never let the knees go past the toes" while doing a squat or lunge. This common movement cue originated from a 1978 Duke University study that found that keeping the lower leg as vertical as possible reduced shearing forces on the knees during a squat (McLaughlin, Lardner & Dillman, 1978). In truth, leaning the trunk too far forward is more likely the cause of any injury.

In 2003, researchers confirmed that knee stress increased by 28% when the knees were allowed to move past the toes while performing a squat (Fry, Smith, & Schilling, 2003). However, hip stress increased by nearly 1,000% when forward movement of the knee was restricted. In addition, in group exercise, the cue "don't let your knees go over your toes" has long been an effective general rule when trying to teach an exercise to a room full of people with different skill levels, abilities, and goals. When a class has a large number of participants, it is difficult to help each individual participant with his or her specific range of motion, so providing this general cue is an effective way of erring on the side of caution for the group fitness instructor.

The general pointer while performing a lunge is to try to keep the knees aligned over the second toe so that the knee is moving in the same direction as the ankle joint. However, in reality, exercisers often find the knee translating forward to the toes or beyond in a squat or lunge movement, so there are other things that must be considered, specifically limb length.

During lunge or squat movements, fitness professionals should always emphasize beginning the movement by pushing the hips backward before lowering toward the floor (an action referred to as "hip hinging"). This technique prevents premature forward movement of the knee by shifting the hips backward. As the exerciser continues to lower his or her body downward, this creates a healthy hinge effect at the knee, but there comes a time where the knee (tibia) will begin to move forward in order to maintain balance (keeping the center of mass within the base of support). If an exerciser happens to have long limbs, then it is realistic to expect the knees to move forward over or beyond the toes. Any attempt to prevent this motion will result in either the individual falling backward or bad squat or lunge technique that places increased loads on the low back. As long as fitness professionals teach the lunge/squat movement correctly by first initiating the movement at the hips and avoid premature forward movement of the knees, then the fact that the knees are moving forward is quite safe.

femoris muscles are needed for lifting heavy objects, walking, and climbing stairs. Squats, lunges, and stepping are important exercises in preparing the quadriceps for most ADL. Many experts agree that the safest approach in exercise programming is to limit knee flexion to no more than 90 degrees during weightbearing exercises.

Posterior Knee Muscles: Knee Flexors and Rotators

The primary knee flexors are the hamstrings muscle group: semitendinosus, semimembranosus, and biceps femoris. The hamstrings are referred to as a biarticular group of muscles, producing knee flexion as well as hip extension when acting concentrically. Additionally, the two medial hamstrings— semimembranosus and semitendinosus—are internal rotators of the knee. The lateral hamstring, the biceps femoris, is an external rotator of the knee. Knee-joint rotation is only possible in flexed-joint positions, as a phenomenon known as the **screw-home mechanism** increases knee-joint stability by locking the femur on the tibia (or vice-versa) when the knee is fully extended.

The sartorius, popliteus, gastrocnemius, and gracilis are secondary knee flexors (Figure 3-17) (also see Figure 1-39, page 48). The popliteus plays a very unique role in that it is responsible for initiating knee flexion and "unlocking" the knee from its extended position.

To stretch the hamstrings effectively, have the individual assume a position that places the targeted limb in hip flexion and knee extension (Figure 3-18). From a standing position, the individual will put the foot of the leg to be stretched on a step and slowly bend forward at the waist, keeping a flat back (**neutral spine position**). This stretch can also be performed while sitting on a stability ball. Both of these positions isolate the stretch to the hamstrings group and avoid overstressing the erector spinae muscles. To increase the intensity of this stretch, have the individual flex the knee and hip of the limb not being stretched.

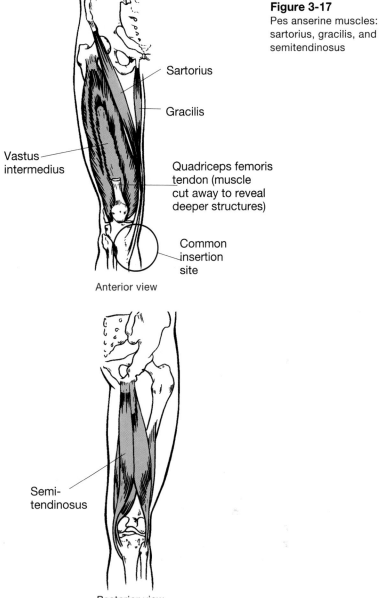

Figure 3-17
Pes anserine muscles: sartorius, gracilis, and semitendinosus

Sartorius

Gracilis

Vastus intermedius

Quadriceps femoris tendon (muscle cut away to reveal deeper structures)

Common insertion site

Anterior view

Semi-tendinosus

Posterior view

Figure 3-18
Standing hamstring stretch; hands can be used for balance—the exerciser should not apply pressure on the knee

ACE Essentials of Exercise Science for Fitness Professionals

Anterior Leg Muscles: Dorsiflexors

The muscles below the knee are organized into four finite compartments. The muscles in the anterior compartment of the lower leg are the anterior tibialis, extensor digitorum longus, and extensor hallucis longus (Figure 3-19) (also see Figure 1-38, page 48). When acting concentrically, these muscles produce **dorsiflexion** of the ankle. These muscles also work together during locomotor activities, such as walking and running, to eccentrically lower the foot to the ground with control. Without the vital eccentric action of the dorsiflexor muscles as dynamic shock absorbers, the foot would slap the ground with each stride or impact. Given that the ground-reaction forces during running are three to five times one's body weight with each stride and that there are approximately 1,500 to 1,800 strides (ground impacts) per mile (1.6 km), the importance of the shock-absorption role of these muscles cannot be overstated.

The anterior tibialis inserts on the medial aspect of the foot and combines with the posterior tibialis to serve as the prime movers for inversion of the foot. A common method of warming these muscles prior to impact activities is to perform toe tapping, stepping either straight ahead or side-to-side. Having people walk for short distances with only their heels touching the ground

is also a good warm-up activity for these anterior-compartment muscles.

Posterior Leg Muscles: Plantarflexors

The large muscles of the superficial posterior tibial compartment (see Figures 1-39 and 3-19) are the primary plantarflexors of the ankle joint. While more easily palpated and more visible than the underlying soleus muscle, the gastrocnemius is actually the smaller of the two. These muscles combine distally to form the Achilles tendon, the largest tendon in the body, which attaches posteriorly to the calcaneus. The gastrocnemius, as mentioned previously, acts at both the knee and the ankle; the soleus only works at the ankle joint. Indeed, there are eight muscles that act as synergists for plantarflexion, evidence of the adaptive importance of plantarflexion force production. The remaining six muscles of the lower leg—the posterior tibialis, flexor hallucis longus, flexor digitorum longus, plantaris, peroneus longus, and peroneus brevis—play secondary functional roles in producing the propulsion force required for human locomotion.

The gastrocnemius and soleus muscles are often inflexible, particularly among individuals who regularly wear high-heeled shoes. To stretch the two-joint gastrocnemius, the hip and knee should be extended and the ankle should be in a dorsiflexed position while the heel remains on the ground. To stretch the soleus, a similar posture is assumed, except that the knee is flexed to about 20 degrees to isolate the soleus. These stretches can be performed while seated or lying down, but more commonly are performed against a real or imagined wall or by utilizing a step aerobics bench (Figure 3-20).

Lateral Leg Muscles: Evertors

The peroneus longus and peroneus brevis are muscles found in the lateral tibial compartment (see Figure 3-19 and Figure 1-40, page 48) that are responsible for eversion of the foot

Figure 3-19
Contents of the muscular compartments of the lower leg

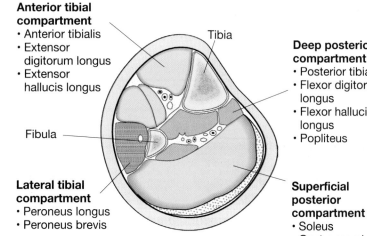

Anterior tibial compartment
• Anterior tibialis
• Extensor digitorum longus
• Extensor hallucis longus

Lateral tibial compartment
• Peroneus longus
• Peroneus brevis

Tibia

Fibula

Deep posterior compartment
• Posterior tibialis
• Flexor digitorum longus
• Flexor hallucis longus
• Popliteus

Superficial posterior compartment
• Soleus
• Gastrocnemius
• Plantaris

Figure 3-20
Stretching of the gastrocnemius (rear leg) and soleus (front leg) muscles

(i.e., pulling the foot laterally in the frontal plane). The tendons of these muscles curve around behind the lateral malleolus and attach on the foot. Both muscles play secondary roles as plantarflexors at the ankle due to their posterior location relative to the axis of motion of the talocrural (ankle) joint. These muscles are active during virtually all locomotor activities to provide dynamic stability at the subtalar joint, acting eccentrically to prevent the joint from rolling too far into inversion and overloading the lateral ankle ligaments, possibly causing a sprain.

Medial Leg Muscles: Invertors

There are two muscles that are primarily responsible for concentric inversion (i.e., pulling the foot toward the midline in the frontal plane): the anterior tibialis and posterior tibialis. A key anatomical point is to focus on the **insertion** sites of the distal tendons of these muscles. As its name suggests, the anterior tibialis muscle

is located on the front of the tibia and is a key muscle for dorsiflexion in the sagittal plane. Its antagonist muscle in the sagittal plane is the posterior tibialis, found on the posterior aspect of the tibia and acting as a plantarflexor. While the functions of these muscles are opposite in the sagittal plane, they function as synergists in the frontal plane to produce inversion when they act concentrically. Similar to the evertors, these muscles are active during most weightbearing activities as **dynamic stabilizers** of the ankle joint and medial arch of the foot.

Kinesiology of the Spine and Pelvis

Posture and Balance

Posture refers to the biomechanical alignment of the individual body parts and the orientation of the body to the environment. In human activities, the body is always experiencing some kind of movement change. Because of the body's dynamic nature, people are constantly performing muscle contractions in an effort to maintain balance. The term balance is often used synonymously with equilibrium and implies movement control. Balance is the ability to maintain the body's position over its base of support within **stability limits,** both statically and dynamically. Stability limits are boundaries of an area of space in which the body can maintain its position without changing the base of support (i.e., without taking a step).

The maintenance of balance is related to a body's COG. As previously described, COG is a location where the body's mass is distributed evenly in all planes. In most individuals, it is located just anterior to, and in line with, the second sacral vertebrae, but it changes from person to person depending on the person's build. For example, a pregnant or obese exerciser has a COG that is displaced more anteriorly than a person of average size, due to the increased abdominal mass associated with each condition. COG is not a tangible place and is not necessarily always located within the body. COG is an abstract concept that is used to define movement of body segments relative to one another. A person's COG changes during movement depending on movement patterns and additional loads (see Figure 3-7).

As mentioned earlier, balance is the ability to maintain the body's position over its base of support within stability limits. In the standing position, a person's base of support is the contact between the feet and the floor, and his or her stability limits are defined by the length of the feet and the distance between them. Efficient standing balance requires that the body's COG be kept within stability limits (i.e., between the feet). A large, wide base of support is more stable than a small, narrow one because the stability limits encompass a larger space for one's COG to move within, resulting in a lesser likelihood that the COG will move outside of the feet. Therefore, standing with the feet apart provides more stability than standing with the feet close together. This is one reason why individuals with balance problems prefer to stand and walk with their feet further apart. If a person's COG shifts beyond the limits defined by the feet, it is likely that a fall will occur unless he or she takes a step to recover balance, thereby shifting the COG to its original position between the feet. To prepare for real world conditions associated with COG changes, weight-shifting exercises can be utilized (e.g., forward or backward lunges).

Posture and the Neutral Spine

Given the wide variation of human body shapes, sizes, and types, there are few people who actually have what can be called an "ideal" posture. Muscularity, flexibility, and pattern of fat deposition are just three of many factors that influence real (versus idealized) posture (Neumann, 2003). The spine of a fully grown healthy adult has 24 movable vertebrae and three normal

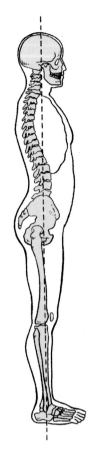

Figure 3-21
Neutral spine alignment with slight anterior (lordotic) curves at the neck and low back and a posterior (kyphotic) curve in the thoracic region

curves: the cervical and lumbar regions are naturally convex anteriorly and concave posteriorly, referred to as a lordotic curvature. In contrast, the thoracic region possesses a curve that first develops *in utero* from the fetal position—concave anteriorly and convex posteriorly—known as a **kyphotic** curve (Figure 3-21).

This idealized neutral spine position requires the mathematical balance of 12 vertebrae that are curved in an anterior direction (seven cervical vertebrae plus five lumbar vertebrae) with the 12 thoracic region vertebrae that are curved in a posterior direction. The normal active ranges of motion of the thoracic and lumbar regions of the spine are presented in Figure 3-22.

A fitness professional can assess muscular balance by having the individual stand in the anatomical position and observing him or her from the back and from the side. If a person stands in this neutral alignment and is viewed from the rear, the line of gravity (envision a plumb bob suspended from above) would pass through the midline of

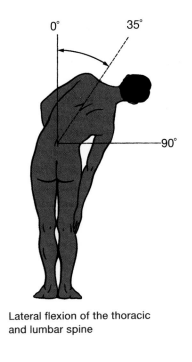

Lateral flexion of the thoracic
and lumbar spine

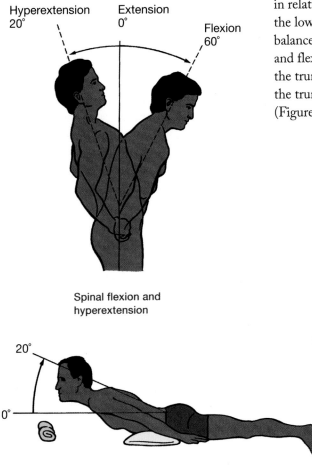

Spinal flexion and
hyperextension

Spinal hyperextension (thoracic and lumbar spine)

Figure 3-22
Active range of motion of the thoracic and lumbar spine

the skull, the center of the vertebral column over the spinous processes, and the vertical crease between the buttocks, and touch the ground midway between the feet. Fitness professionals can promote good posture and muscular balance by having clients and class participants perform all activities with as close to a neutral spine alignment as possible. Effective cueing and correction techniques, combined with verbal and visual feedback, will help people become more aware of their posture. Good posture is a neuromuscular skill that can be achieved or reacquired through repetition and practice.

The position of the pelvis plays a major role in the determination of the forces applied at the lumbar spine. If the lumbar spine is correctly aligned with regard to the pelvis, and the pelvis is properly balanced in relation to the legs, the forces applied to the low back can be reduced. Achieving this balance requires excellent muscular strength and flexibility on both sides of the trunk—the trunk and hip flexors anteriorly and the trunk and spinal extensors posteriorly (Figure 3-23).

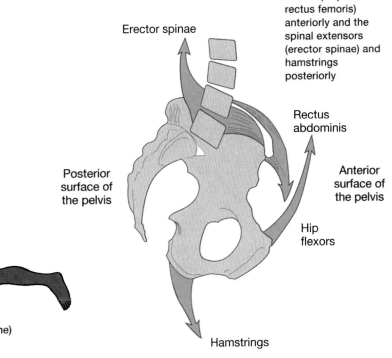

Figure 3-23
Muscular control of the pelvis by the abdominals and hip flexors (iliopsoas and rectus femoris) anteriorly and the spinal extensors (erector spinae) and hamstrings posteriorly

Abnormal and Fatigue-related Postures

Deviations from neutral spine position can be temporary or permanent; muscle spasm and pain following a soft-tissue injury to the back, fatigue, or muscular imbalance may cause these deviations. When applied at the appropriate time with the correct dosage (frequency, intensity, and duration), exercise can help alleviate each of these conditions. Some postural deviations are structural (bony) in nature, and typically do not respond to corrective exercise. The three most common abnormal postures are lordosis, **kyphosis,** and **scoliosis.**

Lordosis is an excessive anterior curvature of the spine that typically occurs at the low back, but may also occur at the neck (Figure 3-24a). This lordotic posture has been linked to low-back pain, a condition commonly experienced by late-term pregnant women and individuals with large concentrations of abdominal fat. Lordotic posture is also often associated with an anterior tilting of the pelvis, placing tension on the anterior longitudinal ligaments of the spine and compression on the posterior part of the intervertebral discs. If this posture is maintained over weeks and months, the back extensor and hip flexor muscles will adapt by losing their extensibility and adaptively shorten. In contrast, the hamstring and abdominal muscles will lengthen under these constant loads, becoming more lax and further decreasing their control of the pelvis. Unlike **obesity,** pregnancy has a finite beginning and end, and most back pain and changes in posture associated with pregnancy are resolved **postpartum.** An overweight or obese individual with lordosis presents a significant challenge to a fitness professional. To correct

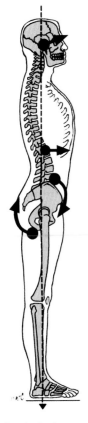

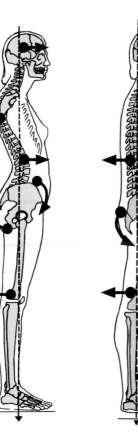

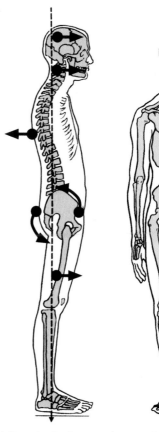

a. Lordosis: increased anterior lumbar curve from neutral

b. Kyphosis: increased posterior thoracic curve from neutral

c. Flat back: decreased anterior lumbar curve

d. Sway back: decreased anterior lumbar curve and increased posterior thoracic curve from neutral

e. Scoliosis: lateral spinal curvature often accompanied by vertebral rotation

Figure 3-24
Postural deviations

the anterior pelvic tilt position associated with lumbar lordosis, the fitness professional should focus on strengthening the individual's abdominal and hip extensor (hamstring) muscles, while stretching the hip flexors (iliopsoas) and spine extensors (erector spinae).

Kyphosis is defined as an excessive posterior curvature of the spine, typically seen in the thoracic region (Figure 3-24b). The presence of kyphosis will give the individual a characteristic "humpback," with associated rounded shoulders, sunken chest, and head-forward posture with neck hyperextension. Kyphosis is a common postural abnormality among older adults with **osteoporosis.** In some instances, the rounded-shoulders posture is caused by weakness or disuse **atrophy** of the muscles that control scapular movement—the rhomboids and trapezius. Strengthening programs intended to correct this postural deformity have had varying levels of success. Excessive tightness in, and overdevelopment of, the chest muscles can also contribute to rounded-shoulder posture.

Flat-back posture (Figure 3-24c) is a decrease in the normal inward curve of the lower back, with the pelvis in posterior tilt. **Sway-back posture** (Figure 3-24d) is a long outward curve of the thoracic spine with a decreased anterior lumbar curve and a backward shift of the upper trunk. It is often accompanied by rounded shoulders, a sunken chest, and a forward-tilted head.

Scoliosis is an excessive lateral curvature of the spine and is more prevalent among women than men (Figure 3-24e). With scoliosis, the pelvis and shoulders often appear uneven and the vertebrae may rotate, causing a posterior shift of the rib cage on one side.

If an individual has one of these three postural abnormalities and cannot actively assume a neutral spine posture, the fitness professional should refer him or her to a physician.

Temporary lordotic (in standing position) or kyphotic (in sitting position) postures may occur every day when people are tired—so-called fatigue postures. Fatigue postures may cause, or be the result of, physical stress,

muscle imbalance, and/or pain. If these postures are continued for extended periods of time (e.g., months or years), the bones of the spine may adapt to these postures, causing skeletal (rather than soft tissue) deviations that become irreversible.

Muscular Balance and Imbalance

When muscular balance is present on all sides of the cylindrical trunk, the neutral spine position can occur. However, a problem in one muscle group often creates problems in the opposing muscle group. If one muscle group is too tight (inflexible), it may pull the body out of the neutral position, causing increased stress and a tendency toward imbalance on the opposite side of the body. Conversely, if a particular muscle group is weakened from injury or fatigue, the body will fall out of alignment in the opposite direction.

The term muscular balance refers to the symmetry of the interconnected components of muscle and **connective tissue.** Specifically, muscular balance involves (1) equal strength and flexibility on the right and left sides of the body (bilateral symmetry); (2) proportional strength ratios in opposing (agonist/antagonist) muscle groups, although they may not be exactly equal; and (3) a balance in flexibility, in that normal ranges of motion are achieved but not exceeded.

One example of agonist/antagonist muscle imbalance is the relationship between the erector spinae and the abdominal muscles. Very commonly, the abdominals are overmatched by the muscles that extend the trunk, and neutral spine is lost. Persons with localized low-back pain from mechanical causes (no intervertebral disk or spinal nerve root involvement) are typically given abdominal-strengthening rehabilitation exercises to regain muscular control of the pelvis and balance with the erector spinae.

While not directly affecting the spine, a common muscular imbalance affects the function of the quadriceps and hamstrings. In untrained individuals, the naturally occurring size of the quadriceps is about twice that of the hamstrings, resulting in a significant imbalance in the agonist/antagonist relationship. With regular training, the ratio of hamstrings-to-quadriceps size and strength will improve, but hamstring strains unfortunately remain an all-too-frequent result of this muscular imbalance. Similarly, strength differences are often present between the dominant and nondominant limbs, particularly in the upper extremity. One method to counteract this is to have clients or class participants perform unilateral resistance exercises with dumbbells, isolating the right and left sides, rather than using a barbell to perform the same activity.

Core Stability

The **axial skeleton** (trunk) forms the "core" of the body, serving as the origin or insertion site for nearly 30 muscles in the abdomen, low back, pelvis, and hips. Biomechanically, the muscles that attach to the axial skeleton work to transfer forces to and from the upper and lower extremities. For example, a baseball pitch begins with generation of muscular force in the lower extremity (i.e., the forward stride toward home plate). These internal forces are transferred upward through a kinetic link system to the axial skeleton and into the throwing arm, concluding with the transfer of momentum to the ball via the fingers. While pitching coaches and athletic trainers go to great lengths to care for the shoulder muscles of professional pitchers, they, along with strength and conditioning specialists, also understand the need to develop trunk and lower-extremity muscular strength and endurance.

While not a particularly new concept, **core stability** is a popular topic of debate among fitness professionals, clinicians, coaches, and athletes. There is an increasing body of knowledge that suggests that core stability is a key component necessary for successful performance of most gross motor activities (Willson et al., 2005). Hip and trunk muscle strength, abdominal muscle endurance, the ability to maintain a particular spinal or pelvic alignment, and the absence of ligamentous laxity in the vertebral column have all been identified as "core stability."

The lumbo-pelvic-hip "core" is formed by the lumbar vertebrae, the pelvis, the hip joints, and the muscles, tendons, ligaments, and other connective tissues that either create or limit movement in any of these segments. **Static stabilizers** (the bony configuration of joints, fibrocartilages, and ligaments) and dynamic stabilizers (the muscles) contribute to the creation of core stability.

When compared to the contributions to core stability made by the dynamic structures (muscles), the contributions of the static tissues are relatively small. There are three mechanisms by which the muscles that comprise the core contribute to the stability of the trunk: intra-abdominal pressure, spinal compressive forces, and hip and trunk **muscle stiffness,** which is the capacity of these tissues to resist internal and external loads (Willson et al., 2005).

Core Anatomy

The different layers of muscles within this region each have specific roles in movement and stabilization. The larger, more **superficial** muscles are primarily responsible for movement and force transfer between the pelvis and rib cage, while the smaller, deeper muscles are more responsible for intersegmental motion and stabilization of the spine.

Cresswell and Thorstensson (1994) demonstrated that the key muscle that works with the neural subsystem is the transverse abdominis. It functions primarily to increase intra-abdominal pressure, reducing compressive forces along the spine. Additionally, in healthy individuals, this muscle fires in anticipation of voluntary or involuntary loading of the spine to reduce compressive forces (Hodges & Richardson, 1996; Hodges et al., 1996). Given the different roles muscles play within this region, it is helpful to review the muscle anatomy by function and location, rather than exclusively by location.

The deep layer, or inner unit, consists of small muscles (rotatores, interspinali, intertransversarii) that span single vertebrae and are generally too small to offer stabilization of the entire spine. They offer segmental stabilization of each vertebra, especially at end ranges of motion, and are rich in sensory nerve endings that provide feedback information to the brain relating to spinal position.

The middle layer forms a box spanning several vertebrae, from the diaphragm to the pelvic floor, with muscles and fascia enclosing the back, front, and sides (Figure 3-25). The group consists of the transverse abdominis, multifidi, quadratus lumborum, posterior fibers of the internal oblique, the diaphragm, and the pelvic floor musculature and adjoining fascia (i.e., linea alba, thoracolumbar fascia). This box allows the spine and sacroiliac joint to stiffen in anticipation of loading and movement, and provides a working foundation from which the body can operate.

The outer layer consists of big powerful muscles that span many vertebrae and are involved in gross movement of the trunk (see Figure 1-29, page 41). These muscles include the rectus abdominis, erector spinae group, external and internal oblique, and iliopsoas.

In healthy individuals without low-back pain, the core musculature functions reflexively to stabilize the spine under voluntary or involuntary loading without the need for conscious muscle control. This anticipatory muscle action aids in postural balance during voluntary movement. During voluntary or involuntary multiplanar loading and movement, effective core action optimizes force production and transfer through the trunk to the extremities, thereby enhancing control of integrated movement; improving the ability to tolerate loading forces; protecting the spine from potential injury; and improving balance, coordination, dynamic postural strength, and control.

Hodges and Richardson (1996) discovered that delayed activation or minimal activation of the transverse abdominis muscle and limited co-contraction of core muscles in individuals suffering from low-back pain indicated some neural control deficits. Delayed onset of the transverse abdominis action may cause inadequate stabilization of the lumbar spine during movements of the upper extremity (Sahrmann, 2002). Deconditioned individuals

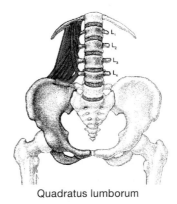
Quadratus lumborum

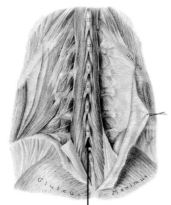
Multifidi

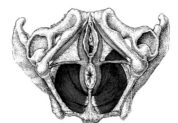
Pelvic floor musculature

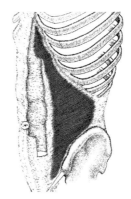
Transverse abdominis

Figure 3-25
Middle layer of core muscles

Source: LifeART image copyright 2008 Wolters Kluwer Health, Inc., Lippincott Williams & Wilkins. All rights reserved.

who spend much of their time sitting may demonstrate similar neural control deficits. Consequently, balance and core training must begin with exercises that emphasize re-education of these faulty motor patterns, which is best achieved by activating the core musculature in isolation in stable, supported environments.

Core muscle involvement is dynamic, and effective core training must ultimately simulate the patterns and planes of natural movement. McGill (2007) states that the development of core endurance should take precedence over core strength, as muscular endurance better correlates with spinal stability and a lower risk of injury. McGill (2007) also states that abdominal hollowing, or "centering," which involves the isolated activation of the inner unit that draws the umbilicus inward and upward, serves essential motor re-education purposes, it does not ensure the same degree of stability as "bracing," which involves the co-contraction of both the core and abdominal muscles to create a more rigid and wider BOS for spinal stabilization. Ultimately, people should implement bracing, as it is a more effective method of stabilizing the spine (McGill, 2007, 2004; Gambetta, 2007).

Intra-abdominal Pressure

Contraction of the inner unit produces a "hoop tension" effect similar to the effect of cinching a belt. This contraction, primarily of the transverse abdominis, pulls on the linea alba, thereby pulling the abdominal wall inward and upward. This contraction compresses the internal organs to push upward against the diaphragm and downward against the pelvic floor musculature. Contraction of the multifidi and transverse abdominis collectively pulls on the thoracolumbar fascia, increasing lumbar extension. Only a small increase in muscle activity of the multifidi and transverse abdominis is required to create this effect (5% of muscle's maximal voluntary contraction for daily activities and approximately 10% of maximal voluntary contraction for more vigorous activities) (Cresswell & Thorstensson, 1994).

Trunk Flexors: Abdominal Muscles

The abdominal muscles are found on the anterior and lateral surfaces of the trunk, and they flex, laterally flex, and rotate the trunk. Trunk flexion occurs in the sagittal plane, right and left lateral flexion occur in the frontal plane, and right and left trunk rotation occur in the transverse plane. The abdominal muscle group is composed of the rectus abdominis, the external oblique, the internal oblique, and the transverse abdominis (see Figure 1-29).

The fibers of the rectus abdominis are superficial and run longitudinally from the lower part of the chest to the pubic bone. Synergistic concentric actions of the right and left rectus abdominis muscles produce flexion of the trunk, as in the upward phase of an abdominal curl or crunch. While the anatomical movement during the return (downward) phase of the crunch is trunk extension, it is the eccentric muscle actions of the right and left rectus abdominis muscles (trunk flexors) that control the slow return to the mat. Unilateral concentric activation of the right or left rectus abdominis will result in lateral flexion of the trunk. Highly effective exercises to develop this muscle are posterior pelvic tilts, supine abdominal curls, reverse abdominal curls (eccentric action emphasized), and abdominal crunches (Figure 3-26a).

The external obliques are also in the superficial layer of trunk muscles. These muscles originate on the ribs and attach to the iliac crest and the **aponeurosis** of the rectus abdominis; their fibers run diagonally downward and forward, as if into the front pockets of a pair of pants. When the right and left external obliques act together concentrically, they produce trunk flexion. The right and left sides can be activated independently to cause lateral flexion and, when combined with concentric action of the opposite internal oblique, produce trunk rotation to the opposite side. An example is the oblique (twisting) abdominal curl with the shoulder moved toward the opposite hip. Effective exercises to develop the external obliques are supine pelvic tilts, abdominal curls with the hips and knees partially extended to create more

Fundamentals of Applied Kinesiology

a. Abdominal curl for rectus abdominis

Figure 3-26
Abdominal strength and endurance exercises

b. Side-lying torso raise for internal and external obliques (modified side plank)

resistance, oblique abdominal curls, side-lying torso raises (Figure 3-26b), and oblique reverse abdominal curls (i.e., lifting the feet toward the ceiling until the buttocks leave the floor).

The internal oblique muscles are found deep to the external obliques, and their fibers run diagonally downward and posteriorly, as if into the back pockets of a pair of pants. Their functions include flexion, lateral flexion, and rotation of the trunk to the same side. Helpful exercises to develop and strengthen the internal obliques are supine pelvic tilts, reverse abdominal curls, oblique reverse abdominal curls, and side-lying torso raises (see Figure 3-26b).

Not long ago, the transverse abdominis, which is found in the deepest layer of the abdominal wall, was thought to have no voluntary motor function; its only known anatomical contributions were to compress the **viscera** and support the spine. A series of studies have shown that the transverse abdominis, together with the multifidi muscles of the spine, play a critical role in core stability (Hodges, 1999; Hodges & Richardson, 1999, 1997). These authors demonstrated that coactivation of the transverse abdominis and multifidi muscles occurred before any movements of the limbs. Specifically, these two muscles were activated an average of 30 milliseconds before shoulder movement and 110 milliseconds before leg movement. What is the importance of this temporal pattern of trunk muscle recruitment? The transverse abdominis and multifidi muscles are thought to play a vital role in providing feedback about spinal joint position, and thus forewarn the **central nervous system** about impending dynamic forces to be

created in the extremities that may destabilize the spine (Fredericson & Moore, 2005).

Knowing how to activate the transverse abdominis muscles is an important aspect of core stability. Have clients or class participants lie on their backs with their knees flexed and feet flat on the floor. While they are relaxed and breathing normally, have them visualize pulling their navel inward toward the spine. They should hold this position for several seconds, relax, and then repeat several times. There are several different floor and standing exercises that will help people learn how to activate their transverse abdominis and multifidi muscles. If an individual has a history of low-back pain or injury, he or she may have difficulty recruiting the transverse abdominis and multifidi muscles early enough to stabilize the spine (Hides, Richardson, & Jull, 1996). A fitness professional may need to refer these individuals to a certified athletic trainer or physical therapist to assist them in learning these exercises. Figure 3-27 provides examples of static core stability exercises (prone plank, side plank) and dynamic core stability exercises (alternate leg bridges with shoulders on a stability ball, abdominal rollout on a stability ball).

There are several effective methods of increasing the resistance and loading pattern during abdominal exercises; one such variation is to change body positions relative to gravity (e.g., partial abdominal curl on an incline bench with the head down rather than on a

Figure 3-27
Core stability exercises

Adapted from Fredericson, M. & Moore, T. (2005). Muscular balance, core stability, and injury prevention for middle- and long-distance runners. *Physical Medicine and Rehabilitation Clinics of North America,* 16, 3, 669–689.

Abdominal roll-out with stability ball; the farther the rollout, the more this exercise targets the latissimus dorsi

Alternate leg bridge with shoulders and head fully supported on a stability ball (extend the raised leg for a greater challenge)

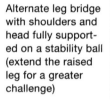

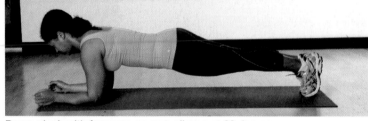
Prone plank with forearms on mat, elbows at 90 degrees

Side plank for abdominals and quadratus lumborum

flat mat). Another variation is to change the end of the muscle that is stabilized and the one that is moved (e.g., perform abdominal curls with the shoulders lifted, and then change to a reverse curl with the hips elevated). Fitness professionals can emphasize endurance training for the abdominals by having the exerciser hold an abdominal curl at various points in the arc of motion while performing exercises for the hip adductors or flexors.

Trunk Extensors: Erector Spinae Group

When acting bilaterally and concentrically, the erector spinae group of muscles, formed by the iliocostalis, longissimus, and spinalis, will produce trunk extension and hyperextension. These muscles also act eccentrically to control flexion of the spine from a standing position, as when bending over to pick up the morning newspaper. When the erector spinae muscles are stimulated unilaterally, they cause lateral flexion to that same side. In normal standing posture, the level of activity in these muscles is quite low.

Exercises that are effective for strengthening this muscle group include the prone trunk hyperextension lift (Figure 3-28a), and, from a kneeling (all-fours) position, simultaneous lifting of the opposite arm and leg (Figure 3-28b). The latter exercise causes the erector spinae muscles to function as stabilizers of the spine to maintain a neutral position. For individuals seeking more advanced challenges, incorporate a BOSU™ into the exercise program to develop balance and proprioception along with trunk extensor strength (Figure 3-29).

To stretch and mobilize the erector spinae group, have the individual assume an all-fours position with the hands directly beneath the shoulders and the knees directly beneath the hips, and arch the back like a cat and then transition to the camel position (Figure 3-30). The posterior pelvic tilt position flattens the anterior (lordotic) curve in the lumbar region of the spine and places the erector spinae in a stretched position.

a. Prone hyperextension

Figure 3-28
Basic and
intermediate
difficulty strength
exercises for the
trunk extensors

b. Birddog: lift the opposite arm and leg simultaneously while keeping the spine in neutral position

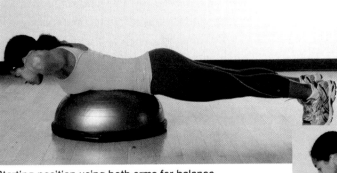

Starting position using both arms for balance

Figure 3-29
Advanced trunk
extension exercise
with a BOSU

Trunk extension exercise (modified "Superman")

Figure 3-30
Cat-camel flexibility
exercise for the
erector spinae muscles

Cat position

Camel position

Kinesiology of the Upper Extremity

Upper-extremity segments include the head and neck, **shoulder girdle [scapulothoracic (S/T) articulation]**, shoulders, elbows, wrists, and hands. Tables 1-7 through 1-10 summarize the muscles in each of these regions, their origins and insertions, primary function(s), and specific examples of exercises involving these muscles. Prior to discussion of the functional relationships of the muscles in the upper extremity, the terms **shoulder joint complex, glenohumeral (G/H) joint,** and shoulder girdle must be differentiated.

The term shoulder joint complex describes the coordinated functioning of four separate upper-extremity segments: the **sternoclavicular (S/C) joint,** the junction of the sternum and the proximal clavicle; the **acromioclavicular (A/C) joint,** the junction of the acromion process of the scapula with the distal clavicle; the G/H joint, the ball-and-socket joint composed of the glenoid fossa of the scapula and the humeral head; and the S/T articulation, the muscles and fascia connecting the scapulae to the thorax (Figure 3-31). The more general term, shoulder girdle, is synonymous with the formal anatomical term, scapulothoracic articulation.

The G/H joint is the most mobile joint in the body, the beneficiary of contributions to range of motion by the other components of the shoulder complex (S/C, A/C, and S/T). Voluntary movement at the G/H joint is possible in all three anatomical planes: flexion and extension in the sagittal plane, abduction and adduction in the frontal plane, **circumduction** in a combination of the sagittal and frontal planes, and internal and external rotation and horizontal flexion and extension in the transverse plane (Figure 3-32).

The glenohumeral joint and the scapulothoracic articulation work together to produce coordinated flexion and extension in the sagittal plane and abduction and adduction in the frontal plane. This relationship is referred to as **scapulohumeral rhythm** and, throughout the available range of motion for flexion/extension and abduction/adduction, approximately 2 degrees of humeral motion occurs for every 1 degree of scapular motion. Translated to absolute terms, to achieve 180 degrees of flexion or abduction, approximately 120 degrees of that motion occurs at the glenohumeral joint and 60 degrees of the motion occurs as the result of movement of the scapula on the thorax (Figure 3-33).

In common activities of daily living, the scapular muscles function primarily as stabilizers, but they also are powerful muscles involved in upper-extremity movements. Anatomical movements of the scapulae on the thorax include **elevation** and **depression,** adduction (also termed "**retraction**") and abduction ("**protraction**"), and upward and downward rotation (Figure 3-34). Scapular muscles are typically divided into two groups based on their location and function. Anterior shoulder girdle muscles connect the scapulae to the front of the trunk, while the posterior shoulder girdle muscles hold the scapulae to the back of the trunk.

There are many anatomical movements possible throughout the upper extremity. However, within the scope of this chapter, only the kinesiology of the scapulothoracic articulation and glenohumeral joint are addressed.

Figure 3-31
The four articulations of the shoulder joint complex

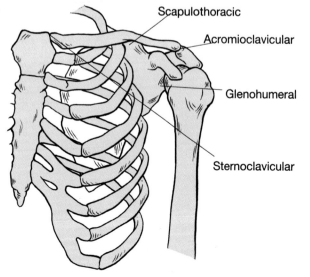

Scapulothoracic

Acromioclavicular

Glenohumeral

Sternoclavicular

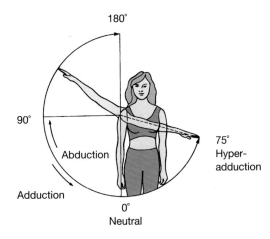

Shoulder range of motion in the frontal plane: abduction 180°, adduction to 0°, hyperadduction 75°

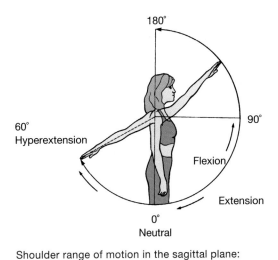

Shoulder range of motion in the sagittal plane: flexion 180°, extension to 0°, hyperextension 60°

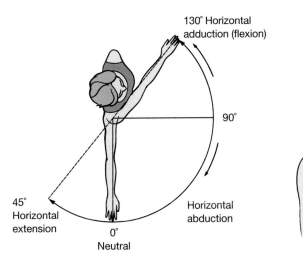

Shoulder range of motion in the transverse plane: horizontal adduction (flexion) 130°, horizontal abduction to 0°, horizontal extension 45° past neutral

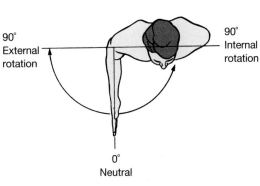

Figure 3-32
Shoulder joint range of motion

Shoulder rotation range of motion in the transverse plane (shoulder is adducted to 0°): external rotation 90°, internal rotation 90°

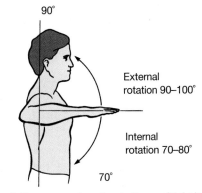

Shoulder rotation range of motion in the sagittal plane: external rotation 90–100°, internal rotation 70–80°

Figure 3-33
The movement of the arm is accompanied by movement of the scapula—a ratio of approximately 2° of arm movement for every 1° of scapular movement occurs during shoulder abduction and flexion; this relationship is known as scapulohumeral rhythm.

Figure 3-34
Scapular
movements

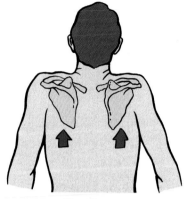

Elevation

Depression

Adduction (retraction)

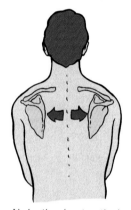

Abduction (protraction)

Upward rotation

Downward rotation (return to anatomical position)

Anterior Shoulder Girdle Muscles

The major anterior shoulder girdle muscles—the pectoralis minor and serratus anterior—attach the scapula to the front of the thorax (Figure 3-35). Concentric and eccentric activity in these muscles results in scapular movement on the thorax; these muscles have no attachment to the humerus, and thus do not directly cause glenohumeral motion. The pectoralis minor originates on the third, fourth, and fifth ribs and inserts on the coracoid process of the scapula. The pectoralis minor can have a positive or negative effect on posture, depending on the amount of muscular tone in the scapular adductors, specifically the middle trapezius and rhomboids. Concentric activity of the pectoralis minor results in abduction, depression, and downward rotation of the scapula. However, if the scapular adductors are weak, fatigued, or injured, the muscular tension created by the pectoralis minor will tilt the scapulae forward and down, worsening a rounded-shoulders posture (kyphosis).

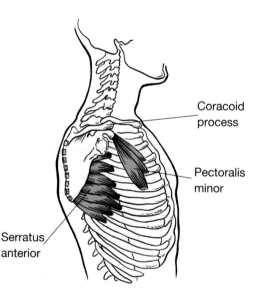

Coracoid process

Pectoralis minor

Serratus anterior

Figure 3-35
Anterior muscles of the shoulder girdle

The serratus anterior is a broad, knife-edged muscle that inserts along the underside of the entire length of the medial border of the scapula and originates on the front parts of the first through ninth ribs. The serratus anterior abducts the scapula and works as a synergist with the upper trapezius to produce upward rotation of the scapula. A key function of the serratus is to hold the medial border of the scapula firmly against the rib cage, preventing "winging" of the scapula posteriorly away from the thorax. Concentric action of the serratus anterior enables powerful forward motion of the arm, as in an overhead throwing motion. Strengthening of the serratus can be done from a supine position with the shoulder flexed to 90 degrees and the elbow extended, by pushing a dumbbell or medicine ball held in the hand toward the ceiling in a "punching" motion without bending the elbow. The shoulder blade(s) should lift off the floor slightly when performing this exercise (Figure 3-36). Another effective method of working the serratus anterior is to have clients or class participants perform push-ups with a "plus"—the addition of scapular abduction at the end of the upward phase of a regular push-up.

Starting position for supine "punches"

Shoulder blades lifted off the floor slightly; elbows fully extended

Figure 3-36
Exercise to strengthen the serratus anterior muscle

Posterior Shoulder Girdle Muscles

The posterior shoulder girdle muscles—the trapezius, rhomboids, and levator scapulae—attach the scapula to the back of the thorax. Since these muscles have no attachment to the humerus, their action does not directly result in glenohumeral motion.

The trapezius is the largest and most superficial of the posterior shoulder girdle muscles; it originates at the base of the skull and has attachments to all 19 vertebrae in the cervical and thoracic regions of the spine. Resembling the shape of a trapezoid, the muscle attaches laterally to the spine of the scapula and the lateral aspect of the clavicle. Looking at the orientation and size of the muscle, it is easy to understand why the different sections of the trapezius have three different names. The trapezius is divided into three distinct units—upper, middle, and lower—because of the different directions and lines of action of its fibers. The fibers of the upper trapezius are angled upward and obliquely, the muscle fibers of the middle trapezius are purely horizontal in their direction and pull, and the fibers of the lower trapezius are angled obliquely downward. Therefore, if the upper fibers are activated concentrically, they will produce elevation and upward rotation of the scapula. Stimulation of the fibers of the middle trapezius will cause pure adduction of the scapula, while concentric activity of the lower trapezius fibers will both depress and adduct the scapula.

The different fibers of the trapezius are alternately activated and relaxed to cause scapular rotation. If the arms are lifted in front (G/H flexion) or out to the side (G/H abduction), the shoulder blades rotate upward and away from the spine. This critical anatomical motion, upward rotation, occurs as the result of the upper and middle trapezius, rhomboids, and serratus anterior pulling on different aspects of the scapula. Concentric action of the lower trapezius, together with eccentric activity in the rhomboids and levator scapulae, will return the shoulder blades to their original (anatomical) position.

ACE Essentials of Exercise Science for Fitness Professionals

To design effective exercises to strengthen each of the sections of the trapezius, fitness professionals should consider the stresses and loads that the muscle encounters regularly. In typical sitting and standing postures, the upper trapezius acts isometrically to support the arms and head. The upper trapezius is also active when a heavy weight or object is held at arm's length. This portion of the trapezius needs stretching and strengthening throughout the full range of motion and does not require long-duration, isometric-resistance activities. The upper trapezius and the levator scapulae are strengthened in an upright standing or a sitting position by performing shoulder shrugs with dumbbells or tubing with the arms extended behind (Figure 3-37).

Figure 3-37
Exercise for the upper trapezius. The exerciser hyperextends the shoulders, then performs a full shoulder shrug.

The middle trapezius is commonly weak or fatigued in individuals who have rounded shoulders (kyphotic) in a standing or sitting posture. Typically, the middle trapezius does not need to be stretched, but rather strengthened in an "antigravity" position; that is, the muscle must be used to lift some resistance against gravity. Simply adducting the scapulae in a standing position does not overload the middle trapezius, because there is no resistance (other than gravity) to overcome. Examples of antigravity positions include a fully prone or a simulated-prone position (e.g., forward lunge, half-kneeling with the torso supported on the front thigh). Using dumbbells, the desired

movement in the modified forward-lunge position is to "squeeze" the shoulder blades together, causing the arms to lift in the direction opposite the pull of gravity (Figure 3-38a). To isolate the middle trapezius in a standing position, use elastic bands or surgical tubing to provide resistance. Instruct exercisers to abduct their G/H joints to 90 degrees, maintain a neutral spine, and then "pull" their scapulae together with no movement at the elbows or wrists (Figure 3-38b).

The rhomboid major and minor work together as one functional unit; the fibers of these muscles run upward and obliquely from the spine to the vertebral border of the scapulae. These muscles act primarily to adduct and elevate the scapulae and assist with downward rotation of the scapulae. When the rhomboids are weak or overstressed, the shoulder blades may tilt and pull away from the thorax due to the unopposed tension exerted by the serratus anterior and pectoralis minor. Bent-over rows with a weighted bar or pulley-machine weights or the use of a rowing ergometer are effective in strengthening the rhomboids (Figure 3-39).

Glenohumeral Joint Muscles

The final muscles discussed in this section are those that directly produce movement at the glenohumeral joint. These prime movers include the pectoralis major, deltoid, rotator cuff, latissimus dorsi, and teres major (Figure 3-40). Due to the complexity of the anatomical functions of the major muscles acting at the G/H joint, they are not listed in groups as adductors, extensors, and so on.

The pectoralis major is a very large muscle that makes up the majority of the muscle mass on the anterior chest wall. The pectoralis major is divided into three sections, with each portion named for its attachment point to the axial skeleton: clavicular, sternal, and costal. The clavicular portion of the pectoralis major, originating on the anterior aspect of the clavicle, is located slightly superior to the G/H joint and acts concentrically as a flexor. The similar downward-oblique angles of the fibers of the sternal and costal portions of the pectoralis major allow them to be considered one

Fundamentals of Applied Kinesiology

Figure 3-38
Exercises for the
middle trapezius

a. The exerciser
should maintain
neutral spine and
pull the scapulae
toward the spine,
keeping the elbows
straight and arms
hanging down.

b. The exerciser
should maintain neu-
tral spine and pull
the scapulae togeth-
er with the elbows
slightly bent and the
wrists neutral.

Figure 3-39
Bent-over row
to strengthen
scapular retractors
(rhomboids and
middle trapezius
muscles)

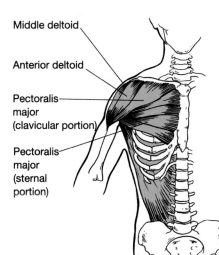

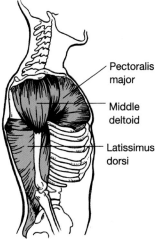

Figure 3-40
Superficial
glenohumeral joint
muscles

Middle deltoid

Anterior deltoid

Pectoralis
major
(clavicular portion)

Pectoralis
major
(sternal
portion)

Pectoralis
major

Middle
deltoid

Latissimus
dorsi

Supraspinatus

Middle deltoid

Infraspinatus

Posterior deltoid

Teres major

Teres minor

Deltoid and
pectoralis major

Latissimus dorsi, pectoralis
major, and deltoid (lateral view)

Posterior muscles of
the glenohumeral joint

functional unit. The inferior location of these muscles relative to the shoulder joint makes the sternal and costal portions powerful shoulder extensors. When considered as a whole unit, the pectoralis major is a prime mover in glenohumeral adduction, internal rotation, and horizontal flexion.

To strengthen the pectoralis major using hand-held weights, clients or class participants can lie supine on a mat or on top of a step bench. From this position, a pectoral fly exercise involving horizontal flexion will overload the pectoralis major. The push-up is also an effective exercise for the pectoral muscles. The pectoralis major, serratus anterior, and triceps brachii act eccentrically to slowly lower the body in the downward phase of the push-up (same direction of movement as the force of gravity). These same muscles act concentrically during the upward phase of the push-up. As an added challenge for an advanced exerciser, utilize a step-bench as the starting position for the hands to increase the level of difficulty of the push-up, or have the individual place two benches close together, positioning one hand on each and performing the push-up between the benches. The increased height off the ground will permit a larger range of motion during the eccentric and concentric phases of the push-up, creating a greater overload of these muscles. A study of 12 different types of push-up exercises reported that ballistic (plyometric) push-ups (e.g., those involving a hand-clap) elicited significantly higher levels of muscle activation in upper-extremity and core musculature than did push-ups performed with the hands on unstable surfaces (e.g., using standard-size basketballs) (Freeman et al., 2006).

The deltoid has a configuration similar to the trapezius in that it has fibers running in three different directions and three names, according to location. As a whole, the deltoid muscle lies superior to the glenohumeral joint and collectively functions as the primary abductor of the shoulder joint. The anterior deltoid is easily palpated in the front of the shoulder, attaching to the lateral one-third of the clavicle. Since the anterior deltoid crosses the shoulder

joint anteriorly, it flexes, internally rotates, and horizontally flexes the arm at the shoulder. The most effective positions to strengthen the anterior deltoid are sitting and standing. Using free weights or elastic tubing, individuals can perform front shoulder raises in sets of eight to 12 repetitions.

The fibers of the middle deltoid are aligned perfectly with the frontal plane, and thus this muscle is the prime mover in concentric abduction of the shoulder joint (e.g., upward phase of a seated shoulder press). During the downward phase of a seated shoulder press, the middle deltoid acts eccentrically to control the lowering of the weight via adduction (Figure 3-41). When performing overhead resistance training, such as a shoulder press, it is important to maintain the glenohumeral joint in neutral or external rotation.

Figure 3-41
Seated shoulder press for the deltoid muscle group

Fundamentals of Applied Kinesiology

Shoulder abduction combined with internal rotation, particularly in people over 40 years of age, will commonly irritate the rotator cuff muscles, impinging their tendons between the acromion process of the scapula, the subacromial bursa, and the head of the humerus. When working with individuals who have existing shoulder pain or who develop impingement symptoms, fitness professionals should avoid recommending resistance exercises that combine shoulder abduction with internal rotation.

The posterior deltoid is located on the back side of the G/H joint and acts as an antagonist to the anterior deltoid. The posterior deltoid has the exact opposite functions as the anterior deltoid; it extends, externally rotates, and horizontally extends the arm at the shoulder. To strengthen the posterior deltoid, have the individual assume a staggered stance position with a neutral spine. Using hand weights, he or she begins with the shoulder flexed, adducted, and internally rotated, and move into extension, abduction, and external rotation (Figure 3-42).

A group of four relatively small muscles comprise the rotator cuff (Figure 3-43). These muscles act synergistically to pull the head of the humerus down and into the glenoid fossa, thus helping to stabilize the G/H joint against the constant downward pull of gravity acting to dislocate the joint. The rotator cuff muscles are sometimes referred to as the "compressor cuff" because they stabilize the humeral head within the joint. The tendons of these muscles cover the head of the humerus, while the muscles themselves are named mostly for their location in relation to the scapula. The acronym **SITS** is used as a memory device to recall the names of the muscles in this group. The supraspinatus, located superior to the spine of the scapula, initiates abduction and is a prime mover through the early abduction range of motion. The infraspinatus, found inferior to (below) the spine of the scapula, and the teres minor are synergists for external rotation of the G/H joint. The subscapularis, located on the anterior undersurface of the scapula, is not easily palpated and attaches to the anterior aspect of the joint. Since it is located anterior and medial, the subscapularis functions as an

Figure 3-42
Strengthening exercise for the posterior deltoid

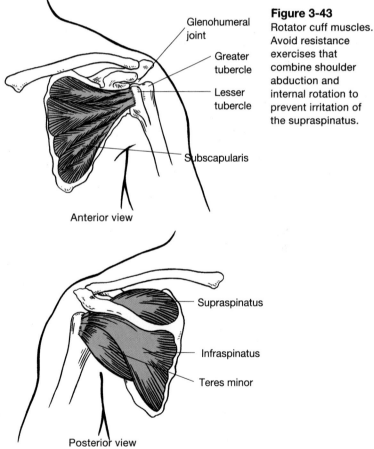

Glenohumeral joint

Greater tubercle

Lesser tubercle

Subscapularis

Anterior view

Supraspinatus

Infraspinatus

Teres minor

Posterior view

Figure 3-43
Rotator cuff muscles. Avoid resistance exercises that combine shoulder abduction and internal rotation to prevent irritation of the supraspinatus.

internal rotator of the humerus.

Caution must be used when working the rotator cuff in isolation; the four musculotendinous attachments (primarily the supraspinatus) can become inflamed as a result of performing many repetitions of movements that involve abduction, flexion, and rotation. For injury prevention, make sure that exercisers' shoulders are in neutral or external rotation any time the arms are abducted or flexed.

The latissimus dorsi and the teres major are similar muscles from a functional perspective (see Figure 1-24, page 37). Kinesiology instructors often nickname the teres major the "little lat" because its functions are identical to the much larger latissimus dorsi. The latissimus dorsi originates over a wide area in the lower thoracic and all of the lumbar regions of the spine, while the teres major arises from the inferior portion of the scapula. What makes these two muscles so functionally similar is the close proximity of their insertion sites on the medial aspect of the proximal humerus. Both muscles act concentrically to produce adduction, extension, and internal rotation of the glenohumeral joint. These muscles can be strengthened with elastic resistance or a cable pulley machine, starting with the arms overhead (elbows extended) and adducting and extending the G/H joint against the resistance provided by the tubing or machine. Performing this same exercise with dumbbells will not involve the latissimus and teres major in adduction, but rather recruit the abductors (deltoids) eccentrically to lower the weights. Regardless of the muscle targeted for strengthening, when working with hand-held weights, fitness professionals must be sure that the initial effort is in a direction opposite the pull of gravity.

Obesity-related Biomechanics

Reports on the negative health effects of **overweight** and obesity, including an increased risk for **hypertension, dyslipidemia, type 2 diabetes, coronary heart disease, stroke,** and gallbladder disease, are seemingly ubiquitous. However, there has been less attention focused on the reporting of the posture and gait abnormalities associated with obesity that pose health risks for the joints and soft tissues of this population. Fitness professionals should recognize

the functional limitations imposed by the additional loading of the locomotor system in obesity that results in abnormal mechanics and the potential for musculoskeletal injury.

Postural Balance

It has been proposed that body size and shape influence static postural stability by altering the location of the COG in overweight and obese individuals. It seems that an anterior displacement of the COG places obese individuals closer to their limits of stability and, as such, at greater risk of falling. Fortunately, regular physical activity has been shown to have a profound positive influence on balance performance in adults. Therefore, exercise programs that focus on weight reduction, balance training, and fall prevention in obese and overweight adults can help reduce the likelihood of falls occurring in this population.

Walking Gait

The calorie cost of walking in the overweight and obese population is greater than for the normal-weight population. Obese people burn more calories during walking, in part because they are much less efficient at it than non-obese persons. In addition to weighing more and thereby expending more calories to perform physical activity, the greater energetic cost of the obese may be due to an altered step frequency (taking more steps to cover the same area), a greater vertical displacement of the COG, and extraneous movements resulting from greater limb dimensions. Additionally, research has shown that obese individuals shift their patterns of walking (i.e., use different muscles in a different order), which results in taking force off the knees and displacing it to the ankles (DeVita & Hortobagyi, 2003).

Individuals who are overweight or obese also increase their risk for the development of **osteoarthritis.** An increase in weight is significantly associated with increased pain in weightbearing joints. Small decreases in body weight [two **body mass index (BMI)** units] over a 10-year period has been associated with decreasing the odds for developing knee osteoarthritis by more than 50%, whereas weight gain is associated with a slight increase in risk (Wearing et al., 2006).

Fitness professionals should encourage physical activity among their obese clients or class participants that will not exacerbate their altered posture and gait biomechanics. Exercise intensities should be kept at a level that does not cause an increase in pain and soreness, since many overweight and obese individuals already have joint pain from simply performing their daily activities. **Cross-training** programs utilizing several exercise modalities within the same session are recommended. For example, cardiovascular-training machines that impart less force and impact to the weightbearing joints, such as the elliptical trainer, stationary bike, and recumbent stepping machine, are popular with overweight and obese individuals. Furthermore, a special effort should be made to steer clear of exercise equipment or positions that may be confining or uncomfortable for obese people. Smaller seat surfaces, positions that allow the abdominal mass to restrict range of motion (e.g., seated leg press machine), and getting up and down from floor-lying positions should be avoided.

Age-related Biomechanics

Biomechanical Considerations for Older Adults

The prevalence of musculoskeletal pain and joint alterations in the older adult population is remarkably high. About half of persons age 65 and older are affected by osteoarthritis (American Geriatrics Society, 2001), approximately half of adults age 80 and older experience **sarcopenia** (Baumgartner et al., 1998), and 55% of Americans age 50 and older have osteopenia or osteoporosis [National Osteoporosis Foundation (NOF), 2008]. Decreased range of motion and loss of spinal flexibility in many older adults results in a "stooped" posture that is associated with a vertical displacement of the COG backward toward the heels. This change in postural alignment can lead to lowered self-confidence, faulty balance, and an increased risk for falls

(Horak, Shupert, & Mirka, 1989). These and other musculoskeletal conditions impart varying levels of discomfort and disability to older adults. Fitness professionals should be knowledgeable in making appropriate exercise and equipment modifications to make physical activity more comfortable for older adults.

Chair-seated Exercise

Whenever possible, training older adults in weightbearing, functional positions is preferred to chair-seated work. However, if an individual has issues related to endurance, mobility, and **self-efficacy,** a chair-seated exercise routine may be appropriate. For example, when working with the frailest older-adult populations, seated exercise may be the only practical method.

Ideally, a chair used for seated exercise should not have armrests. This will increase the potential range of movement and allow a broader variety of possible exercises. However, many individuals who are well-suited for chair exercise use wheelchairs, so it is important for the fitness professional to develop the ability to work effectively using armchairs. During chair exercise, the individual's back should be supported by the back of the chair or by a pillow, pad, or rolled towel if necessary. Additionally, the individual's feet should be in full contact with the floor, which can be accomplished by using a book, stool, or other type of platform. Another option for individuals who have good functional strength while standing, but who have low self-confidence and a fear of falling, is to include standing work using the back of the chair for balance support.

Aquatic Exercise

Exercise in the water provides a great alternative for both aerobic and resistance activities for many older adults. Because water's buoyancy negates the impact of exercise, many older adults who cannot safely jog, jump, or kick on land can successfully perform those activities in the pool. Accessories made for in-pool use, such as water bells, paddles, webbed gloves, and ankle cuffs, can be incorporated to increase intensity and challenge strength or to provide more buoyancy to help an individual float during certain activities. A water temperature of 83 to 88° F (28 to 31° C) works well for most older adults, especially those who suffer from **arthritis.**

The performance of ADL has been shown to improve in older adults who participate in a regular aquatic-based functional training program. Sufferers of chronic back pain who undergo therapeutic water exercise programs experience reduced pain and improved ADL performance (Smit & Harrison, 1991; Landgridge & Phillips, 1988). Furthermore, joint motion and ADL performance for individuals with arthritis and rheumatic diseases have improved after water therapy sessions (Suomi & Lindaur, 1997; Templeton, Booth, & Kelley, 1996). In addition to improved functional abilities, water exercise for older adults has also resulted in increased muscular strength and flexibility, decreased body fat, and improved self-esteem (Sanders, Constantino, & Rippee, 1997).

For older adults diagnosed with osteoporosis, land-based training is preferable to aquatic exercise for stimulating increases in **bone mineral density.** However, joint pain and disability may prohibit many clients with osteoporosis from performing functional activities on land. In these individuals, water-based exercise will help maintain or enhance joint range of motion. Furthermore, with the use of the pool-based equipment, older adults can improve muscular strength, thereby improving functional abilities and reducing the risk of falls on land.

Biomechanical Considerations for Youth

Because children and adolescents are still developing and maturing, their physiology is dynamic, and the measures of health and fitness are in a constant state of evolution. There are also considerable inter-individual differences in physical development between youth of the same age. For example, a 12-year-old girl can be taller and more physically skilled than a 12-year-old boy, and two adolescents of the same age can have considerable differences in height and weight (Servedio, 1997). These differences are related to the timing of puberty, which typically occurs between the ages of eight and 13 in girls and nine and 15 in boys. Sensitivity to inter-individual differences in abilities and physical appearance is especially important when working with children and adolescents.

An area of age-related biomechanical change that clearly affects youth is flexibility. The research on aging and flexibility tends to support the notion that small children are quite supple and that flexibility tends to level off at puberty and then begins to decrease (Alter, 2004; Kendall et al., 2005).

One classic explanation for the decline in flexibility seen in children growing into adolescence is that during periods of rapid growth, bones grow much faster than the muscles stretch. Consequently, there is an increase in musculotendinous tightness at the joints (Kendall & Kendall, 1948; Micheli, 1983). Another theory is that the decrease in flexibility, specifically in the hamstrings, is a direct result of prolonged sitting in school. Most individuals sit with the pelvis in a posteriorly tilted position. Initially, this causes the hamstrings to become slack (Milne & Mierau, 1979; Milne, Mierau, & Cassidy, 1981). Over time, sitting in this position causes the hamstrings to adaptively shorten to take up the slack. An extension of this hypothesis that applies to all age groups is that decreased flexibility and increased tightness could be the result of a less physically active population as a whole.

Fortunately, a program of regular physical activity can contribute significantly to joint stability and flexibility for individuals of any age. Resistance training enhances the tensile strength of tendons and ligaments, and stretching exercises maintain the suppleness of tendons, ligaments, and muscles, thus allowing a full range of motion at each joint. Research has demonstrated that stretching and progressive resistance-training programs can produce the same percentage of improvement in the range of motion of elderly subjects (63 to 88 years) as in young subjects (15 to 19 years) (Chapman, de Vries, & Swezey, 1972).

Summary

Fitness professionals are required to design exercise programs and classes that are safe and effective, and that accomplish the desired fitness and/or personal goals of clients or participants. Without a fundamental understanding of biomechanical principles and kinesiology, this task is virtually impossible. This chapter has provided a region-by-region summary of the functional relationships of skeletal muscles in the upper and lower extremities, as well as a fundamental review of the most current information available related to core stability. With this information, a fitness professional has at his or her disposal sufficient tools to identify specific exercises and physical activities that will safely, effectively, and efficiently accomplish the fitness goals of their clients or class participants.

References

Alter, M.J. (2004). *Science of Flexibility* (3rd ed.). Champaign, Ill.: Human Kinetics.

American Geriatrics Society (2001). Exercise prescription for older adults with osteoarthritis pain: Consensus practice recommendations. *Journal of the American Geriatrics Society*, 49, 808–823.

Baumgartner, R.N. et al. (1998). Epidemiology of sarcopenia among the older persons in New Mexico. *American Journal of Epidemiology*, 147, 755–763.

Chapman, E.A., de Vries, H.A., & Swezey, R. (1972). Joint stiffness: Effects of exercise on young and old men. *Journal of Gerontology*, 27, 218–221.

Clark, J.M. & Haynor, D.R. (1987). Anatomy of the abductor muscles of the hip as studied by computed tomography. *Journal of Bone and Joint Surgery*, 69A, 1021–1031.

Cresswell, A.G. & Thorstensson, A. (1994). Changes in intra-abdominal pressure, trunk muscle activation and force during isokinetic lifting and lowering. *European Journal of Applied Physiology,* 68, 315–321.

DeVita, P. & Hortobagyi, T. (2003). Obesity is not associated with increased knee joint torque and power during level walking. *Journal of Biomechanics,* 36, 9, 1355–1362.

Fredericson, M. & Moore, T. (2005). Muscular balance, core stability, and injury prevention for middle- and long-distance runners. *Physical Medicine and Rehabilitation Clinics of North America,* 16, 3, 669–689.

Freeman, S. et al. (2006). Quantifying muscle patterns and spine load during various forms of the push-up. *Medicine & Science in Sports & Exercise,* 38, 570–577.

Fry, A.C., Smith, J.C., & Schilling, B.K. (2003). Effect of knee position on hip and knee torques during the barbell squat. *NSCA's Journal of Strength and Conditioning Research,* 17, 4, 629–633.

Gambetta, V. (2007). *Athletic Development: The Art and Science of Functional Sports Conditioning.* Champaign, Ill.: Human Kinetics.

Hides, J.A., Richardson, C.A., & Jull, G.A. (1996). Multifidus muscle recovery is not automatic after resolution of acute, first-episode low-back pain. *Spine,* 21, 2763–2769.

Hodges, P.W. (1999). Is there a role for transverse abdominis in lumbo-pelvic stability? *Manual Therapy,* 4, 74–86.

Hodges, P.W. & Richardson, C.A. (1999). Altered trunk muscle recruitment in people with low back pain with upper limb movement at different speeds. *Archives of Physical Medicine and Rehabilitation,* 80, 1005–1012.

Hodges, P.W. & Richardson, C.A. (1997). Contraction of the abdominal muscles associated with movement of the lower limb. *Physical Therapy,* 77, 132–142.

Hodges, P.W. & Richardson, C.A. (1996). Inefficient muscular stabilization of the lumbar spine associated with LBP: A motor control evaluation of the TVA. *Spine,* 21, 2640–2650.

Hodges, P. et al. (1996). Evaluation of the relationship between laboratory and clinical tests of transversus abdominis function. *Physiotherapy Research International,* 1, 1, 30–40.

Horak, F., Shupert, C., & Mirka, A. (1989). Components of postural dyscontrol in the elderly: A review. *Neurobiology of Aging*, 10, 727–745.

Kendall, H.O. & Kendall, F.P. (1948). Normal flexibility according to age groups. *Journal of Bone and Joint Surgery,* 30, 690–694.

Kendall, P.K. et al. (2005). *Muscles: Testing and Function with Posture and Pain* (5th ed.). Philadelphia: Lippincott Williams & Wilkins.

Landgridge, J. & Phillips, D. (1988). Group hydrotherapy exercises for chronic back pain sufferers. *Physiotherapy*, 74, 269–273.

Lindsay, D.M. et al. (1992). Comparison of isokinetic internal and external hip rotation torques using different testing positions. *Journal of Orthopedic and Sports Physical Therapy,* 16, 43–50.

Lundy, J. (2006). Gluteus medius stimulates lower extremity movement. *Biomechanics,* 13, 41–52.

McGill, S.M. (2007). *Low Back Disorders: Evidence-based Prevention and Rehabilitation* (2nd ed.). Champaign, Ill.: Human Kinetics.

McGill, S.M. (2004). *Ultimate Back Fitness and Performance* (3rd ed.). Waterloo, Canada: Backfitpro.com.

McLaughlin, T., Lardner, T., & Dillman, C. (1978). Kinetics of the parallel squat. *Research Quarterly,* 49, 2, 175–189.

Micheli, L.J. (1983). Overuse injuries in children's sport: The growth factor. *Orthopaedic Clinics of North America*, 14, 337–360.

Milne, R.A. & Mierau, D.R. (1979). Hamstring distensibility in the general population: Relationship to pelvic and low back stresses. *Journal of Manipulative and Physiological Therapeutics*, 2, 146–150.

Milne, R.A., Mierau, D.R., & Cassidy, J.D. (1981). Evaluation of sacroiliac joint movement and its relationship to hamstring distensibility (Abstract). *International Review of Chiropractic*, 35, 40.

National Osteoporosis Foundation (2008). www.nof.org.

Neumann, D.A. (2003). *Kinesiology of the Musculoskeletal System.* St. Louis, Mo.: Mosby.

Sahrmann, S. (2002). *Diagnosis and Treatment of Movement Impairment Syndromes.* St. Louis, Mo.: Mosby.

Sanders, M., Constantino, N., & Rippee, N. (1997). A comparison of results of functional water training on field and laboratory measures in older women. *Medicine & Science in Sports & Exercise,* 29, ixx.

Servedio, F. (1997). Normal growth and development: Physiological factors associated with exercise and training in children. *Orthopedic Physical Therapy Clinics of North America,* 6, 4, 417–436.

Smit, T. & Harrison, R. (1991). Hydrotherapy and chronic lower back pain: A pilot study. *Australian Journal of Physiotherapy*, 37, 229–234.

Suomi, R. & Lindaur, S. (1997). Effectiveness of arthritis foundation program on strength and range of motion in women with arthritis. *Journal of Aging and Physical Activity*, 5, 341–351.

Templeton, M.S., Booth, D.L., & Kelley, W.D.O. (1996). Effects of aquatic therapy on joint flexibility and functional ability in subjects with rheumatic disease. *Journal of Orthopaedic and Sports Physical Therapy*, 23, 376–381.

Wearing, S.C. et al. (2006). The biomechanics of restricted movement in adult obesity. *Obesity Reviews,* 7, 13–24.

Willson, J.D. et al. (2005). Core stability and its relationship to lower extremity function and injury. *Journal of the American Academy of Orthopaedic Surgeons,* 13, 316–325.

Suggested Reading

Golding, L.A. & Golding, S.M. (2003). *Musculoskeletal Anatomy and Human Movement.* Monterey, Calif.: Healthy Learning.

Hamilton, N. & Luttgens, K. (2002). *Kinesiology: Scientific Basis of Human Motion* (10th ed.). Boston, Mass.: McGraw-Hill.

Marieb, E.N., Mallatt, J., & Wilhelm, P.B. (2006). *Human Anatomy and Physiology* (4th ed.). Redwood City, Calif.: Benjamin-Cummings.

Mayo Clinic (2005). Core strengthening: Improve your balance and stability. *Mayo Clinic Women's HealthSource,* 9, 7.

Mow, V.C. & Huiskes, R. (Eds). (2005). *Basic Orthopaedic Biomechanics and Mechano-Biology* (3rd ed.). Philadelphia: Lippincott Williams & Wilkins.

Oates, C.A. (2008). *Kinesiology: The Mechanics and Pathomechanics of Human Movement* (2nd ed.). Philadelphia: Lippincott Williams & Wilkins.

Watkins, J. (1999). *Structure and Function of the Musculoskeletal System.* Champaign, Ill.: Human Kinetics.

Chapter 3
Fundamentals of
Applied Kinesiology

Getting Started

This chapter divides the body into three sections—upper extremity, lower extremity, and the spine and pelvis—and explains the functional kinesiology of each region. After reading this chapter, you should have a better understanding of:
- Biomechanical principles applied to human movement
- The kinesiology of the lower extremity
- The kinesiology of the upper extremity
- The kinesiology of the spine and pelvis
- Obesity-related biomechanics
- Age-related biomechanics
- The functions of the various muscles of the body
- Exercises to both strengthen and stretch key muscle groups

Expand Your Knowledge

I. Describe the major differences between the following pairs of words or phrases.

  a. Kinematics and kinetics _____

  _____

  _____

  b. Kyphosis and lordosis _____

  _____

  _____

  c. Posture and balance _____

  _____

  _____

  d. Supraspinatus and infraspinatus _____

  _____

  _____

  e. Base of support and stability limits _____

  _____

  _____

f.   Closed-chain exercises and open-chain exercises _____

_____

_____

II.   Describe Newton's laws of motion

a.   Law of inertia _____

_____

_____

b.   Law of acceleration _____

_____

_____

c.   Law of reaction _____

_____

_____

III.   List the four muscles synergistically responsible for hip flexion.

a.   _____

b.   _____

c.   _____

d.   _____

IV.   List the six external rotators of the hip.

a.   _____

b.   _____

c.   _____

d.   _____

e.   _____

f.   _____

ACE Essentials of Exercise Science for Fitness Professionals

V. Match each muscle with its associated compartment in the lower leg.

a. _____ Extensor hallucis longus   1. Anterior tibial compartment

b. _____ Flexor hallucis longus   2. Lateral tibial compartment

c. _____ Peroneus longus   3. Deep posterior compartment

d. _____ Plantaris   4. Superficial posterior compartment

e. _____ Soleus

f. _____ Anterior tibialis

g. _____ Peroneus brevis

h. _____ Posterior tibialis

i. _____ Gastrocnemius

j. _____ Popliteus

VI. Fill in the blanks.

a. The _____ are two muscles that are often inflexible, particularly among clients who regularly wear high-heeled shoes.

b. An excessive lateral curvature of the spine is known as _____.

c. A phenomenon known as the _____ increases knee-joint stability by locking the femur on the tibia when the knee is fully extended.

d. A key function of the _____ muscle is to hold the medial border of the scapula firmly against the rib cage to prevent "winging" of the shoulder blade.

e. The _____ is the only one of the four muscles of the quadriceps femoris that crosses the hip joint.

f. The _____ muscle is nicknamed the "little lat" because its functions are identical to the much larger latissimus dorsi.

VII. After each abbreviation, write the full name of that segment of the shoulder joint complex and list the bony structures that make up the articulation.

a. S/T articulation _____

_____

b. G/H joint _____

_____

c. S/C joint _____

_____

d. A/C joint _____

_____

VIII. Match the term with its associated descriptive statement.

a. _____ Patella

b. _____ Scapulohumeral rhythm

c. _____ Balance

d. _____ Middle trapezius

e. _____ Serratus anterior

f. _____ Stability

g. _____ Kyphosis

h. _____ Anterior longitudinal ligaments

i. _____ Rotator cuff

1. Commonly weak in individuals who have rounded shoulders in a seated or standing posture
2. Acts synergistically to compress the head of the humerus down and into the glenoid fossa
3. Worked effectively by performing push-ups with a "plus"
4. Relationship of the arm and shoulder blade during shoulder abduction and flexion
5. Rounded shoulders, sunken chest, and forward-head posture with neck hyperextension
6. Increased tension is often placed on these structures due to the anterior tilt of the pelvis in lordotic posture
7. Maintaining the body's position over its base of support within stability limits
8. Sesamoid bone that acts like a pulley to increase the mechanical advantage of the quadriceps at the knee joint
9. Increases as the feet move farther apart, creating a larger base of support

IX. List three factors associated with muscular balance.

a. _____

_____

b. _____

_____

c. _____

_____

X. In addition to the fact that overweight and obese people burn more calories during physical activity simply because they weigh more, what are three reasons why the caloric cost of walking is greater for this population than for the normal-weight population?

a. _____

b. _____

c. _____

XI. Explain the benefits of using chairs without armrests when performing chair-seated exercises. Why is it important for trainers to develop workouts than can be performed in chairs with armrests as well? _____

_____

_____

_____

_____

ACE Essentials of Exercise Science for Fitness Professionals

XII. Provide two possible explanations for the decrease in flexibility seen during adolescence.

a. _____

_____

_____

b. _____

_____

_____

Show What You Know

I. Lou, a new client, is performing abdominal curls and you notice he has a forward-head pos-
    ture. Describe two ways to correct Lou's head position. _____

_____

_____

_____

_____

_____

_____

_____

_____

_____

_____

II. A client, Sue, shows you an exercise for the chest that she really likes. She stands with
    15-pound dumbbells in each hand, and, beginning in 90-degree shoulder abduction, per-
    forms chest flys [i.e., horizontal shoulder flexion (adduction) and extension (abduction)].
    Analyze this exercise to determine its effectiveness and recommend a modification to increase
    the workload placed on the chest muscles. _____

_____

_____

_____

_____

_____

_____

_____

_____

_____

Multiple Choice

1. Which of the following is a closed kinetic chain movement?

    A. Arm movement while throwing a ball

    B. Quadruped hip extensions

    C. Push-ups

    D. Leg movement during swimming

2. Which of the following exercise adjustments would create **INCREASED** stability and balance?

    A. Moving from a position with feet at shoulder width to a position with feet together

    B. Progressing double-leg balance exercises from a wood floor to a foam balance pad

    C. Switching from a forearm plank to a plank in a push-up position

    D. Putting one hand on a bench during a single-arm bent-over row exercise

3. Which muscle provides the **GREATEST** amount of activity and force production during powerful hip extension movements such as those seen during sprinting and running up stairs?

    A. Gluteus medius

    B. Semitendinosus

    C. Gluteus maximus

    D. Semimembranosus

4. Which antagonists for movement in the sagittal plane work together to produce inversion and act as dynamic stabilizers for the ankle joint and medial arch of the foot?

    A. Anterior tibialis and posterior tibialis

    B. Soleus and tibialis anterior

    C. Extensor digitorum longus and posterior tibialis

    D. Gastrocnemius and peroneus brevis

5. The postural deviation most commonly associated with weak abdominal and hip extensor muscles coupled with tight hip flexors and back extensors is _____.

    A. Scoliosis

    B. Lordosis

    C. Sway-back

    D. Kyphosis

6. Which of the following muscle groups is activated to stabilize the core prior to any limb movements?

    A. Quadratus lumborum and rectus abdominis

    B. Multifidi and transverse abdominis

    C. Internal obliques and external obliques

    D. Erector spinae and pelvic floor musculature

7. What is the agonist (prime mover) and the type of muscle contraction performed when lowering the chest to the floor after performing a prone trunk (back) hyperextension?

    A. Erector spinae; eccentric contraction

    B. Rectus abdominis; eccentric contraction

    C. Internal oblique; concentric contraction

    D. Quadratus lumborum; concentric contraction

8. Which two prime movers (agonists) of the scapula originate on the anterior side of the thorax and insert on the scapula?

    A. Pectoralis major and pectoralis minor

    B. Serratus anterior and deltoid

    C. Pectoralis major and coracobrachialis

    D. Serratus anterior and pectoralis minor

9. Which two rotator cuff muscles are prime movers (agonists) for external rotation of the shoulder (glenohumeral) joint?

    A. Teres major and teres minor

    B. Supraspinatus and infraspinatus

    C. Teres minor and infraspinatus

    D. Subscapularis and posterior deltoid

10. Which of the following is a common obesity-related change that affects biomechanics?

    A. Increased pain in weightbearing joints

    B. Decreased step frequency (fewer steps to walk across an area)

    C. Increased stride length during walking

    D. Decreased anterior displacement of the center of gravity (COG)

NATALIE DIGATE MUTH, M.D., MPH, R.D., *is a graduate of the University of North Carolina School of Medicine. She is also a registered dietitian, an ACE Master Trainer, and a freelance nutrition and fitness author. She holds certifications from the American Council on Exercise, the American College of Sports Medicine, and the National Strength and Conditioning Association. She is currently completing her pediatrics residency at UCLA Mattel Children's Hospital.*

Nutrition

Natalie Digate Muth

ACE-certified Fitness Professionals provide nutrition guidance and recommendations within their **scope of practice** to individuals eager to begin or continue an exercise program to improve health, overall fitness, and/or **body composition.** Depending on each person's individual goals, nutritional needs may vary considerably. While a **registered dietitian (R.D.)** may be best equipped to offer a specific and individualized nutrition plan, the fitness professional can be a ready source of general nutrition information and education. Furthermore, a grasp of basic nutrition principles will help the fitness professional to better understand the interplay between diet and exercise, which will help in designing the most effective exercise programs and classes. With discussions of **macronutrient** and **micronutrient** structure and functions, the processes of nutrient **digestion** and **absorption,** nutrition guidelines and resources, and applications in sports nutrition, this chapter prepares fitness professionals to offer scientifically sound practical nutrition information. Moreover, the chapter discusses strategies to help empower clients and class participants to adopt healthful lifestyle changes and achieve their nutrition and fitness goals.

Macronutrient Structure and Function

Food is composed of some combination of three macronutrients: **carbohydrate, protein,** and **fat.** The term macronutrient simply means that the nutrient is needed in large quantities for normal growth and development. Macronutrients are the body's source of **calories,** or energy to fuel life processes.

Carbohydrates

Carbohydrates are the body's preferred energy source. Made up of chains of sugar molecules, carbohydrates contain about 4 calories per gram. A **monosaccharide** is the simplest form of sugar. The three monosaccharides are **glucose, fructose,** and **galactose.** Glucose is the predominant sugar in nature and the basic building block of most other carbohydrates. Fructose, or fruit sugar, is the sweetest of the monosaccharides and is found in varying levels in different types of fruits. Galactose joins with glucose to form the disaccharide **lactose,** the principal sugar found in milk. Other disaccharides include **maltose,** which is two glucose molecules bound together, and **sucrose** (table sugar), which is formed by glucose and fructose linked together.

An **oligosaccharide** is a chain of about three to 10 or fewer simple sugars. A long chain of sugar molecules is referred to as a **polysaccharide. Glycogen,** an animal carbohydrate found in meat products and seafood, and **starch,** a plant carbohydrate found in grains and vegetables, are the only polysaccharides that humans can fully digest. Both are long chains of glucose and are **complex carbohydrates** (versus **simple carbohydrates,** which are short chains of sugar).

Carbohydrates consumed in the diet that are not immediately used for energy are stored as glycogen. Glycogen is stored in the liver and muscle cells and can be broken down into single glucose molecules to provide a rapid source of energy. The amount of stored glycogen can be increased fivefold with physical training (Mahan & Escott-Stump, 2000). **Carbohydrate loading** also increases glycogen stores (refer to "Carbohydrate Loading" on page 176 for more information). Because glycogen contains many water molecules, it is large and bulky and therefore unsuitable for long-term energy storage. Thus, if a person continues to consume more carbohydrates than the body can use or store, the body will convert the sugar into fat for long-term storage.

Protein

Proteins contain 4 calories per gram and are the building blocks of human and animal structure. Proteins serve innumerable functions in the human body, including the following: formation of the brain, nervous system, blood, muscle, skin, and hair; the transport mechanism for iron, **vitamins, minerals,** fats, and oxygen; and the key to acid–base and fluid balance. Proteins form **enzymes,** which speed up chemical reactions to milliseconds that might otherwise take years. Antibodies that the body makes to fight infection are made from proteins. In situations of energy deprivation, the body can break down proteins for energy.

Proteins are built from **amino acids,** which are carbohydrates with a nitrogen-containing amino group and, in some cases sulfur, attached. Proteins, or **polypeptides,** form when amino acids are joined together through **peptide bonds.** Eight to 10 **essential amino acids** cannot be made by the body and must be consumed in the diet. A specific food's protein quality is determined by assessing its essential amino-acid composition, digestibility, and **bioavailability,** or the degree to which the amino acids can be used by the body. Generally, animal products contain all of the essential amino acids (called **complete proteins**), while plant foods do not. One notable exception is soy, which is a plant-based complete protein. Therefore, animal proteins and soy are better sources of quality protein than plants. However, combining complementary incomplete plant proteins that together can provide all of the essential amino acids boosts the protein quality. Excellent combinations include grains-legumes (e.g., rice/beans), grains-dairy (e.g., pasta/cheese), and legumes-seeds (e.g., falafel) (refer to

"Vegetarian Diets" on page 189 for more on **protein complementarity**).

Fats

The most energy-dense of the macro-nutrients, fat provides 9 calories per gram. Ounce for ounce, this is 2.25 times more calories than both carbohydrate and protein. Fats serve many critical functions in the human body, including insulation, cell structure, nerve transmission, vitamin absorption, and **hormone** production. The body stores **adipose tissue** (fat) as **triglyceride. Unsaturated fatty acids** contain one or more double bonds between carbon atoms, are typically liquid at room temperature, and are fairly unstable, making them susceptible to oxidative damage and a shortened shelf life. **Monounsaturated fat** contains one double bond between two carbons. Common sources include olive, canola, and peanut oils. **Polyunsaturated fat** contains a double bond between two or more sets of carbons. Sources include corn, safflower, and soybean oils and cold water fish. **Essential fatty acids** are a type of polyunsaturated fat that must be obtained from the diet. Unlike other fats, the body cannot produce **omega-3 (linolenic acid)** or **omega-6 (linoleic acid) fatty acids**. Omega-3 fatty acids come in three forms: alpha-linolenic acid (ALA), eicosapentaenoic acid (EPA), and docosahexaenoic acid (DHA). ALA is the type of omega-3 found in plants. It can be converted to EPA and DHA in the body, but the research supporting the benefits of ALA is much less compelling than that for EPA and especially DHA. DHA and EPA omega-3 fatty acids are naturally found in egg yolk and cold-water fish and shellfish like tuna, salmon, mackerel, cod, crab, shrimp, and oyster. Overall, omega-3s reduce blood clotting, dilate blood vessels, and reduce inflammation. They are important for eye and brain development (and are especially important for a growing fetus in the late stages of pregnancy); act to reduce **cholesterol** and triglyceride levels; and may help to preserve brain function and reduce the risk of mental illness and attention deficit hyperactivity disorder (ADHD), though more research is needed to confirm these mental

health benefits. Notably, most Americans tend not to get enough omega-3 fatty acids. Though natural food sources are best, people who do not meet this recommendation may benefit from supplementation or from fortified foods. While there is no established **Dietary Reference Intake (DRI)** for the optimal amount of EPA+DHA intake, some expert panels have recommended an intake between 250 and 500 mg per day. This dosage is likely safe and effective to achieve the benefits of the omega-3s without increased risk of complications such as bleeding. Of note, while many products claim to be fortified with omega-3s, it is important for consumers to read the label. If the omega-3s are mostly ALA (as is the case with the omega-3-fortified bread at Subway®), they are unlikely to be optimally converted to EPA and DHA and likely have fewer of the health benefits. If the added omega-3s are of a negligible amount, it is also unlikely that the added cost of the product is worth the limited benefit.

Omega-6, which is generally consumed in abundance, is an essential fatty acid found in flaxseed, canola, and soybean oils and green leaves. It works opposite to omega-3s in that it seems to contribute to inflammation and blood clotting. The balancing act between omega-6 and omega-3 is essential for maintaining normal circulation and other biological processes. In the past, scientists had hypothesized that reducing consumption of omega-6 fatty acids and increasing consumption of omega-3 fatty acids may lower chronic disease risk, but more recent research has shown that maintaining a high consumption of both omega-3 and omega-6 fatty acids has cardiovascular health benefits (Harris, 2010). The American Heart Association recommends that Americans consume 5–10% of calories as omega-6 polyunsaturated fatty acids—that is about 12 g/day for women and 17 g/day for men (Harris et al., 2009).

Some fats—notably **saturated fats** and **trans fats**—lead to clogging of the arteries, increased risk for heart disease, and myriad other problems. **Saturated fatty acids** contain no double bonds between carbon atoms, are typically solid at room temperature, and are very stable. Foods high in saturated fat include red meat, full-fat dairy products, and tropical oils like coconut and palm. Saturated fat increases levels of **low-density lipoprotein (LDL)** cholesterol, the "bad" cholesterol.

Trans fat, which may be listed as "partially hydrogenated" oil on a food ingredient list, results from a manufacturing effort to make unsaturated fat solid at room temperature in order to prolong its shelf life. The process involves breaking the double bond of the unsaturated fat. The product is a heart-damaging fat that increases LDL cholesterol even more than saturated fat. Due to legislation requiring food manufacturers to include the amount of trans fat on the nutrition label if it is more than 0.5 g per serving, many processed foods that used to be high in trans fat, such as chips, crackers, cakes, peanut butter, and margarine, are now "trans-fat free." Clients and participants should be advised to check the label and look on the ingredients list for "partially hydrogenated" oil to determine if a food still contains small amounts of trans fat. If so, they should avoid that food.

Cholesterol, a fat-like, waxy, rigid four-ring structure, plays an important role in **cell membrane** function. It also helps to make bile acids (which are important for fat absorption), metabolize **fat-soluble vitamins** (A, D, E, and K), and make vitamin D and some hormones such as estrogen and testosterone. Saturated fat, converted to cholesterol in the liver, is the main dietary cause of **hypercholesterolemia** (high blood levels of cholesterol), though high levels of cholesterol are also found in animal products such as egg yolks, meat, poultry, fish, and dairy products. Cholesterol causes problems when there is too much of it in the bloodstream. For cholesterol to get from the liver to the body's cells (in the case of endogenously produced cholesterol), or from the small intestine to the liver and adipose tissue (in the case of exogenously consumed cholesterol) it must be transported through the bloodstream.

Because it is fat-soluble, it needs a water-soluble carrier protein to transport it. When the cholesterol combines with this protein en route to the body's cells, it is termed LDL. LDL is susceptible to getting stuck in the bloodstream and clogging the arteries, thus forming a plaque and causing **atherosclerosis.** **High-density lipoprotein (HDL)** cholesterol, the "good cholesterol," removes excess cholesterol from the arteries and carries it back to the liver where it is excreted.

Micronutrient Requirements and Recommendations

The World Health Organization (WHO) refers to micronutrients, so called because they are only needed in small amounts, as the "'magic wands' that enable the body to produce enzymes, hormones, and other substances essential for proper growth and development" (WHO, 2007). When the body is deprived of micronutrients, consequences are severe. But when consumed in just the right amounts, they are key to optimal health and function.

Importantly, though fitness professionals can be a valuable source of nutrition knowledge, when a fitness professionals suspects that an individual may have an inadequate or excessive intake of a particular vitamin or mineral, it is important to refer that individual to a registered dietitian for a nutrition assessment or to the individual's primary care physician. Fitness professionals should avoid advising people to consume specific amounts of food or supplement sources of micronutrients.

Vitamins

Vitamins are **organic,** non-caloric micronutrients that are essential for normal physiologic function. Vitamins must be consumed through food with only three exceptions: vitamin K and biotin can also be produced by normal intestinal flora (bacteria that live in the intestines and are critical for normal gastrointestinal function), and vitamin

D can be self-produced with sun exposure. No "perfect" food contains all the vitamins in just the right amount; rather, a variety of nutrient-dense foods must be consumed to assure adequate vitamin intakes. Many foods (such as breads and cereals) have been fortified with some nutrients to decrease the risk of vitamin deficiency. And some foods contain inactive vitamins—called **provitamins.** Fortunately, the human body contains enzymes to convert these inactive vitamins into active vitamins.

Humans need 13 different vitamins, which are divided into two categories: **water-soluble vitamins** and fat-soluble vitamins. Thiamin, riboflavin, niacin, pantothenic acid, folate, vitamin B6, vitamin B12, biotin, and vitamin C are the water-soluble vitamins. Their solubility in water (which gives them similar absorption and distribution in the body) and their role as **cofactors** of enzymes involved in metabolism (i.e., without them the enzyme will not work) are common traits. With the exception of vitamins B6 and B12, water-soluble vitamins cannot be stored in the body and are readily excreted in urine. This decreases the risk of toxicity from overconsumption and also makes their regular intake a necessity. Folate (vitamin B9; also known as "folic acid" in its supplement form)—named for its abundance in plant foliage (like green leafy vegetables)—deserves special mention due to its crucial role during pregnancy. Folate is essential for production of **deoxyribonucleic acid (DNA),** red and white blood cell formation, **neurotransmitter** formation, and amino-acid metabolism. Deficiency is relatively common, as folate is easily lost during food preparation and cooking and because most people do not eat enough green leafy vegetables. Folate deficiency early in pregnancy can be devastating for a developing fetus, leading to neural tube defects such as spina bifida. Deficiency also causes a megaloblastic **anemia,** skin lesions, and poor growth. Notably, excessive consumption of folate can mask a vitamin B12 deficiency.

Vitamins A, D, E, and K are the fat-soluble vitamins. Often found in fat-containing foods and stored in the liver or adipose tissue until needed, fat-soluble vitamins closely associate with fat. If fat absorption is impaired, so is fat-soluble vitamin absorption. Unlike water-soluble vitamins, fat-soluble vitamins can be stored in the body for extended periods of time and eventually are excreted in feces. This storage capacity increases the risk of toxicity from overconsumption, but also decreases the risk of deficiency.

Choline, called a "quasi-vitamin" because it can be produced in the body but also provides additional benefits through consumption from food, is also important since it plays a crucial role in neurotransmitter and **platelet** function and may help to prevent **Alzheimer's disease** (McDaniel, Maier, & Einstein, 2003). Table 4-1 lists the vitamin's recommended intake level, common food sources, and functions in the human body. See "Dietary Reference Intakes" on page 170 for more on this topic.

Minerals

Serving roles as varied as regulating enzyme activity and maintaining acid–base balance to assisting with strength and growth, minerals are critical for human life. Unlike vitamins, many minerals are found in the body as well as in food. The body's ability to use the minerals is dependent on their bioavailability. Nearly all minerals, with the exception of iron, are absorbed in their free form—that is, in their ionic state unbound to organic molecules and complexes. When bound to a complex, the mineral is considered to not be bioavailable and it will be excreted in feces. Typically, minerals with high bioavailability include sodium, potassium, chloride, iodide, and fluoride. Minerals with low bioavailability include iron, chromium, and manganese. All other minerals, including calcium and magnesium, are of medium bioavailability.

An important consideration when consuming minerals, and particularly when people take mineral supplements, is the possibility of mineral-to-mineral interactions.

Table 4-1

Vitamin Facts

Vitamin	RDA/AI*		Best Sources	Functions
	Men[†]	Women[†]		
A (carotene)	**900 µg**	**700 µg**	Yellow or orange fruits and vegetables, green leafy vegetables, fortified oatmeal, liver, dairy products	Formation and maintenance of skin, hair, and mucous membranes; helps people see in dim light; bone and tooth growth
B1 (thiamin)	**1.2 mg**	**1.1 mg**	Fortified cereals and oatmeals, meats, rice and pasta, whole grains, liver	Helps the body release energy from carbohydrates during metabolism; growth and muscle tone
B2 (riboflavin)	**1.3 mg**	**1.1 mg**	Whole grains, green leafy vegetables, organ meats, milk, eggs	Helps the body release energy from protein, fat, and carbohydrates during metabolism
B6 (pyridoxine)	**1.3 mg**	**1.3 mg**	Fish, poultry, lean meats, bananas, prunes, dried beans, whole grains, avocados	Helps build body tissue and aids in metabolism of protein
B12 (cobalamin)	**2.4 µg**	**2.4 µg**	Meats, milk products, seafood	Aids cell development, functioning of the nervous system, and the metabolism of protein and fat
Biotin	30 µg	30 µg	Cereal/grain products, yeast, legumes, liver	Involved in metabolism of protein, fats, and carbohydrates
Choline	550 mg	425 mg	Milk, liver, eggs, peanuts	A precursor of acetylcholine; essential for liver function
Folate (folacin, folic acid)	**400 µg**	**400 µg[‡]**	Green leafy vegetables, organ meats, dried peas, beans, lentils	Aids in genetic material development; involved in red blood cell production
Niacin	**16 mg**	**14 mg**	Meat, poultry, fish, enriched cereals, peanuts, potatoes, dairy products, eggs	Involved in carbohydrate, protein, and fat metabolism
Pantothenic acid	5 mg	5 mg	Lean meats, whole grains, legumes, vegetables, fruits	Helps release energy from fats and vegetables
C (ascorbic acid)	**90 mg**	**75 mg**	Citrus fruits, berries, and vegetables—especially peppers	Essential for structure of bones, cartilage, muscle, and blood vessels; helps maintain capillaries and gums and aids in absorption of iron
D	5 µg	5 µg	Fortified milk, sunlight, fish, eggs, butter, fortified margarine	Aids in bone and tooth formation; helps maintain heart action and nervous system function
E	**15 mg**	**15 mg**	Fortified and multigrain cereals, nuts, wheat germ, vegetable oils, green leafy vegetables	Protects blood cells, body tissue, and essential fatty acids from destruction in the body
K	120 µg	90 µg	Green leafy vegetables, fruit, dairy, grain products	Essential for blood-clotting functions

* Recommended Dietary Allowances are presented in bold type; Adequate Intakes are presented in non-bolded type.

[†] RDAs and AIs given are for men aged 31–50 and nonpregnant, nonbreastfeeding women aged 31–50; mg = milligrams; µg = micrograms

[‡] This is the amount women of childbearing age should obtain from supplements or fortified foods.

Reprinted with permission from Dietary Reference Intakes (various volumes). Copyright 1997, 1998, 2000, 2001 by the National Academy of Sciences. Courtesy of the National Academies Press, Washington, D.C.

Minerals can interfere with the absorption of other minerals. For example, zinc absorption may be decreased through iron supplementation. Zinc excesses can decrease copper absorption. Too much calcium limits the absorption of manganese, zinc, and iron. When a mineral is not absorbed properly, deficiency may develop.

Serving a variety of functions in the body, minerals are typically categorized as **macrominerals (bulk elements)** and **microminerals (trace elements)**. Macrominerals include calcium, phosphorus, magnesium, sulfur, sodium, chloride, and potassium. Microminerals include iron, iodine, selenium, zinc, and various other minerals that do not have an established DRI and will not be discussed here. See Table 4-2 for mineral DRIs, common food sources, and functions in the human body.

Water

Although it provides no calories and is **inorganic** in nature, water is as important as the oxygen people breathe. Loss of only 20% of total body water may cause death, while a 10% loss causes severe disorders. In general, adults can survive up to 10 days without water, while children can live up to five days (Mahan & Escott-Stump, 2000). Water is the single largest component of the human body, comprising about 50 to 70% of body weight. That is, approximately 85 to 119 lb of a 170-lb man (39 to 54 kg of a 77-kg man) is water weight. Physiologically, this water has many important functions, including regulating body temperature, protecting vital organs, providing a driving force for nutrient absorption, serving as a medium for all biochemical reactions, and maintaining a high blood volume for optimal athletic performance.

Water volume is influenced by a variety of factors, including food and drink intake; sweat, urine, and feces excretion; metabolic production of small amounts of water; and respiratory losses of water that occur with breathing. These factors play an especially important role during exercise when metabolism is increased.

The generated body heat is released through sweat, a solution of water and sodium and other electrolytes. If fluid intake is not increased to replenish the fluid lost, the body attempts to compensate by retaining more water and excreting more concentrated urine; the person is said to be dehydrated. Severe **dehydration** can lead to heat stroke. On the other hand, if someone ingests excessive amounts of fluid to compensate for minimal amounts of water lost in sweat, he or she may become fluid overloaded, or **hyponatremic.** When the blood's water:sodium ratio is severely elevated, excess water can leak into brain tissue, leading to **encephalopathy,** or brain swelling.

Diuretics (whether prescribed for diseases such as **congestive heart failure** or **hypertension** or consumed as beverages such as coffee) increase the excretion of water and electrolytes by the kidneys. The loss of water leads to decreased blood volume, which can predispose an exerciser to dehydration. A person taking a diuretic should be advised to consume ample fluids before, during, and after exercise, especially in warm, humid environments.

The Basic Physiology of Digestion and Absorption

To fully understand the basics of nutrition, fitness professionals not only need to know what the macronutrients do in the body, but also how they are converted from a molecule contained within a piece of food or pill into a usable form. These are the processes of digestion and absorption.

Digestion

The **gastrointestinal tract** forms a long hollow tube from mouth to anus where digestion and absorption occur (Figure 4-1). Digestion takes two forms: **mechanical digestion**—the process of chewing, swallowing, and propelling food through the gastrointestinal tract—and **chemical digestion**—the addition of enzymes that break down nutrients. At the mere sight or smell of a potential meal, the digestive

Table 4-2

Mineral Facts

Mineral	RDA/AI* Men[†]	RDA/AI* Women[†]	Best Sources	Functions
Calcium	1,000 mg	1,000 mg	Milk and milk products	Strong bones, teeth, muscle tissue; regulates heart beat, muscle action, and nerve function; blood clotting
Chromium	35 µg	25 µg	Corn oil, clams, whole-grain cereals, brewer's yeast	Glucose metabolism (energy); increases effectiveness of insulin
Copper	**900 µg**	**900 µg**	Oysters, nuts, organ meats, legumes	Formation of red blood cells; bone growth and health; works with vitamin C to form elastin
Fluoride	4 mg	3 mg	Fluorinated water, teas, marine fish	Stimulates bone formation; inhibits or even reverses dental caries
Iodine	**150 µg**	**150 µg**	Seafood, iodized salt	Component of hormone thyroxine, which controls metabolism
Iron	**8 mg**	**18 mg**	Meats, especially organ meats, legumes	Hemoglobin formation; improves blood quality; increases resistance to stress and disease
Magnesium	**420 mg**	**320 mg**	Nuts, green vegetables, whole grains	Acid/alkaline balance; important in metabolism of carbohydrates, minerals, and sugar (glucose)
Manganese	2.3 mg	1.8 mg	Nuts, whole grains, vegetables, fruits	Enzyme activation; carbohydrate and fat production; sex hormone production; skeletal development
Molybdenum	**45 µg**	**45 µg**	Legumes, grain products, nuts	Functions as a cofactor for a limited number of enzymes in humans
Phosphorus	**700 mg**	**700 mg**	Fish, meat, poultry, eggs, grains	Bone development; important in protein, fat, and carbohydrate utilization
Potassium	4,700 mg	4,700 mg	Lean meat, vegetables, fruits	Fluid balance; controls activity of heart muscle, nervous system, and kidneys
Selenium	**55 µg**	**55 µg**	Seafood, organ meats, lean meats, grains	Protects body tissues against oxidative damage from radiation, pollution, and normal metabolic processing
Zinc	**11 mg**	**8 mg**	Lean meats, liver, eggs, seafood, whole grains	Involved in digestion and metabolism; important in development of reproductive system; aids in healing

* Recommended Dietary Allowances are presented in bold type; Adequate Intakes are presented in non-bolded type.

[†] RDAs and AIs given are for men aged 31–50 and nonpregnant, nonbreastfeeding women aged 31–50; mg = milligrams; µg = micrograms

Reprinted with permission from Dietary Reference Intakes (various volumes). Copyright 1997, 1998, 2000, 2001, 2010 by the National Academy of Sciences. Courtesy of the National Academies Press, Washington, D.C.

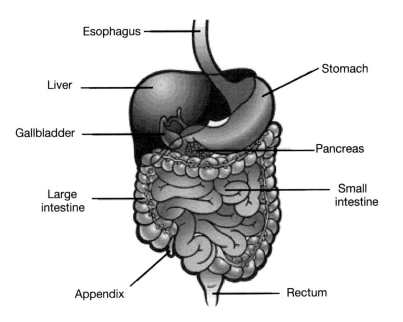

Figure 4-1
The gastrointestinal (GI) tract

This image was provided by KidsHealth, one of the largest resources online for medically reviewed health information written for parents, kids, and teens. www.KidsHealth.org; www.TeensHealth.org. ©1995–2009. The Nemours Foundation/KidsHealth. Reprinted with permission.

system prepares to break down the food into nutrients and usable energy by forming enzyme-rich **saliva.** With the first bite, the saliva begins to digest and moisten the food, forming a **bolus.** Upon swallowing, the food passes through the pharynx to enter the esophagus (the **epiglottis** prevents food from entering the trachea). Muscles in the esophagus push food to the stomach through a wavelike motion called **peristalsis.** The stomach mixes up the food, liquids, and its own digestive juices to physically and chemically break food down into absorbable nutrients and energy. Finally, the stomach empties its contents into the small intestine. The amount of time it takes for the **gastric emptying** depends on the type of food (carbohydrates are emptied the fastest, followed by protein and then fat), the amount of muscle action of the stomach and the receiving small intestine, and several other factors (refer to "Hydration, Gastric Emptying, and Sports Nutrition" on page 181 for additional information).

The gallbladder and pancreas play key roles in digestion, but are not part of the long gastrointestinal tube. With some help from pancreatic digestive juices and bile produced in the liver and stored in the gallbladder, the 22-foot long (6.7 m) small intestine spends about one to four hours further digesting the food, now called **chyme,** and finally absorbing the nutrients and energy into the blood. This blood gets fast-tracked directly to the liver for processing and distribution of nutrients to the rest of the body. All of the waste and indigestibles left over in the small intestine (such as fiber) are passed through the ileocecal valve to the 4-foot long (1.5 m) large intestine, where a few minerals and water are reabsorbed into blood. As more water gets reabsorbed, the waste passing through the colon portion of the large intestine gets harder until it is finally excreted as solid waste from the rectum and anus. Food can stay in the large intestine from hours to days. Total transit time from mouth to anus usually takes anywhere from 18 to 72 hours.

Absorption

Carbohydrates, proteins, lipids, vitamins, and minerals all are absorbed through the walls of the small intestines. To maximize surface area, and thus absorptive capacity, the walls of the small intestine contain many folds and hairlike projections, called **villi** and **microvilli.** These villous structures form a **brush border** where nutrient absorption occurs.

Nutrients are absorbed by different mechanisms depending on their solubility, size, and relative concentration. After passing from the membrane of the small intestine into the bloodstream, sugar, amino acids, water-soluble vitamins, and minerals enter

portal circulation. This system takes nutrients through the bloodstream to the liver. The liver acts to detoxify any harmful substances prior to sending them to the brain or heart. Because broken-down fats that are transported by **chylomicrons** are too large to enter the capillaries, fats and fat-soluble vitamins are transferred into the **lymphatic system** and added to the bloodstream through the thoracic duct, a large lymphatic vein that drains into the heart. Ultimately the nutrients are distributed to muscles, organs, and other tissues.

Federal Dietary Recommendations

Dietary Guidelines

The *2015-2020 Dietary Guidelines*, which are available at www.dietaryguidelines.gov, offer five big-picture recommendations that are key to good nutrition. An overview of these five key recommendations is provided here (U.S. Department of Agriculture, 2015).

Key Guideline 1: Follow a Healthy Eating Pattern Across the Lifespan

All food and beverage choices matter. Choose a healthy eating pattern at an appropriate calorie level to help achieve and maintain a healthy body weight, support nutrient adequacy, and reduce the risk of chronic disease.

The *Guidelines* make a point to emphasize overall eating patterns more so than individual nutrients, recognizing that the overall nutritional value of a person's diet is more than "the sum of its parts." The main components of a healthy eating pattern include:

- A variety of vegetables from five different groups—dark green, red and orange, legumes (beans and peas), starchy, and other
- Fruit
- Grains, primarily whole grains
- Fat-free or low-fat dairy, including milk yogurt, cheese, and/or fortified soy products

- A variety of foods rich in protein, including seafood, lean meats and poultry, eggs, legumes (beans and peas), nuts, seeds, and soy products
- Limited amounts of saturated fats and trans fats (<10% of calories), added sugars (<10% of calories), and sodium (<2,300 mg per day). If alcohol is consumed, it should be consumed in moderation, defined as up to one drink per day for women and two drinks per day for men.

Key Guideline 2: Focus on Variety, Nutrient Density, and Amount

To meet nutrient needs within calorie limits, choose a variety of nutrient-dense foods across and within all food groups in recommended amounts.

The *Guidelines* suggest that Americans are most likely to meet nutrient needs and manage weight by choosing nutrient-dense foods, which provide high levels of vitamins, minerals, and other nutrients that may have health benefits relative to caloric content. Categories of nutrient-dense foods include vegetables, fruits, grains, dairy, protein foods, and oils.

Estimated calorie needs per day according to age, gender, and physical-activity level can be found at www.health.gov/dietaryguidelines/2015/guidelines/appendix-2/.

Key Guideline 3: Limit Calories from Added Sugars and Saturated Fats and Reduce Sodium Intake

Consume an eating pattern low in added sugars, saturated fats, and sodium. Cut back on foods and beverages higher in these components to amounts that fit within healthy eating patterns.

The *Guidelines* urge Americans to pay attention to—and limit—consumption of foods with low to no nutritional value, especially those that are, or may be, harmful to health such as added sugars, saturated fat, and sodium. New to the *2015-2020 Dietary Guidelines* compared to previous editions, dietary cholesterol is no longer noted as a nutrient to limit, as it is likely not harmful to health for most people.

Key Guideline 4: Shift to Healthier Food and Beverage Choices

Choose nutrient-dense foods and beverages across and within all food groups in place of less healthy choices. Consider cultural and personal preferences to make these shifts easier to accomplish and maintain.

While the *Guidelines* advocate an overall healthy and balanced nutrition pattern that is low in added sugars and sodium, the reality is that most Americans eat nothing like the eating patterns recommended by the *Guidelines.* By making shifts in dietary patterns, Americans can achieve and maintain a healthy body weight, meet nutrient needs, and decrease the risk of chronic disease.

Key Guideline 5: Support Healthy Eating Patterns for All

Everyone has a role in helping create and support healthy eating patterns in multiple settings nationwide, from home to school to work to communities.

The *Guidelines* charge all sectors of society to play an active role in the movement to make the United States healthier by developing coordinated partnerships, programs, and policies to support healthy eating.

MyPlate

MyPlate is an interactive online tool (www. ChooseMyPlate.gov) designed to replace the sometimes confusing MyPyramid icon. The goal of MyPlate is to simplify the government's nutrition messages into an easily understood and implemented graphic—a dinner plate divided into four sections: fruits, vegetables, protein, and grains, with a glass of 1% or non-fat milk—and to encourage Americans to eat a more balanced diet that is about 50% fruits and vegetables (Figure 4-2).

Figure 4-2
MyPlate

On the website www.ChooseMyPlate.gov, consumers can input their age, gender, height, weight, and physical-activity level to get an individualized eating plan to meet their caloric needs. The program will calculate estimated energy expenditure based on this demographic information. Within seconds, users will be categorized into one of 12 different energy levels (anywhere from 1,000 to 3,200 calories) and will be given the recommended number of servings—measured in cups and ounces—to eat from each of the five food groups (i.e., vegetables, fruit, protein, grains, and dairy). A set number of discretionary calories (i.e., the leftover calories available for sugar or additional fats or an extra serving from any of the food groups) will also be allocated for that individual. By following these recommendations, users will have the optimal diet for disease prevention and weight maintenance based on their personalized needs.

In general, MyPlate encourages people to:
- Balance calories. People should only eat the amount of calories that the body needs. Physical activity helps to balance calories (this is the only place where physical activity is discussed in the new MyPlate talking points). Individual calorie recommendations are available at www.ChooseMyPlate.gov.
- Enjoy your food, but eat less. The key here is to slow down while eating to truly

enjoy the food (and key in to the body's internal cues of hunger and satiety) and try to minimize distractions like television.

- Avoid oversized portions. MyPlate recommends smaller plates, smaller serving sizes, and more mindful eating.
- Eat more vegetables, fruits, whole grains, and fat-free or 1% milk dairy products for adequate potassium, calcium, vitamin D, and fiber.
- Make half your plate fruits and vegetables. Most Americans need nine servings of fruits and vegetables per day. Few get anywhere near that.
- Switch to fat-free or low-fat (1%) milk. Full-fat dairy products provide excess calories and saturated fat in exchange for no nutritional benefit over fat-free and low-fat versions.
- Make half your grains whole grains (ideally even more than that). This will help to ensure adequate fiber intake and decrease intake of highly processed foods.
- Eat fewer foods high in solid fat (typically saturated and trans fat), added sugars, and salt.
- Compare sodium in foods and then choose the lower sodium versions.
- Drink water instead of sugary drinks to help cut sugar and unnecessary calories.

Online tools and how-to strategies will also become available (see www. ChooseMyPlate.gov to identify the tools currently available). Table 4-3 shows recommended daily amounts of each of the five food groups for a 2000-calorie diet.

Dietary Reference Intakes

In the past, **Recommended Dietary Allowances (RDAs)** were published for the different nutrients based on age and gender. The RDAs were defined as "the levels of intake of essential nutrients that, on the basis of scientific knowledge, are judged by the Food and Nutrition Board to be adequate to meet the known needs of practically all healthy persons." Newer

Table 4-3

MyPlate Recommended Daily Amounts for a 2000-Calorie Diet

Food Group	Daily Average Over 1 Week
Grains	6.2 oz eq
Whole grains	3.8 oz eq
Refined grains	2.4 oz eq
Vegetables	2.6 cups
Vegetable subgroups (amount per week)	
Dark green	1.6 cups per week
Red/orange	5.6 cups
Starchy	5.1 cups
Beans and peas	1.6 cups
Other vegetables	4.1 cups
Fruits	2.1 cups
Dairy	3.1 cups
Protein foods	5.7 oz eq
Seafood	8.8 oz per week
Oils	29 grams
Calories from added fats and sugars	245 calories

Note: oz eq = Ounce equivalents

reference values, known as Dietary Reference Intakes (DRIs), are more descriptive. DRI is a generic term used to refer to three types of reference values:

- RDA
- **Estimated Average Requirement (EAR),** an adequate intake in 50% of an age- and gender-specific group
- **Tolerable Upper Intake Level (UL),** the maximum intake that is unlikely to pose risk of adverse health effects to almost all individuals in an age- and gender-specific group

The term **adequate intake (AI)** is used when a RDA cannot be based on an EAR. Adequate intake is a recommended nutrient intake level that based on research appears to be sufficient for good health.

DRIs have been established for calcium, vitamin D, phosphorus, magnesium, and fluoride; folate and other B vitamins; **antioxidants** (vitamins C and E, selenium);

macronutrients (protein, carbohydrate, fat); trace elements (vitamin A and K, iron, zinc); and electrolytes and water. The complete set of DRIs is available at www.nationalacademies.org.

Food Labels

For people to make healthy nutrition decisions, they first have to be able to understand what nutrients contribute to a healthy diet, and second, know which foods contain those nutrients. While the bulk of a healthy diet is made up of whole, unprocessed foods that do not carry food labels, there are processed or prepared foods (e.g., low-fat milk and milk products) that can be part of a healthy diet and do have food labels. The food label, a required component of nearly all packaged foods, can help people turn knowledge into action (Figure 4-3). It can also be a source of confusion and misunderstanding.

A health and fitness professional can advise individuals to dissect the food label by taking a stepwise approach. Start from the top with the serving size and the number of servings per container. In general, serving sizes are standardized so that consumers can compare similar products. All of the nutrient amounts listed on the food label are for one serving, so it is important to determine how many servings are actually being consumed to accurately assess nutrient intake.

Next, consumers should look at the total calories and calories from fat. The total calories indicate how much energy a person gets from a particular food. Americans tend to consume too many calories, and too many calories from fat, without meeting daily nutrient requirements. This part of the nutrition label is the most important factor for weight control. In general, 40 calories per serving is considered low, 100 calories is moderate, and 400 or more calories is considered high [U.S. Food & Drug Administration (FDA), 2004].

The next two sections of the label note the nutrient content of the food product. Consumers should try to minimize intake of saturated and trans fat and sodium and aim to consume adequate amounts of fiber,

as well as vitamins and minerals, especially vitamin A, vitamin C, calcium, and iron. The food label includes the total amount of sugars (natural and added). Though the label does not separately identify added sugars, natural sugars are found primarily in milk and fruit. Therefore, if the food item does not belong to either of those two food groups, the amount of sugar contained in the product approximates added sugar. For foods that contain milk or fruit, added sugars can be identified in the ingredients list.

The **percent daily values (PDV)** are listed for key nutrients to make it easier to compare products (just make sure that the serving sizes are similar), evaluate nutrient content claims (does 1/3 reduced-sugar cereal really contain less carbohydrate than a similar cereal of a different brand?), and make informed dietary tradeoffs (e.g., balance consumption of a high-fat product for lunch with lower-fat products throughout the rest of the day). In general, 5% daily value or less is considered low, while 20% daily value or more is considered high (FDA, 2004).

The footnote at the bottom of the label reminds consumers that all PDV are based on a 2,000-calorie diet. Individuals who need more or fewer calories should adjust recommendations accordingly. For example, 3 grams of fat provides 5% of the recommended amount for someone on a 2,000-calorie diet, but 7% for someone on a 1,500-calorie diet. The footnote also includes daily values for nutrients to limit (total fat, saturated fat, trans fat, cholesterol, and sodium), recommended carbohydrate intake for a 2,000-calorie diet (60% of calories), and minimal fiber recommendations for 2,000- and 2,500-calorie diets.

Legislation also requires food manufacturers to list all potential food **allergens** on food packaging. The most common food allergens are fish, shellfish, soybean, wheat, egg, milk, peanuts, and tree nuts. This information usually is included near the list of ingredients on the package. Clearly, this information is especially important to clients with food allergies. For clients who follow a gluten-free diet, this is also an easy way to identify if wheat is a product ingredient.

Serving Size
The label presents serving sizes as the amount that most people actually consume in a sitting. This is not necessarily the same as how much one should eat per serving. All of the nutrition information on the label is based on one serving. If you eat one-half of the serving size shown here, cut the nutrient and calorie values in half.

Total Fat
Fat is calorie-dense and, if consumed in large portions, can increase the risk of weight problems. While once vilified, most fat, in and of itself, is not bad.

Cholesterol
Many foods that are high in cholesterol are also high in saturated fat, which can contribute to heart disease. Dietary cholesterol itself likely does not cause health problems.

Sodium
You call it "salt," the label calls it "sodium." Either way, it may add up to high blood pressure in some people. So, keep your sodium intake low—less than 2,300 mg each day. (The American Heart Association recommends no more than 3,000 mg of sodium per day for healthy adults.)

Sugars
Too much sugar contributes to weight gain and increased risk of diseases like diabetes and fatty liver disease. Foods like fruits and dairy products contain natural sugars (fructose and lactose), but also may contain added sugars. It is best to consume no more than 10% of total calories from added sugar, or a total of 50 g per day based on a 2,000-calorie eating plan.

Vitamins and Minerals
Your goal here is 100% of each for the day. Don't count on one food to do it all. Let a combination of foods add up to a winning score.

Nutrition Facts

4 Servings Per Container

Serving Size   ½ cup (114g)

Amount Per Serving
Calories   90

               % Daily Value*

Total Fat 3g	**5%**
Saturated Fat 0g	**0%**
Trans Fat 0g	**0%**
Cholesterol 0mg	**0%**
Sodium 300mg	**13%**
Total Carbohydrate 15g	**4%**
Dietary Fiber 3g	**12%**
Total Sugars 12g	
Includes 10g Added Sugars	**20%**
Protein 3g	
Vitamin D 2mcg	10%
Calcium 260mg	20%
Iron 8mg	45%
Potassium 235mg	6%

* The % Daily Value (DV) tells you how much a nutrient in a serving of food contributes to a daily diet. 2,000 calories a day is used for general nutrition advice.

Daily Value
Daily Values are listed based on a 2,000-calorie daily eating plan. Your calorie and nutrient needs may be a little bit more or less based on your age, sex, and activity level (see https://fnic.nal.usda.gov/fnic/interactiveDRI/). For saturated fat, sugars and added sugars, and sodium, choose foods with a low % Daily Value. For dietary fiber, vitamins, and minerals, your Daily Value goal is to reach 100% of each.

Ingredients: *This portion of the label lists all of the foods and additives contained in a product, in order from the most prevalent ingredient to the least.*

Allergens: *This portion of the label identifies which of the most common allergens may be present in the product.*

(More nutrients may be listed on some labels)

mg = milligrams (1,000 mg = 1 g)
g = grams (about 28 g = 1 ounce)

Calories
Are you trying to lose weight? Cut back a little on calories. Look here to see how a serving of the food adds to your daily total. A 5'4", 138-lb active woman needs about 2,200 calories each day. A 5'10", 174-lb active man needs about 2,900.

Saturated Fat
Saturated fat is part of the total fat in food. It is listed separately because it is an important player in raising blood cholesterol and your risk of heart disease. Eat less!

Trans Fat
Trans fat works a lot like saturated fat, except it is worse. This fat starts out as a liquid unsaturated fat, but then food manufacturers add some hydrogen to it, turning it into a solid saturated fat (that is what "partially hydrogenated" means when you see it in the food ingredients). They do this to increase the shelf-life of the product, but in the body the trans fat damages the blood vessels and contributes to increasing blood cholesterol and the risk of heart disease.

Total Carbohydrate
Carbohydrates are in foods like bread, potatoes, fruits, and vegetables, as well as processed foods. Carbohydrate is further broken down into dietary fiber and sugars. Consume foods high in fiber often and those high in sugars, especially added sugars, less often.

Dietary Fiber
Grandmother called it "roughage," but her advice to eat more is still up-to-date! That goes for both soluble and insoluble kinds of dietary fiber. Fruits, vegetables, whole-grain foods, beans, and peas are all good sources and can help reduce the risk of heart disease and cancer.

Protein
Most Americans get more than they need. Eat small servings of lean meat, fish, and poultry. Use skim or low-fat milk, yogurt, and cheese. Try vegetable proteins like beans, grains, and cereals.

Figure 4-3
How to read a food nutrition label

Carefully review the ingredient list. Note that the ingredient list is in decreasing order of substance weight in the product. That is, the ingredients that are listed first are the most abundant ingredients in the product. The ingredient list is useful to help identify whether or not the product contains trans fat, solid fats, added sugars, whole grains, and refined grains.

- *Trans fat:* Although trans fat is included in the "fat" section of the nutrition label, if the product contains <0.5 grams per serving, the manufacturer does not need to claim it. However, if a product contains "partially hydrogenated oils," then the product contains trans fat.
- *Solid fats:* If the ingredient list contains beef fat, butter, chicken fat, coconut oil, cream, hydrogenated oils, palm kernel oils, pork fat (lard), shortening, or stick margarine, then the product contains solid fats.
- *Added sugars:* Ingredients signifying added sugars are listed in Table 4-4. In many cases, products contain multiple forms of sugar.
- *Whole grains*: To be considered 100% whole grain, the product must contain all of the essential parts of the original kernel—the bran, germ, and endosperm. When choosing products, the whole grain should be the first or second ingredient. Examples of whole grains include brown rice, buckwheat, bulgur (cracked wheat), millet, oatmeal, popcorn, quinoa, rolled oats, whole-grain sorghum, whole-grain triticale, whole-grain barley, whole-grain corn, whole oats/oatmeal, whole rye, whole wheat, and wild rice.
- *Refined grains:* Refined grains are listed as "enriched." If the first ingredient is an enriched grain, then the product is not a whole grain. This is one way to understand whether or not a "wheat bread" is actually whole wheat or a refined product.

Table 4-4
The Many Ways to Say Sugar

Agave syrup	Fructose	Molasses
Anhydrous dextrose	Fruit juice concentrate	Nectar
Brown sugar	Fruit nectar	Pancake syrup
Cane juice	Glucose	Raw sugar
Confectioner's powdered sugar	High-fructose corn syrup	Sucrose
Corn sweetener	Honey	Sugar
Corn syrup	Invert sugar	Sugar cane juice
Corn syrup solids	Lactose	Trehalose
Crystal dextrose	Liquid fructose	Turbinado sugar
Dextrin	Malt syrup	White granulated sugar
Dextrose	Maltose	
Evaporated corn sweetener	Maple syrup	

Nutrition Label Sample Problem

Using the nutrition label from Figure 4-3, determine (1) the number of calories per container; (2) the calories from carbohydrate, protein, and fat per serving; and (3) the percentage of calories from carbohydrate, protein, and fat.

1. 90 calories per serving x 4 servings per container = 360 calories per container

2. *Carbohydrate:* 13 g carbohydrate per serving x 4 calories per gram = 52 calories per serving from carbohydrate

   Protein: 3 g protein per serving x 4 calories per gram = 12 calories per serving from protein

   Fat: 3 g fat per serving x 9 calories per gram = 27 calories per serving from fat

   [*Note:* The nutrition label does this calculation for you and lists the calories from fat on the label. On this label, it states that the product contains the rounded number 30 calories from fat vs. the calculated 27 calories from fat. Also note that the total calories is 91 per the calculations but the label rounds to 90.]

3. *Carbohydrate:* 52 calories from carbohydrate/90 calories = 57% carbohydrate

   Protein: 12 calories from protein/90 calories = 13% protein

   Fat: 27 calories from fat/90 calories = 30% fat

Energy Balance and Weight Control

The *Dietary Guidelines* highlight that the key to weight control is to balance caloric intake from food and beverages with caloric expenditure. When more calories are consumed than expended, an individual is in **positive energy balance.** Positive energy balance is necessary during times of growth such as in infancy, childhood, and pregnancy. Otherwise, positive energy balance results in weight gain. When more calories are expended than consumed, an individual is in **negative energy balance,** which is necessary for weight loss.

Determining Energy Needs

Fitness professionals can help their clients and class participants achieve their weight-loss goals by first determining daily energy needs using the energy expenditure calculator at www. ChooseMyPlate.gov or by utlizing the Mifflin-St. Jeor equation, a fairly accurate estimation of **resting metabolic rate (RMR)** (Frankenfield, Routh-Yousey, & Compher, 2005):

Mifflin-St. Jeor Equation

For men: RMR = 9.99 x wt (kg) + 6.25 x ht (cm) – 4.92 x age (yrs) + 5

For women: RMR = 9.99 x wt (kg) + 6.25 x ht (cm) – 4.92 x age (yrs) – 161

(*Note:* Convert pounds to kilograms by dividing by 2.2; convert inches to centimeters by multiplying by 2.54)

The RMR value derived from the prediction equation is then multiplied by the appropriate activity correction factor:

- Sedentary (little or no exercise): 1.200
- Lightly active (light exercise/sports one to three days per week): 1.375
- Moderately active (moderate exercise/sports six to seven days per week): 1.550
- Very active (hard exercise/sports six to seven days per week): 1.725
- Extra active (very hard exercise/sports and a physical job): 1.900

Note: This equation is more accurate for obese than non-obese individuals.

Note: 1 kg = 2.2 lb; 1 inch = 2.54 cm

The RMR represents the number of calories needed to fuel ventilation, blood circulation, and temperature regulation. Calories are also required to digest and absorb consumed food and fuel the activities of daily life. For weight maintenance, moderately active people are generally advised to consume about 1.550 times the calculated RMR (ADA, 2009). For example, a 30-year-old female who is 5'6" (168 cm), weighs 145 pounds (66 kg), and engages in 40 to 60 minutes of vigorous physical activity most days of the week would maintain her weight with an intake of 2,100 calories per day.

After determining an individual's approximate caloric intake for weight maintenance, the fitness professional should develop an exercise program that creates a sufficient energy deficit to help him or her reach those goals. Individuals trying to lose weight aim for a 500-calorie deficit per day, achieved through decreased caloric intake and/ or increased physical activity. Over the course of a week, the 3,500-calorie deficit should lead to a loss of 1 pound. For optimal long-term success and overall health, gradual weight loss of no more than 1 to 2 pounds per week is best. Fitness professionals should encourage people to consult www.ChooseMyPlate.gov or a registered dietitian if they would like help developing an individualized nutrition plan to complement their fitness program.

Dietary and Lifestyle Approaches to Weight Loss

Most people understand that the most effective way to lose weight is to eat less and exercise more. Still, people are always looking for the newest, quickest, and most popular diet. From super-low-fat and severely carbohydrate-restricted diets to meal replacements and strict calorie counting, every method has its followers. On the other hand, every diet also has people who have failed to achieve their weight-loss goals. This section discusses some of the research on popular diets, though fitness professionals may benefit most from learning how to evaluate popular diets in general (see "Frequently Asked

Questions" on page 192).

A randomized trial, the "gold standard" in research design, compared the following diet plans in more than 300 premenopausal, **overweight,** or obese women:

- Atkins® (very low carbohydrate)
- LEARN® (Lifestyle, Exercise, Attitudes, Relationships, and Nutrition) (low-fat, high-carbohydrate plan based on national recommendations)
- Ornish® (very high carbohydrate)
- Zone® (low carbohydrate)

At 12 months, the Atkins dieters came out ahead, with a modest 10-pound (4.5-kg) weight loss (Gardner et al., 2007). The unimpressive amount of weight loss reflects how people struggle to stick to rigid dietary restrictions, though it is worth noting that even a 5 to 10% weight loss confers significant health benefits (National Institutes of Health, 1998).

A study of 60,000 male and female participants of Jenny Craig®, a commercial weight-loss program, found that those who followed the program for one year lost 16% of their body weight. But only 6.6% of the original dieters stuck with the program for that long (Finley et al., 2007). Another study found that people who ate a 100- to 300-calorie meal replacement per day (such as a nutrition bar or formulated milk shake meal) maintained a substantial (8.4% ± 0.8%) weight loss at four years (Flechtner-Mors et al., 2000). Dansinger et al. (2005) made the following conclusion after a one-year randomized trial to assess the adherence rate and effectiveness of the Atkins, Ornish, Weight Watchers®, and Zone diets: While any of these diets can yield short-term benefit in terms of weight loss and improvements in cardiovascular risk profile, adherence is the primary factor in determining permanent weight management.

The National Weight Control Registry (NWCR) (www.nwcr.ws), a database that tracks more than 5,000 people who have lost at least 30 pounds (13.6 kg) and maintained the loss for at least one year, has uncovered an abundance of tried-and-true tips to help people lose weight and keep it off. Results from several observational research studies further highlight what works and what does not. The following are 10 insights that fitness professionals can offer their clients or class participants:

- *Control portions:* Twenty years ago, a standard cup of coffee with whole milk and sugar was 8 oz and 45 calories. Today, a 16-oz Grande Mocha Frappuccino at Starbucks® adds up to 380 calories. To burn the extra calories, a person would have to walk for an hour. A typical muffin was 1.5 ounces and 200 calories. Today it is 5 ounces and 500 calories— the difference equates to 90 minutes of vacuuming [National Heart, Lung, and Blood Institute (NHLBI), 2004]. As standard portions have gotten larger, so have Americans. The only remedy is to pay attention to serving sizes. Successful "losers" control portions. In fact, some research suggests that portion control is the greatest predictor of successful weight loss (Rogue et al., 2004). Fitness professionals can help people control portions by teaching them to read nutrition labels, carefully measure out servings, eat only one helping, use smaller serving dishes, and resist the urge to "clean the plate."
- *Be mindful:* Encourage people to eat when they are hungry and stop when they are full. That means paying attention to everything they eat. People should ask themselves: Do I eat when I am bored, stressed, sad, tired, and sometimes even when I am full? Emotional eating can wreak havoc on a well-planned weight-management program. People should ask themselves "why" before heading to the pantry.
- *Exercise:* More than 94% of participants in the National Weight Control Registry increased physical activity in their effort to lose weight (NWCR, 2008). In fact, many reported walking for at least one hour per day. And exercise was crucial for those who kept the weight off. People who dropped their fitness programs put on the pounds (NWCR, 2008). As people lose weight, a proportion of each pound

comes from muscle. That slows down metabolism and makes it difficult to keep the weight off. While walking and other cardiovascular exercise is important for burning calories, fitness professionals should be sure to recommend a resistance-training program to preserve lean tissue and maintain metabolic rate.

- *Check the scale:* While it is not advisable to become obsessive about weight to the nearest 0.01 pounds, people who maintain their weight loss keep tabs on the scale, weighing themselves at least once per week. This way they are able to identify small weight increases in time to take appropriate corrective action (NWCR, 2008).

- *Eat breakfast:* Of all NWCR participants, 78% eat breakfast daily, while only 4% never do (Wyatt et al., 2002). And research suggests that breakfast eaters weigh less and suffer from fewer chronic diseases than non-breakfast eaters (Timlin & Pereira, 2007).

- *Monitor intake:* One of the strongest predictors of successful and maintained lifestyle change is monitoring dietary intake (Tinkler et al., 2007). While some people may find it tedious, keeping a food log is a highly effective and proven strategy.

- *Turn off the tube:* Time spent watching TV is time spent: (1) being completely **sedentary** and thus expending minimal amounts of calories; and (2) eating. Most people mindlessly consume snacks while mesmerized in front of the television, not noticing the rapidly multiplying calorie intake. Successful NWCR "losers" watch less than 10 hours of television per week (Raynor et al., 2006).

- *Do not wait until tomorrow to get started— and no cheating:* It is easy to put off starting a serious lifestyle change to a later date. Likewise, it is also easy to "cheat" and eat an extra piece of cake here, a pizza buffet there. But people who do not consistently give themselves a day or two off to cheat are 150% more likely to maintain their weight loss (Gorin et al., 2004). Encourage people to adopt a healthy lifestyle that they can stick with so they do not often feel compelling urges to unwittingly sabotage their weight-management success.

- *Know thy friend:* A study of 12,000 people followed over 30 years concluded that **obesity** spreads through social ties (Christakis & Fowler, 2007). That is, obese people tend to have obese friends. Pairs of friends and siblings of the same sex seem to have the most profound effect. The study authors suspect that the spread of obesity has a lot to do with an individual's general perception of the social norms regarding the acceptability of obesity. The logic works like this: If my best friend and my sister are both obese and I love and admire them all the same, then maybe it is not so bad that I gain a few pounds. People can reverse this psychological phenomenon by inviting pals to work out at the gym or go for a bike ride to stay or get fit.

- *Be optimistic!* Research suggests that people who are optimistic—that is, they have perceived control, positive expectations, empowerment, a fighting spirit, and a lack of helplessness—are more successful at changing behaviors and losing weight (Tinkler et al., 2007).

Nutrition and Hydration Needs for Active Adults

Active adults require conscientious fueling and refueling to maintain optimal performance and overall health. The Institute of Medicine's (IOM) 2005 Dietary Reference Intakes (DRI) recommend that approximately 45 to 65% of calories come from carbohydrates, 10 to 35% from protein, and 20 to 35% from fats (IOM Food and Energy Board, 2005). Although active individuals require ample carbohydrates to maintain blood glucose during exercise and replace muscle glycogen expended during exercise, as well as increased protein for muscle repair, research suggests that active individuals do not need a greater *percentage* of calories from carbohydrate or protein than the average population. However, they are able meet increased demands by a greater overall caloric intake (ADA, 2009).

Carbohydrates and Sports Nutrition

The EAR for carbohydrates is 100 grams (about seven servings) for children and non-pregnant, non-lactating adults; 135 grams (about nine servings) for pregnant women; and 160 grams (about 11 servings) for lactating women. The American Dietetic Association recommends that athletes consume 6 to 10 g/kg (3 to 5 g/lb) of body weight per day depending on their total daily energy expenditure, type of exercise performed, gender, and environmental conditions to maintain blood glucose levels during exercise and to replace muscle glycogen (ADA, 2009).

Carbohydrate Loading

Individuals training for long-distance endurance events lasting more than 90 minutes, such as a marathon or triathlon, may benefit from carbohydrate loading in the days or weeks prior to competition. Eating more carbohydrates helps muscles store more carbohydrates in the form of glycogen. If more glycogen is stored, it will take longer to deplete the body's preferred energy source during a prolonged workout. This effort to maximize available glycogen on race day is the same reason that fitness professionals advise people to taper their workout duration as they approach an event. Fitness professionals should warn clients and class participants that they may gain a few pounds while carbohydrate loading because carbohydrates require a lot of water for storage. Those individuals who are serious about optimizing sports performance may consider a consultation with a sports nutritionist to help them adopt the most appropriate dietary plan and carbohydrate loading regimen.

While various carbohydrate loading regimens exist, the following is a one-week sample plan:

- Days 1–3: Moderate-carbohydrate diet (50% of calories)

- Days 4–6: High-carbohydrate diet (80% of calories). This should be about 4.5 grams of carbohydrate per pound (0.45 kg) of body weight. For a 170-lb (77.2-kg) man, that is 765 grams, or a whopping 3,000 calories from carbohydrates per day.
- Day 7—Competitive event: Pre-event meal (typically dinner the night before the event) with >80% of calories from carbohydrates

Fueling for Exercise

A small snack before strenuous or prolonged exercise will help the individual optimize the training session. The food should be something that is relatively high in carbohydrate to maximize blood glucose availability, relatively low in fat and fiber to minimize gastrointestinal distress and facilitate gastric emptying, moderate in protein, and well-tolerated by the individual. Many people prefer a banana or granola bar, for example.

During extended training sessions, exercisers should consume 30 to 60 grams of carbohydrate per hour of training to maintain blood glucose levels. This is especially important for training sessions lasting longer than one hour; exercise in extreme heat, cold, or high altitude; and when the athlete did not consume adequate amounts of food or drink prior to the training session (ADA, 2009). After exercise, individuals should focus on carbohydrates and protein. Studies show that the best meals for post-workout refueling include an abundance of carbohydrates accompanied by some protein (Figure 4-4). The carbohydrates replenish the used-up energy that is normally stored as glycogen in muscle and liver. The protein helps to rebuild the muscles that were fatigued with exercise. The ADA recommends a carbohydrate intake of 1.0 to 1.5 g/kg of body weight in the first 30 minutes after exercise and then every two hours for four to six hours (ADA, 2009). Certainly, the amount of refueling necessary depends on the intensity and duration of the training session. Fitness professionals should remind people to eat as soon after exercising as possible, preferably within 30 minutes. This is the time when

Figure 4-4
Performance-enhancing post-workout snacks and meals

The following meal ideas provide ample carbohydrate and protein for refueling after an extended early-morning workout. The serving amounts are approximations based on a typical restaurant breakfast.	This sample post-workout plan is for late-starters who ate before their prolonged endurance workout, but still want the performance benefits of post-workout refueling. The snacks should be spaced approximately one to two hours apart:
French toast: Two slices of French toast with powdered sugar, strawberries, and light syrup; two turkey links; and a glass of orange juice • Carbohydrates: 80 grams • Protein: 17 grams • Calories: 510	Snack 1: In the first several minutes after exercise, consume 16 ounces of a sports drink, a power gel, and a medium banana. This snack quickly begins to replenish muscle carbohydrate stores. • Carbohydrates: 73 grams • Protein: 1 gram • Calories: 288
Egg muffin: One poached egg with toasted whole-grain English muffin and low-fat slice of cheese; a glass of low-fat chocolate milk; and an orange • Carbohydrates: 74 grams • Protein: 25 grams • Calories: 490	Snack 2: 12 ounces of orange juice and ¼-cup of raisins • Carbohydrates: 70 grams • Protein: 3 grams • Calories: 295
Oatmeal with fruit: One cup of oatmeal with dried fruit, brown sugar, and skim milk; one egg (sunny side up); and a glass of cranberry juice • Carbohydrates: 80 grams • Protein: 17 grams • Calories: 480	Small meal appetizer: Salad with spinach, tomatoes, chick peas, green beans, and tuna and a whole-grain baguette • Carbohydrates: 69 grams • Protein: 37 grams • Calories: 489
Elvis bagel sandwich: Whole-grain bagel with peanut butter and banana; a glass of water with lemon • Carbohydrates: 76 grams • Protein: 19 grams • Calories: 510	Small meal main course: Whole-grain pasta with diced tomatoes • Carbohydrates: 67 grams • Protein: 2 grams • Calories: 292
Omelet: Egg white omelet with tomatoes, spinach, and feta or mozzarella cheese; two slices of whole-wheat toast with jelly; low-fat yogurt with granola; and a glass of tomato juice • Carbohydrates: 72 grams • Protein: 30 grams • Calories: 490	Dessert: One cup of frozen yogurt and berries • Carbohydrates: 61 grams • Protein: 8 grams • Calories: 280

the muscles are best able to replenish energy stores, enabling the body to prepare for the next workout.

Glycemic Index

As far as refueling goes, not all carbohydrates are created equal. Historically, much debate has centered around whether consumption of simple or complex carbohydrates is better for athletic performance. The role of a particular carbohydrate in athletic performance may be better determined by its **glycemic index (GI)** than its structure. GI ranks carbohydrates based on their blood glucose response: High-GI foods break down rapidly, causing a large glucose spike; low-GI foods are digested more slowly and cause a smaller glucose increase. **Glycemic load (GL)** accounts for GI as well as portion size (GL = GI x grams of carbohydrate). Research suggests that a diet based on consumption of high-GI carbohydrates promotes greater glycogen storage following strenuous exercise (Jentjens & Jeukendrup, 2003). On the other hand, a low-GI eating plan may be better for weight loss (Thomas, Elliott, & Baur, 2007) and for people with **diabetes** (Brand-Miller et al., 2003). Overall, high-GI glucose-rich foods are good for refueling and athletic performance, but as far as heart health goes, lower-GI foods and fruits may be a better choice. The goal is to find a balance. The GI values of various foods are shown in Table 4-5.

Table 4-5

Glycemic Index (GI) of Various Foods

High GI ≥70	Medium GI 56–69	Low GI ≤55
White bread	Rye bread	Pumpernickel bread
Corn Flakes®	Shredded Wheat®	All Bran®
Graham crackers	Ice cream	Plain yogurt
Dried fruit	Blueberries	Strawberries
Instant white rice	Refined pasta	Oatmeal

Protein and Sports Nutrition

Resistance training and cardiovascular exercise induce beneficial muscular and structural damage. As protein helps the muscles and tissues to repair and rebuild themselves, the American Dietetic Association, Dietitians of Canada, and the American College of Sports Medicine reckon that athletes have higher protein needs than the general population and recommend that endurance- and strength-trained athletes consume from 1.2 to 1.7 g/kg (0.5 to 0.8 g/lb) of body weight per day (ADA, 2009). However, a 2005 report from the Institute of Medicine concluded that the scientific evidence for increased requirements for active individuals was not compelling, and suggested that 0.8

g/kg per day was appropriate for athletes and the general population (IOM Food and Energy Board, 2005).

Notably, as Wolfe and Miller argued in a 2008 commentary published in the *Journal of the American Medical Association*, much confusion surrounds the IOM protein recommendations, which the authors note have been widely misinterpreted. The protein intake of 0.8 g/kg/day reflects the RDA, which by definition is the *minimum* daily intake level that meets the nutrient requirements of nearly all healthy individuals; it is not an ideal or maximal level. They note that a variety of studies have shown that higher levels of protein intake benefit muscle mass, strength, and function; bone health; maintenance of energy balance; cardiovascular function; and wound health (Wolfe & Miller, 2008). The authors suggest that the ideal protein intake should be based on the **Acceptable Macronutrient Distribution Range (AMDR),** published in the same IOM document (IOM Food and Energy Board, 2005), of 10 to 35% of daily energy intake (Wolfe & Miller, 2008). Table 4-6 shows the total protein intake at various levels of energy intake within the AMDR for protein.

Protein plays important roles in endurance and resistance-training exercise. Both modes of exercise stimulate muscle protein synthesis (Phillips, 2006), which is further enhanced with consumption of protein around the time of exercise (Hayes & Cribb, 2008). Consumption of protein immediately post-exercise helps in the repair and synthesis of muscle proteins

Table 4-6

Protein Intake (grams) at Various Levels of Energy Intake

Energy intake (kcal/d)	Low-protein diet (<10% kcal)	Average diet (~15% kcal)	High-protein diet (≥20% kcal)	Very-high protein diet (≥30% kcal)
1200	30	45	60	90
2000	50	75	100	150
3000	75	112	150	225

Note: Each gram of protein contains 4 calories.

Reprinted with permission from American Heart Association, Inc.; St. Jeor, S.T. et al. (2001). Dietary protein and weight reduction: A statement for healthcare professionals from the nutrition committee of the Council on Nutrition, Physical Activity, and Metabolism of the American Heart Association. *Circulation, 104,* 1869–1874.

(ADA, 2009). For endurance athletes who may struggle to consume adequate calories to fuel extended training sessions, or for the average exerciser striving to lose weight, research suggests that protein helps to preserve lean muscle mass and assure that the majority of weight lost comes from fat (Phillips, 2006). While these may seem like great reasons to consume high amounts of protein, it is worth noting that protein metabolism likely becomes more efficient with exercise training, thus lending support to the IOM assertion that athletes do not have increased protein needs compared to the more sedentary population (IOM Food and Energy Board, 2005). Further, beyond a certain level of protein intake at which the body has achieved its maximal ability to utilize amino acids to build muscle, any excess protein will be broken down into amino acids and converted to carbohydrate or fat in the liver (ADA, 2009).

Choosing Healthy Proteins

Many factors come into play when choosing a protein source: protein quality, health benefits, dietary restrictions, cost, convenience, and taste—to name a few. While the same protein may not be best for everyone, keeping a few considerations in mind can help people reap maximum benefit from their protein intake.

- *Protein quality varies:* Several scales are used to evaluate protein quality, including the protein efficiency ratio, biological value, net protein utilization, and the **protein digestibility corrected amino acid score (PDCAAS).** The PDCAAS is the most accepted and widely used of the scales. In the PDCAAS, protein quality is calculated through a somewhat complex mathematical formulation that gives each protein food a score determined by its chemical score (essential amino acid content in a protein food divided by the amino acid content in a reference protein food) multiplied by its digestibility. The proteins with highest PDCAAS score are casein, egg, milk, whey, and soy proteins (all 1.0). Beef comes in next (0.92), followed by black beans (0.75), peanuts

(0.52), and wheat gluten (0.25) (Hoffman & Falvo, 2004). Overall, with the exception of soy, the highest quality proteins—whey, casein, egg, and milk—typically come from animal sources such as egg, milk, meat, fish, and poultry. Casein, egg, milk, whey, and soy contain all of the essential amino acids and are easily digestible and absorbed. Fruits, vegetables, grains, and nuts are **incomplete proteins** and must be consumed in complementary combinations over the course of a day to assure intake of each of the essential amino acids.

- *Protein is not the only consideration:* It is important to remember the other non-protein health benefits and harms from consuming certain foods. For example, while beef is a fairly good protein source, it is also high in saturated fat and calories, which can be detrimental to other health goals. The following is an example offered by the Harvard School of Public Health (2008): A 6-ounce broiled porterhouse steak that contains 38 grams of protein is an excellent source of protein. But it also delivers 44 grams of fat, 16 of them saturated. That is almost three-fourths of the recommended daily intake for saturated fat. The same amount of salmon gives you 34 grams of protein and 18 grams of fat, 4 of them saturated. A cup of cooked lentils has 18 grams of protein, but less than 1 gram of fat.

- *Different proteins are best at different times:* For example, whey protein is rapidly digested, resulting in a short burst of amino acids into the bloodstream, while casein is slowly digested, resulting in a slower but more prolonged release of amino acids (Dangin et al., 2002). If the goal is for amino acids to be readily available for muscle regeneration immediately following a workout, exercisers can time protein intake accordingly.

A carefully planned high-protein diet poses few health risks and even benefits cardiovascular health. However, individuals with pre-existing disease such as kidney disease, **osteoporosis,** diabetes, and liver disease should consult with their physicians prior to adopting a high-protein diet (St. Jeor et al., 2001).

Protein and Amino Acid Supplementation

Many people use protein supplements to boost protein intake and assure consumption of a particular protein type or amino acid. For example, some people believe that branched-chain amino acids (leucine, isoleucine, valine) may enhance endurance by delaying the onset of **central nervous system** fatigue and contributing to increased energy availability. Others have found that, following exercise, the branched-chain amino acids, especially leucine, increase the rate of protein synthesis and decrease the rate of protein **catabolism** (Blomstrand et al., 2006). The billion-dollar supplement industry has been quick to respond; many supplement retailers carry at least four different leucine supplements ranging in price from $25 to $60 per container. However, because the research findings are inconsistent and little is known about the safety of these products, the ADA advises against individual amino acid supplementation and protein supplementation overall (ADA, 2009). In general, while some supplements may in fact provide beneficial effects, consumers should purchase and use these products cautiously, as they are not closely regulated by the Food and Drug Administration (FDA) and may prove harmful or, as in the case of ephedra, even deadly. Importantly, no matter how safe a supplement seems, fitness professionals should never recommend supplements to anyone.

Evaluating High-protein Diets

Fitness professionals can help their clients evaluate high-protein diets by keeping the following considerations in mind:

- Total protein intake should not be excessive and should be reasonably proportional (~15% of total caloric intake) to carbohydrate (~55% of total caloric intake) and fat (~30% of total caloric intake) (St. Jeor et al., 2001).
- Not all protein is created equal. Other than soy, vegetable proteins are incomplete proteins. **Vegetarians** and those who eat limited amounts of animal products should be sure to consume a wide variety of high-protein vegetarian foods.
- Carbohydrates should not be omitted or severely restricted, especially for athletes who need large amounts of carbohydrate to fuel optimal performance. A minimum of 100 g of carbohydrate per day is recommended (St. Jeor et al., 2001). Fitness professionals should refer individuals to a registered dietitian for help designing a balanced high-protein diet, if appropriate.
- Selected protein foods should not contribute excess total fat or saturated fat (St. Jeor et al., 2001).
- The eating plan should be safely implemented and provide adequate nutrients (St. Jeor et al., 2001). Fitness professionals should be careful not to advocate a particular "diet."
- Fitness professionals should recommend that protein intake come from whole

ACE Position Statement on Nutritional Supplements

It is the position of the American Council on Exercise (ACE) that it is outside the defined scope of practice of a fitness professional to recommend, prescribe, sell, or supply nutritional supplements to clients. Recommending supplements without possessing the requisite qualifications (e.g., R.D.) can place the client's health at risk and possibly expose the fitness professional to disciplinary action and litigation. If a client wants to take supplements, a fitness professional should work in conjunction with a qualified registered dietitian or medical doctor to provide safe and effective nutritional education and recommendations.

ACE recognizes that some fitness and health clubs encourage or require their employees to sell nutritional supplements. If this is a condition of employment, fitness professionals should protect themselves by ensuring their employers possess adequate insurance coverage for them should a problem arise. Furthermore, ACE strongly encourages continuing education on diet and nutrition for all fitness professionals.

foods rather than supplements (ADA, 2009). If someone expresses continued interest in supplementation, the fitness professional should recommend that he or she discuss the pros and cons with a registered dietitian.

Fats and Sports Nutrition

Fat is an important source of energy, fat-soluble vitamins, and essential fatty acids. The ADA (2009) recommends that athletes consume a comparable proportion of food from fat as the general population—that is, 20 to 25% of total calories. There is no evidence for performance benefit from a very low-fat diet (<15% of total calories) or from a high-fat diet. A complete discussion of the role of fat in maintaining optimal health and fat's impact on blood lipids is presented in the "Fats" section on page 161.

Hydration, Gastric Emptying, and Sports Nutrition

Fluid and Hydration for Optimal Performance

Acutely aware of the health and performance effects of dehydration, health and fitness experts have long warned recreational exercise enthusiasts and athletes alike to hydrate continuously. But the latest research reveals that **hyponatremia**—or severely reduced blood sodium concentration resulting from overhydration—may be of equal or greater concern than dehydration. ACSM and the United States Track and Field Association (USATF) have developed guidelines for optimal hydration during exercise (Table 4-7).

People should also adhere to the following guidelines (Casa, Clarkson, & Roberts, 2005):

- *Use thirst to determine fluid needs:* Advise clients to drink when they are thirsty and stop drinking when they feel hydrated.
- *Aim for a 1:1 ratio of fluid replacement to fluid lost in sweat:* Ideally, people should consume the same amount of fluid as is lost in sweat. Exercisers can compare pre- and post-exercise body weight. Perfect hydration occurs when no weight is lost or gained during exercise. Because people sweat at varying rates, the typical recommendation to consume 3 to 6 ounces of water for every 20 minutes of exercise may not be appropriate for everyone. However, when individual assessment is not possible, this recommendation works for most people. Experts advise slightly less for slower, smaller athletes in mild environmental conditions and slightly more for competitive athletes working at higher intensities in warmer environments (Noakes, 2003).
- *Measure fluid amounts:* When exercisers know how much they are actually drinking, they may be able to better assess if they are consuming appropriate amounts.
- *Drink fluids with sodium during prolonged exercise sessions:* If an exercise session lasts longer than two hours or an athlete is participating in an event that stimulates heavy sodium loss (defined as more than 3 to 4 grams of sodium), experts recommend that the athlete drink a sports drink that contains elevated levels of sodium (Coyle, 2004). Note that researchers did not find a benefit from sports drinks that contained only the 18 mmol/L (100 mg/8 oz) of sodium typical of most sports drinks and thus concluded that higher levels would be needed to prevent hyponatremia during prolonged exercise (Almond et al., 2005). Alternatively, exercisers can consume extra sodium with meals and snacks prior to a lengthy exercise session or a day of extensive physical activity (Casa, 2003).
- *Drink carbohydrate-containing sports drinks to reduce fatigue:* With prolonged exercise,

Table 4-7
Fluid-intake Recommendations During Exercise
2 hours prior to exercise, drink 500–600 mL (17–20 oz)
Every 10–20 minutes during exercise, drink 200–300 mL (7–10 oz) or, preferably, drink based on sweat losses
Following exercise, drink 450–675 mL for every 0.5 kg body weight lost (or 16–24 oz for every pound)

Data from: Casa, D.J. et al. (2000). National Athletic Trainers' Association: Position statement: Fluid replacement for athletes. *Journal of Athletic Training,* 35, 212–224.

muscle glycogen stores become depleted and blood glucose becomes a primary fuel source. To maintain performance levels and prevent fatigue, consume drinks and snacks that provide about 30 to 60 g of rapidly absorbed carbohydrate for every hour of training (Coyle, 2004). As long as the carbohydrate concentration is less than about 6 to 8%, it will have little effect on gastric emptying (Coombes & Hamilton, 2000).

• *Hydrate appropriately pre- and post-event:* To maximize pre-event hydration, USATF recommends consuming 17 to 20 ounces of water or sports drink two to three hours before exercise and 10 to 12 ounces of water or sports drink within 10 minutes of beginning exercise. Following exercise, the athlete should aim to correct any fluid imbalances that occurred during the exercise session. This includes consuming water to restore hydration, carbohydrates to replenish glycogen stores, and electrolytes to speed rehydration (Casa, 2003). Those at greatest risk of hyponatremia should be careful not to consume too much water following exercise and instead should focus on replenishing sodium.

• *Pay attention to environmental conditions:* Athletes who are well-acclimatized to heat will have decreased sodium losses in sweat, which lowers their risk of hyponatremia (Casa, 2003). Risk of heat stroke is elevated in conditions of elevated temperature and humidity and little or no wind due to the diminished ability of the body to dissipate heat into the environment (Noakes, 2003).

The human body is well-equipped to withstand dramatic variations in fluid intake during exercise and at rest with little or no detrimental health effects. For this reason, most recreational exercisers will never suffer from serious hyponatremia or dehydration and should not be alarmed. It is under extreme situations of prolonged or very high-intensity exercise in excessive heat and humidity that risk elevates. And even then, if athletes replenish sweat loss with equal amounts of fluid, hydration problems can be avoided.

The Gut and Gastric Emptying

The gastrointestinal (GI) system must rapidly digest and absorb fluids and nutrients that fuel exercise. Many exercise-induced GI complaints, such as cramps, reflux, heartburn, bloating, side-stitch, gas, nausea, vomiting, the urge to defecate, loose stool, bloody stool, and diarrhea, occur in response to: (1) reduced gastric emptying; (2) delayed transit time; or (3) decreased blood flow. Knowledge of factors that affect the GI system's ability to adapt to exercise-induced stresses can help to prevent GI upset and optimize athletic performance.

Gastric emptying refers to the passage of food and fluid from the stomach to the small intestine for further digestion and absorption. When gastric emptying is reduced, food sloshes around in the stomach for longer, leading to various GI disturbances. High-intensity exercise (>70% $\dot{V}O_2max$); dehydration; **hyperthermia;** and consumption of high-energy (>7% carbohydrate), hypertonic drinks slow gastric emptying. On the other hand, low- to moderate-intensity exercise helps to speed digestion by stimulating intestinal muscles to contract and push more food waste through the digestive system. Endurance-trained athletes enjoy faster gastric emptying than their untrained counterparts. This translates into quicker energy availability and decreased GI discomfort following fueling (Murray, 2006).

Exercise-induced sympathetic stimulation diverts blood flow from the GI system to the heart, lungs, and working muscles. The higher the exercise intensity, the more blood flow and colonic tone decrease, which causes waste to accumulate in the colon and rectum. The high amount of waste at the end of the GI tract may signal the stomach to slow down, leading to reduced gastric emptying and prolonged transit time. A bulky high-fiber snack increases intestinal distention and water content, contributing to decreased gastric emptying as well as discomforts such as loose stool and an urge to defecate. Notably, trained subjects experience higher blood flow to the gut at any given exercise intensity compared to untrained subjects (Murray, 2006). See Table 4-8 for practical suggestions on how to prepare the gut for an athletic competition.

Table 4-8

Practical Tips to Prepare the Gut for Competition

- Get fit and acclimatized to heat.

- Stay hydrated.

- Practice drinking during training to improve race-day comfort.

- Avoid over-nutrition before and during exercise.

- Avoid high-energy, hypertonic food and drinks before (within 30–60 minutes) and after exercise. Limit protein and fat intake before exercise.

- Ingest a high-energy, high-carbohydrate diet.

- Avoid high-fiber foods before exercise.

- Limit nonsteroidal anti-inflammatory drugs (NSAIDs), alcohol, caffeine, antibiotics, and nutritional supplements before and during exercise. Experiment during training to identify triggers.

- Urinate and defecate prior to exercise.

- Consult a physician if gastrointestinal problems persist, especially abdominal pain, diarrhea, or bloody stool.

Data from: Brouns, F. & Beckers, E. (1993). Is the gut an athletic organ? *Sports Medicine,* 15, 242–257.

Heart Disease

Coronary heart disease, a leading killer of both men and women in the United States, develops from atherosclerosis, or an accumulation of fat and cholesterol in the lining of the arteries that supply oxygen and nutrients to the heart muscle. Over time, blood flow is reduced and oxygenation to the heart can become limited, leading to **angina** (chest pain) and **myocardial infarction** (heart attack). Though atherosclerosis usually is not deadly until middle age and beyond, it begins to develop in childhood (McMahan et al., 2006; Haust, 1990). High blood cholesterol levels—in particular, LDL—and cholesterol's susceptibility to **oxidation** are main culprits in the development of atherosclerosis. Cholesterol, **lipoproteins,** and triglycerides—

all factors important in the development of heart disease—are discussed in more detail in the "Fats" section on page 161.

Fitness professionals can play an important role in helping people minimize their **cardiovascular disease** risk by educating them about risk factors and encouraging them to talk with their physicians about their own personal risk (Figure 4-5). It is important to

- What is my risk for heart disease?

- What is my blood pressure? What does it mean for me, and what do I need to do about it?

- What are my cholesterol numbers? (These include total cholesterol, LDL "bad" cholesterol, HDL "good" cholesterol, and triglycerides.) What do they mean for me, and what do I need to do about them?

- What are my body mass index (BMI) and waist measurement? Do they indicate that I need to lose weight for my health?

- What is my blood sugar level? Does it mean that I'm at risk for diabetes?

- What other screening tests for heart disease do I need? How often should I return for checkups for my heart health?

- For smokers: What can you do to help me quit smoking?

- How much physical activity do I need to help protect my heart? What kinds of activities are helpful?

- What is a heart-healthy eating plan for me? Should I see a registered dietitian or qualified nutritionist to learn more about healthy eating?

- How can I tell if I'm having a heart attack?

U.S. Department of Health & Human Services, National Institutes of Health, & National Heart, Lung, and Blood Institute (2005). *Your Guide to a Healthy Heart.* NIH Publication No. 06-5269.

Figure 4-5
Questions that exercisers should ask their doctors

emphasize the importance of keeping close tabs on risk factors, not only for older adults who may have already developed one or more risk factors and now must vigorously work to reverse them, or at least prevent their progression, but also for younger individuals who appear to be perfectly healthy.

Regardless of a person's overall risk, everyone should be encouraged to follow these nutrition recommendations to optimize heart health:

- Eat a diet rich in fruits and vegetables, whole grains, and high-fiber foods.
- Consume fish (in particular oily fish like salmon, trout, and tuna) at least twice per week.
- Limit saturated fat to <10% of total caloric intake (preferably <7%), alcohol to no more than one drink per day, and sodium intake to <2.3 g/day (1 tsp of salt).
- Keep trans fat intake as low as possible.

Studies have shown that following these basic dietary recommendations leads to beneficial changes in reported dietary intake as well as measurable decreases in blood pressure, total cholesterol, and LDL cholesterol (Brunner et al., 2007). Still, implementation is overwhelming and extremely difficult for many people. In fact, only 3% of Americans eat healthfully, engage in regular physical activity, maintain a healthy weight, and do not smoke (Sandmaier, 2007). MyPlate (www.ChooseMyPlate.gov) offers many resources to help people get started, but if this is not enough, fitness professionals should consider referring clients or class participants to a registered dietitian.

Special Nutrition Considerations

A well-balanced eating plan often extends beyond a one-size-fits-all dietary recommendation. At certain times, some individuals need slightly modified dietary recommendations to best meet their health, lifestyle, nutritional, and cultural needs.

Obesity

Obesity is described as a **body mass index (BMI)** of ≥30 kg/m^2, a measurement based solely upon height and weight. While not a perfect measure of body fatness, it accurately categorizes most people. Obesity results from an imbalance of caloric intake and caloric expenditure. It makes sense that obesity treatments target either decreased caloric intake (or in some cases, decreased absorption of calories consumed) or increased caloric expenditure either via increased exercise or by revving up the body's metabolism. In all, there are four potential treatment options: dietary changes, lifestyle changes including exercise and behavioral modification, medications, and surgery. The dietary and lifestyle changes that help prevent or treat obesity are discussed earlier in this chapter.

While pills are never a "quick fix" for an unhealthy lifestyle, in some cases medications may be beneficial for people who are not successful with improved eating and exercise habits. Research suggests that overweight or obese people who eat healthfully, exercise regularly, and take a weight-loss medication may lose more weight than those who use the drug alone or lifestyle treatment alone at one year (Wadden et al., 2005). The two most well-studied weight-loss medications are sibutramine and orlistat. Sibutramine (Meridia®) works by decreasing appetite. It costs about $100 per month, and on average leads to a 10-lb (4.4-kg) weight loss. It is available by prescription only. Orlistat (Xenical® and Alli®) blocks fat absorption. While orlistat used to be available by prescription only, Alli now can be purchased over the counter. Weight loss is modest— about 6 pounds (2.7 kg)—and the cost reaches about $170 per month for the prescription version (Li et al., 2005). In general, an effective weight-loss medication will lead to a 4-lb (1.8-kg)loss within four weeks.

When dietary, lifestyle, and pharmacological approaches do not work, some people may benefit from weight-loss surgery. Ideal candidates are severely obese

(BMI >40); have a BMI >35 with other high-risk conditions, such as diabetes, sleep apnea, or life-threatening cardiopulmonary problems; have an "acceptable" operative risk determined by age, degree of obesity, and other pre-existing medical conditions; have been previously unsuccessful at weight loss with a program integrating diet, exercise, behavior modification, and psychological support; and are carefully selected by a multidisciplinary team that has medical, surgical, psychiatric, and nutritional expertise (Consensus Development Conference Panel, 1991). Weight-loss surgery is not recommended for the overweight or mildly obese person who is trying to lose 20 or 30 lb (9.1 to 13.6 kg). Furthermore, only those individuals who are committed to permanent lifestyle changes—including regular physical activity and a healthy diet—are considered good candidates for surgery (Consensus Development Conference Panel, 1991).

Childhood Obesity

It is no secret that the United States faces an epidemic of childhood obesity. Obesity prevalence among children increased from 5% in the 1960s to 17% in 2004 (Ogden et al., 2006). Black girls (24%), Mexican-American boys (22%), and children from lower-income communities with little access to healthful foods and physical-activity opportunities suffer the highest rates (Ogden et al., 2006). While genes and environment both contribute to obesity risk, the increasing prevalence of childhood obesity has occurred too rapidly to be explained by a genetic shift; rather, changes in physical activity and nutrition are responsible (Barlow et al., 2007).

As with adults, behavior-based weight loss and subsequent weight maintenance prove to be extremely challenging for children. In fact, obesity in childhood, especially among older children and those with the highest BMIs, is likely to persist into adulthood (Whitaker et al., 1997). Social marginalization, **type 2 diabetes,** cardiovascular disease, and myriad other morbidities are real threats for overweight children during childhood and into adulthood (Lobstein, Baur, & Uauy, 2004). Alarmed by these sobering statistics, stakeholders—including fitness professionals—have responded with the development of numerous policies, programs, and interventions aimed to prevent childhood obesity. In fact, the American College of Sports Medicine ranked an increase in childhood obesity prevention programs number two in its list of worldwide fitness trends in 2009 (Thompson, 2008). Nutrition recommendations for children are discussed in "Nutrition in Childhood and Adolescence" on page 190.

Hypertension

Hypertension is defined as having a **systolic blood pressure (SBP)** of ≥140 mmHg, a **diastolic blood pressure (DBP)** of ≥90 mmHg, and/or being on anti-hypertensive medication. According to these criteria, approximately 73 million individuals in the United States and 1 billion individuals worldwide have hypertension [American Heart Association (AHA), 2007]. Millions more are **prehypertensive,** with a blood pressure greater than 120/80 mmHg [Centers for Disease Control and Prevention (CDC), 2004]. Hypertension is the leading cause of **stroke** in the United States, and therefore blood pressure should be carefully controlled. While prescription medications are highly effective in reducing blood pressure, nutrition and physical activity are also important in the treatment and prevention of hypertension. In fact, multiple studies have shown that the **Dietary Approaches to Stop Hypertension (DASH) eating plan** combined with decreased salt intake can substantially reduce blood pressure levels and potentially make blood-pressure medications unnecessary (Champagne, 2006).

The DASH eating plan, while developed to reduce blood pressure, is an overall healthy eating plan that can be adopted by anyone regardless of whether he or she has elevated blood pressure. In fact, some studies suggest that the DASH eating plan may also reduce coronary heart disease risk by lowering total cholesterol and LDL cholesterol in addition to lowering blood pressure (Champagne, 2006). The eating plan is low in saturated fat and total fat. The staples are fruits, vegetables, and low-fat dairy products. Fish, poultry, nuts, and other unsaturated fats as well as whole grains are also encouraged. Red meat, sweets, and sugar-containing beverages are very limited. Table 4-9 describes the DASH eating plan in more detail.

Table 4-9

The DASH Eating Plan

Food Group	Daily Servings (except as noted)	Serving Sizes	Examples and Note	Significance of Each Food Group to the DASH Eating Plan
Grains and grain products	7–8	1 slice bread 1 oz dry cereal* ½ cup cooked rice, pasta, or cereal	Whole-wheat bread, English muffin, pita bread, bagel, cereals, grits, oatmeal, crackers, unsalted pretzels, popcorn	Major sources of energy and fiber
Vegetables	4–5	1 cup raw leafy vegetable ½ cup cooked vegetable 6 oz vegetable juice	Tomatoes, potatoes, carrots, green peas, squash, broccoli, turnip greens, collards, kale, spinach, artichokes, green beans, lima beans, sweet potatoes	Rich sources of potassium, magnesium, and fiber
Fruits	4–5	6 oz fruit juice 1 medium fruit ¼ cup dried fruit ½ cup fresh, frozen, or canned fruit	Apricots, bananas, dates, grapes, orange juice, grapefruit, grapefruit juice, mangoes, melons, peaches, pineapples, prunes, raisins, strawberries, tangerines	Important sources of potassium, magnesium, and fiber
Low-fat or fat-free dairy foods	2–3	8 oz milk 1 cup yogurt 1½ oz cheese	Fat-free (skim) or low-fat (1%) milk, fat-free or low-fat buttermilk, fat-free or low-fat regular or frozen yogurt, low-fat and fat-free cheese	Major sources of calcium and protein
Meats, poultry, and fish	2 or less	3 oz cooked meats, poultry, or fish	Select only lean; trim away visible fats; broil, roast, or boil, instead of frying; remove skin from poultry	Rich sources of protein and magnesium
Nuts, seeds, and dry beans	4–5 per week	⅓ cup or 1½ oz nuts 2 Tbsp or ½ oz seeds ½ cup cooked dry beans	Almonds, filberts, mixed nuts, peanuts, walnuts, sunflower seeds, kidney beans, lentils, peas	Rich sources of energy, magnesium, potassium, protein, and fiber
Fats and oils†	2–3	1 tsp soft margarine 1 Tbsp low-fat mayonnaise 2 Tbsp light salad dressing 1 tsp vegetable oil	Soft margarine, low-fat mayonnaise, light salad dressing, vegetable oil (e.g., olive, corn, canola, or safflower)	DASH has 27% of calories as fat, including fat in or added to foods
Sweets	5 per week	1 Tbsp sugar 1 Tbsp jelly or jam ½ oz jelly beans 8 oz lemonade	Maple syrup, sugar, jelly, jam, fruit-flavored gelatin, jelly beans, hard candy, fruit punch, sorbets, ices	Sweets should be low in fat

* Equals ½–1¼ cups, depending on cereal type. Check the product's Nutrition Facts label.

† Fat content changes serving counts for fats and oils. For example, 1 Tbsp of regular salad dressing equals one serving; 1 Tbsp of a low-fat dressing equals ½ a serving; 1 Tbsp of a fat-free dressing equals 0 servings.

Source: National Heart Lung and Blood Institute of the National Institutes of Health

Diabetes

According to the Centers for Disease Control and Prevention (2005), an estimated 21 million people in the United States have diabetes, with more than 6 million undiagnosed cases, while prevalence is approximately 7.0% of the population. **Diabetes mellitus** is a condition that results from abnormal regulation of blood glucose. **Type 1 diabetes** results from the inability of the pancreas to secrete **insulin,** the hormone that allows the cells to take up glucose from the bloodstream. Type 2 diabetes results from the cells' decreased ability to respond to insulin. In most cases, the nutrition recommendations for individuals with diabetes closely resemble the *Dietary Guidelines.* However, it is especially important for people with diabetes to balance nutrition intake with exercise and insulin or other medications in order to maintain a regular blood sugar level throughout the day. In addition, people who have diabetes should consume five to six equally sized small meals to maintain healthy blood sugar levels throughout the day. All individuals with diabetes who have not already had a comprehensive nutrition consultation prior to beginning an exercise program should be referred to a registered dietitian for an evaluation and nutrition teaching.

Osteoporosis

Osteoporosis is defined as a weakening of the bones, which can lead to bone fracture of the hip, spine, and other skeletal sites. It is estimated that more than 50% of all women and 20% of all men over the age of 50 will suffer an osteoporotic fracture at some time in their lives (U.S. Department of Health & Human Services, 2004). The disease most often affects elderly women, although it can occur in men and younger women. Nutrition therapy for the prevention and treatment of osteoporosis includes adequate calcium intake, which is modestly correlated with **bone mineral density,** and adequate vitamin D intake. Vitamin D deficiency is associated with higher bone turnover, reduced calcium absorption, and decreased bone mass. Adequate vitamin K (found primarily in green leafy vegetables and some vegetable oils) intake might also help decrease fracture risk (Cockayne et al., 2006). Smoking and a sedentary lifestyle also increase the risk of osteoporosis, while engaging in weightbearing physical activity decreases the risk (Mahan & Escott-Stump, 2000).

Pregnancy and Lactation

Good nutrition habits during pregnancy optimize maternal health and reduce the risk for some birth defects, suboptimal fetal growth and development, and chronic health problems in the developing child. According to the American Dietetic Association (2008), the key components of a health-promoting lifestyle during pregnancy include:

- *Appropriate weight gain:* The Institute of Medicine (IOM) recommends that women with a BMI <18.5 gain 28 to 40 pounds (12.7 to 18.2 kg), a BMI of 18.5 to 24.9 gain 25 to 35 pounds (11.4 to 15.9 kg), a BMI of 25.9 to 29.9 gain 15 to 25 pounds (6.8 to 11.4 kg), and a BMI of >30 gain 11 to 20 pounds (5.0 to 9.1 kg) (IOM, 2009).

- *Appropriate physical activity:* Pregnant women should aim to incorporate 30 minutes or more of moderate-intensity physical activity appropriate for pregnancy on most, if not all, days of the week (ADA, 2008).

- *Consumption of a variety of foods and calories in accordance with the Dietary Guidelines for Americans:* MyPlate offers specialized guidance for optimal nutrition for pregnant and lactating women (www.ChooseMyPlate.gov). Women do not have increased caloric needs until the second trimester, at which time needs increase by 340 calories per day. Women need an additional 450 calories above baseline in the third trimester.

- *Appropriate and timely vitamin and mineral supplementation:* Pregnant women need 600 µg of folic acid daily from fortified foods or supplements in addition to food forms of folate from a varied diet (ADA, 2008). Folic acid reduces the risk of neural tube defects if taken prior to conception through the sixth week of pregnancy and may reduce birth defects if taken later in pregnancy. Many pregnant women suffer from iron-deficiency anemia and may benefit from iron supplementation.

- *Avoidance of alcohol, tobacco, and other harmful substances:* Pregnant women should avoid caffeine intakes above 300 mg/day due to increased risk of delayed conception, miscarriage, and low birth weight (ADA, 2008).
- *Safe food handling:* Pregnant women and their fetuses are at higher risk of developing foodborne illness and should take extra precautions to prevent consumption of contaminated foods by avoiding:
  ✓ Soft cheeses not made with pasteurized milk
  ✓ Deli meats, unless they have been reheated to steaming hot
  ✓ Raw or unpasteurized milk or milk products, raw eggs, raw or undercooked meat, unpasteurized juice, raw sprouts, and raw or undercooked fish
  ✓ Cat litter boxes
  ✓ Handling pets when preparing foods
  ✓ Shark, swordfish, king mackerel, or tilefish. Pregnant women can safely consume 12 ounces or less of fish or shellfish per week, provided that it is low in mercury, such as shrimp, canned light tuna, salmon, pollock, and catfish. Consumption of albacore tuna should be limited to 6 ounces or less per week.

Prior to the child's birth, most women will make the decision as to whether they plan to breastfeed. Breastfeeding is thought to provide optimal nutrition and health protection for the first six months of life. From six to 12 months, breastfeeding combined with the introduction of complementary foods is optimal (ADA, 2005a). Women who breastfeed require approximately 500 additional calories per day for weight maintenance. Thus, breastfeeding generally facilitates postpartum weight loss. ACE-certified Fitness Professionals can help women achieve postpartum weight loss by reinforcing the positive nutrition changes made during pregnancy, such as increased fruit, vegetable, and whole-grain consumption. Also, fitness professionals should facilitate entry or re-entry into a regular physical-activity program.

Vegetarian Diets

A growing number of Americans are vegetarians, meaning that they do not eat meat, fish, poultry, or products containing these foods. Vegetarian diets come in several forms, all of which are healthful, nutritionally adequate, and effective in disease prevention if carefully planned. A **lacto-ovo-vegetarian** does not eat meat, fish, or poultry. A **lacto-vegetarian** does not eat eggs, meat, fish, or poultry. A **vegan** does not consume any animal products, including dairy products such as milk and cheese.

Vegetarian diets provide several health advantages. They are low in saturated fat and animal protein and high in fiber, folate, vitamins C and E, carotenoids, and some **phytochemicals.** Compared to omnivores, vegetarians have lower rates of obesity, death from cardiovascular disease, hypertension, type 2 diabetes, and prostate and colon cancer. However, if poorly planned, vegetarian diets may include insufficient amounts of protein, iron, vitamin B12, vitamin D, calcium, and other nutrients (ADA, 2003).

Quality protein intake is crucial for vegetarians. A main determinant of protein quality is whether a food contains all of the essential amino acids. Most meat-based products are higher-quality proteins because they have varying amounts of the essential amino acids, while plant proteins other than soy are incomplete proteins because they do not contain all eight to 10 essential

Figure 4-6
Protein complementarity chart

Adapted with permission from Lappé, F.M. (1992). *Diet for a Small Planet.* New York: Ballantine Books.

amino acids. However, complementary plant products such as rice and beans together provide all essential amino acids. Research suggests that most vegetarians consume adequate amounts of complementary plant proteins throughout the day to meet their protein needs. Thus, the complementary proteins do not need to be consumed in the same meal (Figure 4-6) (ADA, 2003).

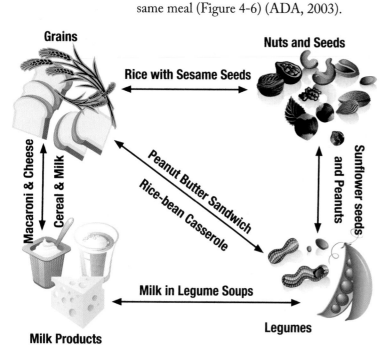

Grains

Nuts and Seeds

Rice with Sesame Seeds

Macaroni & Cheese

Cereal & Milk

Peanut Butter Sandwich

Rice-bean Casserole

Sunflower seeds and Peanuts

Milk in Legume Soups

Milk Products

Legumes

Too few well-conducted research studies exist to determine whether or not a vegetarian diet affects athletic performance (Venderley & Campbell, 2006). However, if vegetarian athletes do not consume enough calories to fuel exercise, performance may suffer. Some suggestions to increase caloric intake include the following:

- Eat more frequent meals and snacks
- Include meat alternatives
- Add dried fruit, seeds, nuts, and other healthful calorie-dense foods

Eating Disorders

Most fitness professionals will at some point face the challenge of helping someone overcome the powerful grips of an eating disorder such as **anorexia nervosa, bulimia nervosa, binge eating disorder,** or other disordered eating. Fitness professionals and coaches who work with young people and others at risk for eating disorders

play a critically important role in helping prevent the onset of an obsession with weight, body image, and exercise. The National Eating Disorders Association (www.nationaleatingdisorders.org) offers the following tips for coaches and fitness professionals to help prevent eating disorders:

- Take warning signs seriously. If a fitness professional believes that someone may have an eating disorder, he or she should share those concerns in an open, direct, and sensitive manner, keeping in mind the following "don'ts" when confronting someone with a suspected eating or exercise disorder: Don't oversimplify, diagnose, become the person's therapist, provide exercise advice without first helping the individual get professional help, or get into a battle of wills if the person denies having a problem.
- De-emphasize weight. Fitness professionals should not weigh individuals they suspect may have an eating disorder. They should also eliminate comments about weight.
- Do not assume that reducing body fat or weight will improve performance.
- Help other fitness professionals recognize the signs of eating disorders and be prepared to address them.
- Provide accurate information about weight, weight loss, body composition, nutrition, and sports performance. Have a broad network of referrals (such as physicians and registered dietitians) that may also be able to help educate individuals when appropriate.
- Emphasize the health risks of low weight, especially for female athletes with menstrual irregularities (in which case, referral to a physician, preferably one who specializes in eating disorders, is warranted).
- Avoid making any derogatory comments about weight or body composition to or about anyone.
- Do not curtail athletic performance and gym privileges to an athlete or exerciser who is found to have eating problems

unless medically necessary. Consider the individual's physical and emotional health and self-image when deciding how to modify exercise participation level.

- Strive to promote a positive self-image and self-esteem in exercisers and athletes.
- Carefully assess one's own assumptions and beliefs as they relate to self-image, body composition, exercise, and dieting.

In addition to being a source of help and **empathy,** fitness professionals can play an important role in developing structured exercise programs for people recovering from eating and exercise disorders who have already sought help from a qualified medical professional. An important first step is to develop a partnership with the individual's treating physician. Seek medical clearance and general recommendations from the physician regarding the maximal duration and intensity of exercise. Note that individuals with a BMI of less than 20 may not receive clearance to exercise until they gain a specified amount of weight. When working with the individual, emphasize the positive psychological and health benefits of appropriate exercise and minimize focus on appearances and weight. Fitness professionals should always strive to develop a balanced and well-rounded program that includes cardiovascular training, resistance training, and flexibility exercises. The goal is to help the individual learn how to exercise in moderation.

Nutrition in Childhood and Adolescence

The American Academy of Pediatrics (AAP) and the AHA recommend a diet rich in fruits, vegetables, whole grains, low-fat and non-fat dairy products, beans, fish, and lean meat for children and adolescents as well as adults (AHA et al., 2006). Strategies to implement these recommendations include the following:

- Balance dietary calories with physical activity to maintain normal growth.
- Perform 60 minutes of moderate to vigorous play or physical activity daily.
- Eat vegetables and fruit daily, and limit juice intake.
- Use vegetable oils and soft margarines low in saturated fat and trans fatty acids instead of butter or most other animal fats in the diet.
- Eat whole-grain breads and cereals rather than refined-grain products.
- Reduce intake of sugar-sweetened beverages and foods.
- Use non-fat (skim) or low-fat milk and dairy products daily.
- Eat more fish, especially oily fish, broiled or baked.
- Reduce salt intake, including salt from processed foods.

As with adults, a wide gap exists between nutrition recommendations for children and what children actually eat. Compared to the recent past, children and adolescents eat breakfast less often, away from home more often, a greater proportion of calories from snacks, more fried and nutrient-poor foods, greater portion sizes, fewer fruits and vegetables, excess sodium, and more sweetened beverages and fewer dairy products (French, Story, & Jeffrey, 2001). As a result, children and especially adolescents eat smaller amounts of many nutrients such as calcium and potassium than the recommended values (IOM, 2004). Some tips for helping children improve nutrition habits are listed in Table 4-10.

Adolescents face unique nutritional challenges due to rapid bone growth and other maturational changes associated with the onset of puberty. While caloric and some micronutrient needs increase to fuel growth, adolescence is also a time of decreasing physical activity for many teens and increased independence when making food choices. With the ready access to soda machines in schools, fast food restaurants on most corners, and peer and media pressure to eat fat- and sugar-laden foods, many teens eat more calories than they expend and are at greater risk for obesity. While

Table 4-10

Improving Nutrition in Young Children

- Parents choose meal times, not children.

- Provide a wide variety of nutrient-dense foods such as fruits and vegetables instead of high-energy-density/nutrient-poor foods such as salty snacks, ice cream, fried foods, cookies, and sweetened beverages.

- Pay attention to portion size; serve portions appropriate for the child's size and age.

- Use nonfat or low-fat dairy products as sources of calcium and protein.

- Limit snacking during sedentary behavior or in response to boredom and particularly restrict the use of sweet/sweetened beverages as snacks (e.g., juice, soda, sports drinks).

- Limit sedentary behaviors, with no more than one to two hours per day of video screen/television and no television sets in children's bedrooms.

- Allow self-regulation of total caloric intake in the presence of normal BMI or weight for height.

- Have regular family meals to promote social interaction and role model food-related behavior.

Reprinted with permission from American Heart Association, Inc.; American Heart Association et al. (2006). Dietary recommendations for children and adolescents: A guide for practitioners. *Pediatrics,* 117, 544–559.

the *Dietary Guidelines* and MyPlate provide scientifically sound nutrition guidelines for teens, any nutrition advice offered must be individualized and consistent with the teen's readiness to change if it is to be successful (AHA et al., 2006).

Nutrition in Aging

Optimal nutrition choices are important for successful aging, which is defined as the ability to maintain a low risk of disease, high mental and physical function, and active engagement in life (Rowe & Kahn, 1998). In fact, research suggests that eating a nutritious diet, engaging in regular physical activity, and not smoking are more important than genetics in terms of helping people avoid the deteriorating effects of aging (CDC, 2008).

While the U.S. suffers from an epidemic of obesity at least partly due to excessive caloric intake, many older adults are at risk of inadequate caloric intake to supply adequate nutrients. Appetite often decreases with age, and as a result many older adults do not consume enough of some nutrients, including calcium, zinc, iron, and B vitamins.

The decreased appetite likely is due to a combination of decreased taste and smell and altered appetite and satiety regulation. Older adults are also at risk of dehydration resulting from a blunted thirst sensation, decreased functioning of the kidneys, medication side effects, and other factors.

Though caloric intake may decrease, many older adults still are overweight or obese, since a decrease in physical activity and metabolic rate with aging is often more pronounced than reduced caloric intake. This leads to positive energy balance and weight gain.

The ADA recommends that older adults consume a variety of healthful foods, including vegetables, fruit, whole grain, poultry, fish, and low-fat dairy, to assure adequate nutrient intake, and also adopt a healthful eating plan such as the DASH or Mediterranean-style eating plan to control chronic disease (ADA, 2005b). Nutrient supplementation may be necessary for some older adults with poor dietary intake. In these situations, referral to a registered dietitian is prudent.

Scope of Practice

While a registered dietitian is best trained to provide specific and individualized eating plans, an ACE-certified Fitness Professional can use well-established guidelines to help individuals adopt healthful and appropriate nutrition habits. Many people may have medical diagnoses that require special nutrition recommendations beyond those discussed in the government guidelines. In these cases, it is advisable that the person work closely with his or her physician and a registered dietitian to develop an individualized eating plan. The role of a fitness professional will often be to provide support and encouragement for the individual to follow the recommended plan. This is especially important when working with individuals with complex medical histories and special nutritional requirements and needs.

While the certified fitness professional's competencies include *knowledge of* basic nutrition and weight-management information, fitness professionals are not expected to—and should not—*calculate, outline, counsel,* or *prescribe* individual nutrition or weight-management plans. As several lawsuits have demonstrated, fitness professionals tread especially treacherous waters if they recommend supplements or other risky substances (Sass et al., 2007).

Ohio legislators passed a statute in 2006 titled the "Unauthorized Practice of Dietetics" that may serve as a useful example to help clarify scope of practice for "nonlicensed individuals"—that is, individuals with occasion to discuss nutrition but without the registered dietitian credential and state license, where necessary (31 states require licensing). Non-licensed individuals should only provide "general nonmedical nutrition information" such as a cooking demonstration; endorsement of government-recommendations such as the *Dietary Guidelines* and MyPlate; discussion of macronutrients and micronutrients and how requirements vary by life stage; information about statistics relating to nutrition and chronic disease; and education about nutrients contained in particular foods or substances (Sass et al., 2007).

Frequently Asked Questions

How should a fitness professional respond to an individual who plans to adopt a popular diet?

Many people will adopt a popular diet in an effort to lose weight quickly. Rather than provide detailed information on the specifics of current popular diets that could quickly become outdated, this section offers 10 questions that fitness professionals should ask when evaluating popular diets:

1. *It is about energy (im)balance: How does the diet cut calories?* The most important concept to understand about dieting is that regardless of diet composition, time of day food is eaten, or any other variable diets tout, people lose weight on diets because they consume fewer calories than they expend.

2. *Is it healthy? All diets that create a caloric deficit cause weight loss—but are they healthy?* First, a 5 to 10% weight loss in the obese or overweight, regardless of how it is attained, leads to an improved health profile. However, the improvements may not be as powerful as the negative health consequences associated with yo-yo dieting, which may include cardiovascular damage, altered metabolism, and decreased functioning of the immune system. Therefore, a healthy diet will encourage slow weight loss [no more than 1 to 2 pounds (0.5 to 0.9 kg) per week] that can be maintained.

3. *What about nutrient density?* The best diets advocate at least nine servings daily of a variety of fruits and vegetables. Fiber-containing whole grains and calcium-rich low-fat dairy products should also be encouraged. If the diet relies primarily on a supplement to assure sufficient vitamins and minerals, it probably is not the healthiest choice. Plus, most fruits and vegetables are low-calorie but filling (due to their fiber content)—ideal for reducing caloric intake.

4. *Does it advocate exercise?* Nutrition is only one component of making a long-term lifestyle change that facilitates weight management. Exercise not only speeds weight loss by increasing the caloric deficit, but it also is essential in keeping the weight off. In fact, studies of the National Weight Control Registry's successful dieters indicate that physical activity is a primary predictor of weight-loss maintenance. The *2015–2020 Dietary Guidelines* recommend 150 minutes of moderate-intensity, or 90 minutes of vigorous-intensity, aerobic physical activity each week (USDA, 2015).

5. *Does it make sense?* Diet plans tend to make unbelievable claims that are often substantiated by dieters' personal

testimony. From promises to lose 8 to 13 pounds (3.6 to 5.9 kg) in the first two weeks of a diet to promotion of magic supplements, diets are often marketed as so easy and effective that they are irresistible—at first. Learn to see through the hype. For instance, it is true that Atkins dieters can lose a lot of weight in the initial stages of the diet. But they are not losing fat. Rather, when carbohydrates are severely limited, carbohydrate stores (glycogen) become depleted. Because water is needed to store glycogen, as glycogen becomes depleted, water, and thus water weight, is lost. As soon as the dieter replaces the glycogen stores (i.e., goes off the diet), the water weight will once again be retained.

6. *Where is the evidence?* Research studies can be a rich source of information on the effectiveness and safety of different diets. Every published diet should provide unbiased research studies that support its claims. Fitness professionals should be sure to check on the validity of any cited research.

7. *Does it meet the person's individual needs?* The most negligent diet is one that prescribes the same plan to all people regardless of their health status and other individual factors. If a person has health problems such as diabetes or heart disease, he or she should consult a physician before starting a diet or exercise regimen.

8. *What are the financial costs?* While some individuals may be able to scrape together enough money to begin an expensive weight-loss program, they might not be able to sustain the cost for an extended period of time. Encourage them to plan ahead and assess their readiness to change and commit to a program before making huge lifestyle adjustments and financial sacrifices.

9. *Is social support part of the plan?* Social support is a key to successful weight loss. If a diet requires that a dieter eat different food than the rest of the family,

he or she probably will not be successful on the diet. If a person's family is not supportive and committed to helping him or her make the healthy change, he or she may struggle.

10. *How is adherence addressed?* Long-term adherence to a program (i.e., lifestyle change) is the most important factor for lifelong weight-loss success. And the specific diet really does not matter very much. Dansinger et al. (2005) conducted a one-year randomized trial to assess the adherence rate and effectiveness of the Atkins, Ornish, Weight Watchers, and Zone diets. The results indicated that all of the diets modestly reduced body weight and cardiovascular risk factors after the one-year trial, and for each of the diets, people who adhered to the diet had greater weight loss and risk factor reductions. Of course, most of the study participants struggled with adherence, which overall was poor for all of the diets. This just drives home the point once again—permanent lifestyle change, not a quick-fix time-bound diet—is essential for successful weight loss and subsequent improved health.

Is it true that food eaten late at night (e.g., after 8:00 p.m.) is more likely to turn into body fat?

The idea that eating late at night leads to greater weight gain is not necessarily true. Weight gain is dependent on caloric intake and caloric expenditure. If people eat more than they expend, they will gain weight—regardless of whether the calories come from breakfast, dinner, or a late-night snack. However, in reality, people who eat a lot of food late at night tend to consume more calorie-dense foods and thus eat more calories, which can cause weight gain. The bottom line: It is not *when* a person eats but *what* and *how much*. If a person finds him- or herself mindlessly eating chips at 10:00 at night while watching TV, then it might be helpful to reverse this fat-promoting behavior by making a behavioral plan that includes not eating after 8:00 p.m.

Which is better for weight control, consuming three square meals or eating five or six small meals spread out over the day?

Weight control is a balance of "calories in" versus "calories out." So ultimately, it does not matter if the calories come in the form of three larger meals or five to six smaller meals; however, some people find that they are better able to control their caloric intake in one way or the other. For instance, people who consume three or fewer meals per day may find that when they eat they feel famished and overeat to compensate. Eating fewer meals spaced throughout the day may help with calorie control. On the other hand, someone who eats five to six meals per day may forget to make them *small* meals and instead end up consuming more calories than he or she would with three meals. In the end, it is a matter of preference. One strategy for effective meal planning is to determine the total number of calories (or, alternatively, total number of servings from each of the food groups) and divide them somewhat equally throughout the day—whether that is three meals or six. Importantly, people who have diabetes should consume five to six equal-sized small meals to maintain healthy blood sugar levels throughout the day.

Does exercise curb appetite?

Research suggests that appetite decreases for about the first hour after strenuous exercise and then normalizes. However, appetite regulation is a very complex process relying on insulin, hormones, psychological factors, and blood sugar levels. This complexity makes it difficult to generalize the effects of exercise on appetite. Overall, people who participate in moderate exercise tend to eat about the same number of calories—or only slightly more—than they would if they did not exercise. Competitive athletes overall do consume a lot more food than usual after exercise, but they usually burn off much more than the excess calories they consumed.

How long should a person wait to exercise after eating?

It is generally recommended that exercisers wait about three hours after eating a full meal to engage in a strenuous exercise program. That is about how long it takes for a balanced meal including some carbohydrate, protein, and fat to move from the stomach into the small intestines, where nutrients are absorbed and energy becomes available. Exercising before food has had time to empty from the stomach can cause cramps and abdominal discomfort. But people respond differently and there is no set amount of time to wait. If an individual exercises in the morning, a quick carbohydrate-dense snack might help to provide some energy during the workout without a lot of discomfort. Generally, carbohydrates are digested in about an hour, while protein takes about two hours and fat about four hours. But remember, most foods are a combination of the three types of macronutrients.

Why do some people have a more difficult time losing weight than others?

Genetics clearly is a factor in how easily someone loses weight. Also, gender differences play a role, in that when men lose weight they tend to lose abdominal fat first, whereas women have a more difficult time losing abdominal fat. However, there are additional, more controllable factors as well. First, the amount of muscle mass an individual has is directly proportional to metabolism, and thus caloric expenditure. People who have a large muscle mass can more easily lose weight when they control caloric intake than someone who has a low muscle mass. Secondly, people who have more weight to lose experience a lot of weight-loss success when they decrease their caloric intake and increase physical activity, because their baseline is often a very high-calorie diet. For example, if someone who weighs 250 pounds (114 kg) normally eats 3,000 calories per day and he or she cuts back to 2,000 calories per day and expends

ACE Essentials of Exercise Science for Fitness Professionals

200 more calories per day with exercise, he or she can easily lose more than 3 pounds (1.4 kg) in one week. On the other hand, if someone who weighs 125 pounds (57 kg) and normally eats 2,200 calories per day cuts back to 2,000 calories per day and expends 200 more calories per day with exercise he or she will only lose about 0.75 pounds (0.34 kg) in a week. Finally, behavioral factors cannot be ignored. Some people are more successful at weight loss because they are better able to adhere to a lower-calorie diet and regularly engage in physical activity.

Are carbohydrates bad? What proportion of carbohydrates, fats, and protein should people eat for optimal weight loss and health?

As far as weight loss goes, the proportion of macronutrients consumed is not what is important. Rather, it is total caloric intake versus caloric expenditure, or "calories in" versus "calories out." However, foods rich in fiber and protein tend to be the most filling, which in theory would lead to decreased intake of food and calories compared to high-fat foods and low-fiber carbohydrates. It is important to remember that people often eat for reasons other than hunger, and as a result occasionally continue to eat even when they are full. An effective weight-loss program addresses both the recommended food intake as well as the behavioral factors that sometimes get in the way of successful weight loss. From a heart health perspective, the healthiest overall meal plan appears to be a Mediterranean-type eating plan, which is rich in fruits, vegetables, whole grains, and omega-3 fatty acids from fish and low in saturated fat, trans fat, sodium, and added sugars.

Should people cut out food groups to lose weight?

The most successful approach to weight loss and weight-loss maintenance is to make permanent lifestyle changes that include a healthful eating plan and ample physical activity. A diet—which implies short-term and hard-to-adhere-to changes—is not the answer. Thus, while certain foods are

prohibited in various "diets," a healthy lifestyle allows for all foods *in moderation*. This means that less healthy foods can fit, as long as they make up only a small portion of the total daily caloric intake. The government's MyPlate plan calls these "discretionary calories." It is essential that an eating plan contain adequate amounts of a variety of foods from each of the food groups to assure balanced nutrient intake.

Should people take a supplement to get adequate nutrition?

The science on multivitamins is inconclusive. In 2006, a National Institutes of Health (NIH) panel convened to evaluate all of the research on multivitamins and develop recommendations for the public. The panel's summary statement was that insufficient high-quality research has been done to be able to assess whether vitamins help in chronic disease prevention. Two exceptions are the strong indications for folic acid supplements for all women of child-bearing age to prevent neural tube defects in the developing baby and fish oil/omega-3 fatty acid supplements in the prevention of heart disease in people who are at risk. In general, most dietitians recommend that people take a multivitamin as "insurance" and more importantly, aim to get optimal nutrition including vitamins and minerals from whole foods such as fruits, vegetables, fish, and low- or non-fat dairy products.

How can a fitness professional help someone lose weight and keep it off?

The key to permanent weight-loss success is making lifestyle changes that include a healthy eating plan and ample physical activity. The changes need to be reasonable enough that a person can maintain them indefinitely and not feel deprived or unhappy. A realistic weight-loss goal for someone who is overweight or obese is to aim to lose 7 to 10% of starting weight over a six-month to one-year period and then to keep the weight off for at least six months before trying to lose more. This amount of weight loss will provide significant health benefits, including decreased blood pressure, cholesterol, and risk of developing diabetes. Also, weight loss is more easily maintained when the weight is lost slowly [about 1 to 2 pounds (0.5 to 0.9 kg) per week].

How can a fitness professional help people who say they do not have time to exercise?

One could argue that the extra time invested each day to healthy meal planning and physical activity will, in the end, add years to life and so is worth the extra time regardless of how busy someone is. While this is true, in a practical sense it may not be enough to encourage someone to make the time for these changes—at least not right away. So it is also important to note that small changes that do not take much extra time, such as taking the stairs instead of the elevator, parking in one of the far away spaces at the grocery store, and getting up to change the TV channel instead of using the remote control, can add up. Also, most fast-food and take-out restaurants now offer healthier choices such as grilled chicken, salads, and kids meals (that adults can order, too) with fruit and milk. Visit www.cdc. gov/physicalactivity/basics/adding-pa/index. htm to learn how to help clients incorporate more physical activity into their lives.

Are low-fat foods also low in calories?

Foods naturally low in fat (e.g., fruits, vegetables, grains) tend to be low in calories. However, foods that are manufactured to be low in fat (e.g., reduced-fat snacks and desserts) can be relatively high in calories. During the process of removing fat, some of the taste and texture of the food items are lost. In an effort to add taste and texture, food manufacturers often add carbohydrates and protein, thus adding calories. Like most foods, low-fat foods should be consumed in moderation to avoid weight gain.

Does caffeine improve athletic performance?

Research findings are clear: Caffeine enhances athletic performance. Caffeine sustains duration, maximizes effort at 85% of $\dot{V}O_2$max in cyclists, and quickens speed in an endurance event. Perceived exertion decreases and high-intensity efforts seem less taxing. Contrary to popular opinion, research suggests that caffeine use combined with exercise does not cause negative effects like water-electrolyte imbalances, hyperthermia, or reduced exercise-heat tolerance. But there is a catch: Performance-enhancing benefits of caffeine are stronger in non-users (<50 mg/day) than regular users (>300 mg/day). In addition to tolerance, chronic caffeine use contributes to high blood pressure, high blood sugar, decreased bone density in women, jittery nerves, sleeplessness, and for many, the dreaded withdrawal symptoms after a brief respite from the stimulant, including headache, irritability, increased fatigue, drowsiness, decreased alertness, difficulty concentrating, and decreased energy and activity levels (Armstrong et al., 2007; Keisler & Armsey, 2006).

Summary

Fitness professionals can serve as credible sources of nutrition knowledge and advice to help individuals develop a healthy eating plan and lifestyle. Fitness professionals should use the *Dietary Guidelines* and MyPlate as the basis for their suggestions and remember to refer to a registered dietitian when someone needs individualized nutrition plans, supplement recommendations, or meal planning for chronic diseases or special populations. And fitness professionals should always remember the overarching objective to help individuals transform nutrition information and recommendations into action.

References

Almond, C.S.D. et al. (2005). Hyponatremia among runners in the Boston Marathon. *New England Journal of Medicine*, 352, 15, 1550–1556.

American Dietetic Association (2009). Position of the American Dietetic Association, Dietitians of Canada, and the American College of Sports Medicine: Nutrition and athletic performance. *Journal of the American Dietetic Association*, 109, 509–527.

American Dietetic Association (2008). Position of the American Dietetic Association: Nutrition and lifestyle for a healthy pregnancy outcome. *Journal of the American Dietetic Association*, 108, 3, 553–561.

American Dietetic Association (2007). Position of the American Dietetic Association and Dietitians of Canada: Dietary fatty acids. *Journal of the American Dietetic Association,* 107, 9, 1599–1611.

American Dietetic Association (2005a). Position of the American Dietetic Association: Promoting and supporting breastfeeding. *Journal of the American Dietetic Association,*105, 5, 810–818.

American Dietetic Association (2005b). Position paper of the American Dietetic Association: Nutrition across the spectrum of aging. *Journal of the American Dietetic Association*, 105, 4, 616–633.

American Dietetic Association (2003). Position of the American Dietetic Association and Dietitians of Canada: Vegetarian diets. *Journal of the American Dietetic Association,* 103, 6, 748–765.

American Heart Association (2007). *Hypertension Statistics.* Dallas: American Heart Association.

American Heart Association et al. (2006). Dietary recommendations for children and adolescents: A guide for practitioners. *Pediatrics,* 117, 544–559.

Armstrong, L.E. et al. (2007). Caffeine, fluid-electrolyte balance, temperature regulation, and exercise-heat tolerance. *Exercise and Sports Science Reviews,* 35, 3, 135–140.

Barlow S.E. and the Expert Committee (2007). Expert committee recommendations regarding the prevention, assessment, and treatment of child and adolescent overweight and obesity: Summary report. *Pediatrics,* 120, S4, S164–S193.

Blomstrand E. et al. (2006). Branched-chain amino acids activate key enzymes in protein synthesis after physical exercise. *Journal of Nutrition,* 136, Suppl. 1, 269S–273S.

Brand-Miller, J. et al. (2003). Low-glycemic index diets in the management of diabetes: A meta-analysis of randomized controlled trials. *Diabetes Care,* 26, 8, 2261–2267.

Brouns, F. & Beckers, E. (1993). Is the gut an athletic organ? *Sports Medicine,* 15, 242–257.

Brunner E.J. et al. (2007). Dietary advice for reducing cardiovascular risk. *Cochrane Database of Systematic Reviews,* 4, CD002128.

Casa D.J. (2003). Proper hydration for distance running—Identifying individual fluid needs: A USA Track & Field advisory. https://www.khsaa.org/sportsmedicine/heat/properhydrationfordistancerunning.pdf

Casa D.J., Clarkson P.M., & Roberts W.O. (2005). American College of Sports Medicine roundtable on hydration and physical activity: Consensus statements. *Current Sports Medicine Reports,* 4, 115–127.

Casa, D.J. et al. (2000). National Athletic Trainers' Association: Position statement: Fluid replacement for athletes. *Journal of Athletic Training,* 35, 212–224.

Centers for Disease Control and Prevention (2008). Healthy aging: Preventing disease and improving quality of life among older Americans. www.cdc.gov/nccdphp/publications/aag/aging.htm

Centers for Disease Control and Prevention (2005). *National Diabetes Fact Sheet: National Estimates and General Information on Diabetes in the United States—2005.* Atlanta, Ga.: U.S. Department of Health & Human Services, Centers for Disease Control and Prevention.

Centers for Disease Control and Prevention (2004). Health, 2004 with chartbook on trends in the health of Americans. www.cdc.gov/nchs/data/hus/hus04trend.pdf#067

Champagne, C.M. (2006). Dietary interventions on blood pressure: The Dietary Approaches to Stop Hypertension (DASH) trials, *Nutrition Reviews,* 64, 2, S53–S56.

Christakis, N.A. & Fowler, J.H. (2007). The spread of obesity in a large social network over 32 years. *New England Journal of Medicine,* 357, 370–379.

Cockayne S. et al. (2006). Vitamin K and the prevention of fractures. *Archives of Internal Medicine,* 166, 1256–1261.

Consensus Development Conference Panel (1991). Gastrointestinal surgery for severe obesity. *Annals of Internal Medicine,* 115, 956–961.

Coombes, J.S. & Hamilton, K.L. (2000). The effectiveness of commercially available sports drinks. *Sports Medicine,* 29, 3, 181–209.

Coyle, E.F. (2004). Fluid and fuel intake during exercise. *Journal of Sports Sciences,* 22, 1, 39–55.

Dangin, M. et al. (2002). Influence of the protein digestion rate on protein turnover in young and elderly subjects. *Journal of Nutrition,* 132, 3228S–3233S.

Dansinger, M.L. et al. (2005). Comparison of the Atkins, Ornish, Weight Watchers, and Zone diets for weight loss and heart disease risk reduction. *Journal of the American Medical Association,* 293, 1, 43–53.

Finley, C.E. et al. (2007). Retention rates and weight loss in a commercial weight loss program. *International Journal of Obesity,* 31, 292–298.

Flechtner-Mors, M. et al. (2000). Metabolic and weight

effects of long-term dietary intervention in obese patients: Four-year results. *Obesity Research, 8,* 399–402.

Frankenfield D., Routh-Yousey L., & Compher C. (2005). Comparison of predictive equations of resting metabolic rates in healthy non-obese and obese adults: A systematic review. *Journal of the American Dietetic Association,* 105, 5, 775–789.

French S.A., Story M., & Jeffrey R.W. (2001). Environmental influences on eating and physical activity. *Annual Reviews of Public Health, 22,* 309–335.

Gardner, C.D. et al. (2007). Comparison of the Atkins, Zone, Ornish, and LEARN Diets for change in weight and related risk factors among overweight premenopausal women: The A TO Z weight loss study: A randomized trial. *Journal of the American Medical Association,* 297, 969–977.

Gorin, A.A. et al. (2004). Promoting long-term weight control: Does dieting consistency matter? *International Journal of Obesity and Related Metabolic Disorders,* 28, 2, 278–281.

Harris, W.S. (2010). Omega-6 and omega-3 fatty acids: Partners in prevention. *Current Opinions in Clinical Nutrition and Metabolic Care,* 13, 2, 125–129.

Harris, W.S. et al. (2009). Omega-6 fatty acids and risk for cardiovascular disease: A science advisory from the American Heart Association Nutrition Subcommittee of the Council on Nutrition, Physical Activity, and Metabolism; Council on Cardiovascular Nursing; and Council on Epidemiology and Prevention. *Circulation,* 119, 6, 902–90

Harvard School of Public Health (2008). Protein: Moving closer to center stage. *The Nutrition Source.* www.hsph.harvard.edu/nutritionsource/what-should-you-eat/protein-full-story/

Haust, M.D. (1990). The genesis of atherosclerosis in pediatric age-group. *Pediatric Pathology,* 10, 1–2, 253–271.

Hayes, A. & Cribb, P.J. (2008). Effect of whey protein isolate on strength, body composition, and muscle hypertrophy during resistance training. *Current Opinions in Clinical Nutrition and Metabolic Care,* 11, 40–44.

Hoffman, J.R. & Falvo, M.J (2004). Protein: Which is best? *Journal of Sports Science and Medicine,* 3, 118–130.

Institute of Medicine Food and Energy Board (2005). Dietary Reference Intakes for energy, carbohydrate, fiber, fat, fatty acids, cholesterol, protein, and amino acids. Washington, D.C.: National Academy Press.

Institute of Medicine (2009). *Weight Gain During Pregnancy: Reexamining the Guidelines.* Washington, D.C.: National Academy Press.

Institute of Medicine (2004). Dietary Reference Intakes for calcium, magnesium, phosphorus, vitamin D, and fluoride. Washington, D.C.: National Academy Press.

Jentjens, R. & Jeukendrup, A.E. (2003). Determinants of post-exercise glycogen synthesis during short-term recovery. *Sports Medicine,* 33, 2, 117–144.

Keisler, B.D. & Armsey, T.D. (2006). Caffeine as ergogenic acid. *Current Sports Medicine Reports,* 5, 215–219.

Lappé, F.M. (1992). *Diet for a Small Planet.* New York: Ballantine Books.

Li, Z. et al. (2005). Meta-analysis: Pharmacologic treatment of obesity. *Annals of Internal Medicine,* 142, 532–546.

Lobstein, T., Baur, L., & Uauy, R. (2004). Obesity in children and young people: A crisis in public health. *Obesity Reviews,* 5, Suppl. 1, 4–85.

Mahan, L.K. & Escott-Stump, S. (2000). *Krause's Food Nutrition and Diet Therapy* (10th ed.). Philadelphia, Pa.: W.B. Saunders Company.

McDaniel, M.A., Maier, S.F., & Einstein, G.O. (2003). "Brain-specific" nutrients: A memory cure? *Nutrition,* 19, 957–975.

McMahan, C.A. et al. (2006). Pathological determinants of atherosclerosis in youth risk scores are associated with early and advanced atherosclerosis. *Pediatrics,* 118, 4, 1447–1455.

Murray, R. (2006). Training the gut for competition. *Current Sports Medicine Reports,* 5, 161–164.

National Heart, Lung, and Blood Institute, National Institutes of Health (2004). *Portion Distortion II.* hp2010.nhlbihin.net/portion/

National Institutes of Health (2006). National Institutes of Health state-of-the-science conference statement: Multivitamin/mineral supplements and chronic disease prevention. *Annals of Internal Medicine,* 145, 5, 364–371.

National Institutes of Health (1998). Clinical guidelines on the identification, evaluation, and treatment of overweight and obesity in adults: The evidence report. www.nhlbi.nih.gov/guidelines/obesity/ob_gdlns.pdf

National Weight Control Registry (2008). NWCR facts. www.nwcr.ws/Research/default.htm

Noakes, T. (2003). Fluid replacement during marathon running. *Clinical Journal of Sport Medicine,* 13, 309–318.

Ogden, C.L. et al. (2006). Prevalence of overweight and obesity in the United States, 1999–2004. *Journal of the American Medical Association,* 295, 13, 1549–1555.

Phillips, S.M. (2006). Dietary protein for athletes: From requirements to metabolic advantage. *Applied Physiology, Nutrition, & Metabolism,* 31, 647–654.

Raynor, D. et al. (2006). Television viewing and long-term weight maintenance: Results from the National Weight Control Registry. *Obesity Research,* 14, 10, 1816–1824.

Rogue, E.E. et al. (2004). Longitudinal relationship between elapsed time in the action stages of change and weight loss. *Obesity Research,* 12, 9, 1499–1508.

Rowe, J.W. & Kahn, R.L. (1998). *Successful Aging.* New York: Pantheon Books.

Sandmaier, M. (2007). *The Healthy Heart Handbook for Women.* Bethesda, Md.: U.S. Department of Health & Human Services: National Institutes of Health, National Heart, Lung, and Blood Institute. https://www.nhlbi. nih.gov/health/educational/hearttruth/downloads/pdf/ handbook-for-women.pdf

Sass, C. et al. (2007). Crossing the line: Understanding the scope of practice between registered dietitians and health/fitness professionals. *ACSM's Health & Fitness Journal,* 11, 3, 12–19.

St. Jeor, S.T. et al. (2001). Dietary protein and weight reduction: A statement for healthcare professionals from the nutrition committee of the Council on Nutrition, Physical Activity, and Metabolism of the American Heart Association. *Circulation,* 104, 1869–1874.

Thomas, D.E., Elliott, E.J., & Baur, L. (2007). Low glycaemic index or low glycaemic load diets for overweight and obesity. *Cochrane Database of Systematic Reviews,* 3, CD005105.

Thompson, W.R. (2008). Worldwide survey reveals fitness trends for 2009. *ACSM's Health and Fitness Journal,* 12, 6, 1–8.

Timlin, M.T. & Pereira, M.A. (2007). Breakfast frequency and quality in the etiology of adult obesity and chronic diseases. *Nutrition Reviews,* 65, 6, 268–281.

Tinkler, L.F. et al. (2007). Predictors of dietary change and maintenance in the Women's Health Initiative Dietary Modification Trial. *Journal of the American Dietetic Association,* 107, 1155–1165.

U.S. Department of Agriculture (2015). *2015–2020 Dietary Guidelines for Americans* (8th ed.). www. health.gov/dietaryguidelines

U.S. Department of Health & Human Services (2004). *Bone Health and Osteoporosis: A Report of the Surgeon General.* Rockville, Md.: U.S. Department of Health & Human Services, Office of the Surgeon General.

U.S. Department of Health & Human Services, National Institutes of Health, National Heart, Lung, and Blood Institute (2005). *Your Guide to a Healthy Heart.* NIH Publication No. 06-5269. www.nhlbi. nih.gov/health/public/heart/other/your_guide/ healthyheart.pdf

U.S. Food and Drug Administration, Center for Food Safety and Applied Nutrition (2004). *How To Understand And Use The Nutrition Facts Label.* https:// www.fda.gov/food/labelingnutrition/ucm274593.htm

Venderley, A.M. & Campbell, W.W. (2006). Vegetarian diets: Nutritional considerations for athletes. *Sports Medicine,* 36, 4, 293-305.

Wadden, T.A. et al. (2005). Randomized trial of lifestyle modification and pharmacotherapy for obesity. *New England Journal of Medicine,* 353, 20, 2111–2120.

Whitaker, R.C. et al. (1997). Predicting obesity in young adulthood from childhood and parental obesity. *New England Journal of Medicine,* 337, 869–873.

Wolfe, R.R. & Miller, S.L. (2008). The Recommended Dietary Allowance of protein. *Journal of the American Medical Association,* 299, 24, 2891–2893.

World Health Organization (2007). Micronutrients. who.int/nutrition/topics/micronutrients/en/index.html

Wyatt, H.R. et al. (2002). Long-term weight loss and breakfast in subjects in the National Weight Control Registry. *Obesity Research,* 10, 78–82.

Suggested Reading

Clark, N. (2008). *Nancy Clark's Sports Nutrition Guidebook* (4th ed.). Champaign, Ill.: Human Kinetics.

Dunford, M. (2006). *Sports Nutrition: A Practice Manual for Professionals* (4th ed.). Washington, D.C.: American Dietetic Association.

Duyff, R.L. & American Dietetic Association (2006). *Complete Food and Nutrition Guide* (3rd ed.). Hoboken, N.J.: John Wiley and Sons.

Kleiner, S.M. (2007). *Power Eating: Build Muscle, Gain Energy, Lose Weight* (3rd ed.). Champaign, Ill.: Human Kinetics.

National Heart Lung and Blood Institute. *The DASH Eating Plan.* www.nhlbi.nih.gov/health-topics/dash-eating-plan

Willett, W. (2006). *Eat, Drink, and Be Healthy: The Harvard Medical School Guide to Healthy Eating* (2nd ed.). New York: Free Press.

Chapter 4
Nutrition

Getting Started

This chapter provides information on the basic nutrients and nutritional needs of physically active adults. It also covers specific nutritional considerations for various "special populations," including youth, older adults, pregnant women, and individuals with hypertension, diabetes, and osteoporosis. After reading this chapter, you should have a better understanding of:

- The structure and function of carbohydrates, fats, and protein
- The structure and function of water, vitamins, and minerals
- The physiology of digestion and absorption
- The MyPlate Food Guidance System and other federal dietary guidelines
- How to read food labels
- Appropriate responses to frequently asked nutrition-related questions

Expand Your Knowledge

I. Describe the major differences between the following pairs of words or phrases.

a. Recommended Dietary Allowances and Dietary Reference Intakes _____

_____

_____

_____

b. Estimated Average Requirement and Tolerable Upper Intake Level _____

_____

_____

_____

c. Complex carbohydrates and simple carbohydrates _____

_____

_____

_____

d. Saturated fatty acids and unsaturated fatty acids _____

_____

_____

_____

e. Complete protein and incomplete protein _____

_____

_____

_____

II. Match the following vitamins to their functions.

a. _____ Vitamin B12

b. _____ Vitamin K

c. _____ Choline

d. _____ Thiamin

e. _____ Vitamin D

f. _____ Pantothenic acid

g. _____ Vitamin E

h. _____ Carotene

1. Helps release energy from fats and vegetables

2. Aids in cell development, function of the nervous system, and the metabolism of protein and fat

3. Protects blood cells, body tissue, and essential fatty acids from destruction in the body

4. Essential for blood-clotting functions

5. Supports formation and maintenance of skin, hair, and mucous membranes

6. Essential for liver function

7. Helps the body release energy from carbohydrates during metabolism

8. Aids in bone and tooth formation

III. Indicate whether each of the following food substances is a monosaccharide (MS), disaccharide (DS), or polysaccharide (PS).

a. _____ Fructose

b. _____ Glycogen

c. _____ Brown sugar

d. _____ Starch

e. _____ Galactose

f. _____ Whole grains

g. _____ Lactose

h. _____ Glucose

IV. Fill in the blanks.

    a. _____ is the result of the binding together of glucose and fructose.

    b. Saturated fat increases levels of _____, which is sometimes called the "bad" cholesterol.

    c. Proteins are essential for the manufacture of _____, which the body uses to fight infection.

    d. _____ is the condition resulting from the ingestion of excessive amounts of fluids.

    e. The degree to which a mineral can be absorbed by the body is called its _____.

V. Match the following minerals to their functions.

    a. _____ Calcium

    b. _____ Magnesium

    c. _____ Iodine

    d. _____ Zinc

    e. _____ Iron

    f. _____ Fluoride

    g. _____ Chromium

    h. _____ Selenium

1. Important in the development of the reproductive system and aids in healing

2. Component of thyroxine, which controls metabolism

3. Essential for strong bones, teeth, and muscle tissue and helps to regulate the heart beat

4. Protects body tissue from oxidative damage

5. Stimulates bone formation and inhibits or reverses dental caries

6. Maintains acid/alkaline balance and aids in the metabolism of carbohydrates, minerals, and glucose

7. Important for hemoglobin formation and improves blood quality

8. Involved in glucose metabolism and may increase the effectiveness of insulin

VI. List the three vitamins that do not have to be consumed through foods, and give a brief statement about how they are manufactured by the body.

    a. _____

    b. _____

    c. _____

VII. List the number of calories per gram provided by the following macronutrients.

Macronutrient	kcal/g
Carbohydrate	_____
Fat	_____
Protein	_____
Alcohol	_____

VIII. Fill in the blanks in the following statements about food labels.

a. All of the nutrient amounts listed on the food label are for one _____.

b. The _____ are listed for key nutrients to make it easier to compare products.

c. The percent daily values listed on a food label are for a _____-calorie diet.

d. Fish, shellfish, soybean, wheat, egg, milk, peanuts, and tree nuts are common food _____.

e. Refined grains are often listed as "_____."

IX. Complete the table by filling in the recommendations from the DASH eating plan for the amount of servings from each food group and the significance of the food group to the plan.

Food Group	Servings	Significance of Food
Grains and grain products	_____	_____
Vegetables	_____	_____
Fruits	_____	_____
Low-fat or fat-free dairy	_____	_____
Meats, poultry, and fish	_____	_____
Nuts, seeds, and dry beans	_____	_____
Fats and oils	_____	_____
Sweets	_____	_____

X. Your client, Sarah, is required to attend business dinners at least three days per week. She is worried that eating the large portion sizes at restaurants will sabotage her goal of eating healthier and losing weight. List five strategies to keep from overeating at restaurants when the main portion sizes are larger than a recommended serving size.

a. _____

_____

ACE Essentials of Exercise Science for Fitness Professionals

b. _____

_____

c. _____

_____

d. _____

_____

e. _____

_____

XI. List the five Key Guidelines to good nutrition offered in the *2015-2020 Dietary Guidelines.*

a. _____

_____

b. _____

_____

c. _____

_____

d. _____

_____

e. _____

_____

XII. Using the Mifflin-St. Jeor equation for estimating resting metabolic rate, as well as recommendations from the American Dietetic Association, help the following clients estimate the appropriate daily caloric intake range to support their moderately active lifestyle:

Client: Michael Scott
Body weight: 176 lb (80 kg)
Height: 6' (183 cm)
Age: 40 years

Client: Claire Scott
Body weight: 135 lb (61 kg)
Height: 5' 7" (170 cm)
Age: 37 years

For men: RMR = 9.99 x wt (kg) + 6.25 x ht (cm) – 4.92 x age (yrs) + 5
For women: RMR = 9.99 x wt (kg) + 6.25 x ht (cm) – 4.92 x age (yrs) – 161
Moderately active individuals need approximately 1.5 to 1.7 times their calculated RMR.

Michael _____

_____

_____

Claire _____

_____

_____

XIII. Describe the major differences between the following pairs of words or phrases.

a. Prehypertension and hypertension _____

_____

_____

b. Glycemic index and glycemic load _____

_____

_____

c. Dehydration and hyponatremia _____

_____

_____

d. Lacto-ovo-vegetarian and vegan _____

_____

_____

e. Mechanical digestion and chemical digestion _____

_____

_____

XIV. List the 10 insights from the National Weight Control Registry that personal trainers can share with clients who are seeking to lose weight or maintain weight loss.

a. _____

b. _____

c. _____

d. _____

e. _____

f. _____

g. _____

h. _____

i. _____

j. _____

Show What You Know

I. Using the Nutrition Facts food label on page 172, calculate the number of calories that come from each of the macronutrients (fat, carbohydrate, and protein) for the entire container. *Note:* Manufacturers are allowed to round numbers when presenting information on nutrition labels. Therefore, the calculated values might be slightly different than the label's values.

_____

_____

_____

_____

_____

_____

_____

_____

II. Determine the required grams of each of the macronutrients based on the following percentages of total daily caloric intake for a 2,000-calorie per day diet.

a. Fat (25% of total daily calories) _____

_____

_____

b. Carbohydrate (55% of total daily calories) _____

_____

_____

c. Protein (20% of total daily calories) _____

_____

_____

Practice What You Know

I. Log on to the MyPlate Food Guidance System interactive online tool (www. ChooseMyPlate.gov) and input your personal lifestyle information to discover your recommended daily calorie needs and physical-activity guidelines. Peruse the entire website to become familiar with its functions and tools to prepare for questions your clients might ask you about using the website and its various tools.

Multiple Choice

1. How many kilocalories (kcal) are in a food that contains 4 grams of protein, 12 grams of carbohydrates, and 2 grams of fat?

    A. 72 kcal

    B. 82 kcal

    C. 92 kcal

    D. 102 kcal

2. Mary is a new client who has goals to lose 10 pounds (4.5 kg) and improve her overall health while training for an upcoming 5K race. She asks for your recommendations on when she should consume low- and high-glycemic carbohydrates and for good sources of each. Which of the following responses is **MOST** appropriate?

    A. Inform her that as a trainer, making recommendations on low- and high-glycemic sources and timing of consumption is outside of your scope of practice and therefore you cannot help her.

    B. Inform her that low-glycemic sources such as sodas and sweets are best consumed to refuel her body after exercise, while high-glycemic sources such as fruits are best consumed throughout the day.

    C. Inform her that high-glycemic sources such as simple sugars are best consumed to refuel her body after exercise, while low-glycemic sources such as bran and oatmeal are best consumed throughout the day.

    D. Inform her that as her trainer, you will develop a meal plan that outlines when and what she should eat to help her achieve her exercise and dietary goals.

3. Fructose is classified in which carbohydrate category?

    A. Monosaccharide

    B. Disaccharide

    C. Oligosaccharide

    D. Polysaccharide

4. According to current dietary guidelines, a 30-year-old moderately active man who consumes 2,500 calories per day requires _____ of daily protein.

    A. 45–150 g

    B. 54–175 g

    C. 63–218 g

    D. 76–253 g

5. The words "partially hydrogenated" on an ingredient list indicate the presence of _____.

   A. Added sugars

   B. Refined grains

   C. Added sodium

   D. Trans fat

6. Which of the following fatty acids contains multiple double-carbon bonds in its backbone?

   A. Saturated fat

   B. Monounsaturated fat

   C. Hydrogenated fat

   D. Polyunsaturated fat

7. Your client would like to lose 20 pounds (9 kg) over the next 15 weeks. What daily caloric deficit is needed to achieve this goal?

   A. 525 kcal

   B. 667 kcal

   C. 750 kcal

   D. 833 kcal

8. Which of the following statements reflects the recommended fluid intake guidelines prior to exercise or an athletic event?

   A. Drink no more than 12 ounces of fluids 2 hours prior to exercise.

   B. Drink a minimum of 17 ounces of fluids 2–3 hours prior to exercise.

   C. Drink 8 ounces of fluid 1–2 hours prior to exercise.

   D. Drink 24 ounces of fluid 4 hours prior to exercise.

9. Your client would like to lose 25 pounds (11.3 kg) over the next 20 weeks. If he agrees to increase his physical-activity levels by 300 kcal daily, how many calories would he need to reduce from his daily intake to reach this goal?

   A. 225 kcal

   B. 275 kcal

   C. 300 kcal

   D. 325 kcal

10. Kristin is a varsity crew athlete who is now beginning her pre-season training in preparation for the upcoming season. If she weighs 155 pounds (70.45 kg), how many grams of carbohydrate per hour will she need to maintain her blood glucose levels during her training sessions?

    A. 10–30 g

    B. 20–35 g

    C. 30–60 g

    D. 60–75 g

IN THIS CHAPTER:

SABRENA JO, M.S., has been actively involved in the fitness industry since 1987, focusing on teaching group exercise, owning and operating her own personal-training business, and managing fitness departments in commercial fitness facilities. Jo is a former full-time faculty member in the Kinesiology and Physical Education Department at California State University, Long Beach. She has a bachelor's degree in exercise science as well as a master's degree in physical education/biomechanics from the University of Kansas, and has numerous fitness certifications. Jo, an ACE-certified Personal Trainer and Group Fitness Instructor and ACE Faculty Member, educates other fitness professionals about current industry topics through speaking engagements at local establishments and national conferences, as well as through educational videos. She is a spokesperson for ACE and is involved in curriculum development for ACE continuing education programs.

CHAPTER 5

Physiology of Training

Sabrena Jo

I t is imperative that ACE-certified Fitness Professionals understand the fundamental anatomy, exercise physiology, and kinesiology principles associated with exercise training (see Chapters 1 through 3). More importantly, it is essential that fitness professionals are able to translate their knowledge of exercise science into the practical application of designing and implementing one-on-one training sessions or group fitness classes. This chapter presents cardiorespiratory-, resistance-, and flexibility-training principles that can be applied during a training session (acute response) and for the progression (chronic adaptation) of an exercise program. The information presented in this chapter takes into account the theoretical material laid out in Chapters 1 through 3 and provides examples of application of these sciences in a practical setting.

ACE Essentials of Exercise Science for Fitness Professionals

Acute Responses to Exercise

Exercise poses a serious challenge to the body's various systems. For example, during high-intensity exercise, the body's total energy expenditure may increase 15 to 25 times above expenditure at rest. Contributions from the cardiorespiratory, nervous, endocrine, muscular, and thermoregulatory systems are vital for the rest-to-exercise transition to be successful.

The respiratory and circulatory systems work together to deliver adequate amounts of oxygen to the body's cells and remove wastes from body tissues. To meet the increased demands of muscle during exercise, two major adjustments in blood flow must occur: an increase in **cardiac output** and a redistribution of blood from inactive organs to the active skeletal muscle.

Recall that cardiac output is the product of **heart rate** and **stroke volume (SV),** which represents the amount of blood pumped per minute by the heart. Thus, cardiac output increases due to a rise in heart rate and/or stroke volume. Regulation of heart rate is controlled intrinsically by the **sinoatrial node (SA node)** located in the posterior wall of the right atrium (Figure 5-1), which serves as the pacemaker for the heart, or extrinsically by the nervous and hormonal systems. Changes in heart rate often involve factors that influence the SA node. The two most prominent

factors that influence heart rate are the parasympathetic and sympathetic divisions of the **autonomic nervous system.**

Parasympathetic and Sympathetic Regulation of Heart Rate

Because of its specialized capacity, cardiac muscle maintains its own rhythm. If left to its inherent rhythm, the heart would beat steadily at about 100 beats per minute (bpm). This occurs as a result of the SA node's ability to spontaneously **depolarize** and **repolarize** to provide an innate stimulus for heart contraction. Impulses originating in the SA node spread across the atria to another small knot of tissue called the **atrioventricular node (AV node)** (see Figure 5-1). The AV node, located in the floor of the right atrium, gives off many branches that facilitate ventricular contraction. This arrangement means that first the atria contract together, and then the ventricles.

Parasympathetic fibers supply the heart via a pair of **vagus nerves.** When these fibers reach the heart, they make contact with both the SA node and AV node. Upon stimulation, vagus nerve endings release **acetylcholine,** which causes a decrease in the activity of both the SA and AV nodes, in turn reducing heart rate. At rest, the heart is primarily under the influence of the vagus nerves, which is referred to as parasympathetic tone. An increase or decrease in heart rate can occur due to the relative influence of parasympathetic activity. For example, a decrease in parasympathetic tone to the heart can elevate heart rate, while an increase leads to a reduction in heart rate.

An increase in sympathetic activity, on the other hand, increases heart rate. Sympathetic fibers reach the heart through **cardiac accelerator nerves,** which innervate the SA node and the ventricles. Stimulation of these nerves causes the release of the **catecholamines** called **epinephrine** and **norepinephrine.** These **hormones** accelerate SA node depolarization, thereby causing the heart to beat faster (chronotropic response) and increase the force of heart contractility (inotropic response). During exercise, the initial increase in heart

Figure 5-1
Sinoatrial (SA) node and atrioventricular (AV) node

Source: LifeART image copyright 2008 Wolters Kluwer Health, Inc., Lippincott Williams & Wilkins. All rights reserved.

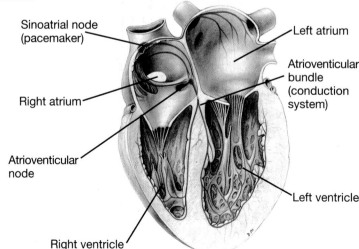

Sinoatrial node (pacemaker)

Left atrium

Atrioventicular bundle (conduction system)

Right atrium

Atrioventicular node

Left ventricle

Right ventricle

rate (up to 100 bpm) is due to a withdrawal of parasympathetic tone. At higher intensities, there is further inhibition of the parasympathetic system, and increased myocardial activation is due to direct stimulation of cardiac accelerator nerves via sympathetic activity.

The strength of ventricular contraction is influenced by the volume of blood in the ventricles at the end of **diastole** (i.e., end-diastolic volume). An increase in ventricular volume at the end of the cardiac cycle stretches the cardiac muscle fibers, which improves the force of contraction similar to what is seen in skeletal muscle. This relationship is known as the **Frank-Starling mechanism** of the heart, named after the physiologists who discovered it. Consequently, a rise in cardiac contractility results in an increased amount of blood pumped per beat.

Sympathetic stimulation also influences blood flow throughout the body by producing **vasoconstriction** in non-exercising muscles, except in the vessels that supply the heart, and **vasodilation** in exercising muscles. At the start of exercise, skeletal muscle arteriole vasodilation prepares the muscle for action by allowing more blood into the tissue. As exercise continues, vasodilation is increased and maintained through various mechanisms that include a reflex that arises from accumulation of metabolites produced during muscle action (e.g., decreased oxygen in the tissues is a potent stimulus for vasodilation in muscle). This feedback system monitors the effectiveness of blood flow in meeting the increased metabolic demands presented by exercise. Additionally, increases in core body temperature; carbon dioxide and acidity levels in the blood; adenosine, magnesium, and potassium ions; and nitric oxide production within the blood vessels all enhance regional blood flow. This process is called **autoregulation** and is thought to be the most important determinant in blood flow regulation to skeletal muscle during exercise. Lastly, sympathetic activity is also responsible for a significant shift of blood flow from the abdominal organs to the active muscles during physical activity via vasoconstriction of the arteries supplying the **viscera.**

Blood Pressure and Blood Distribution During Exercise

Blood pressure during exercise is influenced by the nervous and endocrine systems via alterations in the diameter of active-muscle arterioles (i.e., vasodilation or vasoconstriction). Recall that the highest blood pressure attained is **systolic blood pressure (SBP)** and the lowest is **diastolic blood pressure (DBP).** During ventricular systole, blood is ejected into the aorta and other arteries and the blood pressure increases to a maximum (SBP). As blood drains from the arteries during ventricular diastole (filling phase), the pressure decreases to a minimum (DBP). During physical activity, blood pressure increases as a result of the accompanying increase in cardiac output. SBP is affected more than DBP during exercise due to several factors:

- Increased heart contractility and stroke volume increase the force with which blood leaves the heart.
- Muscle action requires greater force or pressure to deliver blood into the exercising muscles.
- Vasodilation within the exercising muscles allows more blood to drain from the arteries through the arterioles and into the muscle capillaries, thus minimizing changes in diastolic pressure (Figure 5-2).

Figure 5-2
Normal responses to blood pressure during exercise

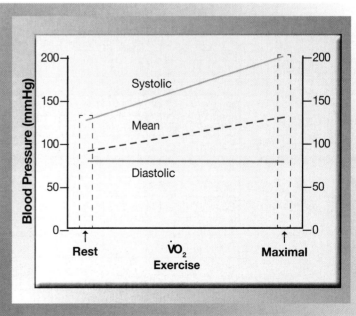

The redistribution of blood flow during exercise affects various organ systems differently (Table 5-1). At rest, approximately 15 to 20% of total cardiac output is directed toward skeletal muscle. During maximal exercise, however, 80 to 85% of total cardiac output is diverted to active skeletal muscle (Sjogaard, Sauard, & Juel, 1988; Laughlin & Korthius, 1987). During intense physical activity, the percentage of total cardiac output to the brain is decreased compared to resting. However, the absolute volume of blood that reaches the brain is slightly increased above resting levels due to the elevated cardiac output during exercise. The percentage of total cardiac output that the heart receives in its coronary circulation is the same at rest and during maximal exercise, even though total coronary blood flow is increased due to the increase in cardiac output during intense exercise. Blood flow to the kidneys and **gastrointestinal tract** diminishes, but does not cease. Blood flow to the skin increases as exercise intensity increases, but at maximal intensities it decreases.

During the early stages of exercise, blood may experience a 10 to 20% decrease in volume due initially to the increased hydrostatic pressure from muscle contraction (which squeezes fluid out of the bloodstream) and an increase in osmotic pressure in the interstitial fluid space around muscle cells due to the accumulation of metabolites. Gradually, fluid lost to sweat will also contribute to a loss of blood volume. Consequently, the following changes take place to preserve blood volume:

- A progressive increase in heart rate at steady-state exercise to maintain cardiac output and offset the small loss in stroke volume associated with the fluid loss
- A compensation in blood pressure via further vasoconstriction in the non-exercising regions to maintain peripheral resistance and blood pressure
- A release of hormones—antidiuretic hormone, or **vasopressin**, and **aldosterone**—to help reduce water and sodium losses from the body

During resistance-training exercise, the working muscles experience a temporary increase in fluid accumulation, which results in a feeling of fullness in the muscle. Weight lifters often refer to this as the "pump." This phenomenon is called **transient hypertrophy** and results from fluid accumulation (i.e., **edema**) in the interstitial and intracellular spaces of the muscle that comes from the blood plasma. As the name implies, it lasts only for a short time. The fluid returns to the blood within hours after exercise.

Because the heart can only pump as much blood as it receives, cardiac output is ultimately dependent on the volume of blood returned to the right side of the heart via the systemic venous circulation (or venous return). Therefore, during maximal exercise, an increase in cardiac output of four to five times the level seen at rest means that venous return must also increase by that amount. An important mechanism that contributes to venous return during exercise is the muscle pump. As muscles contract, their veins are compressed and the blood within them is forced toward the heart. Between contractions, blood fills the veins again and more blood is forced toward the heart with the next contraction. Thus, the muscle pump is the result of the mechanical pumping action produced by rhythmical muscular contractions. Blood is prevented from flowing backward away from the heart

Table 5-1

Blood Flow Distribution at Rest and During Exercise

Organ	Rest	Maximal Exercise
Muscles	15–20%	84%
Liver	27%	2%
Heart	4%	4%
Skin	6%*	2%*
Brain	14%	4%
Kidneys	22%	1%
Other	7%	3%

*During light-intensity exercise in warm climates, skin blood flow might reach 12–14%. Reduced flow is seen during high-intensity exercise.

by one-way valves located in the veins of the limbs. During weightlifting and other types of sustained muscular exercise (e.g., **isometric exercise**), the action of the pump is inhibited and venous return is reduced.

Ventilatory Regulation

For the purposes of this discussion, the remaining function of the cardiorespiratory system that requires attention is ventilatory control. Exercise, especially **aerobic** exercise, results in significant increases in oxygen to working tissues, carbon dioxide returned to the lungs, and **minute ventilation** [measured as the volume of air breathed per minute ($\dot{V}_E$)]. The action of breathing (i.e., **inspiration** and **expiration**) is produced by the contraction and relaxation of the diaphragm during passive or quiet breathing and includes accessory muscles during exercise. Like the cardiovascular control center, the respiratory control center is located within the medulla oblongata region of the brain. Interestingly, immediately before exercise begins, the breathing rate increases. Since this premature acceleration in ventilation is not due to the performance of physical activity, it is most likely due to stimulation from the motor cortex resulting from anticipation of the ensuing exercise bout.

Ventilation is primarily controlled by neural and humoral influences. Humoral receptors (which are sensitive to chemical changes in the blood) and neural receptors offer input to the respiratory control center in the brain, thereby affecting the actions of the neurons that drive respiration. For example, when concentrations of carbon dioxide, hydrogen, and potassium in the blood increase, the humoral receptors located in the brain and carotid and aortic arteries stimulate the respiratory control center to increase ventilation. Decreases in arterial oxygen (as occurs during an ascent to high altitude or in severe pulmonary disease) also trigger the humoral receptors to signal a faster breathing rate.

Neural input to the respiratory control center may come from one of several peripheral receptors, such as the **muscle spindles, Golgi tendon organs (GTO),** or joint pressure receptors. These structures are sensitive to movement generated by the working muscles and may be partly responsible for the rise in ventilation that occurs within a few seconds of initiating activity. Further, mechanoreceptors in the right ventricle of the heart may also send afferent signals to the respiratory control center relative to increases in cardiac output that stimulate breathing. It is important to note that no single factor controls respiration during exercise, and the combined effects of several chemical (i.e., humoral) and neural factors contribute to the regulation of exercise ventilation.

Aerobic exercise accounts for the greatest impact on both oxygen uptake and carbon dioxide production. During submaximal exercise, ventilation increases linearly with oxygen consumption and carbon dioxide production. This occurs primarily through an increase in **tidal volume** (i.e., the volume of air inhaled and exhaled per breath). At higher or near-maximal intensities, the frequency of breathing becomes more pronounced and minute ventilation rises disproportionately to the increases in oxygen consumption (Figure 5-3). This disproportionate rise in breathing rate represents a state of ventilation that is no longer directly linked with oxygen demand at the cellular level and is generally termed

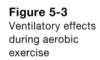

Figure 5-3
Ventilatory effects during aerobic exercise

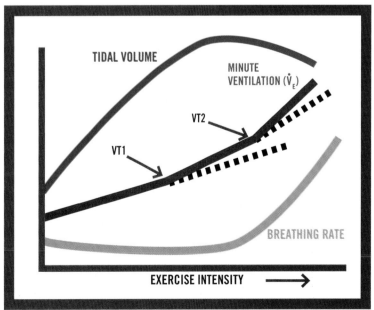

Note: VT1 = First ventilatory threshold; VT2 = Second ventilatory threshold; $\dot{V}_E$ = Minute ventilation

ventilatory threshold (for more information, refer to page 79). The overcompensation in breathing frequency results from an increase in carbon dioxide output related to the **anaerobic glycolysis** that predominates during near-maximal-intensity exercise. During strenuous exercise, breathing frequency may increase from 12 to 15 breaths per minute at rest to 35 to 45 breaths per minute, while tidal volume increases from resting values of 0.4 to 1.0 L up to 3 L or greater (McArdle, Katch, & Katch, 2007).

More specifically, there are two fairly distinct changes in the breathing pattern during incremental exercise. The **first ventilatory threshold (VT1)** occurs at approximately the first time that **lactate** begins to accumulate in the blood, and represents hyperventilation relative to $\dot{V}O_2$. It is caused by the need to blow off the extra carbon dioxide (CO_2) produced by the buffering of acid metabolites. There is a second disproportionate increase in ventilation, the **second ventilatory threshold (VT2),** which occurs at the point where lactate is rapidly increasing with intensity, and represents hyperventilation even relative to the extra CO_2 that is being produced. It probably represents the point at which blowing off CO_2 is no longer adequate to buffer the increase in acidity that is occurring with progressively intense exercise. See Chapter 2 for more on VT1 and VT2.

Fast-acting Hormones

The hormones described in this section are fast-responding substances that quickly return blood **glucose** concentrations back to normal after the body experiences a stressor, such as exercise. Each hormone behaves in a predictable way during exercise to ensure proper blood glucose maintenance.

Catecholamines

Mentioned earlier for their roles in preparing and regulating the body's cardiorespiratory function during exercise, epinephrine and norepinephrine (collectively called the catecholamines) are hormones of the **sympathetic nervous system.** The adrenal gland is actually two distinct glands located atop each kidney—the adrenal medulla (inner portion), which secretes the catecholamines, and the adrenal cortex (outer portion), which secretes steroid hormones.

The adrenal medulla is part of the sympathetic nervous system. Epinephrine and norepinephrine exert widespread effects on the organ systems that are critical for exercise performance. This readying process is often referred to as the "fight-or-flight" response and consists of preparing the body for strenuous physical activity in the face of an emergency or stressful situation.

Epinephrine is the primary hormone released by the adrenal medulla. Under the influence of epinephrine (and to a lesser extent, norepinephrine), the following responses occur:

- The strength of cardiac contraction increases, resulting in increased cardiac output.
- Generalized vasoconstriction in non-exercising muscles acts to increase total peripheral resistance. Combined, these effects cause an increase in SBP, thus ensuring an appropriate driving pressure to force blood to the organs most vital for physical exertion.
- Vasodilation of heart and active skeletal-muscle blood vessels occurs. Skeletal muscle vasodilation is then maintained throughout the course of the exercise session through autoregulation, which is affected by the by-products created during muscle metabolism.
- Epinephrine (but not norepinephrine) dilates the respiratory passages to aid in moving air into and out of the lungs, and reduces digestive activity and bladder emptying during exercise.
- Blood glucose concentration is also influenced by the release of epinephrine.
  - ✓ In general, epinephrine stimulates the mobilization of stored **carbohydrates** and **fats** for the purpose of making them available as energy to fuel muscular work.
  - ✓ Specifically, epinephrine stimulates

the production (**gluconeogenesis**) and release (**glycogenolysis**) of liver **glycogen.** It also stimulates glycogenolysis in skeletal muscles.

✓ Epinephrine also increases blood fatty-acid levels by promoting **lipolysis** [the breakdown of **triglycerides** in **adipose tissue** to **free fatty acids (FFAs)** for use as fuel].

• Lastly, epinephrine affects the **central nervous system** by promoting a state of arousal and increased alertness to permit "quick thinking" to help cope with the impending stressor (or exercise activity).

During physical exertion, blood levels of epinephrine and norepinephrine increase linearly with the duration of exercise. Norepinephrine increases noticeably until exercise intensity approaches 50% $\dot{V}O_2max,$ whereas epinephrine levels remain unchanged until exercise intensity exceeds about 60% $\dot{V}O_2max$ (McArdle, Katch, & Katch, 2007). These fast-acting hormones function to mobilize glucose and free fatty acids to maintain blood glucose concentration.

Insulin

Insulin, a hormone released by the pancreas, is directly involved in the uptake of glucose into tissue. Essentially, insulin exerts a hypoglycemic effect by reducing blood glucose levels and promoting the uptake of glucose, fats, and amino acids into cells for storage. During physical activity, however, the body needs to mobilize stored forms of fuel to use for energy. Therefore, the effects of insulin would generally be considered counterproductive. Activation of the sympathetic system during exercise suppresses insulin release from the pancreas. Glucose uptake by skeletal muscle can increase seven to 20 times over the values observed at rest (Felig & Wahren, 1975). Muscle tissue can take up higher levels of glucose at a faster rate, even when insulin levels are decreasing, partly due to an increase in muscle's sensitivity to insulin even after an acute bout of exercise training. As a result, less insulin is needed to bring about the same effect on glucose uptake into muscle tissue.

Glucagon

Another hormone released by the pancreas, **glucagon,** has the opposite effect of insulin on blood glucose concentrations. Glucagon stimulates an almost instantaneous release of glucose from the liver and is part of a negative feedback loop in which low blood glucose levels stimulate its release. In other words, one of glucagon's primary roles is to facilitate an increase in blood glucose concentration. Glucagon primarily contributes to blood glucose control as exercise progresses and glycogen stores deplete, typically later, rather than earlier, in an exercise bout. Working together, insulin and glucagon favor the maintenance of blood glucose levels at a time when the muscle is using blood glucose at a high rate.

Slow-acting Hormones

The hormones discussed in this section either facilitate the actions of other hormones or respond to stimuli in a slow manner. Each one is involved in the regulation of carbohydrate, fat, and **protein** metabolism.

Cortisol

Cortisol is a **glucocorticoid** released from the adrenal cortex that stimulates FFA mobilization from adipose tissue, mobilizes glucose synthesis in the liver (i.e., gluconeogenesis), and decreases the rate of glucose utilization by the cells. Its effect is slow, however, allowing other fast-acting hormones such as epinephrine and glucagon to primarily deal with glucose and FFA mobilization. Cortisol production increases with exercise intensity and with increasing levels of stress placed upon the body's physiological systems. Extremely high cortisol levels occur after long-duration events such as a marathon. This post-exercise elevation suggests that cortisol plays a role in tissue recovery and repair. However, prolonged elevations in blood cortisol levels have been linked with excessive protein breakdown, tissue wasting, negative nitrogen balance, and abdominal obesity. Individuals who follow very low-carbohydrate, low-calorie weight-loss diets often experience **ketosis** (i.e., dangerously excessive ketoacid concentrations in the extracellular fluid), which is amplified by elevated cortisol secretion.

Growth Hormone

Released from the anterior pituitary gland, **growth hormone** plays a major role in protein synthesis. Growth hormone also supports the action of cortisol by decreasing glucose uptake by the tissues, increasing FFA mobilization, and enhancing gluconeogenesis in the liver. The net effect of these actions is to preserve blood glucose concentration, thus augmenting performance during prolonged exercise. Short-term physical activity stimulates a dramatic increase in serum growth hormone concentrations. It appears that growth hormone increases are more dramatic for previously sedentary exercisers compared to fit exercisers.

Fuel Use During Exercise

Each of the macronutrients—carbohydrates, fats, and proteins—plays an important role in fueling the body during an exercise session. The body stores these energy sources in various locations and releases them for use depending on the type of activity performed.

Carbohydrate as Fuel

Carbohydrate serves as the major food fuel for the metabolic production of **adenosine triphosphate (ATP)**, which is a chemical compound required for all cellular work. Importantly, carbohydrate is the only macronutrient whose stored energy generates ATP anaerobically. This is crucial during maximal exercise that requires rapid energy release above levels supplied by aerobic metabolism.

Carbohydrate is stored as glycogen in both the muscle and the liver. Blood glucose levels are regulated primarily through the glycogen stored in the liver, such that when blood glucose levels are low, glycogen from the liver is broken down to glucose through a process called glycogenolysis and is released into the bloodstream. Once released into the blood, this glucose can be carried to the contracting muscle and used as fuel.

Carbohydrate use during exercise comes from both glycogen stores in muscle tissue and from blood glucose. Exercise intensity and duration determine the relative contribution of muscle glycogen and blood glucose used during a workout (Figure 5-4). During low-intensity exercise, blood glucose plays a greater role in energy metabolism, as the body's ability to deliver glucose is comparable to the rate of glucose utilization. On the other hand, muscle glycogen is the primary source of carbohydrate during high-intensity exercise, as the rate of glucose utilization far exceeds the rate of glucose delivery. The higher rate of utilization of glycogen during high-intensity exercise can be explained by the increased rate of glycogenolysis that occurs in the muscle due to recruitment of **fast-twitch muscle fibers** and elevated blood epinephrine levels. Remember, epinephrine stimulates the production and release of both liver and skeletal muscle glycogen. This generally occurs at exercise intensities exceeding 60% $\dot{V}O_2$max.

As mentioned earlier, the duration of exercise also affects the relative contribution of muscle glycogen and blood glucose. During the first hour of submaximal endurance exercise, much of the carbohydrate metabolized by muscle comes from muscle glycogen. However, as exercise continues and muscle glycogen levels decline, blood glucose derived from glycogenolysis in the liver becomes an increasingly important source of fuel.

Fat as Fuel

Fat used to fuel exercise is mainly stored in the form of triglycerides in **adipocytes** (fat cells). A relatively small amount is also stored in muscle cells. The role of fat as an energy source is mainly determined by its availability to the muscle cell. To be metabolized, triglycerides must be broken down into FFAs and glycerol (via a process called lipolysis). When triglycerides are split, FFAs can be converted into **acetyl coenzyme A (acetyl-CoA)** and enter the **Kreb's cycle.**

As with carbohydrate usage, exercise intensity and duration determine which fat stores are used as fuel. During low-intensity exercise, circulating FFAs from adipocytes (i.e.,

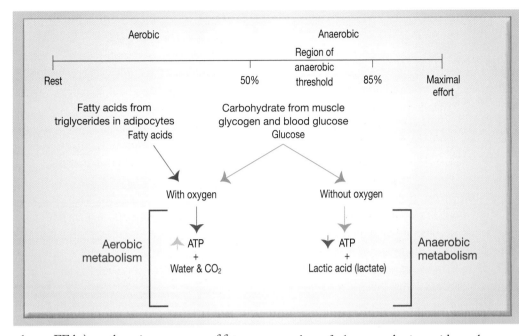

Aerobic   Anaerobic

Region of
anaerobic
Rest   50%   threshold   85%   Maximal
effort

Fatty acids from   Carbohydrate from muscle
triglycerides in adipocytes   glycogen and blood glucose
Fatty acids   Glucose

With oxygen   Without oxygen

Aerobic   ATP   ATP   Anaerobic
metabolism   +   +   metabolism
              Water & CO₂   Lactic acid (lactate)

Figure 5-4
Energy production
and relative intensity
in an exercising
muscle

Note:
ATP = Adenosine
triphosphate

plasma FFAs) are the primary source of fat energy. At higher intensities, metabolism of muscle triglycerides increases. Specifically, at exercise intensities between 65 and 85% $\dot{V}O_2$max, the contribution of fat as a muscle fuel source is approximately equal between plasma FFAs and muscle triglycerides (Coyle, 1995; Romijn et al., 1993).

The contribution of plasma FFAs and muscle triglycerides also changes over the course of a prolonged exercise session. At the beginning of exercise, the use of plasma FFAs and muscle triglycerides is equal. However, as the duration of exercise increases, there is a progressive rise in the role of plasma FFAs as a fuel source. During low-intensity, long-duration exercise, blood levels of epinephrine rise, thus promoting lipolysis. *Note:* This, however, is not justification for the concept of a fat-burning zone with respect to aerobic exercise (see text box on page 76). The process of lipolysis is slow, and an increase in fat metabolism occurs only after several minutes of endurance exercise.

Protein as Fuel

Although the role that protein plays as an energy source to fuel exercise is small, it is important to mention, especially considering its contribution to gluconeogenesis during prolonged exercise. Proteins must be broken down into **amino acids** before they can be

used as a fuel source. Amino acids can be supplied to muscle tissue from the blood and from the amino acid pool that exists in the muscle fiber itself. Skeletal muscle can directly metabolize certain types of amino acids (e.g., valine, leucine, isoleucine) to produce ATP. One fundamental difference between glucose found in muscle versus glucose found in liver cells is that muscle glucose is essentially trapped in the cell and cannot be released into circulation. During exercise, glucose stored in non-exercising muscles can be delivered indirectly to the exercising muscles by entering the glucose-alanine pathway (Figure 5-5). In the non-exercising muscles, glucose is partially metabolized to pyruvate, to which an amino group is added to manufacture

Figure 5-5
The glucose-alanine cycle

Reprinted with permission from McArdle, W.D, Katch, F.I., & Katch, V.L. (2007). *Exercise Physiology: Energy, Nutrition, and Human Performance* (6th ed.). Baltimore: Lippincott Williams & Wilkins.

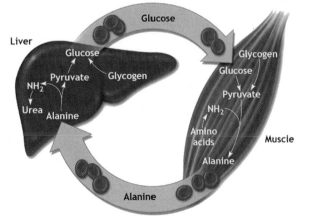

ACE Essentials of Exercise Science for Fitness Professionals

alanine, an amino acid that can be released into circulation. Alanine travels to the liver, where the amino group is removed and the pyruvates are reconstituted back to glucose, which then can be released into circulation to the exercising muscles. During prolonged or intense exercise, this pathway can contribute significantly to the delivery of glucose to muscles cells.

During prolonged endurance exercise (i.e., longer than two hours), amino acids are liberated from their parent proteins, causing a rise in the skeletal muscle amino-acid pool. This results in a small increase in the use of amino acids as fuel for exercise. The process of protein metabolism during exercise is significant because the increased conversion of amino acids to glucose helps prevent **hypoglycemia,** and the oxidation of certain amino acids may provide energy for muscular contraction.

Energy-system Interaction During Exercise

Each of the three energy systems [phosphagen, anaerobic glycolysis (or fast glycolytic or lactate), and aerobic] contributes to the total energy needs of the body during physical activity (Table 5-2). These systems do not work independently of each other. That is, one energy system generally dominates during an activity, but all three are utilized to provide the body with the fuel required to complete the task (Figure 5-6).

- At the onset of activity, or with any increase in intensity, the immediate energy needs are met by the phosphagen system.

- During endurance activities prior to the body achieving a steady state (or **homeostasis**), or during endurance activities when the intensity approaches the **anaerobic** threshold, fuel needs are met by the fast glycolytic (lactate) system.

- The aerobic (or oxidative) system takes over as the predominant energy pathway during endurance activities after the point at which the anaerobic systems (phosphagen and fast glycolytic) fatigue.

For example, during a 100-meter sprint, the lactate system predominates, but both the phosphagen and aerobic systems provide a small portion of the energy needed. At the other extreme, during a 30-minute, 1,000-meter run, the aerobic system predominates, but both the phosphagen and lactate systems contribute a very small amount of energy as well (Table 5-3).

Lactate as Fuel

Once thought of as only a waste product of glycolysis, lactate (i.e., **lactic acid**) can play a beneficial role during exercise by serving as both a compound used in gluconeogenesis in the liver and as a direct fuel source for the skeletal muscles and heart. During exercise, some of the lactate that is produced by skeletal muscles is transported to the liver via the blood. The liver then converts the lactate back to glucose and releases it into the bloodstream to be transported back to the skeletal muscles to be used as an energy source. The cycle of lactate-to-glucose between the muscle and the liver is called the **Cori cycle** (Figure 5-7). This

Table 5-2

The Three Energy Systems and Their Contributions to Total Energy Needs

System	Rate of ATP Production	Substrate	System Capacity	Utilization	Limitations
Phosphagen	Very rapid	Creatine phosphate, ATP	Very limited	High-intensity, very short-duration activities	Limited energy supply
Anaerobic Glycolysis	Rapid	Blood/muscle glucose, glycogen	Limited	High-intensity, short-duration activities	Lactic acid production
Aerobic	Slow	Blood glucose, glycogen, fatty acids, proteins	Unlimited	Lower-intensity, longer-duration activities	Slow rate of oxygen production

Note: ATP = Adenosine triphosphate

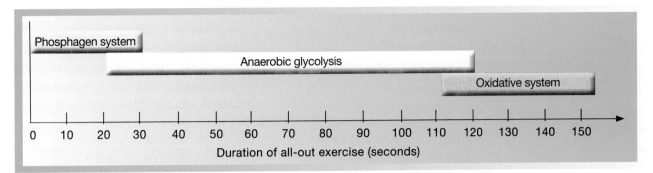

Figure 5-6
Energy-system contributions during all-out physical effort

Table 5-3					
Different Physical Activities and Fuel Use Associated With Each					
	Energy System				
Event	**Phosphagen**	**Anaerobic Glycolysis**	**Aerobic**	**Liver Glycogen**	**Free Fatty Acids**
100-meter run	50.0%	50.0%	Insignificant	Insignificant	Insignificant
200-meter run	25.0%	65.0%	10.0%	Insignificant	Insignificant
400-meter run	12.5%	62.5%	25.0%	Insignificant	Insignificant
800-meter run	6.0%	50.0%	44.0%	Insignificant	Insignificant
1,500-meter run	Insignificant	25.0%	75.0%	Insignificant	Insignificant
5,000-meter run	Insignificant	12.5%	87.5%	Insignificant	Insignificant
10,000-meter run	Insignificant	3.0%	97.0%	Insignificant	Insignificant
Marathon	Insignificant	Insignificant	75.0%	5.0%	20.0%
Ultramarathon	Insignificant	Insignificant	35.0%	5.0%	60.0%
Soccer game	10.0%	70.0%	20.0%	Insignificant	Insignificant

process works to preserve the body's blood glucose levels and to ensure that the muscles have adequate fuel to perform work.

Muscle Contractility

The ability of skeletal muscle to contract depends on three performance characteristics: maximal force production, speed of contraction, and muscle fiber efficiency.

- Maximal force production is expressed by how much force the fiber produces per unit of fiber cross-sectional area. Research suggests that fast-twitch muscle fibers produce 10 to 20% more force than **slow-twitch muscle fibers** because fast-twitch fibers contain more **myosin** cross-bridges per cross-sectional area of fiber (Bottinelli et al., 1994).
- The maximal shortening speed of muscle fibers is determined by the rate of

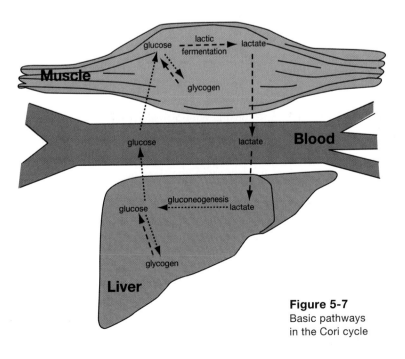

Figure 5-7
Basic pathways in the Cori cycle

cross-bridge movement (called cross-bridge cycling). Fast-twitch fibers exhibit a high maximal shortening velocity, whereas slow-twitch fibers contract more slowly. This appears to be due to the biomechanical properties of muscle fiber, such that fibers containing high levels of **myosin ATPase** (the **enzyme** required for the breakdown of ATP) are able to contract with higher speed. Accordingly, fast-twitch fibers possess higher concentrations of ATPase than slow-twitch fibers.

- A muscle fiber's efficiency is determined by a measure of the fiber's economy. That is, an efficient fiber requires less energy to perform a given amount of work than a less-efficient fiber. Slow-twitch fibers are more efficient than fast-twitch fibers due to their higher concentrations of **myoglobin,** larger numbers of capillaries, and higher mitochondrial enzyme activities. In other words, slow-twitch fibers are more efficient at using oxygen to generate more ATP to fuel continuous muscle contractions for extended periods.

Muscle Fatigue

An acute bout of intense prolonged exercise (e.g., one to two hours) that leads to a decline in muscular performance results in muscle fatigue. The anecdotal description of "hitting the wall" has been used by marathon runners to convey the sensations of fatigue and muscle pain associated with severe glycogen depletion. Thus, muscle fatigue is associated with a reduction in the body's glycogen reserves. In this state, fat from adipose tissue, the liver, and intramuscular stores supplies a progressively greater percentage of energy to the working muscles. A greater reliance on fat during muscle-fatigue states reduces power output because fat mobilization and oxidation are significantly slower than the mobilization and utilization of carbohydrate, and carbohydrates are needed to metabolize fats.

Exercisers who drink a glucose and water solution near the point of fatigue may prolong exercise for a short period, but the muscles' glycogen stores will remain depleted for the duration of the exercise session. Preventing muscle fatigue during prolonged exercise is a strategy that can be addressed by manipulating the macronutrient ratio in the diet. That is, endurance exercisers who eat a high-carbohydrate diet (approximately ≥60% of calories from carbohydrate) and/or who practice carbohydrate loading can extend their performance times before hitting the wall (Applegate & Grivetti, 1997; Rauch et al., 1995; Bergstrom et al., 1967).

Thermoregulation During Exercise

One of the many demands that sustained physical exertion places on the body is increased heat production. Contracting skeletal muscles produce large amounts of heat, and the body must regulate internal temperature by making adjustments in the amount of heat that is lost. In fact, metabolism often rises 20 to 25 times above resting levels during intense aerobic exercise by elite athletes, resulting in a potential increase in body temperature of 1° C every five to seven minutes.

The importance of body-temperature regulation is related to the critical processes of metabolism. That is, enzymes that regulate metabolic pathways are greatly influenced by changes in body temperature. An increase in body temperature above 113° F (45° C) may be destructive to the protein structure of enzymes, resulting in cellular death. A decrease in body temperature below 93.2° F (34° C) may cause a slowed metabolism and abnormal cardiac function. Thus, it is clear that body temperature must be carefully regulated.

An important concept should be kept in mind regarding temperature regulation: within the body, temperature may vary. There is a gradient (i.e., difference) between deep body temperature, such as the area surrounding internal organs, and shell (or skin) temperature. Thus, when referring to body temperature, an emphasis should be placed on using specific, descriptive terms (i.e., core temperature or skin temperature).

The body's temperature regulatory center is located in the hypothalamus in the brain. Receptors in the core and the skin send information to the hypothalamus about temperature changes within the body and the environment, respectively. During a bout of sustained submaximal endurance exercise in a cool/moderate environment (i.e., low humidity and room temperature), muscular contraction produces heat in amounts directly proportional to exercise intensity. The venous blood draining from the exercising muscle carries excess heat throughout the body's core. Thermal core receptors signal the hypothalamus that the core temperature is rising, which directs the nervous system to commence sweating and increase blood flow to the skin. These processes increase body-heat loss and minimize the increase in body temperature.

The four mechanisms the body uses to give off heat are **radiation, conduction, convection,** and **evaporation** (Figure 5-8). Radiation is heat loss in the form of infrared rays, which involves the transfer of heat from the surface of one object to another without any physical contact (e.g., the sun's rays transferring heat to the earth's surface). Conduction is the transfer of heat from the body into the molecules of cooler objects that come in contact with its surface (e.g., the transfer of heat from the body to a metal chair while a person is sitting on it). Convection is a form of conduction wherein heat is transferred to either air or water molecules in contact with the body. As water or air molecules are warmed and moved away from the skin (such as in forced convection when the wind from a fan blows over the skin), cooler molecules replace them. Evaporation occurs when heat is transferred from the body to water on the surface of the skin (e.g., sweat). When this water accumulates sufficient heat, it is converted to a gas (water vapor), removing heat from the body as it vaporizes.

At rest, the body relies predominantly

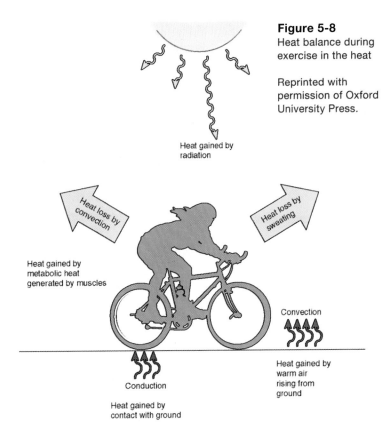

Figure 5-8

Heat balance during exercise in the heat

Reprinted with permission of Oxford University Press.

Heat gained by radiation

Heat loss by convection

Heat loss by sweating

Heat gained by metabolic heat generated by muscles

Convection

Conduction

Heat gained by warm air rising from ground

Heat gained by contact with ground

on conduction, convection, and radiation for thermoregulation. During sustained exercise in a moderate environment, these mechanisms play minor roles in heat loss due to the small temperature gradient between the skin and the room. As environmental temperature and exercise intensity increase, the extent of heat loss due to conduction, convection, and radiation are further reduced due to a decrease in the skin-to-room temperature gradient. Thus, the body relies on evaporation as the primary means of losing heat during exercise (Table 5-4).

Table 5-4		
Mechanisms of Thermoregulation		
Thermoregulatory Mechanism	**Rest**	**Exercise**
Conduction and convection	20% of total	10–15% of total
Radiation	55–60% of total	5% of total
Evaporation	20% of total	80% of total
Excretion/lungs*	5–10% of total	<2% of total

*300 mL in mucus membranes

ACE Essentials of Exercise Science for Fitness Professionals

Exercise in the Heat

Since a hot/humid environment reduces the ability to lose heat through radiation, convection, and evaporation, it is clear that exercising in the heat poses a particularly stressful challenge to the body. Individuals become more at risk for suffering from **hyperthermia,** as exercise in a hot/humid environment produces a greater core temperature and a higher sweat rate (i.e., more fluid loss) (see Table 2-4, page 87).

There are steps that individuals can take to improve exercise tolerance in a hot environment and prevent heat-related illness. First, optimizing exercise performance in the heat can be accomplished through **heat acclimation,** which is the process of physiological adaptation to heat (see "Heat Acclimation" on page 238). Second, consuming appropriate amounts of fluids before and during exercise can help attenuate the fluid losses due to heavy sweating during exercise in the heat (Table 5-5).

Table 5-5

Fluid-intake Recommendations During Exercise

2 hours prior to exercise, drink 500–600 mL (17–20 oz)
Every 10–20 minutes during exercise, drink 200–300 mL (7–10 oz) or, preferably, drink based on sweat losses
Following exercise, drink 450–675 mL for every 0.5 kg body weight lost (or 16–24 oz for every pound)

Adapted with permission from Casa, D.J. et al. (2000). National Athletic Trainers' Association: Position statement: Fluid replacement for athletes. *Journal of Athletic Training*, 35, 212–224.

Exercise in the Cold

Exercising in the cold presents its own set of specific challenges to the body. The chance of heat injury is greatly reduced in the cold, but the risk of developing hypothermia is increased.

When the skin or blood temperature drops, the thermoregulatory center activates mechanisms that conserve body heat and increase heat production. There are three primary ways in which the body avoids excessive heat loss: **peripheral vasoconstriction,** nonshivering **thermogenesis,** and shivering.

Peripheral vasoconstriction is the narrowing of the arterioles (due to sympathetic stimulation), which reduces the blood flow to the shell of the body, thus decreasing the amount of body heat lost to the environment. When altering skin blood flow is not enough to prevent heat loss, nonshivering thermogenesis is increased. This involves stimulation of the metabolism (as directed by the sympathetic nervous system) to increase internal heat production. Shivering is the next bodily process that occurs if peripheral vasoconstriction and nonshivering thermogenesis are not adequate in preventing heat loss. Shivering is a rapid, involuntary cycle of contraction and relaxation of skeletal muscles, which can increase the body's rate of heat production by four to five times.

The two major cold stressors are air and water. The effects of cold air are compounded by wind. As wind increases, so do convective heat loss and the rate of body cooling. An index based on the cooling effect of wind is **windchill,** which refers to the cooling power of the environment (see Table 2-5, page 88). As windchill increases, so does the risk of freezing body tissues. Water, on the other hand, is actually more detrimental than air in terms of heat loss. In general, the body loses heat four times faster in water than it does in air of the same temperature. This rate can be increased even more if the cold water is moving around the individual (e.g., in a current) due to increased heat loss through convection. A body immersed in cold water [≤59° F (15° C)] for prolonged periods can experience extreme hypothermia and even death.

Gender Differences in Thermoregulation

In general, women of comparable aerobic fitness and **heat acclimatization** appear to tolerate heat at least as well as men. Sweating is the most distinct gender difference in thermoregulation. Given that women have more surface area for their body weight (i.e., less lean, dense mass), they rely more on conduction, convection, and radiation to regulate body temperature than do men, who generate greater quantities of heat (due to increased lean mass). Thus, women tend to sweat less than men, and start to sweat at higher skin and core temperatures. In addition, they produce less sweat than men for a given exercise load, even after equivalent acclimatization, because they have less bodily fluid than men due to lower quantities of lean mass (muscle cells are approximately 75% water, whereas fat cells may be up to 10% water). Regardless of the noticeable difference in sweat output, women have a heat tolerance similar to men of the same aerobic fitness level at the same exercise intensity (Stephenson & Kolka, 1993). One explanation for the finding that women sweat less, yet are able to tolerate heat as well as men, is that women use circulatory mechanisms (e.g., shunting more blood to the cooler periphery) for heat dissipation, whereas men make greater use of evaporation. Producing less sweat to maintain body temperature protects women from dehydration during exercise in the heat. With exposure to the cold, there is also little difference between men and women in terms of body temperature regulation.

Chronic Adaptations to Exercise

Throughout this chapter, some of the physiological processes that occur during a single bout of physical exertion have been described. This section is devoted to explaining several adaptations to regular, consistent exercise that allow the body to improve its performance measures.

Cardiorespiratory Changes

Cardiorespiratory endurance capacity is determined by the ability of the cardiovascular and respiratory systems to deliver oxygen to active tissues, and the ability of those tissues to extract and use the oxygen during prolonged bouts of exercise. Numerous cardiorespiratory adaptations occur during the course of a regular training program to enhance the body's endurance capacity (Table 5-6).

Blood Volume

An increase in blood volume (primarily plasma, and to a lesser extent red blood cells) is an initial, rapid adaptation to endurance

Table 5-6	
Summary of Adaptations to Cardiovascular Training	
Cardiac Output Factors	**Oxygen Extraction Factors**
Decreased HR at any submaximal effort, including rest	Increased capillary density
Increased SV at rest, and at all intensities	Increased number of mitochondria
Increased maximum cardiac output	Increased activity of mitochondrial (aerobic) enzymes

Note: HR = Heart rate; SV = Stroke volume

exercise. An increase in plasma volume can be observed within one hour of recovery from the first exercise session. Practically all of the increase in blood volume during the first two weeks of training can be attributed to an increase in plasma volume. In fact, plasma volume can increase up to 12 to 20% after three to six aerobic training workouts (Sawka et al., 2000).

The number of red blood cells may also increase as a result of endurance training, although the evidence of this is unclear. Interestingly, the actual number of red blood cells may increase, while the ratio of red blood cell volume to total blood volume may decrease. A blood volume ratio that favors plasma over red blood cells reduces the blood's viscosity, or thickness. A physical-performance advantage of reduced blood viscosity is that it enhances oxygen delivery to the active skeletal muscles, because the blood flows more easily through the vessels, including the capillaries.

Heart Size

Active individuals tend to have moderately enlarged hearts. Both heart size and heart volume increase as an adaptation to increased work demand and decrease to pre-training measures within several weeks after training is stopped. This enlargement is characterized by an increase in the size of the left ventricular cavity and a slight thickening of its walls. Since the left ventricle is responsible for the forceful propulsion of oxygenated blood through the arterial system, it is the cardiac structure most affected by endurance training.

The extent and type of heart size adaptation

relates to the type of exercise training performed. During resistance training, the left ventricle must contract against an increased **afterload** (i.e., the pressure against which the heart must pump blood, determined by the peripheral resistance in the large arteries). Thus, the thickening of the left ventricular wall is a response to repeated exposure to the increased afterload with resistance training.

The increased cavity size of the left ventricle is largely due to the endurance training–induced increase in plasma volume discussed in the previous section. An increase in plasma volume causes an increase in end-diastolic volume (i.e., the volume of blood in the left ventricle just prior to contraction after it has completed filling). This endurance-training effect of increased left ventricular volume is believed to be due to the stretch imposed by the increased blood volume both during exercise and at rest. Recall from earlier in the chapter the Frank-Starling mechanism of the heart, wherein an increase in ventricular volume at the end of the cardiac cycle stretches the cardiac muscle fibers, which improves the force of contraction similar to that seen in skeletal muscle. Consequently, increased cardiac force and blood volume result in an increased amount of blood pumped per beat. Additionally, a decreased resting heart rate (caused by increased parasympathetic tone) and a decreased exercise heart rate for a given intensity allow for a longer diastolic filling period and a reduced work requirement for the heart. These adaptations lead to improvements in $\dot{V}O_2$max and less cardiac stress.

Fick Equation

In exercise physiology, the Fick equation is used to determine the rate at which oxygen is being used during physical activity. The Fick equation states that systemic oxygen consumption is determined by cardiac output ($\dot{Q}$), which is reflective of the amount of oxygen being delivered to the tissues, and **arterial-mixed venous oxygen difference (a-v̄ O_2 difference)**, which is reflective of the

amount of oxygen extracted by the tissues. Thus, the product of cardiac output and the a-v̄ O_2 difference determines the rate at which oxygen is being consumed:

$$\dot{V}O_2 = \dot{Q} \times a\text{-}\bar{v}O_2 \text{ difference}$$

$$\dot{Q} = \text{stroke volume} \times \text{heart rate}$$
$$a\text{-}\bar{v}O_2 \text{ difference} = \text{oxygen extraction}$$

According to the Fick equation, any improvements in $\dot{V}O_2$max as a response to training over time would have to be due to one or more of the variables on the right side of the first equation. A brief overview of each of the Fick equation variables and their responses to chronic endurance training follows.

Stroke volume at rest and during submaximal and maximal exercise increases as a result of regular training. Typical values for stroke volume at rest and during maximal exercise are compared among untrained, trained, and highly trained athletes in Table 5-7. These increases can be attributed to a greater blood volume, increased left ventricular dimensions, and reduced systemic resistance. The expansion of blood volume and the increase in size of the left ventricular cavity have been described in previous sections. Recall that increased cardiac muscle contractility results from an increase in left ventricular thickness and greater diastolic filling (Frank-Starling mechanism), which makes the heart more efficient with each beat. Further contributing to increased stroke

Table 5-7

Stroke Volumes (SV) for Different States of Training

Subjects	SVrest (mL/beat)	SVmax (mL/beat)
Untrained	50–70	80–110
Trained	70–90	110–150
Highly Trained	90–110	150–220+

Reprinted with permission from J.H. Wilmore, D.L. Costill, & W.L. Kenney (2008). *Physiology of Sport and Exercise* (4th ed.). Champaign, Ill.: Human Kinetics, 226.

volume is the reduction in systemic peripheral resistance observed with chronic endurance training. This decrease in vascular resistance (or decreased afterload) contributes to the increased volume of blood pumped from the left ventricle with each beat.

Heart rate is affected by aerobic endurance training in at least two ways: resting heart rate is typically decreased by more than 10 bpm, and submaximal heart rate is generally 10 to 20 bpm lower during exercise at the same absolute workload. In general, maximal exercise heart rate does not change with endurance training. Although the reasons for the decreases in resting and submaximal heart rates associated with training are not entirely understood, it is believed that regular endurance exercise increases parasympathetic activity while decreasing sympathetic activity.

The two factors of cardiac output (stroke volume and heart rate) have just been described in terms of their responses to a program of consistent endurance training. That is, while stroke volume increases, heart rate generally decreases at rest and during submaximal exercise at a given workload. Interestingly, cardiac output at rest and at a given submaximal exercise intensity does not change much following endurance training, and has even been shown to decrease slightly. This is most likely due to greater oxygen extraction at the tissues (reflecting an increase in the a-$\bar{v}$ O_2 difference). Cardiac output during maximal intensities, however, does change considerably in response to aerobic training. Since maximal heart rate changes little, if at all, the increased cardiac output at maximal intensities is almost exclusively due to an increase in maximal stroke volume.

The last variable of the Fick equation is a-$\bar{v}$ O_2 difference. The a-$\bar{v}$ O_2 difference increases with training, particularly at maximal exercise intensity. Recall that a-$\bar{v}$ O_2 difference stands for arterial-mixed venous oxygen difference, which represents oxygen content in venous blood returning from all body parts, not just active tissues. Thus, an increased a-$\bar{v}$ O_2 difference observed in a trained individual means that he or she has a lower mixed venous oxygen content than an untrained person. This reflects both greater oxygen extraction at the tissue level and a more effective distribution of blood flow to active tissue.

Blood Flow

During exercise, more blood is delivered to active muscles than to inactive ones. With regular endurance training, blood flow to active muscles is enhanced through:

- Increased capillarization of trained muscles
- Greater recruitment of existing capillaries in trained muscles
- More effective blood flow redistribution from inactive areas
- Increased blood volume

New capillaries develop in trained muscles to allow blood to more effectively perfuse the active tissues. Existing capillaries that were not readily open prior to endurance training become more easily recruited and open to blood flow in trained muscles. These factors combine to create more cross-sectional area for exchange between the vascular system and the active muscle fibers.

As mentioned earlier in the chapter, during exercise, blood is shunted from the areas that do not need high blood flow (e.g., organs in the abdominal cavity) and is redirected to active musculature. In addition, the body's total blood volume increases with regular endurance exercise. These factors allow the body to provide more blood to the working muscles during endurance activities.

Blood Pressure

Both aerobic-endurance and resistance-training exercise may have a positive influence on blood pressure. At a given submaximal exercise workload, arterial blood pressure is reduced. While resting blood pressure in response to aerobic training does not change significantly in healthy subjects, both systolic and diastolic pressures tend to be lowered in borderline or moderately hypertensive individuals who exercise regularly. At maximal exercise capacity, SBP increases, while DBP decreases. Lastly, a program of consistent resistance training may also reduce resting SBP (Hagberg et al., 1984).

Oxidative Enzymes

Another important adaptation in response to aerobic-endurance training is an increase in both the size and number of **mitochondria** within the skeletal muscles. Since the mitochondria improve the muscle's capacity to produce ATP, these increases in mitochondrial size and number enhance the muscle's ability to use oxygen and produce ATP via oxidation.

Aerobic training also increases the activity of the mitochondrial oxidative enzymes responsible for catalyzing (or speeding up) the breakdown of nutrients to form ATP. As a consequence of the mitochondrial changes associated with endurance training, there is a slower rate of muscle glycogen utilization and an enhanced reliance on fat as fuel at any given exercise intensity. This has a glycogen-sparing effect, which may allow an exerciser to maintain a higher exercise intensity throughout the duration of a workout.

Neural Changes

Neuromuscular adaptations in response to chronic exercise are more significant as a result of resistance training than aerobic-endurance training. While gains in strength are related to muscle **hypertrophy,** there are many instances when strength gains occur in the absence of hypertrophy. These gains can be best explained by changes that occur in the neuromuscular system. **Motor unit** recruitment and synchronization, **rate coding,** and diminished co-contraction are neurological factors that contribute to strength gains observed in the early part of a resistance-training program (the first one to three weeks), before muscle hypertrophy occurs.

Motor Unit Recruitment and Synchronization

Movement is created when skeletal muscles receive impulses from alpha motor neurons to contract. The functional unit of movement, the motor unit, consists of one alpha motor neuron and all of the specific muscle fibers it innervates. When activated, all of the muscle fibers in a motor unit maximally contract simultaneously. This is known as the **all-or-none principle.** If low-force muscle contraction is required, only a few motor units are activated. In contrast, when higher-force requirements are present, progressively more motor units are called upon (**type I muscle** fibers are recruited first, and then **type II muscle** fibers in a progressive and additive manner). Thus, all motor units within a given muscle are generally not called on to contract at the same time. That is, they are typically recruited asynchronously. However, with regular resistance training, motor units may act more synchronously (i.e., many motor units recruited simultaneously), enhancing contraction and potentially increasing the muscle's ability to generate force.

Rate Coding

A single motor unit can produce varying levels of force depending on the frequency at which it is stimulated. A motor unit's smallest contractile response to a single electrical stimulation is termed a **twitch.** A series of multiple stimuli in rapid sequence, prior to relaxation from the first stimulus, results in even greater force production. This process is termed **summation**. Continued stimulation at even higher frequencies can lead to a state of **tetanus,** resulting in peak force production of the motor unit (Figure 5-9). Rate coding describes the process by which the force production of a given motor unit varies from that of a twitch to that of tetanus by increasing the frequency of stimulation of the motor unit. Rate coding may increase with resistance training, which would result in an increase in the frequency of discharge of the motor units and allow for a faster time to peak force production for the trained muscle. Rapid movement or ballistic (explosive) training may be particularly effective in provoking increases in rate coding.

Diminished Co-contraction

For any given set of opposing muscle groups, to maximize the force generated by an **agonist,** the activation of the **antagonist** must be diminished. In other words, antagonists act to impede the action of the agonists. For

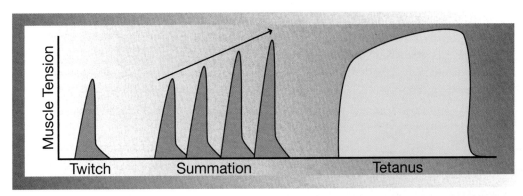

Figure 5-9
Rate coding

example, if the quadriceps and hamstrings were contracting with equal force simultaneously, no movement of the knee would occur. Thus, strength gains that occur early in a resistance-training program could be in small part due to the neurological occurrence of diminished co-activation or co-contraction.

Hormonal Changes

In general, the hormonal response to a given exercise load declines with regular endurance training. This increased efficiency may result from improved target tissue sensitivity and/or responsiveness to a given amount of hormone. Table 5-8 lists a selection of hormones and their general responses to endurance-exercise training.

Adrenal Hormones

Catecholamine (i.e., epinephrine and norepinephrine) output declines significantly during the first several weeks of submaximal endurance training. The favorable training adaptations of a lowered resting heart rate and a smaller rise in blood pressure during submaximal exercise are the most common evidence of decreased catecholamine levels. Circulating cortisol levels tend to increase slightly as a result of exercise training as the body seeks to become more efficient at preserving glucose.

Pancreatic Hormones

Individuals who participate in regular aerobic-endurance exercise maintain blood levels of insulin and glucagon during exercise that are closer to resting values. This is important because the trained state requires less insulin at any specific point from rest through submaximal-intensity exercise.

Table 5-8	
Hormones and Their Responses to Endurance Training	
Hormone	**Training Response**
Epinephrine and norepinephrine	Decreased secretion at rest and at the same absolute exercise intensity after training
Cortisol	Slight elevation during exercise
Insulin	Increased sensitivity to insulin; normal decrease in insulin during exercise greatly reduced with training
Glucagon	Smaller increase in glucose levels during exercise at absolute and relative workloads
Growth hormone	No effect on resting values; less dramatic rise during exercise

Date from: McArdle, W.D, Katch, F.I., & Katch, V.L. (2007). *Exercise Physiology: Energy, Nutrition, and Human Performance* (6th ed.). Baltimore: Lippincot Williams & Wilkins.

Further, the combination of resistance exercise and aerobic training improves active muscles' insulin sensitivity more than aerobic training alone. Thus, individuals with blood glucose regulation problems (i.e., those with the **metabolic syndrome** or **diabetes**) stand to benefit from both modes of exercise training.

Growth Hormone

Endurance-trained individuals show less rise in circulating blood growth hormone levels at a given exercise intensity than their untrained counterparts. This can be attributed to the reduction in stress that arises as a result of the exercise stimulus as training progresses and fitness improves. In contrast, resistance training augments growth hormone release (via increases in **testosterone**) and interacts with nervous system function to increase muscle force production, especially in men (Davis et al., 2000; Kraemer et al., 1999).

Testosterone

In addition to growth hormone, testosterone is a primary hormone that affects resistance-training adaptations. Heavy resistance exercise [i.e., 85 to 95% of **one-repetition maximum (1 RM)**], or moderate- to high-volume training with multiple sets and/or exercises with less than one-minute rest intervals, along with training larger muscle groups, leads to an increase in testosterone release (Kraemer, 1988). Following long-term resistance training in men, resting testosterone levels increase, which is associated with strength improvement over time (Hakkinen et al., 2000).

General Adaptation Syndrome

In the mid-1930s, a Canadian endocrinologist, Dr. Hans Selye, observed that a wide variety of stressful events (including heavy exercise) led to predictable increases in cortisol. He called this response the **general adaptation syndrome.** According to Selye, the general adaptation syndrome has three distinct stages (Selye, 1936):

- The shock or alarm reaction, involving cortisol secretion
- The stage of adaptation or resistance, where bodily repairs occur
- The stage of exhaustion, in which repairs are inadequate and sickness or death results

When stress (such as physical exertion) causes tissue damage, cortisol stimulates the breakdown of tissue protein to form amino acids, which can then be used at the site of tissue damage for repair. Performing large amounts of high-intensity activity can have negative effects on adaptation such that the muscles become chronically depleted of their energy reserves and symptoms of chronic fatigue or overtraining set in.

The following list illustrates how the body responds to an overload of chronic exercise training (Figure 5-10).

- Shock or alarm phase
  - ✓ The individual generally exhibits initial symptoms of fatigue, weakness, and soreness, but soon experiences what appear to be remarkable gains
  - ✓ Usually lasts two to three weeks, with strength gains attributed to neuromuscular adaptations only
- Adaptation or resistance phase
  - ✓ Generally begins around weeks four through six and represents major muscular adaptations (biochemical, mechanical, and structural)
  - ✓ Characterized by progressive increases in muscle size and strength
- Exhaustion phase
  - ✓ May occur at any time, demonstrates symptoms similar to the first phase, but inadequate repair or recovery time leads to burnout, overtraining, reduction or elimination of overload, injury, illness, or lack of adherence

Overtraining

Overtraining as a result of overloading the body's physiological capacities in an effort to improve future performance is a distinct problem, especially in athletes trying to achieve a competitive edge. During periods of intense overload, athletes may experience symptoms of overtraining, collectively referred to as overtraining syndrome. It is important to realize that these symptoms are subjective and identifiable only after an athlete's performance and physiological function have suffered. Primary signs and symptoms of overtraining include the following:

- A decline in physical performance with continued training
- Elevated heart rate and blood lactate levels at a fixed submaximal work rate
- Change in appetite
- Weight loss
- Sleep disturbances
- Multiple colds or sore throats
- Irritability, restlessness, excitability, and/or anxiousness
- Loss of motivation and vigor

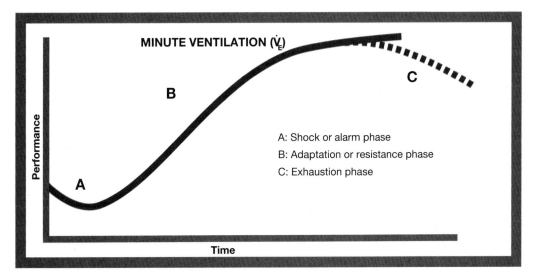

Figure 5-10
The body's response
to an overload of
chronic exercise
training

- Lack of mental concentration and focus
- Lack of appreciation for things that are normally enjoyable

Notice that the symptoms of overtraining are a complex combination of both physiological and emotional factors. This suggests that the anxiety and psychological demands associated with physical competition may be sources of intolerable emotional distress. Interestingly, some researchers have pointed to the similarities between overtraining syndrome and clinical **depression,** including physical signs and symptoms, as well as disturbances in **neurotransmitter** levels, endocrine pathways, and immune responses (Armstrong & VanHeest, 2002).

Since the symptoms of overtraining are highly individualized, they cannot be universally applied to all individuals. The presence of just one or more of these symptoms may be sufficient to alert a coach or fitness professional that an individual might be experiencing the overtraining syndrome. The importance of designing exercise programs or classes to include both rest and variation of training intensity and volume to prevent overtraining cannot be overstated.

The best way to prevent overtraining is to follow **periodization** training models, which alternate easy, moderate, and hard periods of training. As a general rule, one or two days of intense training should be followed by an equal number of easy training days. Similarly, a week or two of hard training should be followed by a week or two of easier effort. This type of

alternate-intensity training allows the hardest working muscle fibers to replenish their energy stores and be prepared to take on the next intense training session.

Delayed Onset Muscle Soreness

While many theories have been proposed to explain the occurrence of **delayed onset muscle soreness (DOMS),** present evidence suggests it is caused by tissue injury from excessive mechanical force, particularly **eccentric** force, exerted on muscle and **connective tissue** (Clarkson & Sayers, 1999; Friden & Lieber, 1992; Smith, 1991). DOMS is defined as muscle soreness that generally appears 24 to 48 hours after strenuous exercise. Although not completely understood, the following series of events is thought to lead up to DOMS:

- First, structural damage to muscle and connective tissue occurs as a result of strenuous eccentric muscle actions.
- As a result, calcium leaks out of the **sarcoplasmic reticulum** and collects in the mitochondria to the extent that ATP production is halted.
- Next, the buildup of calcium activates enzymes that break down cellular proteins, including contractile proteins.
- This breakdown of muscle proteins causes an inflammatory process.
- Lastly, the accumulation of histamines, potassium, prostaglandins, and edema surrounding muscle fibers stimulates free

nerve endings (i.e., pain receptors), which results in the sensation of DOMS.

Efforts to prevent DOMS should include beginning a new training program gradually, starting at a very low intensity and progressing slowly through the first few weeks (e.g., five to 10 training sessions). Further, since eccentric exercise is associated with greater suffering from DOMS, attempts should be made to minimize eccentric actions early in the program. Activities that involve strenuous eccentric actions (e.g., dead lifts) can be introduced later in the program after muscles have had a chance to adapt to the new stress of exercise.

General Training Principles

The basic training principles presented in this section apply to all forms of physical training. An understanding of these principles aids fitness professionals in developing the safest and most effective training programs or classes.

Specificity

The principle of **specificity** explains the outcome of a given type of training program such that the exercise response is specific to the mode and intensity of training. In other words, only the physiological systems emphasized during a training program will improve. For example, a program of long-distance endurance running will improve an exerciser's aerobic capacity, but it will do nothing to enhance the exerciser's performance on a heavy bench press.

At the cellular level, specificity refers to the types of adaptations that occur in the muscle fibers themselves. Endurance training results in the primary adaptations of increased capillary and mitochondria number, which improve the capacity of the muscle to produce energy aerobically. Heavy resistance training, on the other hand, results in an increase in the quantity of contractile proteins, while the mitochondrial and capillary densities actually decrease. These adaptations allow the muscle to produce more contractile force while improving the muscle's efficiency during anaerobic metabolism. Thus, a

training program must include activities of the appropriate mode and intensity to match the desired performance outcome.

Overload and Progression

Overload and **progression** are two distinct principles, but they are often combined to describe one of the most important foundations of training—progressive overload. Overload refers to strategically applying increased load on a tissue or system above and beyond the point at which that tissue or system is normally loaded. An example of overload is when a weightlifter performing a bench press lifts 5 to 10 more pounds (2.3 to 4.5 kg) during a set than he or she did the last time performing the same exercise. Variables that can be manipulated to apply overload include the frequency, intensity, duration, and mode of an exercise-training program.

Progression refers to the systematic process of applying overload. In resistance training, progression implies that as the muscles become stronger, proportionately greater resistance is required to stimulate further strength gains. In long-distance endurance training, progression implies that appropriate increases in the duration of a workout session result in increased distance outcomes. An important point related to progressive overload is that the increased physical demand placed on the body must be done gradually and within appropriate exercise guidelines to avoid overtraining and musculoskeletal injuries.

Diminishing Returns

People respond to specific exercise programs based on their own individual genetic composition. In many instances, regardless of the physical-activity programming being used, some individuals will demonstrate improvement, while others will not. Thus, performance outcomes among various exercisers are highly individualistic. The principle of diminishing returns suggests that the rate of fitness improvement diminishes over time as fitness approaches its ultimate genetic potential. The response to physical activity is not only associated with heredity, but is also highly influenced by an individual's current level of fitness. The more fit a person is, the less likely he or she is to improve further. Figure 5-11 demonstrates the principle of diminishing returns such that the individual with the lowest fitness level showed the greatest magnitude of improvement.

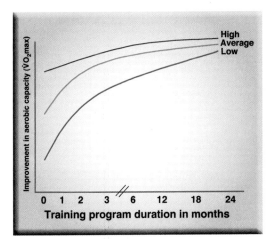

Figure 5-11
Hypothetical relationship between training program duration and improvements in aerobic capacity for three cardiorespiratory fitness levels (in healthy individuals)

Reversibility

The principle of **reversibility** pertains to the losses in function experienced after the cessation of a training program. Regardless of the gains in fitness achieved through a regular exercise program, those improvements will be reversed to pre-training levels and may ultimately decrease to a point that meets only the demands of daily use. The principle of reversibility supports the concept that a training program must include a maintenance plan to avoid functional losses throughout life.

Muscle Growth

Earlier in this chapter, neurological adaptations to resistance training were discussed. It was mentioned that early gains in strength are attributed to changes in the nervous system. Muscle growth, or **chronic hypertrophy,** is responsible for the strength gains experienced after a prolonged period of resistance training. Chronic hypertrophy is associated with structural changes in the size of existing individual muscle fibers (fiber hypertrophy), in the number of muscle fibers (fiber **hyperplasia**), or both.

Fiber Hypertrophy

Muscle fiber hypertrophy is most likely the result of one or more of the following: an increased number of myofibrils, a greater number of **actin** and **myosin** filaments, more **sarcoplasm,** and more connective tissue. An increase in muscle protein synthesis stimulated by resistance training appears to be the mechanism responsible for fiber hypertrophy in trained individuals. The ingestion of adequate amounts of carbohydrate and protein immediately after a training session, as well as the presence of testosterone, are factors that enhance muscle protein synthesis.

Research on the type of resistance training that evokes the most muscle hypertrophy suggests that eccentric actions combined with high-velocity training promote greater increases in hypertrophy than **concentric** actions and slower-velocity training (Shepstone et al., 2005). Thus, limiting a resistance-training program to include only concentric muscle actions could have a negative impact on an individual's ability to increase muscle size and strength.

Fiber Hyperplasia

Most evidence points to muscle fiber hypertrophy as the primary cause of increased muscle size associated with resistance training. However, fiber hyperplasia may also contribute to the muscle growth related to resistance training. It is thought that individual muscle fibers may have the capacity to split into two daughter cells, each of which can develop into new muscle fibers. Located within each muscle fiber are satellite cells, which are myogenic stem cells involved in the generation of new muscle fibers. Stress to the muscle in the form of stretch, injury, immobilization, or intense training (especially eccentric action) stimulate satellite cells to migrate to the damaged region to possibly fuse existing muscle fibers and/or produce new fibers (Hawke & Garry, 2001).

*Enhancing Muscle
Growth Through Exercise*

A resistance-training program that induces the stimulation of protein synthesis, and thus muscle growth, is a program that naturally increases levels of testosterone and growth hormone. It is presumed that growth hormone increases the availability of amino acids for protein synthesis by decreasing tissue glucose uptake, increasing FFA mobilization, and enhancing liver gluconeogenesis. Growth hormone also stimulates the release of **insulin-like growth factor 1 (IGF-1)**, which works together with growth hormone to stimulate muscle cell growth. Testosterone promotes the release of growth hormone from the pituitary gland and interacts with the neuromuscular system to stimulate muscle growth as well.

A training program that stresses and manipulates the endocrine system to bring about increases in these muscle-building (i.e., **anabolic**) hormones includes large-muscle-group or multijoint exercises (e.g., dead lift, power clean, squat) performed at high intensities with short rest intervals between sets. Serum testosterone levels are increased when heavy resistance (85 to 95% 1 RM) is used, multiple sets or multiple exercises are performed, or short rest intervals (30 to 60 seconds) are incorporated (Kraemer et al., 1991). Growth hormone levels are increased when high-intensity (10 RM or heavier) exercises are performed for multiple sets with short rest periods (e.g., 60 seconds) (Kraemer et al., 1990). Consuming adequate amounts of carbohydrate and protein before and after a training session is also important for optimizing the anabolic effects of growth hormone.

Muscle Fiber Adaptations

The principle of specificity is apparent when looking at how specific types of training cause adaptations in muscle fibers. With anaerobic training (e.g., sprint training and resistance training), type II fibers are recruited to a greater extent than type I fibers. Consequently, both type IIa and type IIx fibers experience an increase in their cross-sectional areas. Type I fibers also undergo an increase in cross-sectional area, but to a lesser extent since the contribution of type I fibers is not as predominant in anaerobic activities. In addition, sprint training (i.e., 15- to 30-second all-out sprinting) can cause a reduction in type I fibers with a simultaneous increase in the number of type II fibers. This type of shift from type I to type II fibers is associated with sprint training, and is not typically seen with resistance training alone. Although early research contradicted the concept that one muscle fiber type could be converted into another, later studies have shown that a combination of high-intensity resistance training and short-interval speed work can, in fact, cause the conversion of type I fibers into type IIa fibers (Anderson et al., 2000; Staron et al., 1990).

In contrast, a program of aerobic-endurance training causes type I fibers to increase in size. Accordingly, with aerobic training, type II fibers do not show an increase in size because they are typically not recruited to the same extent during endurance activities. In some instances, long-duration exercise (e.g., a 20-week program of aerobic-endurance training) may eventually recruit type IIa fibers and even cause some type IIx fibers to take on the characteristics of the more oxidative type IIa fibers. Furthermore, some evidence suggests that while the magnitude of change is very small (not more than a few percentage points), there might also be an actual conversion of type II fibers to type I fibers (Rico-Sanz et al., 2003).

Muscle Glycogen Storage

The body stores approximately 300 to 400 grams of glycogen in the skeletal muscles and approximately 70 to 100 grams in the liver. Since exercise requires the breakdown and use of glycogen to fuel bodily movement, physically active individuals should take care to ensure they are replenishing their glycogen stores regularly. Exercise intensity determines the rate at which glycogen is depleted such that as exercise intensity increases, muscle glycogenolysis also increases. During moderate- and high-intensity exercise (i.e., intensities equal to or greater than 60% of **maximal oxygen uptake**) muscle glycogen is the predominant energy source, whereas liver glycogen is more important during low-intensity exercise.

Strategies to enhance muscle glycogen storage include eating a carbohydrate-rich diet and consuming carbohydrates immediately after high-intensity exercise (i.e., within 30 minutes). It is possible to load trained skeletal muscle with nearly twice its normal capacity for glycogen storage by eating a high-carbohydrate diet (i.e., 55 to 65% of total calories from carbohydrates). Endurance athletes are able to increase the duration and intensity of their workouts if they are performing with full glycogen stores. They also perceive training as easier if their muscle glycogen is maintained throughout a workout. Further, since prolonged endurance exercise and high-intensity training deplete muscle glycogen stores, athletes should take advantage of the most favorable time period to replenish glycogen stores—immediately after a training session.

Rates of glycogen resynthesis are very high during the first two hours after high-intensity or long-duration workouts, and progressively level off thereafter (Figure 5-12). It takes about 24 hours to fully restore muscle glycogen, assuming that the appropriate post-workout nutrients are consumed and that nutrition goals for the athlete to properly fuel the activity are met (Table 5-9). Eating a combination of carbohydrate and protein in the post-workout meal has been shown to enhance glycogen replenishment and may also improve muscle tissue repair (Ivy, 2004; Ivy et al., 2002).

Muscle-buffering Capacity

The ability of muscles to neutralize the lactic acid that accumulates in them during high-intensity exercise is the muscle's buffering capacity. As lactic acid increases, the pH of the muscle tissue decreases, which inhibits the cells' enzymatic activity and other metabolic processes, resulting in a decrease in the

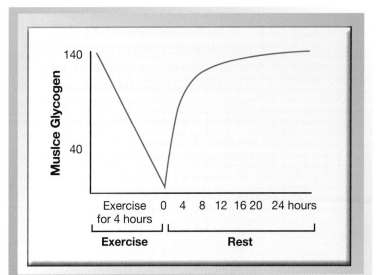

Figure 5-12
It takes 24 hours to replenish muscle glycogen after strenuous exercise.

Table 5-9	
Nutrition Goals for Athletes	
Energy	Ensure adequate total energy intake to support physical activity; maintain appropriate body weight
Carbohydrate	6–10 g/kg/day
Protein	1.2–1.4 g/kg/day for endurance-based sports
	1.6–1.7 g/kg/day for strength-based sports

available energy and muscle contraction force during exercise. Thus, an increase in a muscle's buffering capacity delays the onset of fatigue and allows the exerciser to perform at a higher intensity and for a longer duration before "hitting the wall."

Lactic acid is converted to its salt, lactate, by buffering systems in the muscle and blood. Lactate is not a fatigue-producing substance. In fact, lactate may be circulated in the blood and used as an energy source, especially in type I and cardiac muscle fibers. Recall that lactate may also be transported to the liver, where it is converted to glucose via the Cori cycle (see Figure 5-7). Blood lactate concentrations are measured as markers for lactic acid production and clearance such that the clearance of lactate from the blood reflects a return to homeostasis and thus is reflective of a person's recovery status.

It has been demonstrated that both aerobically trained and anaerobically trained athletes are able to clear lactate from their blood faster than untrained individuals (McMillan et al., 1993; Pierce et al., 1987; Gollnick, Bayly, & Hodgson, 1986). Evidence suggests that when individuals train at near or above their lactate thresholds (the point at which lactate begins an abrupt increase above baseline levels), they are able to perform at higher intensities without as much lactate accumulation in the blood (Donovan & Brooks, 1983; Davis et al., 1979).

Lactate threshold is typically observed at 50 to 60% of $\dot{V}O_2$max in untrained individuals and at 70 to 80% of $\dot{V}O_2$max in trained individuals. Thus, consistently training at these intensities will enhance an individual's muscle-buffering capacity and delay muscle fatigue during subsequent training sessions.

Recall that during submaximal exercise, ventilation parallels oxygen uptake until the point at which exercise approaches the lactate threshold. VT1, or the point at which ventilation begins to increase disproportionately to the increase in oxygen consumption, is an indirect representation of an exerciser's lactate threshold. At this point, an increase in the production of lactate, or a decrease in the clearance of lactate, results in the combining of lactic acid and sodium bicarbonate (which buffers acid) to form sodium lactate, water, and carbon dioxide. As the formation of carbon dioxide increases, chemoreceptors signal an increase in ventilation. This increase in ventilation reflects the need to remove excess carbon dioxide from the blood.

With exercise training, an individual's ability to sustain exceptionally high levels of submaximal ventilation improves. Furthermore, a decrease of approximately 20 to 30% in submaximal ventilation is observed at the same relative workloads after a training program compared with pre-training levels (Casburi et al., 1987). This contributes to the finding that after a program of regular endurance training, exercise causes less disruption in the acid–base balance, as evidenced by less lactate accumulation (Spengler et al., 1999; Vrabas et al., 1999). Other factors, including increased aerobic enzyme levels and oxidative capacity of the respiratory muscles, also enhance ventilatory muscle function.

Thermoregulatory Changes

As mentioned earlier in the chapter, the body's thermoregulatory center adjusts to repeated exercise in a hot environment, thereby allowing an individual to better tolerate thermal stress. Repeated exercise in the heat causes a relatively rapid adjustment—called heat acclimation—that enables the exerciser to perform better in hot conditions. Similar to heat acclimation, but more gradual in onset, is the process of heat acclimatization, which occurs in people who live in hot environments for months or years. Heat acclimation is discussed here because it is more applicable to outdoor exercise during warmer seasons.

Heat Acclimation

The positive adaptations to exercising in the heat can take place as early as nine to 14 days after beginning the acclimation process. The critical changes that occur to facilitate heat tolerance include an expansion of plasma volume, a decrease in heart rate and core temperature, and an increase in sweat rate during exercise, as well as a reduced threshold to initiate sweating (i.e., sweating will start at a lower core temperature).

The increased plasma volume occurs over the first one to three days of acclimation. This early process is important because an increased plasma volume supports increased stroke volume, allowing the maintenance of adequate cardiac output while additional physiological adjustments are made. The decreased heart rate and core temperature experienced with acclimation allow the body to perform more work before the onset of fatigue or exhaustion in the heat. The increased sweat rate associated with acclimation occurs up to 10 days or more after starting to exercise in the heat and allows the body to dissipate heat more effectively. Furthermore, at the beginning of exercise, sweating starts earlier in an acclimated person, which also improves heat tolerance. Lastly, the sweat that is produced is more dilute (i.e., has a lower concentration of **electrolytes**), which acts to conserve sodium.

An exercise program that involves heat acclimation should include low-intensity workout sessions in the heat for one hour or more each day for nine to 14 days. In addition, proper hydration before, during, and after exercise should be carefully planned.

Flexibility Training

Tissue Elasticity

Elasticity is the mechanical property that allows a tissue to return to its original shape or size when an applied force is removed (often defined as "temporary deformation") (Figure 5-13). **Ballistic** and **dynamic stretching** are examples of this principle. While they offer no permanent improvement to tissue extensibility, these stretching modalities activate neuromuscular patterns in preparation for activity.

A critical region called the "elastic limit" is reached when a tissue is stretched beyond the point where it can return to its normal length after the tensile force is removed (Figure 5-14). The difference (or deformity) between the original resting length of the tissue and the new resting length, after being stretched beyond its elastic limit, is termed permanent set, permanent deformation, or strain. This new state of permanent elongation is also called plastic stretch. This transition is called the yield point. **Static stretching,** which illustrates this principle, improves tissue extensibility, as the tissue deformation remains after the tension is removed. If further tensile force is applied to a tissue beyond its yield point, gradual tissue failure occurs.

Tissue Plasticity

The mechanical property known as plasticity allows a tissue to deform when it is loaded past its elastic limit. Once a tissue is set past its yield point, it may succumb to considerable amounts of additional

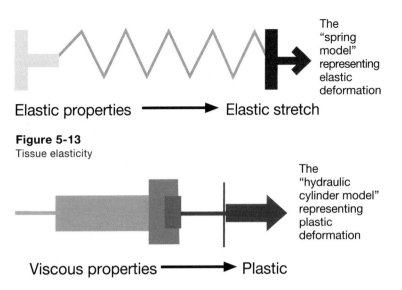

Elastic properties ⟶ Elastic stretch

The "spring model" representing elastic deformation

Figure 5-13
Tissue elasticity

Viscous properties ⟶ Plastic

The "hydraulic cylinder model" representing plastic deformation

Figure 5-14
Plastic stretch

deformation with relatively small increases in force. Plasticity of tissues can be observed with long-term, repetitive microtrauma. This type of chronic stress leads to tissues that are less stable and less efficient. An unmistakable example of long-term microtrauma is the deformation that occurs in postural muscles as a result of poor posture when sitting in a chair. Over time, the body adapts to a faulty sitting posture by increased deformation of the back tissues and shortening of the anterior trunk tissues. This ultimately leads to reduced **range of motion** and the development of pain. In this example, one would want to correct the problem by promoting plasticity of the anterior trunk muscles through stretching exercises and developing strength in the back muscles through resistance training.

Tissue Viscoelasticity

Viscosity is the property of tissues that allows them to resist loads and, unlike elasticity and plasticity, is dependent on time and temperature. Tissue viscosity is an important principle for exercisers and athletes. Properly warming up the body's tissues and fluids reduces viscosity and allows adequate extensibility.

As the name implies, viscoelasticity is the property that allows tissues to exhibit both plastic and elastic behaviors. Most structures in the body are neither completely elastic nor completely plastic. Instead, they exhibit a combination of both properties. When subjected to low loads, most tissues exhibit elastic behavior. Conversely, when subjected to higher loads, tissues exhibit a plastic response. Furthermore, when loads are repeated over time, tissues exhibit viscous deformation.

Although the evidence is unclear, many fitness and sports professionals engage in regular flexibility training to improve performance and reduce the risk of musculoskeletal injuries. It is clear, however, that losses in flexibility can result in a reduction of movement efficiency and place individuals at risk for low-back pain. This section presents commonly used stretching techniques and the acute improvements and chronic adaptations to flexibility training.

Neurological Properties of Stretching

Autogenic inhibition is a principle stating that activation of a GTO inhibits a muscle spindle response.

- When a static stretch is initially performed (low-force, longer-duration), the small change in muscle length stimulates low-grade muscle spindle activity and a temporary increase in muscle tension.
- This low-grade muscle response progressively decreases due to a gradual desensitization of the muscle spindle activity as the duration of the stretch progresses. This response is referred to as stress-relaxation.
- After seven to 10 seconds of a low-force stretch, the increase in muscle tension activates a GTO response.
- Under GTO activation, muscle spindle activity and any tension in the muscle are temporarily inhibited, allowing further muscle stretching.
- Now that the muscle tension is removed, holding the stretch beyond 10 seconds places stresses along the collagen fibers,

remodeling them as they pull apart (plastic deformation) and lengthen the tissue. The lengthening that occurs when a stretch force is applied is called **creep**. Reductions in tension (stress-relaxation response) and creep are possible explanations for the increases in range of motion observed after an acute static-stretching session

- After terminating the stretch, the muscle spindle quickly reestablishes its stretch threshold again (approximately a 70% recovery of the muscle spindle within the first five seconds).
- Repeating the static stretch a finite number of times produces a gradual increase in muscle extensibility.
- As an example, holding a hamstrings stretch for seven to 10 seconds will inhibit the muscle and allow greater stretching.

Reciprocal inhibition is the principle stating that activation of a muscle on one side of a joint (i.e., the agonist) coincides with neural inhibition of the opposing muscle on the other side of the joint (i.e., the antagonist) to facilitate movement. When a contraction or active movement in an agonist is performed (<50% of maximum force is suggested) for more than six seconds, the antagonist muscle becomes inhibited (reduced muscle spindle activity), allowing it to be stretched. For example, firing the gluteus maximus for six to 15 seconds reciprocally inhibits the hip flexors temporarily, thereby allowing the hip flexors to be then stretched.

Static Stretching

A static stretch is performed by moving the joints to place the targeted muscle group in an end-range position and holding that position for up to 30 seconds. Static stretching is one of the most commonly practiced forms of flexibility training because it is easily performed without the requirement of a partner and it does not elicit the **stretch reflex** (i.e., a reflexive muscle contraction that occurs in response to rapid stretching of the muscle), reducing the likelihood of injury. As long as the stretch is not too intense (i.e., does not provoke pain), there are no real disadvantages to static stretching if proper technique is used.

Static stretching can be performed actively or passively. An active stretch occurs when the individual applies added force to increase the intensity of the stretch. For example, leaning further to the side during a side bend stretch increases the intensity of the stretch to the lateral flexors on the opposite side of the torso. Since the side-bending action is performed by the person stretching, he or she is "actively" involved in the exercise. In contrast, a passive stretch occurs when a partner or assistive device provides added force for the stretch. An example of a passive stretch is an individual performing a lying hamstring stretch with the leg propped against a sturdy table or door jamb (Figure 5-15). Another example is when a fitness professional applies a slight force to the back of the person's leg to allow the client to reach the point of resistance in his or her range of motion.

Figure 5-15
Passive static stretch of the hamstrings

Proprioceptive Neuromuscular Facilitation

Originally developed and used to treat increased tissue tonicity in the rehabilitation setting, **proprioceptive neuromuscular facilitation (PNF)** capitalizes on the principles of autogenic inhibition and reciprocal inhibition. There are three basic types of PNF stretching techniques: hold-relax, contract-relax, and hold-relax with agonist contraction. For each of the three techniques, a partner provides a passive pre-stretch of 10 seconds as the initial step. The actions that follow the passive pre-stretch are different for each technique. These unique differences give each technique its name.

Hold-relax

After the passive 10-second pre-stretch, the hold-relax technique requires the individual to hold and resist the force provided by the fitness professional so that an isometric muscle contraction occurs for six seconds in the muscle group targeted for the stretch. Then, the individual relaxes the muscle group and allows a passive stretch force from the fitness professional (held for 30 seconds) to increase the range of motion in the muscle group that was previously in isometric contraction. This final stretch should be of greater magnitude due to autogenic inhibition. Figure 5-16 illustrates proper technique for a hold-relax stretch of the hamstrings.

Figure 5-16
Hold-relax hamstrings stretch

Contract-relax

After a passive 10-second pre-stretch, the contract-relax technique requires the individual to push against the force provided by the fitness professional so that a concentric muscle contraction occurs throughout the full range of motion of the muscle group targeted for the stretch. In other words, the fitness professional provides enough resistance to slightly counteract the individual's force of contraction, but not so much that he or she cannot move the joint through its range of motion. Then, similar to the hold-relax method, the individual relaxes the muscle group and allows a passive stretch force from the fitness professional (held for 30 seconds) to increase the range of motion in the muscle group that was previously in concentric contraction. This final stretch should be of greater magnitude due to autogenic inhibition. Figure 5-17 illustrates proper technique for a contract-relax stretch of the hamstrings.

Figure 5-17
Contract-relax hamstrings stretch

Hold-relax With Agonist Contraction

The hold-relax with agonist contraction technique is identical to the hold-relax technique, except a concentric action of the opposing muscle group is added during the final passive stretch to add to the stretch force. With this technique, the final stretch should be of greater magnitude primarily due to reciprocal inhibition and, secondarily, to autogenic inhibition. This PNF technique is considered the most effective since it utilizes both reciprocal and autogenic inhibition. Figure 5-18 illustrates proper technique for a hold-relax with agonist contraction stretch of the hamstrings.

Dynamic Stretching

A dynamic stretch mimics a movement pattern to be used in the upcoming workout or sporting event. It is commonly used to help athletes prepare for competition by allowing them to increase sport-specific

Figure 5-18
Agonist hold-relax hamstrings stretch

flexibility. An example of an athlete preparing for an event using dynamic stretches would be a track sprinter performing long walking strides that emphasize hip extension while maintaining a posterior pelvic tilt. This type of activity-specific movement enhances the flexibility of the hip joints and prepares the tissues for the upcoming intense physical exertion.

Ballistic Stretching

A stretch that incorporates bouncing-type movements is a ballistic stretch. Ballistic stretching has been used in athletic drills and in pre-training warm-ups. The bouncing movements associated with ballistic stretching usually trigger the stretch reflex and thus may be associated with an increased risk for injury. As a result, the use of ballistic stretching has not been widely advocated. However, the absolute exclusion of ballistic stretching from flexibility programs has been questioned, particularly in the case of athletes whose functional demands include ballistic-type movements.

Zachazewski and Reischl (1986) state that, "Ballistic activities may play a vital role in the conditioning and training of the athlete. If ballistics are utilized, they should be preceded by static stretching and confined to a small range of motion, perhaps no more than 10% beyond the static range of motion." A safe ballistic stretching program has been developed by Zachazewski (1990), who recommends a progressive velocity flexibility program preceded by a warm-up. After consistently practicing this program, the athlete goes through "a series of stretching exercises in which the velocity and range of lengthening are combined and controlled on a progressive basis" (Zachazewski, 1990). This gradual program permits the muscle and its associated tendon to adapt progressively to functional ballistic movements, thus reducing the risk of injury. Zachazewski (1990) briefly describes the program as follows:

The athlete progresses from an environment of control to activity simulation, from slow-velocity methodical activity to high-velocity functional activity. After static stretching:

- *Begin with slow, short end-range (SSER) ballistic movements.*
- *Progress to slow, full-range (SFR) movements.*
- *Progress to fast, short end-range (FSER) movements.*
- *End with fast, full-range (FFR) movements.*

Control and range are the responsibility of the athlete. No outside force is exerted by anyone else.

Active Isolated Stretching

Active isolated stretching (AIS), a technique originally used during rehabilitation for surgery patients, follows a design similar to a traditional strength-training workout. Instead of holding stretches for 15 to 30 seconds at a point of resistance (i.e., mild discomfort), stretches are never held for more than two seconds. The stretch is then released, the body segment returned to the starting position, and the stretch is repeated for several repetitions, with each subsequent movement exceeding the resistance point by a few degrees. Increasing the stretch by a few degrees at a time allows the muscle to adjust more gradually to the stretch. The stretches are typically performed in sets of a specified number of repetitions, with a goal of isolating an individual muscle in each set. Proponents of AIS claim that this technique targets specific muscles and prepares the body for physical activity better than static

stretching can, while also protecting the joint attachments that static stretching can sometimes weaken.

To better understand AIS, consider the traditional hamstrings stretch, in which the exerciser lifts the leg onto a bench. This requires work not only from the target muscles, but also from the calf, gluteal muscles, and back muscles. This creates a passive stretch of the hamstrings, and their natural response is to contract, thereby negating the benefit of the stretch. In AIS, the quadriceps are contracted and the hamstrings are stretched in a supine position using a rope or towel as an aid (Figure 5-19). It is believed that this allows the hamstrings to relax more completely and fully benefit from the stretch. It should be noted that some experts believe that holding a stretch for only two seconds is not adequate to have an effect on the connective tissue that surrounds and runs through muscles.

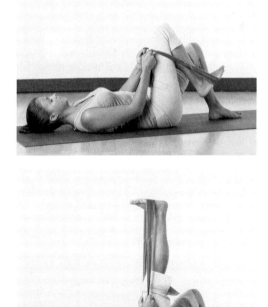

Figure 5-19
Active isolated stretching

Myofascial Release

Understanding the concept behind **myofascial release** requires an understanding of the fascial system itself. Fascia is a densely woven, specialized system of connective tissue that covers and unites all of the body's compartments. The result is a system where each part is connected to the other parts through this web of tissue. Essentially, the purpose of the fascia is to surround and support the bodily structures, which provides stability as well as a cohesive direction for the line of pull of muscle groups. For example, the fascia surrounding the quadriceps keeps this muscle group contained in the anterior compartment of the thigh (stability) and orients the muscle fibers in a vertical direction so that the line of pull is more effective at extending the knee.

In a normal healthy state, fascia has a relaxed and wavy configuration. It has the ability to stretch and move without restriction. However, with physical trauma, scarring, or inflammation, fascia loses its pliability. It becomes tight, restricted, and a potential source of pain. An acute injury, habitual poor posture over time, and repetitive stress injuries can be damaging to the fascia. As a result, the damaged fascia can exert excessive pressure, producing pain or restriction of motion, which in turn may induce adaptive shortening of the muscle tissue associated with the fascia.

Myofascial release is a technique that applies pressure to tight, restricted areas of fascia and underlying muscle in an attempt to relieve tension and improve flexibility. It is thought that applying sustained pressure to a tight area can inhibit the tension in a muscle by stimulating the GTO to bring about autogenic inhibition. Tender areas of soft tissue (also called trigger points) can be diminished through the application of pressure (myofascial release) followed by static stretching of the tight area.

The practical application of myofascial release in the fitness setting is commonly done through the use of a foam roller, where the exerciser controls his or her own intensity and duration of pressure. A common technique is to instruct individuals to perform small, continuous, back-and-forth movements on a foam roller, covering an area of 2 to 6 inches (5 to 15 cm) over the tender region for 30 to 60 seconds (Figure 5-20). Because exerting pressure on an already tender area requires a certain level of pain tolerance, the intensity of the application of pressure determines the duration in which the individual can withstand the discomfort. For example, a person with a high pain tolerance can position his or her body on the foam roller directly over a tender area and hold the applied pressure for 30 seconds. On the other hand, an individual with low pain tolerance can position his or her body near the focal point of the tender area and hold the applied pressure for 60 seconds.

Ultimately, myofascial release realigns the elastic muscle and connective tissue fibers from a bundled position (called a knot or adhesion) into a straighter arrangement, and resets the proprioceptive mechanisms of the soft tissue, thus reducing **hypertonicity** within the underlying muscles.

Figure 5-20
Myofascial release for gluteals/external rotators

Myofascial release for the quadriceps

Myofascial release for the hamstrings

Acute Responses to Flexibility Training

Soft tissues possess certain mechanical and dynamic properties that allow for performance of necessary functions as well as protection from forces they may encounter. Whenever a tissue is subjected to a force, a change in the shape of the tissue may occur. These changes are called deformations. The extent of deformation depends on variables such as the type of tissue, the amount of force applied, and the temperature of the tissue. When a tensile, or horizontal, force is applied to a tissue, its length is increased. This lengthening is called tensile deformation. In general terms, "stretching" refers to the process of elongation and "stretch" refers to the elongation itself.

Chronic Adaptations to Flexibility Training

One of the major determinants of long-term adaptations in flexibility is the collagen found in connective tissues. The two major physical properties of collagen fibers are their tensile strength and relative inextensibility. In other words, structures containing large amounts of collagen tend to limit motion and resist stretch. Thus, collagen fibers are the main constituents of tissues such as ligaments and tendons that are subjected to a pulling force.

One of the mechanisms behind collagen's great tensile strength and relative inextensibility is its banded, or striated, structure (much like the pattern observed in muscle tissue). When viewed under a microscope, the collagen of a tendon is arranged in wavy bundles called **fascicles.** The fascicle is composed of fibrils, which in turn consist of bundles of subfibrils. Each subfibril is composed of bundles of collagen filaments. In addition to a striated pattern, connective tissues contain wavelike folds of collagen fibers known as **crimp.** The mechanical properties of collagen fibers are such that each fibril behaves as a mechanical spring—thus, each fiber is a collection of springs. When a fiber is pulled, its crimp straightens and its length increases. As in a mechanical spring, energy is stored within the fiber, and it is the release of this energy that returns the fiber to its resting state when the stretch force is removed.

Compared to a **sarcomere,** a collagenous fiber is relatively inextensible. In fact, one classic study demonstrated that the collagen fiber is so inelastic that a weight 10,000 times greater than its own will not stretch it (Verzar, 1964). Collagen fibers may undergo an extension of about 3% before the slack in their wavy bundles (crimp) is taken up. If the stretch continues, a critical point will be reached at which the tissue ruptures.

Collagen fibers are almost always found together with elastic fibers. Since elastic fibers surround the sarcomere, they are responsible for determining the possible range of extensibility of muscle cells. As their name implies, elastic fibers succumb readily to stretching, and when released they return to their former length. Elastic fibers are responsible for what is called reverse elasticity (i.e., the ability of a stretched material to return to its original resting state). Only when elastic fibers are stretched to more than 150% of their original length do they reach their rupture point. Collagen and elastic fibers work together to support and facilitate joint movement, as they are both found in connective tissues such as tendons and ligaments.

Static Stretching and Permanent Tissue Elongation

Techniques that result in elastic, or short-term, deformation are characterized by high-force, short-duration stretching. In contrast, a program favoring low-force, longer-duration stretches at elevated tissue temperatures (i.e., after a warm-up) is more likely to result in plastic, or permanent, lengthening.

To ensure a safe and effective approach to developing flexibility, the simplest tactic is to perform a moderate, activity-specific warm-up (i.e., dynamic stretching) for the muscle groups involved in the upcoming activity. Gentle static stretching after an adequate warm-up may be incorporated and appears to do no harm. However, due to time constraints, it may be more practical to perform static stretching at the conclusion of the training session rather than at the beginning *and* the end.

Recommendations for the optimal time for holding a static stretch vary, ranging from as little as three seconds to as much as 60 seconds. However, stretches lasting longer than 30 seconds seem to be uncomfortable for many people, especially when they exhibit muscular tightness. The practice of holding a static stretch for 15 to 30 seconds appears to be the most effective for increasing range of motion. A stretch of this nature should be repeated three or four times and, as mentioned previously, after the muscle group is warm (preferably at the conclusion of a workout).

Summary

The practical application of the cardiorespiratory-, resistance-, and flexibility-training principles presented in this chapter will enhance the ACE-certified Fitness Professional's leadership and exercise programming skills. This information is essential for proper program design and progression from the first training session or group fitness class with an individual to the last. The understanding that exercise poses a serious challenge to the body's various systems is an important concept for fitness professionals to grasp. This chapter describes the significant contributions from the cardiorespiratory, nervous, endocrine, muscular, and thermoregulatory systems that are vital for the rest-to-exercise transition to be successful, as well as the adaptations that these systems undergo after a period of regular exercise training.

References

Anderson, J.L. et al. (2000). Muscle, genes, and athletic performance. *Scientific American,* 283, 48–55.

Applegate, E.A. & Grivetti, L.E. (1997). Search for the competitive edge: A history of dietary fads and supplements. *Journal of Nutrition,* 127, 869S–873S.

Armstrong, L.E. & VanHeest, J.L. (2002). The unknown mechanism of the overtraining syndrome. *Sports Medicine,* 32, 185–209.

Bergstrom, J. et al. (1967). Diet, muscle glycogen and physical performance. *Acta Physiologica Scandinavica,* 71, 140–150.

Bottinelli, R.M. et al. (1994). Myofibrillar ATPase activity during isometric contractions and isomyosin composition of rat single skinned muscle fibers. *Journal of Physiology,* 481, 663–675.

Casa, D.J. et al. (2000). National Athletic Trainers' Association: Position statement: Fluid replacement for athletes. *Journal of Athletic Training,* 35, 212–224.

Casburi, R. et al. (1987). Mediation of reduced ventilatory response to exercise after endurance training. *Journal of Applied Physiology,* 63, 1533–1538.

Clarkson, P. & Sayers, S. (1999). Etiology of exercise-induced muscle damage. *Canadian Journal of Applied Physiology,* 24, 234–248.

Coyle, E.F. (1995). Substrate utilization during exercise in active people. *American Journal of Clinical Nutrition,* 61, 968S–979S.

Davis, J.A. et al. (1979). Anaerobic threshold alterations caused by endurance training in middle-aged men. *Journal of Applied Physiology,* 46, 1039–1046.

Davis, S.N. et al. (2000). Effects of gender on neuroendocrine and metabolic counterregulatory measures responses to exercise in normal man. *Journal of Clinical Endocrinology and Metabolism,* 85, 224–230.

Donovan, C.M. & Brooks, G.A. (1983). Endurance training affects lactate clearance, not lactate production. *American Journal of Physiology,* 244, E83–E92.

Felig, P. & Wahren, J. (1975). Fuel homeostasis in exercise. *New England Journal of Medicine,* 293, 1078–1084.

Friden, J. & Lieber, R. (1992). Structural and mechanical basis of exercise-induced injury. *Medicine & Science in Sports & Exercise,* 24, 521–530.

Gollnick, P.D., Bayly, W.M., & Hodgson, D.R. (1986). Exercise intensity, training diet and lactate concentration in muscle and blood. *Medicine & Science in Sports & Exercise,* 18, 334–340.

Hagberg, J.M. et al. (1984). Effect of weight training on blood pressure and hemodynamics in hypertensive adolescents. *Journal of Pediatrics,* 104, 141–151.

Hakkinen, K.A. et al. (2000). Basal concentrations and acute responses of serum hormones and strength development during heavy resistance training in middle-aged and elderly men and women. *Journals of Gerontology Series A: Biological Sciences and Medical Sciences,* 55, B95–B105.

Hawke, T.J. & Garry, D.J. (2001). Myogenic satellite cells: Physiology to molecular biology. *Journal of Applied Physiology,* 91, 534–551.

Ivy, J.L. (2004). Regulation of muscle glycogen repletion, muscle protein synthesis and repair following exercise. *Journal of Sports Science and Medicine,* 3, 131–138.

Ivy, J.L. et al. (2002). Early postexercise muscle glycogen recovery is enhanced with a carbohydrate-protein supplement. *Journal of Applied Physiology,* 93, 1337–1344.

Kraemer, W.J. (1988). Endocrine responses to resistance exercise. *Medicine & Science in Sports & Exercise,* 29, S152–S157.

Kraemer, W.J. et al. (1999). Acute hormonal responses to a single bout of heavy resistance exercise in trained power lifters and untrained men. *Canadian Journal of Applied Physiology,* 24, 524–537.

Kraemer, W.J. et al. (1991). Endogenous anabolic hormone and growth factor responses to heavy resistance exercise in males and females. *International Journal of Sports Medicine,* 12, 228–235.

Kraemer, W.J. et al. (1990). Hormonal and growth factor responses to heavy resistance exercise. *Journal of Applied Physiology,* 69, 1442–1450.

Laughlin, M.H. & Korthius, R. (1987). Control of muscle blood flow during sustained physiological exercise. *Canadian Journal of Applied Sport Sciences,* 12, 775S–835S.

McArdle, W.D, Katch, F.I., & Katch, V.L. (2007). *Exercise Physiology: Energy, Nutrition, and Human Performance* (6th ed.). Baltimore: Lippincott, Williams, & Wilkins.

McMillan, J.L. et al. (1993). 20-hour physiological responses to a single weight-training session. *Journal of Strength and Conditioning Research,* 7, 9–21.

Pierce, K. et al. (1987). The effects of weight training on plasma cortisol, lactate, heart rate, anxiety and perceived exertion. *Journal of Applied Sports Science Research,* 1, 58.

Rauch, L.G. et al. (1995). The effects of carbohydrate loading on muscle glycogen content and cycling performance. *International Journal of Sports Nutrition,* 5, 25–36.

ACE Essentials of Exercise Science for Fitness Professionals

Rico-Sanz, J. et al. (2003). Familial resemblance for muscle phenotypes in The Heritage Family Study. *Medicine & Science in Sports & Exercise,* 35, 1360–1366.

Romijn, J. et al. (1993). Regulation of endogenous fat and carbohydrate metabolism in relation to exercise intensity. *American Journal of Physiology,* 265, E380–E391.

Sawka, M.N. et al. (2000). Blood volume: Importance and adaptations to exercise training, environmental stresses, and trauma/sickness. *Medicine & Science in Sports & Exercise,* 32, 332–348.

Selye, H. (1936). A syndrome produced by diverse nocuous agents. *Nature,* 138, 32.

Shepstone, T.N. et al. (2005). Short-term high vs. low-velocity isokinetic lengthening training results in greater hypertrophy of elbow flexors in young men. *Journal of Applied Physiology,* 98, 1768–1776.

Sjogaard, G., Sauard, G., & Juel, C. (1988). Muscle blood flow during isometric activity and its relation to muscle fatigue. *European Journal of Applied Physiology,* 57, 327–335.

Smith, L. (1991). Acute inflammation: The underlying mechanism in delayed onset muscle soreness. *Medicine & Science in Sports & Exercise,* 23, 542–551.

Spengler, C.M. et al. (1999). Decreased exercise blood lactate concentrations after respiratory endurance training in humans. *European Journal of Applied Physiology*, 79, 299–305.

Staron, R.R. et al. (1990). Muscle hypertrophy and fast fiber type conversions in heavy-resistance-trained women. *European Journal of Applied Physiology,* 60, 71–79.

Stephenson, L.A. & Kolka, M.A. (1993). Thermoregulation in women. *Exercise and Sport Science Reviews,* 21, 231–262.

Verzar, F. (1964). Aging of collagen fiber. In: Hall, D.A. (Ed.). *International Review of Connective Tissue Research,* 2, 244–300. New York: Academic Press.

Vrabas, I.S. et al. (1999). Endurance training reduces the rate of diaphragm fatigue in vitro. *Medicine & Science in Sports & Exercise,* 31, 1605–1611.

Wilmore, J.H., Costill, D.L., & Kenney, W.L. (2008). *Physiology of Sport and Exercise* (4th ed.). Champaign, Ill.: Human Kinetics.

Zachazewski, J.E. (1990). Flexibility for sports. In: Sanders, B. (Ed.). *Sports Physical Therapy* (pp. 201–238). Norwalk, Conn.: Appleton & Lange.

Zachazewski, J.E. & Reischl, S.R. (1986). Flexibility for the runner: Specific program considerations. *Topics in Acute Care Trauma Rehabilitation,* 1, 9–27.

Suggested Reading

Atler, M.J. (2004). *Science of Flexibility* (3rd ed.). Champaign, Ill.: Human Kinetics.

Baechle, T.R. & Earle, R.W. (2008). *Essentials of Strength Training and Conditioning* (3rd ed.). Champaign, Ill.: Human Kinetics.

McArdle, W.D., Katch, F.I., & Katch, V.L. (2007). *Exercise Physiology: Energy, Nutrition, and Human Performance* (6th ed.). Baltimore: Lippincott Williams & Wilkins.

Wilmore, J.H., Costill, D.L., & Kenney, W.L. (2008). *Physiology of Sport and Exercise* (4th ed.). Champaign, Ill.: Human Kinetics.

Chapter 5
Physiology of Training

Getting Started

This chapter covers the acute responses to a single bout of exercise, as well as the chronic adaptations made by the major physiological systems in response to an ongoing training program. It also discusses the physiological responses to various forms of flexibility exercise, including proprioceptive neuromuscular facilitation, static stretching, dynamic stretching, ballistic stretching, and active isolated stretching. After reading this chapter, you should have a better understanding of:

- The acute responses to exercise, including blood pressure and blood distribution during exercise, fuel use during exercise, muscle contractility and fatigue, and thermoregulation
- The chronic adaptations to exercise, including cardiorespiratory, neural, and hormonal changes
- Muscle growth and muscle fiber adaptations made as a result of an ongoing exercise regimen
- General training principles, including specificity, progressive overload, diminishing returns, and reversibility
- The acute and chronic adaptations to flexibility training

Expand Your Knowledge

I. What two major adjustments in blood flow must occur to meet the increased demands of muscle during exercise?

a. _____

b. _____

II. Describe the major differences between the following pairs of words or phrases.

a. SA node and AV node _____

_____

_____

_____

b. Chronotropic response and inotropic response _____

_____

_____

_____

c. VT1 and VT2 _____

_____

_____

_____

_____

_____

d. Heat acclimation and heat acclimatization _____

_____

_____

e. Twitch and summation _____

_____

_____

f. Fiber hypertrophy and fiber hyperplasia _____

_____

_____

III. Give three reasons why systolic blood pressure is affected more by exercise than diastolic blood pressure.

a. _____

_____

_____

b. _____

_____

_____

c. _____

_____

_____

IV. Explain how the redistribution of blood flow during exercise affects each of the following organ systems, taking into consideration both the percentage of total cardiac output and the absolute volume of blood.

a. Skeletal muscle _____

_____

_____

b. Brain _____

_____

_____

c. Heart _____

_____

_____

_____

d. Kidney and gastrointestinal tract _____

_____

_____

_____

e. Skin _____

_____

V. Match each of the following hormones with its description.

a. _____ Epinephrine

b. _____ Insulin

c. _____ Glucagon

d. _____ Cortisol

e. _____ Growth hormone

1. One of two fast-acting hormones that exert widespread effects on the organ systems that are critical for exercise performance; triggers the "fight-or-flight response"

2. Slow-acting hormone that plays a major role in protein synthesis and decreases glucose uptake by the tissues, increases free fatty acid mobilization, and enhances gluconeogenesis in the liver

3. Fast-acting hormone that reduces blood glucose levels and promotes the uptake of glucose, fats, and amino acids into cells for storage

4. Slow-acting hormone that stimulates free fatty acid mobilization from adipose tissue, mobilizes glucose synthesis in the liver, and decreases the rate of glucose utilization by the cells

5. Fast-acting hormone that stimulates an almost instantaneous release of glucose from the liver and is part of a negative feedback loop in which low blood glucose levels stimulate its release

VI. Read each of the following facts about the use of macronutrients as fuel during exercise, and place a (C) if it describes carbohydrate, an (F) if it describes fat, and a (P) if it describes protein.

    a. _____ Its role as an energy source is mainly determined by its availability to the muscle cell

    b. _____ Must be broken down into amino acids before being used as fuel

    c. _____ Use increases slightly during prolonged exercise lasting more than two hours

    d. _____ The major food fuel for the metabolic production of ATP

    e. _____ Mainly stored in the form of triglycerides in adipocytes

    f. _____ The only macronutrient whose stored energy generates ATP anaerobically

    g. _____ Crucial during maximal exercise that requires rapid energy release above levels supplied by aerobic metabolism

    h. _____ Plays the smallest role of the three macronutrients in terms of fuel during exercise

VII. Match each of the energy systems to the appropriate descriptions by placing a (P) if it describes the phosphagen system, an (A) if it describes the aerobic system, and (AG) if it describes the anaerobic glycolysis system.

    a. _____ The energy system used to meet the immediate energy needs at the onset of exercise or with any increase in activity

    b. _____ The energy system used during endurance activities prior to the body achieving homeostasis, or during activities when the intensity approaches the anaerobic threshold, or VT1

    c. _____ The energy system that takes over as the predominant energy pathway during endurance activities after the other two systems fatigue

    d. _____ Has an unlimited system capacity

    e. _____ Has a slow rate of oxygen production

    f. _____ Has a very rapid rate of ATP production

    g. _____ The primary system used during high-intensity, short-duration activities

    h. _____ The primary system used during high-intensity, very short-duration activities

    i. _____ The primary system used during lower-intensity, long-duration activities

ACE Essentials of Exercise Science for Fitness Professionals

VIII. Explain the Cori cycle and its role in fuel production during exercise. _____

_____

_____

_____

_____

_____

_____

IX. List and describe the four mechanisms the body uses to give off heat during exercise. Give an example of each.

a. _____

_____

_____

b. _____

_____

_____

c. _____

_____

_____

d. _____

_____

_____

X. Consider each of the following weather scenarios for outdoor exercise and describe any risks involved.

a. 95° F (35° C) with 40% humidity: _____

b. 85° F (29° C) with 50% humidity: _____

c. 30° F (–1° C) with calm winds: _____

d. 10° F (–12° C) with 10 mph (16 km/h) winds: _____

XI. Explain why women tend to sweat less than men and start to sweat at higher skin and core temperatures. How does this gender difference affect heat tolerance during exercise? _____

_____

_____

_____

_____

_____

XII. Answer the following questions about various chronic adaptations to exercise.

a. How long after the initiation of an exercise program can an increase in plasma volume be observed? _____

_____

_____

b. What is the physical-performance advantage of reduced blood viscosity? _____

_____

_____

c. Why is the left ventricle the cardiac structure most affected by endurance training? _____

_____

_____

d. Explain how regular endurance training creates more cross-sectional area for exchange between the vascular system and the active muscle fibers. _____

_____

_____

e. Why is the increase in size and number of mitochondria within the skeletal muscles an important adaptation to long-term exercise? _____

_____

_____

XIII. Why is an increase in rate coding due to resistance training so important to overall performance? _____

_____

_____

XIV. Match each hormone with its response to endurance training.

a. _____ Epinephrine and norepinephrine

b. _____ Cortisol

c. _____ Insulin

d. _____ Glucagon

e. _____ Growth hormone

1. Slight elevation during exercise

2. Smaller increase in glucose levels during exercise at absolute and relative workloads

3. No effect on resting values; less dramatic rise during exercise

4. Decreased secretion at rest and at the same absolute exercise intensity after training

5. Increased sensitivity; normal decrease during exercise greatly reduced with training

XV. Match each phase of the general adaptation syndrome to the appropriate descriptions by placing an (S) beside each item that describes the shock or alarm phase, an (A) beside each item that describes the adaptation phase, and an (E) beside each item that describes the exhaustion phase.

a. _____ Repairs are inadequate and sickness or death occurs

b. _____ Strength gains are attributed to neuromuscular adaptation only

c. _____ Characterized by progressive increases in muscle size and strength

d. _____ Can indicate a lack of adherence

e. _____ Represents major muscular adaptations

f. _____ Involves cortisol secretion

XVI. List the primary signs and symptoms of overtraining.

a. _____

b. _____

c. _____

d. _____

e. _____

f. _____

g. _____

h. _____

i. _____

j. _____

XVII. Define the following training principles.

a. Specificity _____

_____

b. Overload _____

_____

c. Progression _____

_____

d. Diminishing returns _____

_____

e. Reversibility _____

_____

Practice What You Know

Ask a fellow fitness professional to partner with you to practice the three methods of proprioceptive neuromuscular facilitation (PNF) presented in this chapter (i.e., hold-relax, contract-relax, and hold-relax with agonist contraction). Take turns with your partner as you each practice performing the assistive techniques and receiving the stretch. Make note of your experiences as both the "trainer" and the "participant" to further your understanding of the PNF techniques and apply them to your role as a fitness professional.

Multiple Choice

1. During cardiorespiratory exercise at higher intensities, which of the following results in the **GREATEST** change in percentage of total-body blood flow regulation?
   A. Decreased blood flow to the liver
   B. Increased blood flow to the working muscles
   C. Decreased blood flow to the kidneys
   D. Increased blood flow to the skin

2. What increases after catecholamines are released from the adrenal medulla?
   A. Strength of contraction in the cardiac muscle cells
   B. Air pressure in the lungs due to constriction of the respiratory passages
   C. Systolic blood pressure due to vasoconstriction in the working muscles
   D. Transport of free fatty acids from the blood to fat-cell stores

3. During exercise, which hormone causes increases in the production and release of liver glycogen and the availability of free fatty acids in the blood?
   A. Glucagon
   B. Norepinephrine
   C. Insulin
   D. Epinephrine

4. "Hitting the wall" during a marathon or other endurance event is **PRIMARILY** associated with _____.
   A. Severe amino acid depletion
   B. Depleted free fatty acid in the blood
   C. Severe glycogen depletion
   D. Depleted free fatty acids and dehydration

5. Which mechanism is **PRIMARILY** responsible for thermoregulation during exercise?
   A. Conduction
   B. Radiation
   C. Convection
   D. Evaporation

6. According to the recommendations of the National Athletic Trainers' Association (NATA), approximately how much fluid should a participant consume after a 60-minute cardiorespiratory workout?
   A. At least 200–300 mL (7–10 oz) for every 20 minutes of exercise
   B. 450–675 mL (16–24 oz) for every 0.5 kg (1.0 lb) lost during exercise
   C. Up to 200–300 mL (7–10 oz) for every 10 minutes of exercise
   D. 500–600 mL (17–20 oz) within 1–2 hours following exercise

7. The increased oxygen extraction at the tissue level resulting from long-term cardiorespiratory training is attributed **LEAST** to an increase in _____.
   A. Stroke volume
   B. Mitochondrial density
   C. Capillary density
   D. Mitochondrial enzyme activity

8. After conducting a reassessment with a client, you note that he has an elevated resting HR and has recently lost 5 pounds. As you work with him to review and modify his goals, he seems to be distracted and lacking motivation. Which of the following program modifications would be **MOST** appropriate?
   A. Adding one interval workout to his current program to help him push through this plateau
   B. Encouraging him to add 1–2 group exercise classes per week to his current program to reinvigorate his workouts
   C. Decreasing exercise intensity and volume for several weeks to help him recover, as he appears to be overtrained
   D. Increasing the intensity of his resistance-training workouts to prevent further loss of lean body mass

9. You design an exercise program for a client who is training for a three-week hiking trip in the Rocky Mountains. The program includes strengthening exercises for the hip flexors and extensors, knee extensors, ankle plantarflexors, and spinal stabilizers, along with cardiorespiratory training that includes hiking with a weighted pack. This program is **MOST** representative of which training principle?
   A. Overload
   B. Progression
   C. Reversibility
   D. Specificity

10. Contracting the hip flexors during a supine hamstring stretch is an example of which stretching principle?
    A. Reciprocal inhibition
    B. Active isolated stretching
    C. Proprioceptive neuromuscular facilitation
    D. Autogenic inhibition

APPENDIX

Study Guide Answer Key

Chapter 1: Human Anatomy

Expand Your Knowledge

I. (a) 4; (b) 2; (c) 8; (d) 5; (e) 3; (f) 1; (g) 7; (h) 6

II. (a) Carries carbon dioxide and metabolic wastes from the cells; (b) Maintains acid-base balance; (c) Helps regulate body temperature

III. (a) Superior vena cava; (b) Pulmonary veins; (c) Right atrium; (d) Pulmonary valve; (e) Tricuspid valve; (f) Right ventricle; (g) Inferior vena cava; (h) Aorta; (i) Pulmonary arteries; (j) Pulmonary trunk; (k) Left atrium; (l) Mitral valve; (m) Left ventricle; (n) Aortic valve. (1) a&g; (2) c; (3) e; (4) f; (5) d; (6) j; (7) i; (8) b; (9) k; (10) l; (11) m; (12) n; (13) h

IV. (a) 1; (b) 8; (c) 4; (d) 3; (e) 6; (f) 2; (g) 5; (h) 7

V. (a) The central nervous system is completely enclosed in bone, such as the spinal cord and brain, while the peripheral nervous system is connected to the extremities. (b) The axial skeleton is made up of the 74 bones of the head, neck, and trunk, while the appendicular skeleton consists of the 126 bones that form the extremities. (The six auditory ossicles are a separate group of bones.) (c) Formed elements are living, such as red blood cells, while plasma is composed of nonliving water and dissolved solutes. (d) Skeletal muscle contracts voluntarily, while cardiac and visceral muscle contract involuntarily. (e) Arteries carry blood away from the heart, while veins carry blood toward the heart.

VI. (a) Have a space, or joint, between the bones that form them; a variety of movements can occur; (b) Have no joint cavity and are held together by cartilage; little or no motion occurs; (c) Have no joint cavity and are held together by fibrous tissue; very little movement occurs

VII. (a) Saddle: flexion and extension; abduction and adduction; circumduction; opposition; (b) Ball and socket: flexion and extension; abduction and adduction; circumduction; internal and external rotation; (c) Modified hinge: flexion and extension; internal and external rotation; (d) Hinge: flexion and extension;
(e) Condyloid: flexion and extension; abduction and adduction; circumduction

VIII. (a) Tendons: Transmit force from muscle to bone, thereby producing motion; provide 10% of the resistance experienced during joint movement; (b) Ligaments (joint capsule): Support joints by attaching bone to bone; provide 47% of the total resistance experienced during joint movement; (c) Fasciae: Provide a framework that ensures proper alignment of muscle fibers, blood vessels, and nerves; enable the safe and effective transmission of forces throughout the whole muscle; provide the necessary lubricated surface between muscle fibers that allows muscles to change shape during contraction and elongation; provide 41% of the total resistance experienced during joint movement

IX. (a) Aging brings about a decrease in normal muscle function, including strength, endurance, flexibility, and agility. (b) Females are generally more flexible than males, possibly due to anatomical and physiological differences. (c) Injuries to bony structures may cause a joint to lose its ability to fully extend. Injury or surgery that involves tearing, incision, or laceration of the skin will leave inelastic scar tissue, thereby limiting joint movement. (d) Intramuscular temperature should be increased prior to stretching or dynamic movement activity via an appropriate warm-up. (e) Joint stiffness has been associated with specific times of day, often the early morning hours.

X. See Figures 1-20, 1-24, 1-26, 1-29, 1-32, 1-34, 1-35, and 1-39.

Show What You Know

I. The "burning" feeling is a feedback mechanism that warns the body of possible injury if the current activity level is not reduced. It is the body's way of saying "slow down."

II. (a) Rectus femoris, vastus lateralis, intermedius and medialis; (b) Pectoralis major and latissimus dorsi; (c) External and internal obliques and rectus abdominis; (d) Peroneus brevis and longus, posterior tibialis, gastrocnemius, and soleus; (e) Biceps brachii, brachioradialis, brachialis, flexor carpi radialis, flexor carpi ulnaris, pronator teres; (f) Rhomboid major and minor and trapezius

Multiple Choice

1. D
2. B
3. C
4. A
5. C
6. B
7. B
8. C
9. D
10. A

Chapter 2: Exercise Physiology

Expand Your Knowledge

I. (a) Muscular fitness (muscular strength and endurance); (b) Cardiovascular or cardiorespiratory endurance; (c) Flexibility; (d) Body composition

II. (a) Muscular strength is the maximal force that a muscle or muscle group can exert during a single contraction, while muscular endurance is the ability of a muscle or muscle group to exert force against a resistance over a sustained period of time.

(b) Essential fat is the amount of body fat necessary for the maintenance of life and reproductive function (2–5% body fat for men; 10–13% body fat for women), while storage fat is body fat that is stored in excess of essential fat; excess body-fat storage is referred to as overweight or obesity. (c) Tidal volume is the volume of air moved with each breath and represents the depth of ventilation, while stroke volume is the quantity of blood pumped per heart beat. (d) Aerobic glycolysis is the metabolic pathway that produces ATP in the presence of oxygen, while anaerobic glycolysis is the metabolic pathway that produces ATP in the absence of oxygen. (e) Heat exhaustion is a moderate form of heat stress due to inadequate circulatory adjustments to exercise in the heat and humidity coupled with fluid loss, while heat stroke is a severe form of heat stress resulting from a complete failure of the body's heat-regulating mechanisms, with the core body temperature exceeding 104° F (40° C). (f) First ventilatory threshold (VT1) occurs at approximately the first time lactate begins to accumulate, represents hyperventilation relative to $\dot{V}O_2$, and is caused by the need to blow off the extra CO_2 produced by the buffering of acid metabolites. VT1 is approximately the highest intensity that a trained individual can sustain for one to two hours of exercise. Second ventilatory threshold (VT2) occurs at the point where lactate is rapidly increasing with intensity, and represents hyperventilation even relative to the extra CO_2 that is being produced. VT2 is approximately the highest intensity that a trained individual can sustain for 30 to 60 minutes.

III. (a) 5; (b) 3; (c) 7; (d) 9; (e) 2; (f) 8; (g) 10; (h) 1; (i) 4; (j) 6; (k) 12; (l) 11

IV. (a) Getting oxygen into the blood via pulmonary ventilation and the hemoglobin content of the blood; (b) Delivering oxygen to the active tissues through increased cardiac output; (c) Extracting oxygen from the blood to complete the metabolic production of ATP

V. (a) CA; (b) CA; (c) AR; (d) CA;
    (e) CA; (f) AR; (g) AR; (h) CA; (i) AR;
    (j) AR
VI. (a) 2; (b) 5; (c) 4; (d) 8; (e) 7; (f) 1; (g) 6;
    (h) 3
VII. (a) 85%; 15%; (b) lean body mass;
    (c) heart rate; stroke volume; (d) 5 kilo-
    calories; (e) diastolic blood pressure;
    (f) excess post-exercise oxygen con-
    sumption; (g) Motor neurons; (h)
    fast-twitch muscle fibers; (i) amenor-
    rhea; (j) Early morning
VIII. (a) 2; (b) 4; (c) 3; (d) 1
IX. Heat exhaustion: weak, rapid pulse; low
    blood pressure; headache; nausea; diz-
    ziness; general weakness; paleness; cold,
    clammy skin; profuse sweating; elevated
    core temperature (≤104° F; 40° C).
    Heat stroke: hot, dry skin; bright red
    skin color; rapid, strong pulse; labored
    breathing; elevated core temperature
    (≥105° F; 41° C)
X. (a) Recording daily body weights is
    important for preventing accumulative
    dehydration; the amount of water lost
    (in pounds) after aerobic exercise should
    be replaced before exercising again the
    next day. (b) Cotton is a good choice for
    exercising in the heat because it readily
    soaks up sweat and allows evaporation.
    (c) Wearing several layers allows gar-
    ments to be removed and replaced as
    needed; as exercise intensity increases,
    garments can be removed, whereas gar-
    ments can be replaced during periods
    of rest, warm-up, or cool-down. This
    prevents excessive cooling during low-
    intensity exercise periods. (d) Without
    adequate ventilation, sweating during
    exercise can soak inner garments; wet
    garments can drain the body of heat
    during periods of low-intensity exercise
    or rest.
XI. (a) AN; (b) AN; (c) A; (d) AN; (e) A;
    (f) AN

Show What You Know

I. A common misconception is that low-
    intensity exercise is the best way to lose
    body fat because a higher percentage of
    fat is used as fuel at lower intensities.
    However, at higher intensities, more
    total calories are burned. Therefore,
    even though a higher percentage of fuel
    comes from fat during low-intensity
    exercise, more total calories are burned
    during exercise at higher intensities,
    thereby increasing the amount of fat
    burned. Working at higher intensi-
    ties improves body composition more
    effectively and also contributes to larger
    increases in cardiorespiratory fitness
    than does working at low intensities.
    Additionally, on average, men weigh
    more than women, so Bob's progres-
    sion toward his fat-loss goal may also be
    a function of his greater body weight.
    Larger people burn more calories while
    exercising than do smaller people.
II. Short-duration, high-intensity training,
    such as interval training, utilizes more
    anaerobic pathways for energy than
    long-distance training, such as running,
    which relies on aerobic metabolism.
    Interval training emphasizes fast-twitch
    muscle fiber recruitment and calls upon
    "intermediate" fast-twitch muscle fibers
    in the process. Adding interval training
    to Maria's exercise program will de-
    emphasize the slow-twitch muscle fiber
    endurance she has developed through
    long-distance running, and promote
    better performance of high-intensity
    activities such as sprinting and jumping.

Multiple Choice

1. C
2. C
3. B
4. D
5. A
6. B
7. D
8. B
9. A
10. D

Chapter 3:
Fundamentals of
Applied Kinesiology

Expand Your Knowledge

I. (a) Kinematics is the study of the form, pattern, or sequence of movement without regard for the forces that produce that movement, while kinetics is the study of the effects of internal and external forces on the body. (b) Kyphosis is an excessive posterior curvature of the thoracic spine, while lordosis is an excessive anterior curvature of the lumbar spine. (c) Posture refers to the biomechanical alignment of body parts and the orientation of the body to the environment, while balance is the ability to statically and dynamically maintain the body's position over its base of support within stability limits. (d) The supraspinatus is a rotator cuff muscle located superior to the spine of the scapula that functions to stabilize the head of the humerus in the shoulder joint and initiate abduction of the arm, while the infraspinatus is a rotator cuff muscle located inferior to the spine of the scapula that functions to stabilize the head of the humerus in the shoulder joint and externally rotate the arm. (e) Base of support is defined by a person's body surface contact with the floor (e.g., the feet during standing), while stability limits are boundaries of an area of space in which the body can maintain its position without changing the base of support (i.e., the length of the feet and the distance between them when standing). (f) In a closed-chain exercise, the end of the chain farthest from the body is fixed (e.g., squat). Such movements emphasize compression of the joints, which helps stabilize the joints. In an open-chain exercise, the end of the chain farthest from the body is free (e.g., seated leg extension). Such movements tend to involve more shearing forces at the joints.

II. (a) The law of inertia states that a body at rest will stay at rest and that a body in motion will stay in motion (with the same direction and velocity) unless acted upon by an external force. (b) The law of acceleration states that a force (F) acting on a body in a given direction is equal to the body's mass (m) multiplied by the body's acceleration (a) in that direction (F = ma). (c) The law of reaction states that every applied force is accompanied by an equal and opposite reaction force.

III. (a) Iliopsoas; (b) Rectus femoris; (c) Sartorius; (d) Tensor fascia latae

IV. (a) Piriformis; (b) Superior gemellus; (c) Obturator internus; (d) Obturator externus; (e) Inferior gemellus; (f) Quadratus femoris

V. (a) 1; (b) 3; (c) 2; (d) 4; (e) 4; (f) 1; (g) 2; (h) 3; (i) 4; (j) 3

VI. (a) gastrocnemius and soleus; (b) scoliosis; (c) screw-home mechanism; (d) serratus anterior; (e) rectus femoris; (f) teres major

VII. (a) Scapulothoracic articulation: muscles and fascia that connect the scapulae to the thorax; (b) Glenohumeral joint: glenoid fossa of the scapula and the humeral head; (c) Sternoclavicular joint: sternum and proximal clavicle; (d) Acromioclavicular joint: acromion process of the scapula and the distal clavicle

VIII. (a) 8; (b) 4; (c) 7; (d) 1; (e) 3; (f) 9; (g) 5; (h) 6; (i) 2

IX. (a) Bilateral strength/flexibility symmetry; (b) Proportional strength ratios in agonist/antagonist muscle groups; (c) A balance in flexibility resulting in normal ranges of joint motion

X. (a) Altered step frequency; (b) Greater vertical displacement of the center of gravity; (c) Extraneous movements resulting from greater limb dimensions

XI. Chairs without armrests increase the potential range of movement and allow a broader variety of possible exercises. Because many clients who are well-suited to chair-seated exercises use wheelchairs, it is important to be able to work effectively using chairs with armrests.

XII. (a) One classic explanation for the decline in flexibility seen in children growing into adolescence is that during periods of rapid growth, bones grow much faster than the muscles stretch. Consequently, there is an increase in musculotendinous tightness at the joints. (b) Another theory is that the decrease in flexibility, specifically in the hamstrings, is a direct result of prolonged sitting in school. Most individuals sit with the pelvis in a posteriorly tilted position. Initially, this causes the hamstrings to become slack. Over time, sitting in this position causes the hamstrings to adaptively shorten to take up the slack.

Show What You Know

I. One method is to place your hand on the back of Lou's neck in the correct position and help him hold this neutral position by maintaining contact throughout the exercise. Another method would be to place your hand in front of (but not touching) Lou's forehead during the abdominal curl exercise. To maintain a proper neutral position of the head and neck, he must not touch your hand with his forehead.

II. Although the pectorals may be responsible for the joint action, the line of gravity is not in line with the weight movement (i.e., Sue is not lifting or lowering the dumbbells against the line of gravity). An easy way to increase the effectiveness of this exercise would be to place Sue in the supine position on a bench and perform the same horizontal flexion (adduction) and extension (abduction) against the line of gravity.

Multiple Choice

1. C
2. D
3. C
4. A
5. B
6. B
7. A
8. D
9. C
10. A

Chapter 4: Nutrition

Expand Your Knowledge

I. (a) The Recommended Dietary Allowances (RDAs) are levels of intake of essential nutrients based on age and gender that are judged to be adequate to meet the known needs of practically all healthy persons. The Dietary Reference Intakes (DRIs) are a revised, more detailed version of the RDAs and refer to three types of reference values: Estimated Average Requirement (EAR), Tolerable Upper Intake Level (UL), and Adequate Intake (AI). (b) The Estimated Average Requirement indicates an adequate intake in 50% of an age- and gender-specific group, while the Tolerable Upper Intake Level is the maximum intake that is unlikely to pose a risk of adverse health effects to almost all individuals in an age- and gender-specific group. (c) Complex carbohydrates are long chains of glucose molecules including glycogen and starch, while simple carbohydrates are short chains of glucose molecules and are referred to as sugars. (d) Saturated fatty acids are chains of hydrocarbons with no double bonds between carbon atoms. They are stable, typically solid at room temperature, and are found in foods such as red meat, full-fat dairy products, and tropical oils. Unsaturated fatty acids contain one or more double bonds between carbon atoms, are fairly unstable, and are typically liquid at room temperature. Sources include olive, canola, peanut, corn, safflower, and soybean oils, and cold-water fish. (e) A complete protein is a food source that contains all of the essential amino acids, such as any animal product, while an incomplete protein is a food source that does not contain all of the essential amino acids, such as a plant product.

II. (a) 2; (b) 4; (c) 6; (d) 7; (e) 8; (f) 1; (g) 3; (h) 5

III. (a) MS; (b) PS; (c) DS; (d) PS; (e) MS; (f) PS; (g) DS; (h) MS

IV. (a) Sucrose; (b) low-density lipoprotein (LDL); (c) antibodies; (d) Hyponatremia; (e) bioavailability

V. (a) 3; (b) 6; (c) 2; (d) 1; (e) 7; (f) 5; (g) 8; (h) 4

VI. (a) Vitamin K: produced by normal intestinal flora; (b) Biotin: produced by normal intestinal flora; (c) Vitamin D: produced when the skin is exposed to sunlight

VII. Carbohydrate: 4; fat: 9; protein: 4; alcohol: 7

VIII. (a) Serving; (b) Percent daily value; (c) 2,000; (d) Allergens; (e) Enriched

XII. Michael: $(9.99 \times 80 \text{ kg}) + (6.25 \times 183 \text{ cm})$ $- (4.92 \times 40) + 5 = 1,751$
$1,751 \times 1.5 = 2,626$ calories
$1,751 \times 1.7 = 2,977$ calories
Michael's daily energy requirement is between 2,626 and 2,977 calories.
Claire: $(9.99 \times 61 \text{ kg}) + (6.25 \times 170 \text{ cm}) - (4.92 \times 37) - 161 = 1,329$
$1,329 \times 1.5 = 1,993$
$1,329 \times 1.7 = 2,259$
Claire's daily energy requirement is between 1,993 and 2,259 calories.

XIII. (a) Prehypertension is defined as blood pressure greater than 120/80 mmHg, but less than 140/90 mmHg, while hypertension is defined as blood pressure greater

IX.

Food Group	Servings	Significance of Food
Grains and grain products	7–8 servings daily	Major sources of energy and fiber
Vegetables	4–5 servings daily	Rich sources of potassium, magnesium, and fiber
Fruits	4–5 servings daily	Important sources of potassium, magnesium, and fiber
Low-fat or fat-free dairy	2–3 servings daily	Major sources of calcium and protein
Meats, poultry, and fish	2 or fewer servings daily	Rich sources of protein and magnesium
Nuts, seeds, and dry beans	4–5 servings per week	Rich sources of energy, magnesium, potassium, protein, and fiber
Fats and oils	2–3 servings daily	DASH has 27% of calories as fat, including fat in or added to foods
Sweets	5 per week	Sweets should be low in fat

X. (a) Order an appetizer or side dish instead of an entrée. (b) Share a main dish with a friend. (c) If chilling extra food right away is possible, take leftovers home in a "doggy bag." (d) When the food is delivered, immediately set aside or pack half of it to go. (e) Avoid cleaning the plate—leave the rest of the food when you've eaten enough.

XI. (a) Follow a healthy eating pattern across the lifespan. (b) Focus on variety, nutrient density, and amount. (c) Limit calories form added sugars and saturated fats and reduce sodium intake. (d) Shift to healthier food and beverages choices. (e) Support healthy eating patterns for all.

than 140/90 mmHg. (b) Glycemic index is a system for ranking carbohydrates based on their blood glucose response, while glycemic load takes into account the glycemic index as well as the portion size of foods. (c) Dehydration is a loss of body water resulting in impaired function and performance, while hyponatremia is severely reduced blood sodium concentration resulting from overhydration. (d) A lacto-ovo-vegetarian is an individual who chooses to not eat meat, fish, or poultry, but does eat dairy products and eggs. A vegan is an individual who does not consume any animal products, including dairy products and eggs. (e) Mechanical digestion is the process of chewing, swallowing, and propelling food through the gastrointestinal tract, while chemical digestion is the addition of enzymes that break down nutrients.

XIV. (a) Control portions; (b) Be mindful; (c) Exercise; (d) Check the scale; (e) Eat breakfast; (f) Monitor intake; (g) Turn off the tube; (h) Do not wait until tomorrow to get started—and no cheating; (i) Know thy friend; (j) Be optimistic!

Show What You Know

I.   Fat: 3 g x 9 cal/g = 27 calories x 4 servings per container = 108 calories from fat. Carbohydrate: 13 g x 4 cal/g = 52 calories x 4 servings per container = 208 calories from carbohydrate. Protein: 3 g x 4 cal/g = 12 calories x 4 servings per container = 48 calories from protein.

II.   (a) 2,000 cal/day x 0.25 = 500 cal/day from fat; 500 fat cal/9 cal/g = 56 g of fat per day. (b) 2,000 cal/day x 0.55 = 1,100 cal/day from carbohydrate; 1,100 carbohydrate cal/4 cal/g = 275 g of carbohydrate per day. (c) 2,000 cal/day x 0.20 = 400 cal/day from protein; 400 protein cal/4 cal/g = 100 g of protein per day.

Multiple Choice

1. B
2. C
3. A
4. C
5. D
6. D
7. B
8. B
9. D
10. C

Chapter 5: Physiology of Training

Expand Your Knowledge

I.   (a) An increase in cardiac output; (b) A redistribution of blood from inactive organs to the active skeletal muscle

II.   (a) The SA node is located in the posterior wall of the right atrium and intrinsically controls the regulation of heart rate, while the AV node is located on the floor of the right atrium and gives off many branches that facilitate ventricular contraction. (b) A chronotropic response is an increase in heart rate, while an inotropic response is an increase in the force of heart contractility. (c) The first ventilatory threshold (VT1) occurs at approximately the first time that lactate begins to accumulate in the blood, and represents hyperventilation relative to $\dot{V}O_2$. It is caused by the need to blow off the extra carbon dioxide (CO_2) produced by the buffering of acid metabolites. The second ventilatory threshold (VT2) occurs at the point where lactate is rapidly increasing with intensity, and represents hyperventilation even relative to the extra CO_2 that is being produced. It probably represents the point at which blowing off CO_2 is no longer adequate to buffer the increase in acidity that is occurring with progressively intense exercise. (d) Heat acclimation is the relatively rapid (several days or weeks) process of physiological adaptation to exercise in the heat, while heat acclimatization is more gradual in onset and occurs in people who live in hot environments for months or years. (e) A twitch is a motor unit's smallest contractile response to a single electrical stimulation, while summation is a series of multiple stimuli in rapid sequence, prior to relaxation from the first stimulus; this results in greater force production. (f) Fiber hypertrophy is an increase in the size of existing muscle fibers, while fiber hyperplasia is an increase in the number of muscle fibers.

III. (a) Increased heart contractility and stroke volume increase the force with which blood leaves the heart. (b) Muscle action requires greater force or pressure to deliver blood into the exercising muscles. (c) Vasodilation within the exercising muscles allows more blood to drain from the arteries through the arterioles and into the muscle capillaries, thus minimizing changes in diastolic pressure.

IV. (a) Blood flow to the skeletal muscles increases from 10 to 15% at rest to 80 to 85% at maximal exercise. (b) During intense physical activity, the percentage of total cardiac output to the brain is decreased compared to resting, but the absolute volume of blood that reaches the brain is slightly increased due to the elevated cardiac output. (c) The percentage of total cardiac output that the heart receives in its coronary circulation is the same at rest and during maximal exercise, even though total coronary blood flow is increased due to the increase in cardiac output during intense exercise. (d) Blood flow to the kidneys and gastrointestinal tract diminishes, but does not cease. (e) Blood flow to the skin increases as exercise intensity increases, but at maximal intensities it decreases.

V. (a) 1; (b) 3; (c) 5; (d) 4; (e) 2

VI. (a) F; (b) P; (c) P; (d) C; (e) F; (f) C; (g) C; (h) P

VII. (a) P; (b) AG; (c) A; (d) A; (e) A; (f) P; (g) AG; (h) P; (i) A

VIII. During exercise, some of the lactate that is produced by skeletal muscles is transported to the liver via the blood. The liver then converts the lactate back to glucose and releases it into the bloodstream to be transported back to the skeletal muscles to be used as an energy source. This process works to preserve the body's blood glucose levels and to ensure that the muscles have adequate fuel to perform work.

IX. (a) Radiation is heat loss in the form of infrared rays, which involves the transfer of heat from the surface of one object to another without any physical contact (e.g., the sun's rays transferring heat to the earth's surface). (b) Conduction is the transfer of heat from the body into the molecules of cooler objects that come in contact with its surface (e.g., the transfer of heat from the body to a metal chair while a person is sitting in it).

(c) Convection is a form of conduction wherein heat is transferred to either air or water molecules in contact with the body (e.g., wind from a fan blowing over the skin, replacing warm molecules with cooler ones). (d) Evaporation occurs when heat is transferred from the body to water on the surface of the skin (e.g., sweating). When this water accumulates sufficient heat, it is converted to a gas, removing heat from the body as it vaporizes.

X. (a) Heat cramps or heat exhaustion possible; (b) No risks involved; (c) Little danger for a properly clothed person; (d) Danger for freezing of exposed flesh

XI. Women have more surface area for their body weight (i.e., less lean, dense mass), so they rely more on conduction, convection, and radiation to regulate body temperature than do men, who generate greater quantities of heat (due to increased lean mass). Despite the noticeable difference in sweat output, women have a heat tolerance similar to men of the same aerobic fitness level at the same exercise intensity.

XII. (a) Within one hour of recovery from the first exercise session; (b) Reduced blood viscosity enhances oxygen delivery to the active skeletal muscles because the blood flows more easily through the capillaries. (c) The left ventricle is responsible for the forceful propulsion of oxygenated blood through the arterial system. (d) New capillaries develop in trained muscles to allow blood to more effectively perfuse the active tissues. Existing capillaries that were not readily open prior to endurance training become more easily recruited and open to blood flow in trained muscles. (e) Since the mitochondria improve the muscle's capacity to produce ATP, increases in mitochondrial size and number enhance the muscle's ability to use oxygen and produce ATP via oxidation.

XIII. An increase in rate coding results in an increase in the frequency of discharge of the motor units and allows for a faster time to peak force production for the trained muscle.

XIV. (a) 4; (b) 1; (c) 5; (d) 2; (e) 3

XV. (a) E; (b) S; (c) A; (d) E; (e) A; (f) S

XVI. (a) A decline in physical performance with continued training; (b) Elevated heart rate and blood lactate levels at a fixed submaximal work rate; (c) Change in appetite; (d) Weight loss; (e) Sleep disturbances; (f) Multiple colds or sore throats; (g) Irritability, restlessness, excitability, and/or anxiousness; (h) Loss of motivation and vigor; (i) Lack of mental concentration and focus; (j) Lack of appreciation for things that are normally enjoyable

XVII. (a) The principle of specificity explains the outcome of a given type of training program such that the exercise response is specific to the mode and intensity of training. (b) Overload refers to strategically applying increased load on a tissue or system above and beyond the point at which that tissue or system is normally loaded. (c) Progression refers to the systematic process of applying overload. (d) The principle of diminishing returns suggests that the rate of fitness improvement diminishes over time as fitness approaches its ultimate genetic potential. (e) The principle of reversibility pertains to the losses in function experienced after the cessation of a training program. Regardless of the gains in fitness achieved through a regular exercise program, those improvements will be reversed to pre-training levels and may ultimately decrease to a point that meets only the demands of daily use.

Multiple Choice

1. B
2. A
3. D
4. C
5. D
6. B
7. A
8. C
9. D
10. A

GLOSSARY

Abduction Movement away from the midline of the body.

Absorption The uptake of nutrients across a tissue or membrane by the gastrointestinal tract.

Acceptable Macronutrient Distribution Range (AMDR) The range of intake for a particular energy source that is associated with reduced risk of chronic disease while providing intakes of essential nutrients.

Acetyl coenzyme A (acetyl-CoA) An important molecule in metabolism, used in many biochemical reactions. Its main use is to convey the carbon atoms within the acetyl group to the citric acid cycle to be oxidized for energy production. This compound forms the common entry point into the Kreb's cycle for the oxidation of carbohydrate and fat.

Acetyl-CoA *See* Acetyl coenzyme A (acetyl-CoA).

Acetylcholine A white crystalline neurotransmitter and derivative of choline that is released at the ends of nerve fibers in the somatic and parasympathetic nervous systems and is involved in the transmission of nerve impulses in the body.

Acromioclavicular (A/C) joint The junction of the acromion process of the scapula with the distal clavicle.

Actin Thin contractile protein in a myofibril.

Active isolated stretching (AIS) A stretching technique modeled after traditional strength-training workouts. Stretches are held very briefly in sets of a specified number of repetitions, with a goal of isolating an individual muscle in each set.

Activities of daily living (ADL) Activities normally performed for hygiene, bathing, household chores, walking, shopping, and similar activities.

Adduction Movement toward the midline of the body.

Adenosine diphosphate (ADP) One of the chemical by-products of the breakdown of adenosine triphosphate (ATP) during muscle contraction.

Adenosine monophosphate (AMP) Substance found in muscle cells that participates in energy released by working muscle.

Adenosine trisphosphate (ATP) A high-energy phosphate molecule required to provide energy for cellular function. Produced both aerobically and anaerobically and stored in the body.

Adequate intake (AI) A recommended nutrient intake level that, based on research, appears to be sufficient for good health.

Adipocyte A fat cell.

Adipose tissue Fatty tissue; connective tissue made up of fat cells.

Adrenocorticotropin hormone (ACTH) A hormone released by the pituitary gland that affects various important bodily functions; controls the secretion in the adrenal gland of hormones that influence the metabolism of carbohydrates, sodium, and potassium; also controls the rate at which substances are exchanged between the blood and tissues.

Aerobic In the presence of oxygen.

Aerobic glycolysis A metabolic pathway that requires oxygen to facilitate the use of glycogen for energy (ATP).

Afterload The pressure in the aorta and pulmonary trunk, respectively, that the left and right ventricles of the heart must overcome to eject blood.

Agonist The muscle directly responsible for observed movement; also called the prime mover.

Aldosterone One of two main hormones released by the adrenal cortex; plays a role in limiting sodium excretion in the urine.

All-or-none principle The principle of muscle contraction that states that when a motor unit is activated, all of the muscle fibers will maximally contract.

Allergen A substance that can cause an allergic reaction by stimulating type-1 hypersensitivity in atopic individuals.

Alpha cells Endocrine cells in the islets of Langerhans of the pancreas responsible for synthesizing and secreting the hormone glucagon, which elevates the glucose levels in the blood.

Alveoli Spherical extensions of the respiratory bronchioles and the primary sites of gas exchange with the blood.

Alzheimer's disease An age-related, progressive disease characterized by death of nerve cells in the brain leading to a loss of cognitive function; the cause of the nerve cell death is unknown.

Amenorrhea The absence of menstruation.

Amino acids Nitrogen-containing compounds that are the building blocks of protein.

Anabolic Muscle-building effects.

Anaerobic Without the presence of oxygen.

Anaerobic glycolysis The metabolic pathway that uses glucose for energy production without requiring oxygen. Sometimes referred to as the lactic acid system or anaerobic glucose system, it produces lactic acid as a by-product.

Anaerobic threshold (AT) The point during high-intensity activity when the body can no longer meet its demand for oxygen and anaerobic metabolism predominates. Also called lactate threshold or the first ventilatory threshold (VT1).

Anatomical position Standing erect with the feet and palms facing forward.

Androgenic Effects related to developing masculine characteristics associated with manhood.

Anemia A reduction in the number of red blood cells and/or quantity of hemoglobin per volume of blood below normal values.

Anemic *See* Anemia.

Angina A common symptom of coronary artery disease characterized by chest pain, tightness, or radiating pain resulting from a lack of blood flow to the heart muscle.

Anorexia nervosa An eating disorder characterized by refusal to maintain body weight of at least 85% of expected weight; intense fear of gaining weight or becoming fat; body-image disturbances, including a disproportionate influence of body weight on self-evaluation; and, in women, the absence of at least three consecutive menstrual periods.

Antagonist The muscle that acts in opposition to the contraction produced by an agonist (prime mover) muscle.

Antidiuretic hormone (ADH) A hormone released by the posterior pituitary gland during exercise; reduces urinary excretion of water and prevents dehydration.

Antioxidant A substance that prevents or repairs oxidative damage; includes vitamins C and E, some carotenoids, selenium, ubiquinones, and bioflavonoids.

Anus The end point of the gastrointestinal tract through which semisolid waste is passed from the body.

Anxiety A state of uneasiness and apprehension; occurs in some mental disorders.

Aorta The major artery of the cardiovascular system; arises from the left ventricle of the heart.

Aponeurosis A white, flattened, tendinous expansion that mainly serves to connect a muscle to the parts that it moves.

Applied force An external force acting on a system (body or body segment).

Arterial-mixed venous oxygen difference (a-$\bar{v}$O$_2$ difference) The difference in oxygen content between arterial and mixed venous blood, which reflects the amount of oxygen removed by the whole body.

Arterioles Small-diameter blood vessels that extend and branch out from an artery and lead to capillaries; the primary site of vascular resistance.

Arteriosclerosis A chronic disease in which thickening, hardening, and loss of elasticity of the arterial walls result in impaired blood circulation; develops with aging, and in hypertension, diabetes, hyperlipidemia, and other conditions.

Artery A blood vessel that carries oxygenated blood away from the heart to vital organs and the extremities.

Arthritis Inflammation of a joint; a state characterized by the inflammation of joints.

Articulation A joint.

Asthma A chronic inflammatory disorder of the airways that affects genetically susceptible individuals in response to various environmental triggers such as allergens, viral infection, exercise, cold, and stress.

Atherosclerosis A specific form of arteriosclerosis characterized by the accumulation of fatty material on the inner walls of the arteries, causing them to harden, thicken, and lose elasticity.

Atrioventricular node (AV node) The specialized mass of conducting cells in the heart located at the atrioventricular junction.

Atria The two upper chambers of the heart (right and left atrium).

Atrium *See* Atria.

Atrophy A reduction in muscle size (muscle wasting) due to inactivity or immobilization.

Autogenic inhibition An automatic reflex relaxation caused by stimulation of the Golgi tendon organ (GTO).

Autonomic nervous system The part of the nervous system that regulates involuntary body functions, including the activity of the cardiac muscle, smooth muscles, and glands. It has two divisions: the sympathetic nervous system and the parasympathetic nervous system.

Autoregulation Local control of blood distribution (through vasodilation) in response to a tissue's changing metabolic needs.

Axial skeleton The bones of the head, neck, and trunk.

Axis of rotation The imaginary line or point about which an object, such as a joint, rotates.

Axon A nerve fiber that conducts a nerve impulse away from the neuron cell body;

efferent nerve fiber.

Balance The ability to maintain the body's position over its base of support within stability limits, both statically and dynamically.

Ballistic stretching Dynamic stretching characterized by rhythmic bobbing or bouncing motions representing relatively high-force, short-duration movements.

Base of support (BOS) The areas of contact between the feet and their supporting surface and the area between the feet.

Beta cells Endocrine cells in the islets of Langerhans of the pancreas responsible for synthesizing and secreting the hormone insulin, which lowers the glucose levels in the blood.

Beta oxidation Metabolic pathway involving the breakdown of fatty acids (digested dietary fat) for the production of ATP.

Bile A greenish-yellow or brownish emulsifier that prepares fats and oils for digestion; produced in and secreted by the liver, stored in the gallbladder, and released into the small intestine.

Binge eating disorder (BED) An eating disorder characterized by frequent binge eating (without purging) and feelings of being out of control when eating.

Bioavailability The degree to which a substance can be absorbed and efficiently utilized by the body.

Biomechanics The mechanics of biological and muscular activity.

Body composition The makeup of the body in terms of the relative percentage of fat-free mass and body fat.

Body mass index (BMI) A relative measure of body height to body weight used to determine levels of weight, from underweight to extreme obesity.

Bolus A food and saliva digestive mix that is swallowed and then moved through the digestive tract.

Bone mineral density (BMD) A measure of the amount of minerals (mainly calcium) contained in a certain volume of bone.

Bronchi The two large branches of the trachea leading into the lungs.

Bronchioles The smallest tubes that supply air to the alveoli (air sacs) of the lungs.

Brush border The site of nutrient absorption in the small intestines.

Bulimia nervosa (BN) An eating disorder characterized by recurrent episodes of uncontrolled binge eating; recurrent inappropriate compensatory behavior such as self-induced vomiting, laxative misuse, diuretics, or enemas (purging type), or fasting and/or excessive exercise (non-purging type); episodes of binge eating and compensatory behaviors occur at least twice per week for three months; self-evaluation is heavily influenced by body shape and weight; and the episodes do not occur exclusively with episodes of anorexia.

Bulk element An element (such as certain minerals) that animals require in large amounts. *See also* Macromineral.

Calorie A measurement of the amount of energy in a food available after digestion. The amount of energy needed to increase 1 kilogram of water by 1 degree Celsius. Also called a kilocalorie.

Capillaries The smallest blood vessels that supply blood to the tissues, and the site of all gas and nutrient exchange in the cardiovascular system. They connect the arterial and venous systems.

Carbohydrate The body's preferred energy source. Dietary sources include sugars (simple) and grains, rice, potatoes, and beans (complex). Carbohydrate is stored as glycogen in the muscles and liver and is transported in the blood as glucose.

Carbohydrate loading Up to a week-long regimen of manipulating intensity of training and carbohydrate intake to achieve maximum glycogen storage for an endurance event.

Cardiac accelerator nerves Part of the sympathetic nervous system that stimulates the SA node to increase heart rate.

Cardiac cycle The period from the beginning of one heartbeat to the beginning of the next heartbeat; the systolic and diastolic phases and the interval in between.

Cardiac output The amount of blood pumped by the heart per minute; usually expressed in liters of blood per minute.

Cardiac sphincter Sits at the upper portion of the stomach; prevents food and stomach acid from splashing back into the esophagus from the stomach; also called the esophageal sphincter.

Cardiorespiratory endurance The capacity of the heart, blood vessels, and lungs to deliver oxygen and nutrients to the working muscles and tissues during sustained exercise and to remove metabolic waste products that would result in fatigue; the ability to perform large muscle movements over a sustained period; also called cardiovascular endurance.

Cardiovascular disease (CVD) A general term for any disease of the heart, blood vessels, or circulation.

Cardiovascular endurance *See* Cardiorespiratory endurance.

Catabolism Metabolic pathways that break down molecules into smaller units and release energy.

Catecholamine Hormone (e.g., epinephrine and norepinephrine) released as part of the sympathetic response to exercise.

Cell membrane The enveloping capsule of a cell composed of proteins, lipids, and carbohydrates.

Center of gravity (COG) *See* Center of mass (COM).

Center of mass (COM) The point around which all weight is evenly distributed; also called center of gravity.

Central nervous system (CNS) The brain and spinal cord.

Chemical digestion A form of digestion that involves the addition of enzymes that break down nutrients.

Cholesterol A fatlike substance found in the blood and body tissues and in certain foods. Can accumulate in the arteries and lead to a narrowing of the vessels (atherosclerosis).

Chronic hypertrophy   An increase in muscle size that results from repeated long-term resistance training.

Chylomicron   A large lipoprotein particle that transfers fat from food from the small intestines to the liver and adipose tissue.

Chyme   The semiliquid mass of partly digested food expelled by the stomach into the duodenum.

Circumduction   A biplanar movement involving the sequential combination of flexion, abduction, extension, and adduction.

Co-contraction   The mutual coordination of antagonist muscles (such as flexors and extensors) to maintain a position.

Cofactor   A substance that needs to be present along with an enzyme for a chemical reaction to occur.

Collagen   The main constituent of connective tissue, such as ligaments, tendons, and muscles.

Colon   The lower portion of the large intestine, the primary function of which is to absorb water; its segments are the ascending colon, the transverse colon, and the sigmoid colon.

Complete protein   A food that contains all of the essential amino acids. Eggs, soy, and most meats and dairy products are considered complete proteins.

Complex carbohydrate   A long chain of sugar that takes more time to digest than a simple carbohydrate.

Concentric   A type of isotonic muscle contraction in which the muscle develops tension and shortens when stimulated.

Conduction   The direct flow of heat through a material resulting from physical contact.

Congestive heart failure (CHF)   Inability of the heart to pump blood at a sufficient rate to meet the metabolic demand, or the ability to do so only when the cardiac filling pressures are abnormally high, frequently resulting in lung congestion.

Connective tissue   The tissue that binds together and supports various structures of the body. Ligaments and tendons are connective tissues.

Convection   The transfer of heat through surrounding air or water molecules.

Core stability   When the muscles of the trunk function in harmony to stabilize the spine and pelvis to provide a solid foundation for movement in the extremities. A key component necessary for successful performance of most gross motor activities.

Cori cycle   The cycle of lactate-to-glucose between the muscle and the liver.

Coronal plane   Vertical plane that divides the body into anterior and posterior portions. Also called the frontal plane.

Coronary artery disease (CAD)   *See* Coronary heart disease (CHD).

Coronary heart disease (CHD)   The major form of cardiovascular disease; results when the coronary arteries are narrowed or occluded, most commonly by atherosclerotic deposits of fibrous and fatty tissue; also called coronary artery disease (CAD).

Cortical bone   Compact, dense bone that is found in the shafts of long bones and the vertebral endplates.

Cortisol   A hormone that is often referred to as the "stress hormone," as it is involved in the response to stress. It increases blood pressure and blood glucose levels and has an immunosuppressive action.

Creatine phosphate (CP)   A storage form of high-energy phosphate in muscle cells that can be used to immediately resynthesize adenosine triphosphate (ATP).

Creep   The tendency of connective tissue to slowly deform permanently (or lengthen) under the influence of applied stress such as a stretching force.

Crimp   The zigzag structure of collagen, which gradually straightens out when the tissue is subjected to high tensile forces.

Cross-training   A method of physical training

in which a variety of exercises and changes in body positions or modes of exercise are utilized to positively affect compliance and motivation, and also stimulate additional strength gains or reduce injury risk.

Deep   Anatomical term meaning internal; that is, located further beneath the body surface than the superficial structures.

Dehydration   The process of losing body water; when severe can cause serious, life-threatening consequences.

Delayed onset muscle soreness (DOMS)   Soreness that occurs 24 to 48 hours after strenuous exercise, the exact cause of which is unknown.

Dendrite   The portion of a nerve fiber that transmits impulses toward a nerve cell body; receptive portion of a nerve cell.

Deoxyribonucleic acid (DNA)   A large, double-stranded, helical molecule that is the carrier of genetic information.

Depolarize   To decrease the electrical potential across a membrane, as when the inside of a neuron becomes less negative to the outside.

Depression   1. The action of lowering a muscle or bone, or movement in an inferior or downward direction. 2. A condition of general emotional dejection and withdrawal; sadness greater and more prolonged than that warranted by any objective reason.

Diabetes   *See* Diabetes mellitus.

Diabetes mellitus   A disease of carbohydrate metabolism in which an absolute or relative deficiency of insulin results in an inability to metabolize carbohydrates normally.

Diaphysis   The shaft of a long bone.

Diastole   The period of filling of the heart between contractions; resting phase of the heart.

Diastolic blood pressure (DBP)   The pressure in the arteries during the relaxation phase (diastole) of the cardiac cycle; indicative of total peripheral resistance.

Dietary Approach to Stop Hypertension (DASH) eating plan   An eating plan designed to reduce blood pressure; also serves as an overall healthy way of eating that can be adopted by nearly anyone; may also lower risk of coronary heart disease.

Dietary Reference Intake (DRI)   A generic term used to refer to three types of nutrient reference values: Recommended Dietary Allowance (RDA), Estimated Average Requirement (EAR), and Tolerable Upper Intake Level (UL).

Digestion   The process of breaking down food into small enough units for absorption.

Distal   Farthest from the midline of the body, or from the point of origin of a muscle.

Diuretic   Medication that produces an increase in urine volume and sodium excretion.

Dorsiflexion   Movement of the foot up toward the shin.

Duodenum   The top portion of the small intestine.

Dynamic stabilizers   Muscles that actively contribute to core stability.

Dynamic stretching   Type of stretching that involves taking the joints through their ranges of motion while continuously moving. Often beneficial in warming up for a particular sport or activity that involves the same joint movements.

Dyslipidemia   A condition characterized by abnormal blood lipid profiles; may include elevated cholesterol, triglyceride, or low-density lipoprotein (LDL) levels and/or low high-density lipoprotein (HDL) levels.

Eccentric   A type of isotonic muscle contraction in which the muscle lengthens against a resistance when it is stimulated; sometimes called "negative work" or "negative reps."

Edema   Swelling resulting from an excessive accumulation of fluid in the tissues of the body.

Eicosanoids   Oxygenated fatty acids that the body uses to signal cellular responses; includes omega-3 and omega-6 fatty acids.

Ejection fraction The percentage of the total volume of blood that is pumped out of the left ventricle during the systolic contraction of the heart.

Elastin A protein, similar to collagen, found in connective tissue that has elastic properties.

Electrolyte A mineral that exists as a charged ion in the body and that is extremely important for normal cellular function.

Elevation The action of raising a muscle or bone, or a movement in a superior or upward direction.

Empathy Understanding what another person is experiencing from his or her perspective.

Emphysema An obstructive pulmonary disease characterized by the gradual destruction of lung alveoli and the surrounding connective tissue, in addition to airway inflammation, leading to reduced ability to effectively inhale and exhale.

Encephalopathy Brain swelling; can result from hyponatremia.

Endomysium A layer of connective tissue that surrounds individual muscle fibers and contains capillaries, nerves, and lymphatics.

Endosteum A soft tissue lining the internal surface of the diaphysis on a long bone.

Enzyme A protein that speeds up a specific chemical reaction.

Epiglottis The cartilage in the throat that guards the entrance to the trachea and prevents fluid or food from entering it during the act of swallowing.

Epimysium A layer of connective tissue that encloses the entire muscle and is continuous with fascia and other connective-tissue wrappings of muscle, including the endomysium and perimysium.

Epinephrine A hormone released as part of the sympathetic response to exercise; also called adrenaline.

Epiphyseal cartilage Cartilaginous layer between the head and shaft of a long bone where bone growth occurs. Also called a growth plate.

Epiphysis The end of a long bone, usually wider than the shaft (plural: epiphyses).

Epithelial tissue Tissue that covers the surface of the body and lines the body cavities, ducts, and vessels.

Esophagus The food pipe; the conduit from the mouth to the stomach.

Essential amino acids Eight to 10 of the 23 different amino acids needed to make proteins. Called essential because the body cannot manufacture them; they must be obtained from the diet.

Essential fat *See* Essential fatty acids.

Essential fatty acids Fatty acids that the body needs but cannot synthesize; includes linolenic (omega-3) and linoleic (omega-6) fatty acids.

Estimated Average Requirement (EAR) An adequate intake in 50% of an age- and gender-specific group.

Estrogen Generic term for estrus-producing steroid compounds produced primarily in the ovaries; the female sex hormones.

Evaporation The process by which molecules in a liquid state (e.g., water) spontaneously become gaseous (e.g., water vapor).

Eversion Rotation of the foot to direct the plantar surface outward.

Excess post-exercise oxygen consumption (EPOC) A measurably increased rate of oxygen uptake following strenuous activity. The extra oxygen is used in the processes (hormone balancing, replenishment of fuel stores, cellular repair, innervation, and anabolism) that restore the body to a resting state and adapt it to the exercise just performed.

Exercise physiology The study of how the body functions during physical activity and exercise.

Expiration The act of expelling air from the lungs; exhalation.

Extension The act of straightening or extending a joint, usually applied to the muscular movement of a limb.

Fascia Strong connective tissues that perform a number of functions, including developing and isolating the muscles of the body and providing structural support and protection. Plural = Fasciae.

Fasciae *See* Fascia.

Fascicle A bundle of skeletal muscle fibers surrounded by perimysium.

Fast-twitch muscle fiber One of several types of muscle fibers found in skeletal muscle tissue; characterized as having a low oxidative capacity but a high gylcolytic capacity; recruited for rapid, powerful movements such as jumping, throwing, and sprinting; also called type II fibers.

Fat An essential nutrient that provides energy, energy storage, insulation, and contour to the body. 1 gram of fat equals 9 kcal.

Fat-soluble vitamins Vitamins that, when consumed, are stored in the body (particularly the liver and fat tissues); includes vitamins A, D, E, and K.

Fatty acids Long hydrocarbon chains with an even number of carbons and varying degrees of saturation with hydrogen.

Female athlete triad A condition consisting of a combination of disordered eating, menstrual irregularities, and decreased bone mass in athletic women.

First ventilatory threshold (VT1) Intensity of aerobic exercise at which ventilation starts to increase in a non-linear fashion in response to an accumulation of metabolic by-products in the blood.

Flat-back posture A position of the spine that minimizes the natural curve by placing the pelvis in a slight posterior tilt.

Flexibility The ability to move joints through their normal full ranges of motion.

Flexion The act of moving a joint so that the two bones forming it are brought closer together.

Foramina Holes or openings in a bone or between body cavities.

Frank-Starling mechanism The mechanism by which an increased amount of blood in the ventricle places a stretch on the cardiac muscle fibers, thereby causing a stronger ventricular contraction to increase the amount of blood ejected.

Free fatty acid (FFA) A fatty acid that is only loosely bound to plasma proteins in the blood. Fatty acids are used by the body as a metabolic fuel.

Frontal plane A longitudinal section that runs at a right angle to the sagittal plane, dividing the body into anterior and posterior portions.

Fructose Fruit sugar; the sweetest of the monosaccharides; found in varying levels in different types of fruits.

Fulcrum The support on which a lever rotates when moving or lifting something.

Galactose A monosaccharide; a component of lactose.

Ganglia A group of nerve cell bodies usually located in the peripheral nervous system.

Gastric emptying The process by which food is emptied from the stomach into the small intestines.

Gastrointestinal tract A long hollow tube from mouth to anus where digestion and absorption occur.

General adaptation syndrome A three-stage (alarm, adaptation, and exhaustion) universal process first defined by researcher Hans Selye in 1936 that describes the body's response to stress.

Glenohumeral (G/H) joint The ball-and-socket joint composed of the glenoid fossa of the scapula and the humeral head.

Glucagon A hormone released from the alpha cells of the pancreas when blood glucose levels are low; stimulates glucose release from the liver to increase blood glucose. Also releases free fatty acids from adipose tissue to be used as fuel.

Glucocorticoid An adrenocortical steroid hormone that increases gluconeogenesis, exerts an anti-inflammatory effect, and influences many bodily functions.

ACE Essentials of Exercise Science for Fitness Professionals

Gluconeogenesis The production of glucose from non-sugar substrates such as pyruvate, lactate, glycerol, and glucogenic amino acids.

Glucose A simple sugar; the form in which all carbohydrates are used as the body's principal energy source.

Glycemic index (GI) A ranking of carbohydrates on a scale from 0 to 100 according to the extent to which they raise blood sugar levels.

Glycemic load (GL) A measure of glycemic response to a food that takes into consideration serving size; GL = Glycemic index x Grams of carbohydrate.

Glycogen The chief carbohydrate storage material; formed by the liver and stored in the liver and muscle.

Glycogenolysis The breakdown of liver and muscle glycogen to yield blood glucose.

Glycolysis The breakdown of glucose or of its storage form, glycogen.

Golgi-Mazzoni corpuscle A specialized mechanoreceptor located in the joint capsule responsible for detecting joint compression. Any weightbearing activity stimulates these receptors.

Golgi tendon organ (GTO) A sensory organ with a tendon that, when stimulated, causes an inhibition of the entire muscle group to protect against too much force.

Growth hormone A hormone secreted by the pituitary gland that facilitates protein synthesis in the body.

Heart rate The number of heart beats per minute.

Heat acclimation The physiological adaptation to repeated exposure to physical exertion in the heat, occurring over a relatively brief period of time (days to weeks).

Heat acclimatization The gradual onset of the processes that prepare the body to tolerate heat stress. Occurs in people who live in hot climates for months or years, whereas as heat acclimation occurs in individuals in response to a warm season (shorter term).

Heat index Guidelines regarding when exercise can be safely undertaken or when it should be avoided based on measures of heat and humidity.

Hemoglobin The protein molecule in red blood cells specifically adapted to carry oxygen molecules (by bonding with them).

Hemopoiesis The formation of blood cells.

High-density lipoprotein (HDL) A lipoprotein that carries excess cholesterol from the arteries to the liver.

Homeostasis An internal state of physiological balance.

Hormone A chemical substance produced and released by an endocrine gland and transported through the blood to a target organ.

Hypercholesterolemia An excess of cholesterol in the blood.

Hyperextension Extension of an articulation beyond anatomical position.

Hyperplasia Increased cell production in normal tissue. An excess of normal tissue.

Hypertension High blood pressure, or the elevation of resting blood pressure above 140/90 mmHg.

Hyperthermia Abnormally high body temperature.

Hypertonic Having extreme muscular tension.

Hypertonicity *See* Hypertonic.

Hypertrophy An increase in the cross-sectional size of a muscle in response to progressive resistance training.

Hyperventilation A greater-than-normal rate of breathing that results in an abnormal loss of carbon dioxide from the blood; dizziness may occur.

Hypoglycemia A deficiency of glucose in the blood commonly caused by too much insulin, too little glucose, or too much exercise. Most commonly found in the insulin-dependent diabetic and characterized by symptoms such as fatigue, dizziness, confusion, headache, nausea, or anxiety.

Hyponatremia   Abnormally low levels of sodium ions circulating in the blood; severe hyponatremia can lead to brain swelling and death.

Hyponatremic   *See* Hyponatremia.

Hypothermia   Abnormally low body temperature.

Ileum   One of three sections of the small intestine.

Iliotibial (IT) band   A band of connective tissue that extends from the iliac crest to the knee and links the gluteus maximus to the tibia.

Incomplete protein   A protein that does not contain all of the essential amino acids.

Inextensibility   The property of a tissue that makes it unable to be extended; tissues (e.g., ligaments) contribute to limiting the range of motion of a joint when they are inextensible.

Inorganic   Descriptive of non-carbon-containing compounds of mineral, as opposed to biologic, origin.

Insertion   The point of attachment of a muscle to a relatively more movable or distal bone.

Inspiration   The drawing of air into the lungs; inhalation.

Insulin   A hormone released from the pancreas that allows cells to take up glucose.

Insulin-like growth factor   Polypeptide structurally similar to insulin that is secreted either during fetal development or during childhood and that mediates growth hormone activity.

Insulin-like growth factor I (IGF-I)   *See* Insulin-like growth factor.

Interstitial fluid   Fluid between the cells or body parts.

Inversion   Rotation of the foot to direct the plantar surface inward.

Ion   A single atom or small molecule containing a net positive or negative charge due to an excess of either protons (positive) or electrons (negative).

Ischemia   A decrease in the blood supply to a bodily organ, tissue, or part caused by constriction or obstruction of the blood vessels.

Islets of Langerhans   Irregular clusters of endocrine cells scattered throughout the tissue of the pancreas that secrete insulin (beta cells) and glucagon (alpha cells).

Isometric   A type of muscular contraction in which the muscle is stimulated to generate tension but little or no joint movement occurs.

Jejunum   One of three segments of the small intestine.

Ketosis   An abnormal increase of ketone bodies in the body; usually the result of a low-carbohydrate diet, fasting, or starvation.

Kinematics   The study of the form, pattern, or sequence of movement without regard for the forces that may produce that motion.

Kinesiology   The study of the principles of mechanics and anatomy in relation to human movement.

Kinetics   The branch of mechanics that describes the effects of forces on the body.

Kreb's cycle   A series of chemical reactions that act to break pyruvate down to carbon dioxide, water, and many hydrogen-powered molecules known as NADH and FADH2.

Kyphosis   Excessive posterior curvature of the spine, typically seen in the thoracic region.

Kyphotic   *See* Kyphosis.

Lactate   A chemical derivative of lactic acid, which is formed when sugars are broken down for energy without the presence of oxygen.

Lactate threshold (LT)   The point during exercise of increasing intensity at which blood lactate begins to accumulate above resting levels, where lactate clearance is no longer able to keep up with lactate production.

Lactic acid   A metabolic by-product of anaerobic glycolysis; when it accumulates it increases blood pH, which slows down enzyme activity and ultimately causes fatigue.

Lacto-ovo-vegetarian   A vegetarian that does not eat meat, fish, or poultry.

Lactose   A disaccharide; the principal sugar found in milk.

Lacto-vegetarian A vegetarian that does not eat eggs, meat, fish, or poultry.

Larynx The organ of the voice; located between the trachea and the base of the tongue.

Law of acceleration Newton's second law of motion stating that the force acting on a body in a given direction is equal to the body's mass times its acceleration in that direction.

Law of gravity Newton's theory stating that every object in the universe attracts every other object with a force that is proportional to the product of the masses of the two objects and inversely proportional to the square of the distance between them.

Law of inertia Newton's first law of motion stating that a body at rest will stay at rest and a body in motion will stay in motion unless acted upon by an external force.

Law of reaction Newton's third law of motion stating that for every applied force there is an equal and opposite reactive force.

Lean body mass The components of the body (apart from fat), including muscles, bones, nervous tissue, skin, blood, and organs.

Lever A rigid bar that rotates around a fixed support (fulcrum) in response to an applied force.

Ligament A strong, fibrous tissue that connects one bone to another.

Line of gravity A theoretical vertical line passing through the center of gravity, dissecting the body into two hemispheres.

Linoleic acid *See* Omega-6 fatty acid.

Linolenic acid *See* Omega-3 fatty acid.

Lipid The name for fats used in the body and bloodstream.

Lipolysis The release of triglycerides from fat cells.

Lipoprotein An assembly of a lipid and protein that serves as a transport vehicle for fatty acids and cholesterol in the blood and lymph.

Lordosis Excessive anterior curvature of the spine that typically occurs at the low back (may also occur at the neck).

Low-density lipoprotein (LDL) A lipoprotein that transports cholesterol and triglycerides from the liver and small intestine to cells and tissues; high levels may cause atherosclerosis.

Lymphatic system A network of lymphoid organs, lymph nodes, lymph ducts, lymphatic tissues, lymph capillaries, and lymph vessels that produces and transports lymph fluid from tissues to the circulatory system.

Macromineral A mineral needed in large amounts (100 milligrams or more per day); includes calcium, phosphorus, magnesium, sulfur, sodium, chloride, and potassium.

Macronutrient A nutrient that is needed in large quantities for normal growth and development.

Maltose Two glucose molecules bound together; used to make beer.

Maximal aerobic capacity *See* Maximal oxygen consumption ($\dot{V}O_2$max).

Maximal oxygen consumption ($\dot{V}O_2$max) The point at which oxygen consumption plateaus with an additional workload; represents a person's capacity for the aerobic synthesis of ATP. Also called maximal aerobic capacity or maximal oxygen uptake.

Maximal oxygen uptake *See* Maximal oxygen consumption ($\dot{V}O_2$max).

Maximum heart rate (MHR) The highest heart rate a person can attain. Sometimes abbreviated as HRmax.

Mechanical digestion The process of chewing, swallowing, and propelling food through the gastrointestinal tract.

Mediastinum The portion of the thoracic cavity between the lungs.

Meissner's corpuscle A specialized mechanoreceptor located in the superficial aspect of the skin responsible for detecting light touch; occur abundantly in the skin of the fingertips, palms, soles, lips, tongue, and face.

Metabolic syndrome (MetS) A cluster of factors associated with increased risk for coronary heart disease and diabetes—

abdominal obesity indicated by a waist circumference ≥40 inches (102 cm) in men and ≥35 inches (88 cm) in women; levels of triglyceride ≥150 mg/dL (1.7 mmol/L); HDL levels <40 and 50 mg/dL (1.0 and 1.3 mmol/L) in men and women, respectively; blood-pressure levels ≥130/85 mmHg; and fasting blood glucose levels ≥110 mg/dL (6.1 mmol/L).

Micromineral A mineral needed in small amounts (less than 100 milligrams per day); includes iron, iodine, selenium, zinc, and various others.

Micronutrient A nutrient that is needed in small quantities for normal growth and development.

Microvilli Tiny hairlike projections on each cell of every villus that can trap nutrient particles and transport them into the cells for absorption.

Mind/body vitality An individual's ability to minimize or alleviate unnecessary stress and tension from the body through the integration of physical exercise and mental focus.

Mineral Inorganic substances needed in the diet in small amounts to help regulate bodily functions.

Minute ventilation ($\dot{V}_E$) A measure of the amount of air that passes through the lungs in one minute; calculated as the tidal volume multiplied by the ventilatory rate.

Mitochondria The "power plant" of the cells where aerobic metabolism occurs.

Mobility The degree to which an articulation is allowed to move before being restricted by surrounding tissues.

Monosaccharide The simplest form of sugar; it cannot be broken down any further.

Monounsaturated fat A type of unsaturated fat (liquid at room temperature) that has one open spot on the fatty acid for the addition of a hydrogen atom (e.g., oleic acid in olive oil).

Motive force The force that starts or causes a movement.

Motor end plate The location of the synapse of a motor neuron and muscle cell; also called the neuromuscular junction.

Motor neuron Nerve cells that conduct impulses from the central nervous system to the periphery signaling muscles to contract or relax, regulating muscular movement.

Motor unit A motor nerve and all of the muscle fibers it stimulates.

Muscle spindle The sensory organ within a muscle that is sensitive to stretch and thus protects the muscle against too much stretch.

Muscle stiffness The capacity of muscle tissues to resist internal and external loads.

Muscular balance The symmetry of the interconnected components of muscle and connective tissue.

Muscular endurance The ability of a muscle or muscle group to exert force against a resistance over a sustained period of time.

Muscular strength The maximal force a muscle or muscle group can exert during contraction.

Myelin The fatty insulation of nerve fibers that is important for the conduction of nerve impulses. These fibers are damaged in individuals with multiple sclerosis.

Myocardial infarction (MI) An episode in which some of the heart's blood supply is severely cut off or restricted, causing the heart muscle to suffer and die from lack of oxygen. Commonly known as a heart attack.

Myofascial release A general manual massage technique used to eliminate general fascial restrictions; typically performed with a device such as a foam roller.

Myofibril The portion of the muscle containing the thick (myosin) and thin (actin) contractile filaments; a series of sarcomeres where the repeating pattern of the contractile proteins gives the striated appearance to skeletal muscle.

Myoglobin A compound similar to hemoglobin, which aids in the storage and transport of oxygen in the muscle cells.

Myosin Thick contractile protein in a myofibril.

Myosin ATPase An enzyme found in muscle tissue that is responsible for actin-based motility.

Negative energy balance A state in which the number of calories expended is greater than what is taken in, thereby contributing to weight loss.

Neuromuscular junction The site at which a motor neuron transmits information to a muscle fiber.

Neuron The basic anatomical unit of the nervous system; the nerve cell.

Neurotransmitter A chemical substance such as acetylcholine or dopamine that transmits nerve impulses across synapses.

Neutral spine position The balance of vertebrae in the three naturally occurring curves: two slight anterior curves at the neck and low back and one slight posterior curve in the thoracic region.

Norepinephrine A hormone released as part of the sympathetic response to exercise.

Obesity An excessive accumulation of body fat. Usually defined as more than 20% above ideal weight, or over 25% body fat for men and over 32% body fat for women; also can be defined as a body mass index of >30 kg/m^2 or a waist girth of ≥ 40 inches (102 cm) in men and ≥ 35 inches (89 cm) in women.

Oligosaccharide A chain of about three to 10 or fewer simple sugars.

Omega-3 fatty acid An essential fatty acid that promotes a healthy immune system and helps protect against heart disease and other diseases; found in egg yolk and cold water fish like tuna, salmon, mackerel, cod, crab, shrimp, and oyster. Also known as linolenic acid.

Omega-6 fatty acid An essential fatty acid found in flaxseed, canola, and soybean oils and green leaves. Also known as linoleic acid.

One-repetition maximum (1 RM) The amount of resistance that can be moved through the range of motion one time before the muscle is temporarily fatigued.

Onset of blood lactate accumulation (OBLA) The point in time during high-intensity exercise at which the production of lactic acid exceeds the body's capacity to eliminate it; after this point, oxygen is insufficient at meeting the body's demands for energy.

Organic Descriptive of a compound that contains carbon.

Origin The attachment site of a tendon of a muscle attached to the relatively more fixed or proximal bone.

Osmolality Measure of the concentration of ionic substances in the blood, such as sodium, potassium, and glucose.

Osteoarthritis A degenerative disease involving a wearing away of joint cartilage. This degenerative joint disease occurs chiefly in older persons.

Osteoblast A bone-forming cell.

Osteoclast A cell that reabsorbs or erodes bone mineral.

Osteoporosis A disorder, primarily affecting postmenopausal women, in which bone density decreases and susceptibility to fractures increases.

Overload The principle that a physiological system subjected to above-normal stress will respond by increasing in strength or function accordingly.

Overweight A term to describe an excessive amount of weight for a given height, using height-to-weight ratios.

Oxidation The addition of oxygen to a compound with a resulting loss of electrons.

Oxidative glycolysis *See* Aerobic glycolysis.

Oxygen consumption ($\dot{V}O_2$) The process by which oxygen is used to produce energy for cellular work; also called oxygen uptake.

Oxygen extraction The amount of oxygen taken from the hemoglobin molecule and used in exercising muscle cells; often referred to as the arteriovenous oxygen difference or a-$\bar{v}$ O$_2$ diff.

Pacinian corpuscle A specialized bulblike mechanoreceptor located in the subcutaneous tissue of the skin responsible for detecting pressure; occur abundantly in the skin of palms, soles, and joints.

ACE Essentials of Exercise Science for Fitness Professionals

Parasympathetic nervous system A subdivision of the autonomic nervous system that is involved in regulating the routine functions of the body, such as heartbeat, digestion, and sleeping. Opposes the physiological effects of the sympathetic nervous system (e.g., stimulates digestive secretions, slows the heart, constricts the pupils, dilates blood vessels).

Partial pressure The pressure of each gas in a multiple gas system, such as air, which is composed of nitrogen, oxygen, and CO_2.

Peptide bond The chemical bond formed between neighboring amino acids, constituting the primary linkage of all protein structures.

Percentage daily value (PDV) A replacement for the percent RDA on the newer food labels. Gives information on whether a food item has a significant amount of a particular nutrient based on a 2,000-calorie diet.

Perimysium A sheath of connective tissue that covers a bundle of muscle fibers.

Periodization The systematic application of overload through the pre-planned variation of program components to optimize gains in strength (or any specific component of fitness), while preventing overuse, staleness, overtraining, and plateaus.

Periosteum A double-layered connective tissue sheath surrounding the outer surface of the diaphysis of a long bone; serves to cover and nourish the bone.

Peripheral nervous system (PNS) The parts of the nervous system that are outside the brain and spinal cord (central nervous system).

Peripheral vasoconstriction The narrowing of blood vessels resulting from contraction of the muscular wall of the vessels, particularly in the periphery of the body (limbs).

Peripheral vasodilation Widening of the blood vessels (vasodilation) of the peripheral vasculature in the systemic circulation.

Peristalsis The process by which muscles in the esophagus and intestines push food through the gastrointestinal tract in a wave-like motion.

Pharynx The muscular, membranous tube extending from the base of the skull to the esophagus.

Phosphagen High-energy phosphate compounds found in muscle tissue, including adenosine triphosphate (ATP) and creatine phosphate (CP), that can be broken down for immediate use by the cells.

Physical fitness The physical components of well-being that enable a person to function at an optimal level.

Phytochemical A biologically active, nonnutrient component found in plants; includes antioxidants.

Plantarflexion Distal movement of the plantar surface of the foot; opposite of dorsiflexion.

Plasma The liquid portion of the blood.

Platelet One of the disc-shaped components of the blood; involved in clotting.

Plyometrics High-intensity movements, such as jumping, involving high-force loading of body weight during the landing phase of the movement.

Polypeptide A linear chain of amino acids.

Polysaccharide A long chain of sugar molecules.

Polyunsaturated fat A type of unsaturated fat (liquid at room temperature) that has two or more spots on the fatty acid available for hydrogen (e.g., corn, safflower, soybean oils).

Portal circulation A circulatory system that takes nutrients directly from the stomach, small intestines, colon, and spleen to the liver.

Positive energy balance A situation when the storage of energy exceeds the amount expended. This state may be achieved by either consuming too many calories or by not using enough.

Postpartum The period of time after childbirth.

Posture The arrangement of the body and its limbs.

Prehypertension A systolic pressure of 120

to 139 mmHg and/or a diastolic pressure of 80 to 89 mmHg. Having this condition puts an individual at higher risk for developing hypertension.

Prehypertensive *See* Prehypertension.

Prime mover A muscle responsible for a specific movement. Also called an agonist.

Progression The systematic process of applying overload. For example, in resistance training, more resistance is added to progress the training stimulus.

Progesterone Female sex hormone secreted by the ovaries that affects many aspects of female physiology, including menstrual cycles and pregnancy.

Pronation Internal rotation of the forearm causing the radius to cross diagonally over the ulna and the palm to face posteriorly.

Proprioception Sensation and awareness of body position and movements.

Proprioceptive neuromuscular facilitation (PNF) A method of promoting the response of neuromuscular mechanisms through the stimulation of proprioceptors in an attempt to gain more stretch in a muscle; often referred to as a contract/relax method of stretching.

Proprioceptors Somatic sensory receptors in muscles, tendons, ligaments, joint capsules, and skin that gather information about body position and the direction and velocity of movement.

Protein A compound composed of a combination 20 amino acids that is the major structural component of all body tissue.

Protein complementarity Combinations of incomplete plant proteins that together provide all of the essential amino acids.

Protein digestibility corrected amino acid score (PDCAAS) Estimates protein quality by multiplying a particular food protein's chemical score (essential amino acid content in a protein food divided by the amino acid content in a reference protein food) by its digestibility.

Protraction Scapular abduction.

Provitamin Inactive vitamin; the human body contains enzymes to convert a provitamin into an active vitamin.

Proximal Nearest to the midline of the body or point of origin of a muscle.

Pulmonary circuit The circulatory vessels of the lungs; involved in the circulation of blood from the right ventricle of the heart to the lungs and back to the left atrium of the heart.

Pulmonary ventilation The total volume of gas inspired or expired per minute.

Pyloric sphincter Separates the stomach from the small intestines.

Pyruvate A biochemical involved in the Kreb's cycle that facilitates adenosine triphosphate production.

Q 10 effect The physiological phenomenon wherein chemical reactions occur twice as fast when the temperature is increased by $10°$ C.

Radiation Heat transferred from one body to another which are not in contact, such as heat transferring from the sun to a roof.

Range of motion (ROM) The number of degrees through which an articulation will allow one of its segments to move.

Rate coding The frequency of impulses sent to a muscle. Increased force can be generated through an increase in either the number of muscle fibers recruited or the rate at which the impulses are sent.

Reciprocal inhibition The reflex inhibition of the motor neurons of antagonists when the agonists are contracted.

Recommended Dietary Allowance (RDA) The levels of intake of essential nutrients that, on the basis of scientific knowledge, are judged by the Food and Nutrition Board to be adequate to meet the known needs of practically all healthy persons.

Registered dietitian (R.D.) A food and nutrition expert who has met the following criteria: completed a minimum of a bachelor's

ACE Essentials of Exercise Science for Fitness Professionals

degree at a U.S. accredited university, or other college coursework approved by the Commission on Accreditation for Dietetics Education (CADE); completed a CADE-accredited supervised practice program; passed a national examination; and completed continuing education requirements to maintain registration.

Repolarize To restore the difference in charge between the inside and outside of the plasma membrane of a muscle fiber or cell following depolarization.

Resistive force A force that resists the motion of another external force.

Respiration The exchange of oxygen and carbon dioxide between the cells and the atmosphere.

Respiratory compensation threshold (RCT) *See* Second ventilatory threshold (VT2).

Respiratory exchange ratio (RER) A ratio of the amount of carbon dioxide produced relative to the amount of oxygen consumed.

Resting metabolic rate (RMR) The number of calories expended per unit of time at rest; measured early in the morning after an overnight fast and at least eight hours of sleep; approximated with various formulas.

Retraction Scapular adduction.

Reversibility The principle of exercise training that suggests that any improvement in physical fitness due to physical activity is entirely reversible with the discontinuation of the training program.

Sagittal plane The longitudinal plane that divides the body into right and left portions.

SAID principle A training principle that states that the body will adapt to the specific challenges imposed upon it, as long as the program progressively overloads the system being trained; SAID stands for specific adaptation to imposed demands.

Saliva Water, salt, and enzyme secretion from the salivary glands that begins digestion.

Sarcomere The basic functional unit of the myofibril containing the contractile proteins that generate skeletal muscle movements.

Sarcopenia Decreased muscle mass; often used to refer specifically to an age-related decline in muscle mass or lean-body tissue.

Sarcoplasm A gelatin-like tissue surrounding the sarcomere.

Sarcoplasmic reticulum The form of endoplasmic reticulum where calcium is stored to be used for muscle activation; located in striated muscle fibers.

Saturated fat *See* Saturated fatty acid.

Saturated fatty acid A fatty acid that contains no double bonds between carbon atoms; typically solid at room temperature and very stable.

Scapulohumeral rhythm Combined action of scapular and humeral movement.

Scapulothoracic (S/T) articulation The articulation of the scapula with the thorax beneath it.

Sciatica Pain radiating down the leg caused by compression of the sciatic nerve; frequently the result of lumbar disk herniation.

Scoliosis Excessive lateral curvature of the spine.

Scope of practice The range and limit of responsibilities normally associated with a specific job or profession.

Screw-home mechanism A phenomenon that increases knee joint stability by locking the femur on the tibia (or vice-versa) when the knee is fully extended.

Second ventilatory threshold (VT2) Metabolic marker which represents the point at which high-intensity exercise can no longer be sustained due to an accumulation of lactate. Also called the Respiratory compensation threshold (RCT) or the onset of blood lactate accumulation (OBLA).

Sedentary Doing or requiring much sitting; minimal activity.

Self-efficacy One's perception of his or her ability to change or perform specific behaviors (e.g., exercise).

Sensory neuron Nerve cells that convey

electrical impulses from sensory organs in the periphery (such as the skin) to the spinal cord and brain (i.e., the central nervous system).

Shoulder girdle The articulation of the scapula with the thorax.

Shoulder joint complex The three segments of the shoulder: the scapula, clavicle, and humerus.

Simple carbohydrate Short chains of sugar that are rapidly digested.

Sinoatrial node (SA node) A group of specialized myocardial cells, located in the wall of the right atrium, that controls the heart's rate of contraction; the "pacemaker" of the heart.

SITS A pneumonic device for naming the rotator cuff muscles: the supraspinatus, which abducts the arm; the infraspinatus and teres minor, which externally rotate the arm; and the subscapularis, which internally rotates the arm.

Slow-twitch muscle fiber A muscle fiber type designed for use of aerobic glycolysis and fatty acid oxidation, recruited for low-intensity, longer-duration activities such as walking and swimming; Also called type I muscle fiber.

Somatic nervous system Division of the peripheral nervous system that conducts signals from sensory receptors to the central nervous system (afferent signals) and signals from the central nervous system to skeletal muscles (efferent signals).

Specificity Exercise training principle explaining that specific exercise demands made on the body produce specific responses by the body; also called exercise specificity.

Stability Characteristic of the body's joints or posture that represents resistance to change of position.

Stability limits Maximum distance a person can intentionally displace his or her center of gravity (i.e., lean) in a given direction without losing balance, stepping, or reaching for assistance.

Starch A plant carbohydrate found in grains and vegetables.

Static stabilizer Bony configuration of joints,

fibrocartilages, and ligaments that contribute to core stability.

Static stretching Holding a nonmoving (static) position to immobilize a joint in a position that places the desired muscles and connective tissues passively at their greatest possible length.

Steady state Constant submaximal exercise below the lactate threshold where the oxygen consumption is meeting the energy requirements of the activity.

Sternoclavicular (S/C) joint The junction of the sternum and the proximal clavicle.

Storage fat Fat contained within adipose tissue that acts as an energy store and thermal insulation, and also cushions the internal organs.

Stretch reflex An involuntary motor response that, when stimulated, causes a suddenly stretched muscle to respond with a corresponding contraction.

Stroke A sudden and often severe attack due to blockage of an artery into the brain.

Stroke volume The amount of blood pumped from the left ventricle of the heart with each beat.

Subluxation An incomplete dislocation; though the relationship is altered, contact between joint surfaces remains.

Sucrose Table sugar; a disaccharide formed by glucose and fructose linked together.

Summation The repeated stimulation of a muscle that leads to an increase in tension compared to a single twitch.

Superficial External; located close to or on the body surface.

Supination External rotation of the forearm (radioulnar joint) that causes the palm to face anteriorly.

Supine Lying face up (on the back).

Sway-back A long outward curve of the thoracic spine with a backward shift of the trunk starting from the pelvis.

Sympathetic nervous system A branch of

the autonomic nervous system responsible for mobilizing the body's energy and resources during times of stress and arousal. Opposes the physiological effects of the parasympathetic nervous system (e.g., reduces digestive secretions, speeds the heart, contracts blood vessels).

Synapse   The region of communication between neurons.

Synergist   A muscle that assists another muscle in function.

Systemic circuit   The circulatory vessels of the body.

Systole   The contraction phase of the cardiac cycle.

Systolic blood pressure (SBP)   The pressure exerted by the blood on the vessel walls during ventricular contraction.

Talk test   A method for measuring exercise intensity using observation of respiration effort and the ability to talk while exercising.

Tendon   A band of fibrous tissue forming the termination of a muscle and attaching the muscle to a bone.

Tensile strength   The amount of longitudinal pulling stress that a material (e.g., soft tissue) can withstand before being pulled apart.

Testosterone   In males, the steroid hormone produced in the testes; involved in growth and development of reproductive tissues, sperm, and secondary male sex characteristics.

Tetanus   The highest tension developed by a muscle in response to a high frequency of stimulation.

Thermogenesis   The process by which the body generates heat from energy production.

Thorax   The portion of the trunk above the diaphragm and below the neck.

Tidal volume   The volume of air inspired per breath.

Tolerable Upper Intake Level (UL)   The maximum intake of a nutrient that is unlikely to pose risk of adverse health effects to almost all individuals in an age- and gender specific group.

Torque   The result of a force pushing or pulling an object around an axis; often described as a "twisting" or rotation action.

Trabecular bone   Spongy or cancellous bone composed of thin plates that form a honeycomb pattern; predominantly found in the ends of long bones and the vertebral bodies.

Trace element   An element essential to nutrition or physiologic processes, found in such minute quantities that analysis yields a presence of virtually none.

Trachea   The cartilaginous and membranous tube extending from the larynx to the bronchi; windpipe.

Trans fats   *See* Trans fatty acid.

Trans fatty acid   An unsaturated fatty acid that is converted into a saturated fat to increase the shelf life of some products.

Transient hypertrophy   The "pumping" up of muscle that happens during a single exercise bout, resulting mainly from fluid accumulation in the interstitial and intracellular spaces of the muscle.

Transverse plane   Anatomical term for the imaginary line that divides the body, or any of its parts, into upper (superior) and lower (inferior) parts. Also called the horizontal plane.

Triglyceride   Three fatty acids joined to a glycerol (carbon and hydrogen structure) backbone; how fat is stored in the body.

Twitch   The tension-generating response following the application of a single stimulus to muscle.

Type 1 diabetes   Form of diabetes caused by the destruction of the insulin-producing beta cells in the pancreas, which leads to little or no insulin secretion; generally develops in childhood and requires regular insulin injections; formerly known as insulin-dependent diabetes mellitus

(IDDM) and childhood-onset diabetes.

Type 2 diabetes Most common form of diabetes; typically develops in adulthood and is characterized by a reduced sensitivity of the insulin target cells to available insulin; usually associated with obesity; formerly known as non-insulin-dependent diabetes mellitus (NIDDM) and adult-onset diabetes.

Type I muscle fibers *See* Slow-twitch muscle fiber.

Type II muscle fibers *See* Fast-twitch muscle fiber.

Unsaturated fatty acids Fatty acids that contain one or more double bonds between carbon atoms; typically liquid at room temperature and fairly unstable, making them susceptible to oxidative damage and a shortened shelf life.

Vagal withdrawal Effect produced on the heart when the parasympathetic nerve fibers (which are carried in the vagus nerve) controlling the heart rate are inhibited by the sympathetic nervous system during exercise, thus increasing the heart rate.

Vagus nerve The tenth cranial nerve; parasympathetic, general sensory nerve.

Vascularity An increase in the number and size of blood vessels enhancing blood supply and oxygen delivery to muscle cells.

Vasoconstriction Narrowing of the opening of blood vessels (notably the smaller arterioles) caused by contraction of the smooth muscle lining the vessels.

Vasodilation Increase in diameter of the blood vessels, especially dilation of arterioles leading to increased blood flow to a part of the body.

Vasopressin Hormone released by the posterior pituitary gland during exercise; reduces urinary excretion of water and prevents dehydration.

Vegan A vegetarian that does not consume any animal products, including dairy products such as milk and cheese.

Vegetarian A person who does not eat meat, fish, poultry, or products containing these foods.

Veins Blood vessels that carry deoxygenated blood toward the heart from vital organs and the extremities.

Ventilatory threshold (VT) Point of transition between predominately aerobic energy production to anaerobic energy production; involves recruitment of fast-twitch muscle fibers and identified via gas exchange during exercise testing.

Ventricles The two lower chambers of the heart (right and left ventricles).

Venules Smaller divisions of veins.

Vestibular system Part of the central nervous system that coordinates reflexes of the eyes, neck, and body to maintain equilibrium in accordance with posture and movement of the head.

Villi Finger-like projections from the folds of the small intestines.

Viscera The collective internal organs of the abdominal cavity.

Vitamin An organic micronutrient that is essential for normal physiologic function.

$\dot{V}O_2$max Considered the best indicator of cardiovascular endurance, it is the maximum amount of oxygen (mL) that a person can use in one minute per kilogram of body weight. Also called maximal oxygen uptake and maximal aerobic capacity.

Water-soluble vitamins Vitamins that require adequate daily intake since the body excretes excesses in the urine; dissolvable in water.

Windchill A chill factor created by the increase in the rate of heat loss via convection and conduction caused by wind.

Wolff's Law A principle stating that bone is capable of increasing its strength in response to stress (e.g., exercise) by laying down more bone

INDEX